Theatre, education and the making of meanings

Theatre, education and the making of meanings

Art or instrument?

Anthony Jackson

MANCHESTER UNIVERSITY PRESS

MANCHESTER AND NEW YORK ▪ distributed exclusively in the USA by Palgrave

Published by Manchester University Press
Oxford Road, Manchester M13 9NR, UK
and Room 400, 175 Fifth Avenue, New York, NY 10010, USA
www.manchesteruniversitypress.co.uk

Distributed exclusively in the USA by
Palgrave, 175 Fifth Avenue, New York,
NY 10010, USA

Distributed exclusively in Canada by
UBC Press, University of British Columbia, 2029 West Mall,
Vancouver, BC, Canada V6T 1Z2

British Library Cataloguing-in-Publication Data
A catalogue record for this book is available from the British Library

Library of Congress Cataloging-in-Publication Data applied for

ISBN   978 0 7190 6542 2 *hardback*

ISBN   978 0 7190 6543 9 *paperback*

First published 2007

16 15 14 13 12 11 10 09 08 07   10 9 8 7 6 5 4 3 2 1

Typeset by Servis Filmsetting Ltd, Manchester
Printed in Great Britain
by Biddles, King's Lynn

Contents

Illustrations

Table

Figures

Plates

Acknowledgements

This book has been germinating for many years. Sections of some chapters have appeared in one form or another as journal articles, conference papers or chapters in books, and I am grateful particularly to the editors of the following journals for the opportunities they provided to give the material an initial airing: *Critical Quarterly*, *Cultura Moderna*, *Journal of Aesthetic Education*, *Research in Drama Education* and *Theatre Research International*. Some of the papers are recent, prepared with the book in mind, while others appeared many years ago and have afforded me an invaluable opporunity to revisit and, in some cases, completely revise earlier ideas and approaches. I am grateful too to all the extraordinary actors, directors, administrators and others working in theatre companies and heritage organisations who have allowed me to watch, share in and interrogate their practice, to my university colleagues for their continuing support, to Robinson College Cambridge for the opportunity, as a Bye Fellow during 2001/2, to get down (at last) to serious work on the book, and not least to the numerous students who have opted to work with me over the years on project-based courses in theatre in education and site-specific and museum theatre – there has always been an element of experiment involved in those courses and my fascination with and understanding of the field has benefited enormously from their critically enthusiastic input. I must also record my thanks to the British Academy and the Arts & Humanities Research Council for various small grants that enabled me to undertake the field work on which several chapters are based. Finally I wish to thank the members of my family whose patience with the evolution of this book has been epic, whose tolerance and support have been vital to its completion, and to whom the book is lovingly dedicated.

Introduction

This is a study of theatre's educational role during the twentieth and the first years of the twenty-first centuries. It examines the variety of ways in which the theatre's educational potential has been harnessed and theorised, the claims made for its value and the tension between theatre as education and theatre as 'art': between theatre's aesthetic dimension and the 'utilitarian' or 'instrumental' role for which it has so often been pressed into service. In charting and foregrounding the distinct *educational* function of theatre in a variety of social, cultural and artistic contexts, the book attempts to meet the need for a study of theatre *as* education in a broad sense – seen from a variety of perspectives and manifested in a variety of ways, but stemming from what has been a recurrent preoccupation in much of the theatre of the past hundred years. By 'educational theatre', I refer to the variety of theatre forms that have been deployed for explicit educational ends, many of which – but by no means all – involve some form of active audience engagement: whether full-scale in-role participation or performance culminating in a workshop or debate, as commonly found in practices as diverse as theatre in education, Augusto Boal's forum theatre and the various examples of theatre for development in Africa and other parts of the developing world.

'Theatre of the oppressed', 'theatre in education', 'theatre in health education', 'outreach theatre', 'museum theatre', 'theatre in prisons', 'theatre for development', 'theatre for liberation', 'agit-prop', and, more recently, 'applied theatre', 'social theatre' and 'interventionist theatre' – the list of terms related to this field of work seems endless. Most are intended to signify forms of theatre practice that aim to effect a transformation in people's lives, whether that be the activation of a process of *attitudinal* or *behavioural change* on the part of the audience or the creation or consolidation of *consciousness* about the audience's place in the world or, more modestly, the *triggering of curiosity* about a specific issue. But do these terms signify differences of approach, differences in the target audience, differences in rationale, or indeed differences in the agendas of those who fund the work? To some extent they do. Some are quite specific in identifying the agenda which drives the work (such as theatre in health education) or the location in which they operate and by implication the audiences whom they target (prison theatre and museum theatre, for example). But far more difficult to untangle are the hidden, assumed premises on which the work is based and the unstated purposes that may drive it. Some practice may be called theatre but operates primarily by means of participatory workshops with only a nod towards conventional performance; other work is wholly performance-based. The connection between 'art' and 'social agenda' can often be tenuous and fraught, the leakage of one into the other confusing or confused. In the interests of meeting certain 'given' objectives (attitudinal change, for example), the theatre practice may sometimes subordinate the artistic aspects to the function of 'sugaring the pill' or even eradicate them altogether.

In an attempt to disentangle some of the key elements in the way theatre functions, Richard Schechner and others (Schechner 2002, Schechner and Thompson 2004, Schinina 2004) have sought to separate out theatre that is 'social' from 'aesthetic theatre' – that is, theatre that claims a social, interventionist purpose in the real world, as distinct from conventional theatre in which artistic effect and entertainment are the principal functions. While Schechner acknowledges that social theatre will often include aesthetic elements and aesthetic theatre may sometimes include 'social' or 'instrumental' elements, the two are seen as being at opposite ends of the spectrum. It is a dichotomy that has been widely accepted and one that is certainly useful in highlighting often quite profound functional differences between different types of theatre practice. But it is also a problematic distinction because it appears to suggest that social and aesthetic functions cannot be equally at work in the same performance at the same moment or that, if they are, it will be the exception proving the rule. It is a distinction to which I will return several times in the course of this study.

One of the concerns of this book, and one of the premises upon which its argument is built, is the place of 'art' in such theatre practice, and the recurring tensions – manifested in theatre work throughout the last hundred years – between educational goals and the art form through which practitioners endeavour to achieve them. What *is* the aesthetic power of the medium through which the work is undertaken – and why does it matter?

Theatre as education: the scope of the study

I should make clear what the book is *not* about. It is not a study of the place of drama in the school curriculum (drama in education or DIE), or about 'youth theatre' (theatre produced and acted by young people themselves); nor indeed is it exclusively about the movement known as 'theatre in education' (TIE) although that forms a significant part of the study. While much 'social theatre' and 'applied theatre' often centres on participatory workshop activity, I have restricted my focus to overtly *performance-based* work, although I do consider workshop practice when it arises directly out of or is designed to complement a performance. Given the breadth of what 'educational' can mean, it does not attempt to cover all possible ramifications of the term (arguably, *all* theatre is in one sense or another educational), but rather focuses on those manifestations in which the educational aims and claims are explicit or in which educational intent is clearly embodied in the work. That intent may well not be the primary, and rarely if ever the sole, goal, but it will be manifest in some unmistakable way, if not always explicit. I have also not attempted to write a comprehensive history of educational theatre practice, which would be well beyond the scope of one book, nor tried to cover the full range of practice across the world. At the risk of appearing to ignore important examples of educational theatre elsewhere, I have focused on the work I know best: work I have observed, researched and to a limited extent practised, in Britain and the United States. The enormous variety of work that can be found across Europe and in Africa, Asia, Australasia and South America is not covered therefore except where that practice has been particularly influential beyond its own borders – the most notable example of which being the work of the South American director and pioneer of the 'theatre of the oppressed', Augusto Boal. Recent 'theatre for development' practice is, for the same reason, acknowledged but not examined. This is not in any way to devalue work in non-western countries, merely a recognition of the need to place realistic limits on the scope of the book. If the limitation is unavoidable, my hope is that the variety of examples given, the concepts discussed and the questions raised will be more or less applicable to much of the theatre practice across the world that shares similar goals. Finally, this is not a book about what Etherton and Prentki have termed 'monitoring and evaluation' or 'impact assessment' (Etherton & Prentki 2006: 139–40). It does not pretend to be a study of the measurable effects of educational theatre programmes on individuals and communities, nor of the ideological or strategic implications of different evaluative methods. Evaluation is touched on, some chapters draw on the author's

own evaluative studies to illustrate particular aspects of the work discussed and inescapably value judgements are made in the course of
analysing various examples of theatre practice. Evaluation is however a
subject of vital importance and complexity in its own right and certainly
warrants more attention than is possible within these pages.[1]

This book's primary aims then are, firstly, to identify some important
and recurring trends in twentieth- and early twenty-first-century theatre,
in which can be found a distinct *educational* function for theatre in a
variety of social, cultural and artistic contexts, and manifested in work
both for adults and for young people; secondly, to explore, through focus
upon a number of specific examples of practice, some of the problematic
interconnections between art form and educational purpose; and, finally,
to develop an argument about how we might better understand and
value these kinds of theatre, both philosophically and pragmatically.

One of the hypotheses I have set out to test is that such varieties of
theatre, when most effective, constitute *wholly artistic forms*: that the
education takes place *through* the theatrical form, rather than merely
using theatre as a vehicle for message delivery. Theatre that sets out to
educate a specific audience in a specific context, in other words, and
despite many views to the contrary, has an aesthetic function. And any
theatre project that aims to educate will do so effectively only *if* it is also
conceived as an artistic entity. Indeed, artistic criteria may actually offer
some very helpful insights into what makes for excellent education. Of
course this begs all kinds of questions about what is meant by 'aesthetic'
and 'art' let alone education, questions that will be introduced in Chapter
1. There are, too, interesting practices at the margins of what we conventionally conceive as theatre (such as the interactive workshop in
which characters from the play just seen are interrogated by the audience,
and the use of first-person interpretation at historic sites) that will test
the validity of this hypothesis. Likewise, theatre that from our own perspective looks and reads like naive propaganda may, when understood
in the context of its time, be seen to reach its audiences in ways that transcend the negative associations that 'propaganda' conventionally suggests. Whether or not such theatre constitutes education is a question
that will be posed, if not conclusively answered. The fuzzy lines that
often separate propaganda from education may themselves fluctuate
according to the mood of the time, the preconceptions of its audience and
the style of playing.

The concern of the book is then, in part, to explore arguments about
what characterises some of the most innovative theatre of the past
hundred years as well as to offer a study in concrete terms of a number
of representative forms in practice. While views will emerge about what

can often make for good educational theatre, this study is certainly not a prescription for what it should be.

Questions, premises and genealogies

Following a preliminary discussion (in Chapter 1) of some key theoretical approaches to aesthetics, dramatic art and learning and, above all, the relationships between them, the book is organised into two broad chronological periods: early developments in European and American theatre up to the end of the Second World War (Chapters 2–4); and participatory theatre and education since the Second World War (Chapters 5–9). Within each period, a cluster of key themes is introduced and then revisited and examined through a number of specific examples – seen within their cultural contexts – in subsequent chapters. In this way, the approach resists being driven by a primarily chronological imperative, but recognises the value of locating and interrogating notions and examples of educational theatre practice within historical contexts. The historical roots and precedents of educational (and applied and interventionist) theatre have tended to get ignored in recent years, and the loss of that broader perspective has sometimes resulted in overly narrow concepts of theatre's social function.

Among the key questions and themes to be considered (though the book is not pretentious enough to attempt final answers) are these. Does art, can art, indeed should art change perceptions and understandings? When art is used to teach, is there not a substantial, perhaps severely damaging, compromise involved that derails what many consider to be the true function of art, that is, to remove us from the mundane so that we reconnect with our inner selves or with larger matters to do with human purpose, spirituality and value? Or is the latter idea an elitist, art-for-art's-sake notion, outdatedly clinging to traditional, bourgeois or even aristocratic views of art, something that requires sophisticated training and background to be able to appreciate in the first place? If theatrical art is capable of generating an educational, transformative process in its audiences and participants, what are the means at its disposal, and what are the aesthetic processes involved? Is it possible to identify those characteristic elements, elastic and eclectic and culturally specific though they will inevitably be, that contribute to the educational process?

In order to avoid the neat but unproductive separation of theory and practice, theories (of performance, of learning, of art) are discussed rather as interconnected themes which recur through the book. Among the elements of theatre dramaturgy and related concepts of learning theory that will be discussed are: the shifting concepts of education and learning that

have impacted theatre and drama practice; 'audience reception' and
notions of 'meaning making'; the nature of 'aesthetic distance' and 'theatrical frame'; the 'dialogic' process involved in artistic expression and
equally in educational encounters; and the 'ludic' or the playful in theatrical performance. I acknowledge recent developments in performance
theory while insisting upon the need to recognise the theatre event as a
distinctive enterprise with boundaries – fluid and subject to redefinition
as they may be – that mark it out from some of the wider notions of 'performance' (such as religious ritual, sporting events and political conventions) that have been expounded by performance theorists such as
Richard Schechner, Marvin Carlson, Baz Kershaw and others.

At this point, I need to declare some working assumptions and to indicate the main theoretical premises on which the ensuing discussion is
based. Whether explicit or not, there will inevitably be conceptual frameworks, ways of viewing the world, that will inform the author's choice of
subject matter, methods of approach, starting points and hypotheses. In
a book that has 'theatre' and 'education' in its title, some explanation of
those terms especially is necessary – all the more so given the contentious
meanings that these words have taken on over the last decade or so. Is it
still relevant to discuss theatre without conceding that it has become, in
the eyes of many, a kind of sub-set of 'performance'? Schechner's evan-
gelical call for the serious study of performance as a much wider, more
challenging and more appropriate site for the investigation and debate of
ideas about drama on and off stage, about performance events rather than
texts, and about performance as a fundamental and recurring feature of
cultural life across many different social and cultural configurations, has
chimed resonantly with an increased fascination with links between
theatre, sociology and anthropology. This rethinking of theatre has
inevitably corresponded with, and been driven by, the concerns – and anxieties – of a postmodern age.

In his important and penetrating book *The Radical in Performance*,
Baz Kershaw argued that, at the end of the twentieth and beginning of
the twenty-first centuries, we were possibly on the cusp of a major cultural 'paradigm shift', one that appeared (and still appears) to be affecting theatre and performance practice and the ways we think about that
practice, in profound ways (Kershaw 1999: 23). Such words as 'possibly' and 'appears' are important qualifiers since, as Kershaw points out,
any attempt to pin down a shift from modernity to postmodernity is
bound to be at best provisional, at worst a fictional construct. Definitions
have become increasingly problematic, just as have perceptions of the
practice itself. 'Theatre' has now, it seems, at least in some academic
circles and among many avant-garde practitioners, been superseded by

'performance' – appropriate for the 'performative society' in which many claim we now live. If, in the view of Kershaw and others, theatre has become commodified and shorn of its radical potential, performance beyond the confines of theatre buildings may offer more challenging opportunities for the future.

We live in an age in which the experiences that occur 'betwixt and between' the traditional boundary lines of cultural practice have come to seem as important as those practices which operate comfortably within them, if not more so. It is that fascination with what happens at the borderlines, within the margins, that has contributed to the shift in the academy from 'theatre' to 'performance'. Not everyone has welcomed that shift. Willmar Sauter in 1997 expressed the doubts of many about relegating theatre to a minor and rather diminishing place on the cultural scene, and called for a broader concept of theatre and a more systematic study of the 'wide field of theatrical events', not least 'the live interaction between stage and auditorium' and the contexts in which it occurs (Sauter 1997: 39). More recently, Stephen Bottoms has, too, regretted 'the strangely dichotomous situation in which much that once would have been regarded as "theatrical" has been annexed off and relabelled as "performative", the implication being that "performance" has "real effects in the real world", unlike theatre which is seen as "emptily ostentatious" ' (Bottoms 2003: 174).

Ideas about education have been just as vexed. Following Lyotard (1984), we have had to reconsider the modernist assumptions about education and development on which so much of educational theatre practice has in the past been based. Those assumptions – such as the notions of progress, of the straightforward transmission of knowledge, of unified, shared beliefs that can be widely disseminated – have now become intensely problematic. Do the grand narratives of modernism – those overarching stories that cultures tell themselves to explain and reassure and offer hope – no longer hold? Can we no longer rely on the aspirations and beliefs that have underpinned most educational philosophy since the Enlightenment – looking towards a better tomorrow, reached by the 'natural' civilising processes of human societies seeking betterment, climbing the ladder of civilisation, taking with us, as and when we can, those more unfortunate than ourselves? Are the only knowledges that matter those that are local, that can be developed out of particular circumstances with particular groups and at particular times? If so, what does that tell us about the kinds of education we can foster through theatre practice?

To take 'development', for example: the authors of the classic handbook for development workers in the Third World (Hope & Timmel

1999) point out that 'development' in the initial western sense of the word was to do with fostering 'economic growth, increased production of commodities, capital accumulation and growth of Gross National Product'; but that later, 'development education' programmes instead began to focus on 'enabling communities and individuals to identify their own needs and find ways of satisfying them together' (Hope and Timmel, p. vii). Development must, in the authors' views, 'involve local people actively in the transformation of their own reality', a view that has been strengthened by the recognition through the 1990s that 'the only change which effectively transforms the lives of the poor is one in which they have been active participants' (pp. vii–viii).

In formal schooling, too, just as in much community and development theatre, the emphasis has shifted towards participation. The one-way, top-down, delivery systems for educating young people about health, or citizenship, have increasingly given way to 'interactive workshops' and 'experiential learning' methods in the classroom. Likewise, in literature and the arts, recognition has grown of the active role readers and spectators play in the process of making meanings. Even in the most conventional of theatre performances, audiences do not merely sit passively, absorbing like blotting-paper a set of meanings pre-prepared for them by author and director. But if participation and experience are to be privileged, where does that leave the role of critical pedagogy (Usher and Edwards 1994) or of theatre practice that seeks to intervene in order to promote real change in people's lives? Facile assumptions about being able to 'make a difference' in people's lives by the very act of engaging them in a participatory drama experience can all too easily lead to patronisation, even to a certain kind of oppression, and have to be balanced against the risks of doing nothing or of letting participants go their own way. There are perhaps few worse experiences in this field of work than to find oneself belittled or one's dignity undermined within a supposedly participatory event from which there is no ready escape; while there is ample evidence that 'group dynamics' can all too often lead to 'participatory decisions that reinforce the interests of the already powerful' (Cooke and Kothari 2001: 8). The risks of theatre practitioners disempowering the very people they set out to liberate are well articulated by Boon and Plastow (2004) and Thompson (2003).

One of the dangers of postmodernism is that it can induce a resigned 'anything goes' syndrome – one that allows us to opt out of the task of trying to work towards human betterment because it rests on an outdated notion of 'progress', which, once deconstructed, is difficult to reconstruct; or because beset by so many qualifications (for example, that 'betterment' has to be in quotation marks because it is someone else's construct rather than a reality). Further traps lie in wait: if we now privilege the audience in meaning making, do we lose out on art itself? Does the very thing that draws an audience to the theatre, whether in purpose-built arts centre, school hall, prison or outside performance given at a village crossroads in Kenya, risk being compromised? If demand-led market forces or crisis management are to dictate, where does that leave the opportunities to experiment, to surprise, to challenge? There have been heated debates about the relevance, or even the existence, of 'postmodernity'. Thus, the playwright and director John McGrath (1988: 157–8) declared himself to be a premodernist because of postmodernism's seeming imperviousness to – and impotence in the face of – the need for social change, while Terry Eagleton has cast a scep-tical eye on the academic relish of meaninglessness in all texts, and indeed in all means of literary or artistic or, for that matter, everyday social expression (Eagleton 1983). It has seemed sometimes to be a spiral into cultural space in which our only response can be to deconstruct and to stare helplessly into a world that makes no sense (if it can be said to exist at all) and is certainly not changeable. For not dissimilar reasons, the playwright Edward Bond rejects the idea of postmodernism because it constitutes a retreat from reason and belief in justice (Bond 2005: 5): 'Post-modernism is not concerned with answers because it does not think there are any serious questions any more. There are only problems and solutions' (Bond 2002).

For present purposes, it is important to note that the profound social and cultural changes we find ourselves in the midst of – of which post-modernism is undoubtedly a symptom – are ones that those of us working in this field have at least to acknowledge and deal with in our work. The questions abound and can serve to help us critically interro-gate the practice. They can also, sometimes unnecessarily, especially when posed at the wrong moment, undermine confidence in that prac-tice. The questions will not go away and they have to become embedded in the very process of the work, and feed the very questioning that lies at the heart of all good educational theatre practice. As Kathleen Gallagher (Gallagher and Booth 2003: 11) has succinctly put it, theatre, with its distinctive educational force, *dialectics*, invites us to 'take up points of intersection *and* confrontation, so that our dramatic explorations do not simply calcify cultural and ethnic boundaries'.

In brief, and inevitably with considerable oversimplification at this stage in the argument, the three key premises on which this book is pred-icated can be stated as follows.

Firstly, 'theatre' is an art form that still matters. For present purposes, I will define it, if broadly, as performance practice that signals itself to be theatre, that presents plays and various performance and participatory events before an audience that itself knows it is an audience, even if at times it may be invited to participate physically in the event. The theatre may take place in conventional theatre buildings or in school halls or on street corners, or in museums or historic sites. What happens in such events is moreover as much about audiences as it is about 'texts'. Our perceptions of what happens in a theatrical event will be shaped (if not determined) by the cultural codes and experiences that surround us and influence our habits of mind and our assumptions about value; and by the cultural capital (Bourdieu 1979) we may or may not have acquired through our social upbringing and the educational opportunities bestowed on us. One of the challenges faced by theatre seeking to educate is that its potential or target audience may lack that cultural capital that Bourdieu suggests appreciation of the arts generally requires. But then much of the work of educational theatre is at the same time engaged in crossing those very barriers that deny those outside the middle-class mainstream full access to what theatre has to offer. The question that follows, and one that will hover over much of the later discussion, is whether or not the attempt to reach inexperienced audiences necessitates a dilution of theatrical art, to make it easily digestible, or a reduction to mere message-carrying.

Secondly, it matters that we set our understandings of theatre's function in the contemporary world in the larger context of what has happened in the past. We may not always be aware of it, but current practice builds on, even if sometimes it consciously rebels against, what has gone before. And where it does not, it may be that something important has been missed, insights lost. 'History' in this sense matters, and this book is predicated on the belief that we need to locate present practice within a longer tradition or series of cultural practices – partly to increase awareness of how present work has been influenced by what has gone before, partly to see how work from the past diverges from the present (perhaps necessarily so) and partly because there may be lessons we can learn from the past. That does not of course mean that history can be taken as given, as a set of events that sit simply waiting to be uncovered. There is 'History' and there are 'histories'. For Foucault, 'effective history' – or 'genealogy' – was not about the highly suspect pursuit of 'origins' or the attempt to 'capture the exact essence of things' (Foucault 1971: 78), or the manipulation of events into some presumed, overarching and unified 'linear development' or 'evolution' towards an ultimate goal (p. 76). Rather, genealogy looks for 'emergence' rather than evolution (pp. 83–4), for discontinuities, divergences and 'marginal elements' (p. 87) in events and for the 'unstable assemblage of faults, fissures and heterogeneous layers' (p. 82). Such history 'refuses the certainty of absolutes' (p. 87). History is from this perspective as much of a construct as any fiction, all the more problematic because so often presented as undisputed fact. The historical moments and events I have chosen to dwell on constitute just one more attempt at a recovery of aspects of a past we may have overlooked – biased and selective as any such attempt is bound to be. But, just as Foucault cautions against attempting a unified and unifying chronology, the perspectives offered here are provisional and do not claim to provide a neatly ordered narrative of the evolution of educational theatre. In the same way, 'educational theatre' is not seen as a genre but rather as a set of artistic and educationally driven practices that often share values, characteristics and methodologies but which may often diverge in their approaches and philosophical assumptions not only across time and space but even within one given period and cultural setting. In Foucault's terms, then, this study perhaps comes closer to his notion of 'genealogy' than 'History': the accounts of practice given attempt to trace some genealogies across a hundred-year span but avoid as far as possible suggesting that they are part of a progressive evolution towards an ultimate goal. They indicate both discontinuities and some often-overlooked influences and congruences.

Thirdly, 'education' matters – even though our understandings of what it is and what it can do may have been subject to serious challenge and reassessment in recent years. Perhaps it no longer means 'leading out' the young from their state of ignorance into the light of a confident adult world; nor eking out from young, immature minds what may reside in them in some potential but unformed state. We have learned to talk now of learning rather than teaching, of the teacher as a facilitator of that learning; and, from the social constructivists, of the processes by which we build knowledge as much out of our existing knowledges as out of what is explicitly taught us in school; and that learning can, and does, happen as much in informal settings as in formal. The shifting ideas about what constitutes learning inevitably impact upon the kinds of theatre which seek to promote learning.

In linking 'theatre' and 'education' together, in exploring the interconnections between them, and in contemplating the possibility that in certain contexts, at certain times and in certain texts they may be identical, or at least so intertwined as to be inseparable and symbiotic in their function, some preliminary working definitions of terms are needed. These offered definitions are provisional, since perceptions of the function of theatre, of the purpose of education and of the ways in which people learn change over time – they are historically contingent and they reflect important shifts in cultural practice. Across a hundred years, education has shifted its meaning both chronologically – as fashions emerge and get overtaken by new ones, as public policy gets recalibrated, as structural and ideological changes in society make ever-changing demands – and geographically, from country to country. My purpose here is not to try to provide a chronological overview of these changes but rather to point to some of the most significant shifts that have occurred in order to underline how changes in the idea and practice of educational theatre must always be seen against the backdrop of ongoing cultural tides. As Raymond Williams has suggested, from a Marxist perspective, social and cultural change is always a mix of and a constant tension between competing sets of ideologies. At any one historical moment it is usually possible to detect not only the dominant ideology of the period but also the residual ideology, often surprisingly active even in its fading embers, and the emergent ideology, sometimes clearly evident, sometimes hidden or so marginal as to be noticeable only to a few (Williams 1977).

I do not want to suggest either that there are two discrete domains – education and theatre – that somehow, from time to time, coincide to produce 'educational theatre'. There is, to reiterate, no such thing as a distinct genre called educational theatre. Rather, I want to identify the much more intangible but none the less discernible manifestations of a theatre practice driven by the impulse to explain, persuade, cajole, provoke, in order to change, or at least to influence, people's lives, opinions or actions. This does not mean that what follows will essentially be a discussion of theatre that purports to work for social change. There are of course many overlaps and some precise coincidences of radical political theatre and educational theatre (as I suggest for example in Chapter 3). My focus here, though, is less on a practice that has as its primary goal a radical change in the social order but rather on one that endeavours to produce a change in action, behaviour or opinion, or even just attitude; that aims to generate new understandings about the world for an identifiable audience (with identifiable needs, concerns or interests); and that is intended to 'make a difference' in their lives and the way they see the world around them. Thus agit-prop and Brecht will be discussed but not comprehensively, the aim being to highlight aspects that inform directly the argument being developed about how theatre can educate. There is a further aspect to consider in distinguishing theatre-for-learning from the broader notion of theatre-for-social-change. Most educational theatre tends to articulate its goals in terms of the intended effect upon individual attitudes and behaviours, and only indirectly upon society at large. Thus, the play that addresses drug abuse and is aimed at teenagers is likely to seek to put on stage the full realities of what drug abuse can mean for the individual and to influence attitudes among the teenage members of the audience, perhaps their behaviour too. It may set the theme against the larger social context of drug pushers, of social deprivation, perhaps of the commercial interest the tobacco and alcohol industries might have in inducing other kinds of drug dependency, factors that might be seen as formative and requiring government action. But the play is likely to pose questions for individuals and their peers rather than advocate social change at the macrocosmic level. The emphasis tends to be on cognitive change at behavioural or attitudinal levels rather than on the need for social action, although social action is not necessarily debarred. (See Balfour 2000 for a discussion of this tendency in prison theatre.)

Before we move on to explain the spectrum of educational theatre practice that the book will cover, some mention must be made of developments in theories of audience reception and response.

Response theory and the role of the audience

It is now commonplace in discussions of the semiotics of the theatre to stress the interrelationship, indeed the interdependence, of the actor and the audience, the stage and the auditorium. To investigate how signs are generated in the theatre means inevitably some consideration of the reception of those signs by the spectator. After all, 'significance' has no existence on its own: it must be interpreted as such by the percipient. No matter what the author, director or actors intend their work on stage to mean, it has no intrinsic meaning as theatre unless it is communicated to and understood (and remade) by an audience. But until relatively recently, many semioticians, taking as their model the study of signification in literature (or film) have all too readily applied the same principles and method of analysis to the theatre, failing to recognise adequately the ways in which theatre comprises a live, *two-way* communication process, that audiences may not just interpret differently from night to night (or indeed from individual to individual) but that may actually *influence* performance – a characteristic unique to live performance.[2]

More recently, as reader-response theory and subsequently *audience-response* theory have acknowledged more openly the *active* role played by readers and spectators, so a variety of empirical audience research projects have sought to describe, analyse and understand the complex process of audience response. (See Bennett 1990: 34, also Cremona et al. 2004, Sauter 2000 and Schoenmakers 1992.) Ethnography has begun to play a major part in uncovering the multiple narratives that can be told by all involved in a theatrical event (from audience to performer to front-of-house staff). The theoretical field of phenomenology, too, has brought new insights – and new perspectives – to the task of understanding how 'recipients' not only respond but actively contribute to the meanings of an artistic text. As Mark Fortier (1997: 30) has observed, phenomenology has been dismissed by some (such as Terry Eagleton) who consider the underlying philosophy to be elitist, assuming an already-sophisticated set of cultural lenses through which the novel reader, or audience member, will view and be able to interpret actively and intelligently the artwork in front of them. But, as Fortier and others have persuasively pointed out, the strength of the approach for those seeking to understand theatre processes is that it does embrace those very qualities that semiotics has found difficult to codify: those of performativity, liveness, spontaneity, unpredictability and the symbiotic relationship between actor and audience – what Willmar Sauter has called its 'eventness' (Sauter 2000: 11).

But, as we get more sophisticated in developing and applying our analytic apparatus, I am still troubled by the inadequacy of the means we have of describing, let alone analysing, certain kinds of non-traditional contemporary theatre forms. Above all, it is a concern that manifests itself when dealing with participatory theatre forms such as TIE, forum theatre and other practice in which interactive workshops or in-role enactments constitute a pivotal and integrated part of the activity. Much of the discussion through this book is devoted to the attempt to analyse and understand the processes involved in designing and delivering theatre driven by educational objectives and having some form of audience participation at its core.

Some terms

Richard Schechner identifies seven interconnected functions of performance (2002: 37), one of which clearly relates to the subject of this study. They are:

- to entertain
- to make something that is beautiful
- to mark or change identity
- to make or foster community
- to heal
- to teach, persuade or convince
- to deal with the sacred and/or the demonic.

Of course, as Schechner readily acknowledges, they overlap and any one performance is likely to contain several of these functions. What follows in the next few pages is an attempt to open up the 'teach, persuade or convince' category, and simultaneously to suggest ways in which it necessarily crosses over into other functions – not as an accidental straying into foreign territory but rather as an integral part of the very process of 'teaching' or 'persuading'. To entertain may often be central to the very process of teaching. I will therefore attempt to expand Schechner's sixth category, to create room for seepage between this and the other categories, and endeavour to distinguish between the different facets and tendencies of educational theatre. To this end, I shall deploy a variety of terms to try to capture some of the distinctions between different types of work according to their stated or unstated purposes. I propose six possible, overlapping categories, allowing that any one play is likely to contain more than one of these. These are not fixed or impermeable and the reader may understandably wish to take note and quickly abandon them. Plays discussed later in the book which exemplify an aspect of those categories are given in parentheses; several appear against more than one category.

1. *Theatre as propaganda* (or 'campaigning theatre'). The theatre that sets out, sometimes evangelically, to persuade its audience of the rightness of its views; it will usually involve a degree of active campaigning for that view, and there is rarely any question of other views being taken into account unless it is to undermine or reject them, or demonstrate how little credence should be paid to them. Questions may be raised but answers, or at least ways forward, are readily provided. (Examples of plays that manifest this tendency, at least in part, include: *Justice, Waiting for Lefty, Section 218, Spirochete*.)[3]

2. *Theatre as wake-up call.* This theatre is driven by a sense of urgency, a belief that humankind, or, more locally, a specific sector of the community, faces a crisis that needs immediate attention; it sounds an alarm, requires immediate attention and calls for action from its audience. There may be answers, but of more importance is the arousal of the audience to a heightened awareness of the issue and the urgency of decisions being made or action being taken. The target audience tends to be seen collectively rather than as individuals. (Examples include *One Third of a Nation, Uranium 235, Spirochete, E=mc²*.)

3. *The didactic theatre.* The model of education implicitly followed is that in which authoritative teaching is paramount: there is an identifiable body of knowledge about a specific subject that needs to be conveyed directly or indirectly to its audience. While the material is geared specifically to the needs of its target audience, and while it may allow for interaction, the model privileges the one-way transmission of knowledge. A change in behaviour is not necessarily sought, though it may be hoped

for, but a change in attitude usually is and a demonstrable grasp of the information is often expected. (Examples include *Flight*, *One Third of a Nation*, *Love Trouble*, *Forever*.)

4. *Interventionist theatre.* Theatre that targets a specific age group, client group or other sector of the community with the intent of changing minds and/or behaviour. I shall use the term 'interventionist theatre' to embrace the range of theatre work that is driven by clear social agendas, that operates in a far more specifically targeted way than 'didactic theatre'. Interaction with its audience is usually pivotal. The purpose (if not the message) is made quite explicit and a change of attitude or a new, active, observable engagement with the issue is expected; a resulting change in behaviour is hoped for, though not necessarily as an immediate outcome of the theatre experience. (Examples include *Gutted*, *Stay*, *Forever*, *Love Trouble*.)

5. *The dialogic theatre.* Theatre which attempts to embody in its structure and text a genuine (heteroglossic) dialogue between characters and between different views of the world; and which incorporates a dialogic, interactive relationship with its audience. The active participation of the audience at some stage in the process is characteristic if not essential. Decisions on whether to apply the lessons learnt, and how, are handed to the audience, and a fixed or explicit message is avoided. Indeed, it is the audience who must decide for themselves what that message, if any, may be. (Examples include *Home and Away*, *For Any Field?*, the interactions at Plimonth Plantation.)

6. *The playful theatre.* Here the overt emphasis is upon entertainment: inviting laughter, relaxation, and often a celebration of the community's values or beliefs, or of its vitality and *camaraderie* in fighting a common cause. It may seek to release energies and unblock fixed mental attitudes through the sheer playfulness of its approach. The performance style is generally non-naturalistic and may involve music, song, masks or choreography. Any message will be, as far as possible, undetectable, even if educational agendas lie behind the creation of the event; and the production will work to counter any expectations of a message that the audience may initially have. (Examples include *Gutted*, *Forever*.)

On a spectrum these categories might be positioned as in Figure 1. At one end one might characterise the actor–audience relationship as one-way: there is a message to be conveyed, and as directly and unambiguously as possible. At the other, that relationship is fundamentally two-way: any message being imparted is invisible, implied and, at least for the audience, completely subordinate to the enjoyment and playfulness of the event itself. Within the spectrum my focus will be mainly on those aspects covered by the central portions – at the same time recog-

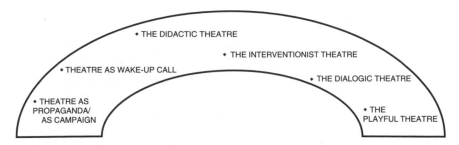

Figure 1 Spectrum of types of educational theatre

nising how other elements necessarily overlap. Thus 'playfulness and celebration' can sometimes be important elements of educative theatre when incorporated as part of a deliberate strategy to reach and engage with specific audiences (as discussed in Chapter 8). Propaganda and campaigning theatre, at the other end of the spectrum, may also be identified as an element of certain kinds of educational theatre. I will not however look at the full range of propagandist theatre since most of the obvious examples (from the Nazi rallies at Nuremberg to admonitory plays about smoking) tend to be fixed on the message (or vision of some new world order), aiming rather to impress or shock their audiences than genuinely to engage or persuade, and therefore lie at the edges of what I am describing as educational. The interesting area for discussion is in those plays where propaganda is accompanied by a discernible openness to dialogue, where an exchange with the audience is at least hinted at or experimented with (as with Piscator's *Section 218*, discussed in Chapter 3).

Subsequent chapters will expand and explore these categories but not be constrained by them: they are offered as a kind of working shorthand for the varieties – and varied permutations – of forms that educational theatre can take.

The examples of theatre practice that appear in the chapters that follow are not meant to be representative of the whole of educational theatre. Rather they provide an opportunity to examine selective examples of work in detail – of different kinds of theatre event and of the varying nature of the relationship with their target audiences – from which some observations and provisional conclusions can be drawn. These examples of educative theatre in action are considered within the larger social, cultural, ideological and theatrical contexts from which inevitably they derive much of their meaning.

Organisation of chapters

The first chapter examines one key aspect of the link between theatre and education, one on which a great deal of my argument through the rest of the book will hinge. That is the question of how far any theatre, or for that matter any form of art, that claims explicitly to be performing an educational function might be considered not just 'art' but 'aesthetic'. The claims made for theatre as an art form are posed against those made for its instrumental function and the possibility that theatre can be both is examined. The connections between certain theories of performance and of learning, both of which place the audience member or learner at the centre of the meaning-making process, are also discussed.

Developments in European and American theatre up to the Second World War

The function of theatre as an educational medium was not exclusive to the twentieth century. But it did re-emerge in the early decades of that century in a whole array of new forms and contexts, and challenged many basic assumptions about the nature and function of theatre: the relationships between actor and audience, playwright and actor, theatre and the state, theatre and actuality, theatre and propaganda. The purpose of these three chapters is to identify some of the more significant developments in theatre as an educational medium during the first half of the century. The first, shorter, Chapter 2 sets the pre-1914 context for the more in-depth studies of theatre in the 1930s in the following two chapters; it is synoptic rather than analytical, and makes particular reference to what was known in Britain as the 'New Drama' of the early twentieth century and to early experiments in children's theatre. One production is however selected for more detailed discussion: John Galsworthy's *Justice*, 1910, an early example of 'theatre as campaign' together with its impact upon the criminal justice legislation of the time.

In Chapter 3 the rise and fall of agit-prop during the 1920s and 1930s is given some prominence because it highlights one of the book's sub-themes: the relationship between campaigning (or propaganda) and education, and the cultural shift detectable as agit-prop rapidly declined to be followed by forms that evidenced much of the same political intent and deployed many of the same techniques but illustrated more sophisticated understandings of the possibilities of the art form. Discussed are Piscator and his experiments with documentary and audience participation; agit-prop companies in Europe and the USA in the 1920s and 1930s; Odets's seminal *Waiting for Lefty*; and the significant American variants of the living newspaper developed as part of the Federal Theatre Project in the USA in the late 1930s. The Project, and the innovative living newspaper especially, stands as an instructive example of a theatre striving for a close, active and educative relationship with its society and for a widening of its audience base, and indeed of the political and artistic risks that that entailed.

Chapter 4 looks at a number of examples of auditorium-based theatre which attempted in various ways to sound alarm-bells, provoke awareness of issues of immediate public concern and influence public opinion – in particular illustrating ways in which theatre attempted to respond to advances in science. *Spirochete*, a living newspaper produced by the Federal Theatre Project in 1938, less well known than other similar examples, was an attempt to raise public awareness of syphilis and of the measures being taken to eradicate it. Three dramas produced within a few years of each other immediately following the end of the Second World War illustrate some of the ways in which the theatre responded to the most frightening scientific advance of the time, the invention and exploitation of the atom bomb: *Uranium 235* by Ewan MacColl and Theatre Workshop, Flanagan-Davis's $E=mc^2$ and Brecht's *Life of Galileo*. The latter offers an instructive contrast: a play that deals, at least on one level, with the same issues but indirectly, metaphorically, and that is certainly less *overtly* educational in style.

Postwar developments and issues in educational theatre

Some of the most interesting and challenging forms of educational theatre have attempted to create a dynamic and physical relationship with their audiences as an educational strategy. The focus in Chapters 5–7 therefore will be on audience participation and the viability of aesthetic criteria when audiences are drawn into the event as *participants* rather than as passive observers. British theatre in education is possibly the best known contemporary practice of this kind. At their best, professional TIE companies gear the resources of theatre to explicit educational ends, and provide an experience for children that, largely through their deployment of participatory techniques, can be intensely absorbing and challenging. Funding crises and the changed cultural perceptions of what theatre can do have led, during the past twenty years, to a marked decrease in the number of professional TIE companies in Britain – but at the same time to an increase in the use of theatre for health education, theatre in prisons and probation services and museum theatre. Examples drawn from both TIE and other related practice such as theatre in prisons will be used to examine different participatory formats and their appropriateness to the different kinds of subject matter and age or type of audience. Even more than the living newspapers, TIE programmes beg fundamental questions about the extent to which educational theatre can still be viewed as 'art'. These accounts of practice will be used to advance the discussion of the interconnections in such work between the educational and the aesthetic. For that reason, examples are taken not only from recent work but from 'classic' TIE productions spanning a period of some thirty years. The aim is not to discuss contemporary practice *per se*, but to look at the issues and problems demonstrated in as wide a variety of practice as possible. Later, in chapter 7, discussion focuses on the notion of the 'dialogic', and suggests connections between the Freirean and Bakhtinian notions of the term as a way of arguing that the aesthetic and the 'instrumental' do not have to be opposed, rather that the dialogic can be (should be) at the heart of any theatre experience that is powerful, moving and educationally provocative.

In Chapter 8, I will pose against each other two contrasting notions: that of the 'targets and outcomes culture' and that of a 'playing culture' and will argue that it is often the ludic qualities of the drama that impacts upon audiences and participants far more than the overtly serious, message-driven elements. Because the arts in education are often constrained and indeed driven by notions of value-for-money and cost-effectiveness, and the agendas are often determined by agencies who prioritise 'crisis management' or narrowly conceived notions of 'development', the creative and aesthetic nature of the work done frequently gets marginalised and under-valued. The 'playing culture' on the other hand (a term I take from Sauter's illuminating study *The Theatrical Event*), represents the opposite end of the spectrum even though the two cultures frequently overlap. It refers to those qualities that lie at the root of theatre's ludic character – qualities associated with spontaneity, unpredictability, celebration and collective endeavour. Examples are offered of varieties of theatre practice – from prison theatre and from TIE – that manage to work creatively within the framework of given agendas (often government-led) in the interests of achieving an effective educational outcome.

Interactive theatre is being used increasingly and in a variety of ways at heritage sites and museums – in the UK and USA especially but in many other countries too – in order to interpret, and arouse curiosity about, the past or aspects of the collections being exhibited. The practice raises interesting questions about the ways drama is used in cultural expression and redefinition and as a medium of learning. Chapter 9 offers a perspective upon such practice by focusing on some contrasting examples of 'living history' projects such as (but not confined to) Plimoth Plantation (a site-specific year-round project based at a replica early Puritan-settler village in Massachusetts) and the work of the Young

National Trust Theatre (until recently the Trust's professional theatre in education company). I will look at the particular dynamic and the dialectical tensions that arise from the relationship between actors in role, the specific historic location they operate within and the audience of visitors, and especially school pupils. The chapter also highlights the problematic issue of how far, and in what ways, first-person interpretation might constitute 'theatre' rather than educationally driven 'historical roleplay'.

The Afterword revisits some of the themes and theoretical implications arising out of the historical survey and the studies of recent and contemporary practice and offers some final (but far from conclusive) reflections.

But, first, what are the implications for theatre as an art form when pressed into service to perform an 'instrumental' function – when designed to achieve some particular, socially useful goal, specified in advance, a goal which can then be checked when the performance is done? And how might a consideration of aesthetic concepts and of developments in theories of learning contribute to a grasp of theatre's potential as a learning medium?

Notes

1 For further discussion of evaluation see the special edition of *Research in Drama Education*, 11.2 (2006) devoted to 'impact assessment' in applied drama; see also Matarasso (1997), a sustained evaluation of the impact upon ordinary (non-professional) people's lives as a result of participating in arts activities.

2 Erika Fischer-Lichte's meticulous and comprehensive study was one of the first to grapple with the complexity of theatre semiotics in a sustained way. See Fischer-Lichte (1992); also Bennett (1990), Carlson (1990), Counsell (1996) and Melrose (1994).

3 The reader may also wish to compare Marion Frank's discussion (Frank 1995: 13) of what she terms 'Campaign Theatre'. Seen as a specific and limited subcategory of theatre for development, it is 'concerned with raising the consciousness of people on such topics as child care, environmental issues, health care, etc.'; see also Breitinger (1994) on propaganda theatre in African contexts, p. 212.

1

Theatre, learning and the aesthetic dimension: preliminary perspectives

Theatre – art or instrument?

A Doll's House will be as flat as ditchwater when *A Midsummer Night's Dream* will still be as fresh as paint; but it will have done more work in the world; and that is enough for the highest genius, which is always intensely utilitarian. (George Bernard Shaw 1895: 63)

People have tried for centuries to use drama to change people's lives, to influence, to comment, to express themselves. It doesn't work. It might be nice if it worked, but it doesn't. The only thing dramatic form is good for is telling a story. (David Mamet 1994: 386)

These two assertions, some hundred years apart, were of course meant to be contentious – but they do point to one of the recurring questions about the role that theatrical art plays in modern western culture, and neatly encapsulate the contrasting claims made by practitioners and critics alike for the 'work in the world' that drama can do. The implication of Shaw's assertion would seem to be that there are broadly two kinds of plays: first, high art that appeals to what is often described as our aesthetic sensibility, universal, timeless, free of that concern with current issues which usually renders the work before long hopelessly dated; and, secondly, the 'issue drama' designed to raise questions, point a finger, change attitudes or even the world. I doubt if, now, many of us would subscribe to such a narrow 'either/or' view of different types of plays (and to be fair this was not wholly Shaw's view either). Even *A Midsummer Night's Dream*, as most scholars would acknowledge, can be fully understood only in terms of the age in and for which it was written; while 'universality' and 'timelessness' now have little critical currency (except when enclosed in quotation marks). But it does underscore an attitude to 'the aesthetic' and to the way different types of drama are valued that is still prevalent in the minds of critics, funders, sponsors, governments and audiences. Does a play that is written to make a social point, or educate or in some other way does 'work in the world', warrant less attention than a 'classic'? Does a play have to survive a hundred years to prove itself as a work of art? Is there not a place for the 'artistic text' that also does work in the world (including educating), even if it may not last the test of time? Much of the theatrical work produced in the 1930s, for example, might seem to us now to be little more than propagandist in nature, but some – notably a number of the living newspapers produced by the Federal Theatre Project in the USA – was clearly educative rather than dogmatic and is still capable of exciting my own students in the twenty-first century, not because the plays are 'as fresh as paint' but because they are obviously highly effective, powerful theatrical expressions of a mood and of a belief in the illuminative function of theatre at a time of severe economic and political strain. If you take enough time to locate these plays within their context (social, economic, cultural), it does not then take much effort to imagine the power of these plays or to see vibrant connections with our own world some seventy years on.

To return to the two polarised views of the function of theatre, then, it is argued on the one hand that what is conventionally thought of as great dramatic art will not achieve the social impact that plays such as *A Doll's House* have done. These plays have a different function: they can be directly useful to us in the 'real world' beyond the theatre walls, perhaps capable of influencing that world or at least influencing the way we think about and operate in the world – but they may not, consequently, have much shelf life. *A Doll's House* still, of course, obstinately refuses to leave both shelf and stage, but in this respect may be an exception to the rule; the vast majority of 'interventionist' dramas rarely outlive their historical moment. A play such as *Spirochete*, a living newspaper written in 1938 in Chicago with the aim of heightening public awareness of the widespread (but barely discussed) problem of syphilis and of the cures available, and discussed in Chapter 4, undoubtedly did much effective work in the world but remains of and for its time.

On the other hand, the playwright David Mamet douses with cold water the whole notion of 'useful' dramatic art. Let us not delude ourselves, he argues, into thinking drama is good for anything else than telling a story – the value of good dramatic story-telling is important enough as it is. It serves the art form – and possibly those we wish to influence – badly if we insist on trying to change the world using drama as our lever. A genuine work of art cannot be didactic or 'instrumental'.

The novel, play or poem that sets out to convey information or to preach a message risks surrendering those very qualities we usually value in art – complexity, multi-layered meanings, richness of imagination. Jonathan Levy, in his *A Theatre of the Imagination*, argues that 'the impulse to create theatre for children is the impulse to give a gift, without strings. It is this impulse . . . we should . . . call upon when we find ourselves in the theatre tempted to teach' (Levy 1987: 9). Further, he insists that 'when art is used to teach, either the teaching or the art must suffer' (Levy, p. 8). In this analysis, teaching and dramatic art are clearly seen to make awkward bedfellows: it has to be one or the other, not both. Lowell Swortzell took a not dissimilar line in his provocative essay on theatre in education, 'Trying to like TIE' (Swortzell 1993), regretting that all too often the didactic intent of the TIE pieces has led to well-intentioned but ill-crafted dramas that in the end diminish the children's experience. Many practitioners of children's and young people's theatre have likewise resisted having their work categorised as educational or in any way curriculum-driven. The work must have its own justification, as art, as story-telling, offering young people an experience that may complement but is fundamentally different from anything else they get in school.

This is a matter that arouses similar if not identical passions beyond British and American shores. During a research collaboration between colleagues in Manchester and Helsinki (in 1998), we encountered similar such attitudes fervently held by writers and directors of plays for young people in the thriving and popular children's theatres in Helsinki.[1] Interestingly, if unsurprisingly, difficulties quickly emerged during the research over our definition of terms. From what began – naively – as an assumption that 'educational' would mean the same in Finnish as in English, we soon discovered that there were significant cultural differences that made the term 'educational theatre' particularly fraught. While 'theatre as an educational tool' was certainly understood, our phraseology carried with it the implication that the education was primary and the art form secondary (for example that theatre was being used to teach language skills, or to communicate or reinforce a body of knowledge). For Finnish theatre directors and actors especially, 'educational' was usually taken to mean 'didactic' – the one-way transmission of information – and to refer to 'institutional education'. Many could not see why on earth actors should have anything to do with it. In the UK, however, 'educational' tends to be used rather more loosely as an umbrella term but is none the less often distinguished from the more narrow and restrictive 'didactic'. All theatre can of course, at some level or other, be thought of as broadly educational; but in Britain it has been possible to speak of 'theatre with an educational purpose' without quite the same pejorative didactic associations. TIE has been a major influence in opening up the field of theatre as an educational medium and allowing more nuanced ideas of what education might involve. In bringing theatre into the classroom, in exploring multi-layered approaches to subject matter, and in its interactive modes, it has, alongside developments in the teaching of classroom drama, done much to reclaim the term 'education' (quite properly) as a legitimate concern for the arts, within and beyond the confines of the official curriculum.

The dichotomy that separates theatre art and theatre for learning has been reinforced and rearticulated, if from a wholly different theoretical angle, within the field of performance studies. Richard Schechner, for example, makes a strong claim for the idea of a social-theatre/aesthetic-theatre binary; he is careful to avoid suggesting a complete separation of the two, but sees two quite distinct, opposing tendencies and clearly privileges the social (or instrumental) over the aesthetic (see Schechner 2002, Schechner and Thompson 2004). Thus, while the aesthetic theatre has been in 'decline' for the past half century, 'many different kinds of theatres' have since emerged, and especially 'social theatre' which is defined as 'theatre with specific social agendas; theatre where aesthetics is not the ruling objective' (Schechner and Thompson 2004: 12).[4] Augusto Boal too has at times appeared to further bolster the dichotomy. Arguing for a theatre that can serve the immediate needs of the marginalised, the oppressed and the disadvantaged, he has opened up important aspects of theatre's social function for debate and interrogated the artistic and social implications of his own practice. But here is what he wrote in 1992:

> Should the presentation of a forum tend towards the theatrical? Should one seek to produce . . . good theatre . . . or should one, on the contrary, aim to stimulate reflection, argument, action? (Boal 1992: 234).

He is of course referring to the whole process of 'forum theatre' (Boal 1979, 1992) – not only to the presentation in dramatic form of the problem being addressed culminating in a dilemma or crisis for the protagonist (the 'oppressed' character) but also to the interactive investigation that follows: the attempts to find alternative ways through the crisis, by the 'spect-actors'. Elsewhere, he qualifies the apparent dichotomy, suggesting that the use of music and dance can inspire audience participation 'with much greater enthusiasm', much more so than 'unadorned speech' (Boal 1992: 235). In the later *Legislative Theatre*, he insists on creativity to enliven and shape dialogue (Boal 1998: 77); and in his latest book (published just before the present study went to press) he appears to have moved further towards giving full weight to 'the aesthetic process' – the means by which participants will develop their perceptions and expressiveness, a fundamental part of what he now calls 'the aesthetics of the oppressed' – which will, at best culminate in and enrich 'the artistic product, the work of art' which can be shared with other persons (Boal 2006: 18). But it is interesting that 'good theatre' and the stimulus of 'reflection, argument, action' should have been posed as alternatives at all. It is characteristic, I think, of how the discourse in the field is so often framed.

In the remainder of this chapter, I want to suggest that the dichotomy that so frequently plagues debates about theatre for young people and whether or not it should have an educational or 'interventionist' agenda, may be misconceived, that the use of theatre in 'applied contexts' (whether schools, museums, young offender institutions, prisons or other community settings), and driven by agendas other than artistic, *can* be both interventionist and aesthetically appealing, indeed that the artistic and the instrumental are – at least in the best practice – interdependent. This is not a new proposal. Horace in *Ars Poetica* spoke of 'delighting' the reader at the same time as 'instructing him'.[2] And, in 1936, Bertolt Brecht had averred that theatre for instruction and theatre for entertainment were not mutually exclusive. Usefulness does not have to preclude enjoyment – the two may exist side by side:

> the contrast between learning and amusing oneself is not laid down by divine rule; . . . theatre remains theatre, even when it is instructive theatre, and in so far as it is good theatre it will amuse. (Brecht 1974a: 72–3)

His advocacy in 1930 of an 'epic theatre' rather than a 'narrative theatre' (Brecht 1972: 37) stemmed largely from a conviction that good theatre could be instrumental in working for social change, but that the particular qualities that would characterise such theatre were necessarily different from those of traditional, Aristotelian, narrative-driven theatre. Thus the epic theatre would value the rational over the emotional; and would foreground the theatricality of the story being told as a means of accentuating its social and ideological implications: that human actions are not inevitable but the product of conscious or unconscious choices, that things might have been, and in our day would be, different. My argument will however attempt to push the boat out just a little further, into waters that would have been less familiar to Brecht: to consider theatre that involves not only performance but active audience participation of the kind that characterises TIE and forum theatre. I will argue that, at its best, theatre that aims to educate or influence can truly do so *only* if it values entertainment, the artistry and craftsmanship that are associated with resonant, powerful theatre, and the aesthetic qualities that – by definition – will appeal to our senses. I will argue too that, even in the most proactive interventionist theatre, the aesthetic dimension of the work is pivotal. Lose sight of the aesthetic and the *capacity* of such theatre to intervene is seriously diminished. It is through the aesthetic indeed that effective theatre will achieve its goals – so long as those goals go beyond the mere imparting of a message, moral or otherwise. There are many examples of educationists, social workers and development agencies turning to theatre in order to convey a message simply because it is inherently an entertaining medium and will therefore make the message more palatable. In this respect, I take issue with those – such as Marion Frank (1995) in her otherwise powerful justification of the use of popular theatre forms in development work in Africa – who imply that the primary reason for using theatre to convey important messages is that it is popular, unthreatening and easy to digest: the sugar coating around the bitter pill. Frank's argument is very much of the 'instrumentalist' tendency: 'theatre through its inherent entertainment value is better suited to convey that message (about health care, the environment, etc) than, for instance, a series of lectures' (Frank 1995: 13).

Surprisingly few writings on theatre for development, applied theatre, interventionist theatre or theatre in education (all of which for convenience I am subsuming here under the title of educational theatre) deal directly and in detail with artistic concerns. There are eminent exceptions of course, but, considering the pivotal place of the word 'theatre' in our terminologies, it does seem strange, if not wholly surprising, that the artistic dimension of this theatre is so rarely addressed head-on. If art is referred to at all in interventionist theatre discourse, it is generally not the primary concern but rather the means towards a larger end: putting 'empowerment', 'ownership' and the voices of the participants at the centre of the work. Process is valued above product. It is of course wholly understandable. There are two main, fairly obvious factors at work: external and internal. There is the pressure from outside agencies (not least from those that provide the funding) to demonstrate the work to be socially beneficial rather than artistic; and there are the internal pressures as companies work to make their performances and workshops accessible and directly useful to the audiences they care about. When faced with the needs of community groups under stress and when the theatre is pressed into service by agencies that inevitably prioritise outcomes and behavioural and attitudinal change, a debate about art and aesthetics can seem pretty irrelevant. Moreover, art is often associated with classical, elitist concepts, and (to borrow Bourdieu's telling phrase) with a cultural capital that is more readily available to those in the more privileged, well-educated strata of society (Bourdieu 1979) – and by definition, less

available to the client groups for which interventionist theatre practitioners most often work. Do we really want to spend time and effort inducting them into the cultural codes we take for granted but which may have
little if any relevance for groups inevitably far more absorbed in the
popular culture that surrounds them? Better surely to focus on those
aspects that demand our immediate attention – how to reach and connect
with young men at risk, teenagers for whom unprotected sex is already
part of their accepted social behavioural norms – with theatre the means,
providing a repertoire of techniques that can be adapted as part of a
process of engagement, challenge and, it is to be hoped, emancipation.

However, I want to argue here that those of us who practise, teach or
write about educational theatre need to be clearer and more assertive
about the aesthetic dimension of the work. This should not be misun-
derstood as appearing to undermine or compromise work that is social,
progressive, transformative and educative. It may be that the artistic and
the transformative may not be awkward bedfellows; that a more open
embrace of the artistic may actually contribute to the very goals of intervention and provide a means by which audiences can be reached in non-
didactic and empowering ways. To seek the art within interventionist
theatre practice is not necessarily about changing the work done; rather
it is about the need constantly to test, question and develop our practice,
and where necessary to reconceptualise it.

The artistic and the aesthetic

Let me first try to tease out one of the problems of definition that bedev-
ils any attempt to bridge the domains of the artistic and the instrumental:
that is, the common association of art with high art. As the cultural
anthropologist Clifford Geertz reminds us, art as it has been practised
across the ages and across cultures is not as universal or timeless as the
western classical tradition or dictionary definitions of art might have us
believe (Geertz 1997). He objects strongly to one such, all too typical, definition of art, namely as the conscious production or arrangement of
colours, forms, movements . . . in a manner that affects a sense of beauty,
because it seems to imply that 'men are born with the power to appreciate . . . and have only to be provided with the occasions to exercise it'
(Geertz 1997: 117–18). 'Not true', he argues – the sense of beauty or
'ability to respond intelligently to [artworks] is no less a cultural artefact
than the objects and devices concocted to "affect" it'. Our relationship
with art, our ability to understand it and talk about it, is culturally constructed. One might add that such traditional assumptions about art stem
from classical theories of art and aesthetics, notably those propounded by

Kant and still, as John Carey in *What Good Are the Arts?* observes, per-
versely exerting a hold on much of our contemporary thinking (Carey
2005). It was in particular Kant's essentialist view of the arts – as a means
of putting us in touch with a deeper, otherwise inaccessible level of
Reality, Goodness and True Worth – that has led to the enshrinement of
the arts as something special, extraordinary and the product of genius,
and by extension appreciated only by highly educated and sensitive
people. Bourdieu's analysis of the social status and social hierarchies that
are involved in the appreciation of the arts is in large measure predicated
upon this notion of the arts as a 'thing' that requires the acquisition of
'taste' and certain social skills in order to understand and value art in all
its complexity and historic significance. The value of art may lie as much
in the sophisticated eye of the beholder as in the art itself. But Bourdieu's
critique – penetrating as it is in its sociological analysis of how literature
and the fine arts are learned, appropriated and become markers of social
class – is much less illuminating about theatre and even less so about
'social theatre', that is, about forms of theatre that make it their business
to reach the marginalised, the underprivileged, the young.

Despite the cultural relativism that Geertz sees as inevitable in any
attempt to understand the social function of art, there is, none the less,
he suggests, some artistic commonality across cultures, and that is, its
aesthetic quality – it appeals to the senses, it is perceptual and tends to
be non-utilitarian. What seems to be shared by most societies is the practice of engaging in symbolic activities that bracket off and give expression to aspects of human life which are seen to have some significance
and value for that society. While such activities may often be functional,
their main purpose is not primarily utilitarian. The bucket is noticeably
different from the decorated vase or pot. The decoration is not actually
needed for the effective storage of water or wine, though it may add
something to the enjoyment of life if and when such tasks are carried out.
Decorated pots may indeed be constructed solely to give pleasure, with
no utilitarian value whatever. This notion of art being non-utilitarian is
one of the stumbling blocks for advocates of educational theatre. Isn't
such theatre by its very nature utilitarian? Is it not designed, and often
funded, to do a specific job with a particular social group with a specific
outcome in mind? If art is not supposed to be 'useful', then no wonder
practitioners often feel suspicious if anyone questions them rather about
artistry and style than about whether or not their practice 'works'.
Perhaps we might stand with Shaw and argue that different criteria, different standards apply to theatre that does 'work in the world': cultural
'shelf life' (if that is what art often seems to imply) is really not a concern.
It must work in the here and now. To quote John McGrath, the erstwhile

director of the radical theatre company 7:84, and speaking of political theatre practice, 'It works if the audience get it with the same sense of wonder and rightness and relevance that you as a group "got it" with, if the instinctive reaction is not jarred by any incongruous worries, if the subterranean connections are made and the scene itself is gripping, for good reasons. That's the end of aesthetics' (McGrath 1979: 47).

It is not quite the end of aesthetics of course. McGrath's pragmatic (and persuasive) assertion of 'what works' still begs the question of the role played by the audience or percipient. Does 'getting it' imply a rather uncomplicated direct transfer of knowledge and experience from performers to audience? Or does audience reception involve a more interactive process? While art and artistry, and the value we assign them, may be culturally constructed, it is in what Geertz calls 'aesthetic activity' that we may find the most resonant and productive concept for educational theatre practice. The conclusion that Geertz draws is that aesthetic activity seems specifically designed 'to demonstrate that ideas are visible, audible and . . . tactible [sic], that they can be cast in forms where the senses, and through the senses the emotions, can reflectively address them' (Geertz 1997: 118). Aesthetic activity then has as much to do with reception and response as with the art forms themselves.

At this point, I need to try to narrow down further my use of this slippery term 'aesthetic', and consider how it differs from 'artistic'. The term 'aesthetic' often gets a rather bad press and it often, confusingly, gets appropriated for a whole range of competing uses.[3] Indeed, so commonly is it associated with 'feelings' or 'refinement' or 'beauty' – the decorative rather than the functional – that one could be forgiven for believing a discussion of the aesthetics of educational theatre to be somewhat peripheral to the tough realities of the social world which educational, and especially interventionist, theatre usually addresses. I want to make the case here, though, that a concern with the aesthetic – far from being diversionary, elitist or secondary to the 'real' business of what the play is 'about' – is actually central to the effectiveness of educational theatre; that the aesthetic dimension must form an integral part of any serious attempt to understand the educational experience of audiences.

An anecdote will help me explain, and to identify some of the key questions I wish to address. Almost thirty years ago, I recall seeing a TIE play[4] that made an enduring impression on me. It was performed in a very ordinary school hall with an audience of about sixty thirteen-year-olds circled closely round the acting area so the audience sense of involvement was strong. It was about a teenage boy suffering from athetosis, a form of cerebral palsy. It told his story, simply but very effectively, by a combination of flashback, direct-address narration and naturalistic action.

Its ingenuity, and its memorability, lay in one particular dramatic strategy. While for most of the play we saw the teenager as others saw him – physically handicapped with a speaking deficiency that made it impossible for virtually anyone except his mother to understand him (and played with great persuasiveness by the actor) – at other moments the play gave us the world from his point of view. At pivotal points in the drama, the boy would suddenly turn to us and speak and move without any impediment – he was 'normal' to us; we now could see him in a new light, as he shared his thoughts, fears, anger, with us. He was bright, articulate, reflective and immensely frustrated – not the 'dumbo' others (and perhaps some in the audience) had taken him for. A simple but stunningly effective device – suddenly illuminating, for me, a fact that I had known intellectually (physical and vocal disability does not mean stupidity) but had never quite seen or understood in that empathetic way.

The theatre had not so much *taught* me, in the sense of conveying new information, but had thrown new light on something I thought I knew already. It had *dramatically* enhanced my understanding. That fleeting but profoundly resonant image, that way of seeing from another's viewpoint, embedded itself in my consciousness and provided me with a personal resource. To my surprise it has remained with me ever since as an intuitive reference point, a quick way of reminding myself – when for example meeting someone with a speech disability – that the lack of a conventionally articulate, fluent way of speaking cannot be equated with intellectual inadequacy. There is another voice within (and more) to which I need to be alert.

The experience of seeing (participating in) that play was one that I will argue is usefully described as an aesthetic experience. Art had done its work on me and it is above all the relationship forged between the play and me, as audience-participant, that I wish to term aesthetic. To describe what I had gone through as 'educational' or 'artistic', or even a combination of the two, would somehow be inadequate. This was not learning as some kind of by-product of the artistic experience; it was rather an organic process of learning through the art. Indeed, it was not thought of as learning at all until after the event was over. And that process, the journey that such a play can take its audience on, is a key part of what I am calling 'aesthetic'.

Aesthetic experience and the making of meaning

Precise and robust definitions of what constitutes 'aesthetic' are virtually impossible to find, and attempts to pin down its meanings are invariably inflected by the age and culture in which they are made. But my purpose here is not to add yet another definition to the list: rather to start from some working assumptions, and focus on the applicability and the relevance of the term to the type of theatre I am discussing. I am indebted particularly to the writings on aesthetics and education of such philosophers and educationists as Peter Abbs (1987), David Best (1991), Maxine Greene (1995), Louis Arnaud Reid (1969) and Malcolm Ross (1984). And I will take as given that the arts are a product of human endeavour of the highest order and that they offer alternative ways of knowing the world. Or, as Boal, puts it, in his most recent excursion into the possibilities afforded by the theatre of the oppressed, 'Art is a special form of knowledge' (Boal 2006: 20).

David Best is surely right to argue not only that the arts are about the world of feelings but that cognition and rationality too are an integral part of the way we experience and make sense of the arts: they are not the exclusive preserve of the sciences (Best 1991). Best further points out that the common separation of cognition from feelings, as though they were two quite distinct mental operations, is false. Rational understanding and the emotions of, say, joy or terror are interconnected. The emotion will often be prompted by our recall and understanding of similar feelings in previous circumstances; while our decision-making will frequently be informed by our intense feelings from past situations. (See also Allen et al. 1999, whose research into the impact of a TIE programme, ostensibly about 'joy-riding' but also, more challengingly, about morals and values, supports Best's argument.) The association of the arts primarily with feelings has undoubtedly been limiting. Even more so has been the Kantian conception of the arts and, by extension, of the 'aesthetic', as a field of human activity essentially concerned with what is beautiful or gives pleasure (especially the pleasure gained by retreating from everyday life) – a conception that has driven debate about the arts for some two centuries. (For a succinct discussion of Kant's influence see Sheppard 1987: 65–73; also Carey 2005: 8–12.) It is especially problematic when trying to account for literary works or the performing arts that appear to offer the reader the total opposite of 'beauty', that rather seek to disturb than give pleasure.

Art is not necessarily always beautiful. Dickens's depiction of life in Victorian London in *Bleak House* is hardly one that induces a delight in the beauties of the landscape or architecture or fine living. It was in part a novel motivated by anger at current injustices, and especially at the destructive impact of a self-serving legal system. No, art is often concerned with depicting aspects of the world that have significance but in ways that can reconnect us with the real world, in ways that are revelatory, striking, disturbing – and perhaps (is this what makes it art?) uplifting or liberating. Susanne Langer attempts to resolve the beauty/ugliness issue by arguing that the beauty that is for many the measure of all 'good art' resides not in what art depicts (content) but in its 'expressive form' (Langer 1953: 396). 'Beautiful works may contain elements that, taken in isolation, are hideous', she acknowledges, but, when taken as a whole, the 'emergent form . . . is alive and therefore beautiful, as awful things may be – as gargoyles, and fearful African masks, and the Greek tragedies of incest and murder, are beautiful' (Langer 1953: 395). In this sense, then, one might acknowledge that the 'beauty' of *Bleak House* derives not from the subject matter but from the expressive power of the writing. But 'beauty' alone is of course insufficient to capture the full sense of that expressive form. By extension one would have to include within the expressiveness of the form its capacity to shock and disturb. That power is embedded in the very essence of classic tragedy but has become particularly characteristic of much twentieth-century theatre, from Strindberg and the expressionists through to the work of Sarah Kane. Aristotle endeavoured to explain and justify it in his concept of tragic catharsis, seeing its value not so much in the beauty of the expressive form but rather in the beneficial effect it would have upon the audience. The emotional process undergone by the tragic protagonist in his journey of discovery was one that (in the great tragic dramas known to Aristotle) was not merely witnessed by the audience. By means of empathy with the hero, it was a process they too, if vicariously, shared. In turn, they would be 'purged' of the distressing emotions of pity and fear that that empathy had generated. Whether or not the audience does indeed experience the identical emotion felt by the protagonist is a moot point (see for example Schoenmakers 1992). The emotions of the character are of course fictitious, a construct of the author. The emotions of the audience members, while triggered by imaginative involvement in the unfolding story, can only be those of observers, at least one step removed from the plight of the protagonist. We may feel for Oedipus in his gathering horror at what his own actions have unwittingly led him towards, but at the same time we are not (thankfully) in Oedipus' position, and the playwright ensures that we can also see the bigger picture: we see things coming that Oedipus cannot, the beneficiaries of Sophocles' larger artistic vision in which patterns of ironies and coincidences and privileged prior knowledge all play their part in helping us understand as well as feel for Oedipus in his predicament. Moreover, while 'fear' suggests an intensely involved response, the very notion of 'pity' implies a degree of distance from the dramatic action: we feel fear; we take pity.

Brecht, and later Boal, famously rejected the notion of catharsis as socially retrograde, one that merely pacified an audience, leaving them emotionally neutralised and therefore reconciled to the status quo. (Boal (2006: 23) warns of the potency of empathy 'when imposed by the Protagonist in Tragedy on passive spectators'.) Recent interpretations of catharsis have however emphasised its more positive function of unblocking, release or liberation. Seamus Heaney, for example, speaks of catharsis as 'that momentary release from confusion which comes from seeing a drama complete itself in accordance with its own inner necessities rather than in accordance with the spectator's wishes' (Heaney 1993: 229). In a discussion of drama and moral education, Joe Winston suggests that with catharsis may come illumination, stressing that catharsis underlines the 'cognitive aspect of emotion' (Winston 1996: 194).

While Langer's definition of beauty in art, bound up with art's 'intrinsically expressive' function, helps us to sidestep some of the limiting associations art can have, it does not entirely eliminate the related association of 'fixedness'. Langer's focus upon expressiveness places primary emphasis upon the qualities of the artwork itself with the role of the percipient being to 'grasp' the beauty of the form through which the subject matter is given full expression. Even her discussion of 'responsiveness' to art privileges 'direct aesthetic experience' (1953: 397), achieved when one can clear the mind of inhibiting 'interpretive prejudices and false conceptions' (p. 396) and respond intuitively to the revelations the artwork inspires. She quotes Charles Morgan's account of the power of great theatre which 'transmutes [the spectator] not his opinions . . . We surrender and are changed.' Dramatic art, Morgan continues, must 'still the preoccupied mind . . . then to impregnate it' (p. 398). Great dramatic art, as with all art, is, for Morgan and Langer alike, an entity that wins us over through the power to touch us and move us; in the auditorium, our role is to be open and receptive. We are percipients rather than participants. Opportunities to grasp, or contemplate, the beauty of the form are however more available with some forms of art than with others. Performance, unlike more concrete or stable art forms such as poetry and the fine arts, is essentially dynamic, fluid, ephemeral; participatory theatre is not only dynamic but calculatedly dependent upon the interactive response from its audiences or participants. As Schechner suggests (2002: 41), Langer's 'classical notions of aesthetics' are challenged by the deliberately unpredictable, boundary-breaking work of performance artists and of other forms of postmodern art – and indeed, one might add, of participatory theatre.

The opportunity to contemplate, then, is not necessarily an essential component of all contemporary art forms. We may be on safer ground to suggest that art – whether the decorated vase or the epic poem or the dance-drama or even the work of the performance artist – is at root a meaning-making activity in which symbolic forms are deployed to take us on some kind of a journey – psychological, emotional – the kind of journey we might not have taken otherwise. It may involve us in a retreat from the everyday, or it may be a detour, offering us vantage points from which to see the everyday in a new light or from a new angle. We may often agree to go on the journey not quite knowing where it will take us, nor how far to trust those who take us, but we are always fellow-travellers, tacit or active participants. Recent years have seen increased recognition of the active role the audience itself plays in the process of making meanings (for example Bennett 1990, Carlson 1990, Schechner 2002), even in the most conventional of theatre performances. We do not merely sit passively, deciphering the codes prepared for us by playwright and director, or unwrapping carefully prepackaged meanings.

The recognition of the participatory role of the audience returns us to the question of the aesthetic and especially to the distinction to be drawn between the artistic and the aesthetic. John Dewey argued in 1934 (though he was not the first to do so) that the aesthetic has more to do with *perception* than with qualities inherent in the artwork itself, in this way drawing a clear distinction between the work of art and aesthetic experience. It is the art form through which the artist's vision is given shape that enables us to see, perhaps understand, what in real life would merely sicken or confuse us; and it is the process of receiving, being moved by and making sense of that vision that constitutes aesthetic perception. At its best, the aesthetic experience is (as one commentator has expressed it) 'arresting, intense and utterly engrossing'; it 'seizes one's whole mind or imagination and conveys [its subject] so vividly that the result is delight and knowledge' (Collinson 1992: 115). Pleasure *may* therefore be found in, for example, a moment of recognition, even if what we are recognising is a truthful rendition of man's inhumanity. As Eric Bentley argues, art is a matter not of cognition but of re-cognition: 'it does not tell you anything you didn't know . . . it tells you something you "know" and makes you realise' (Bentley 1965: 53–4). This is not quite the same argument as Langer's about the beauty that resides in true artistic form. The emphasis suggested by Dewey, Collinson and others is not just upon that which gives pleasure (form) but upon the percipient's pleasurable *act* of recognition. Dewey went on to argue that 'knowledge is transformed in an aesthetic experience': it becomes 'something more than knowledge because it is merged with non-intellectual elements to form an experience worthwhile *as* an experience' (Dewey 1980: 290; quoted in Collinson 1992: 156). Perhaps this goes some way to explaining my response to the TIE play thirty years ago, deriving as it did from a kind of knowing qualitatively different from the kind we normally associate with the classroom.

It is, I think, especially important when trying to understand the impact of educational theatre experiences (even more so when trying to design systematic evaluations) that we identify and differentiate as precisely and productively as we can what constitutes the 'artistic' and what the 'aesthetic' in any such theatre event. One further helpful way of articulating the distinction is offered by the literary critic Wolfgang Iser in his phenomenological account of reader-response in the novel (Iser 1988: 212). He suggests that the *artistic* and the *aesthetic* constitute between them the two main poles in any literary work. While the 'artistic' refers to the text created by the author, the 'aesthetic' refers to the *realisation created by the reader*. (Applied to the theatre, for 'author' we may read the author, directors and actors; while for 'reader' we can substitute 'audience'.) In other words, rather than conflating the two terms in ways that only serve to confuse, we maintain a distinction between, on the one hand, the work and the intended meanings generated by the artists and, on the other, the total experience of the work once it has been shared with an audience. While the artist creates the art and invests it with significance, it is in the appeal to our aesthetic imaginations and sensibilities that the reader or observer becomes an active maker of meaning. It is the percipient who completes the circle, contributes the imaginative filling-in of the gaps left in the text and becomes a co-author in the work of art. Any analysis of that experience must take full account of the perception of the work by an audience (which may not always be quite as the author or director intended), and, further, the active involvement of the audience in the creative process. Thus the aesthetic refers both to that quality of the work that makes its appeal directly to the sense-perceptions of those who read or watch it, and to the response itself. In theatrical contexts, therefore, the aesthetic may have more to do with the role played by the audience in making meaning, with the dynamic relationship that develops between audience and artwork, than with the artwork itself. As playwright David Hare once so succinctly put it, speaking of political theatre in the 1970s (and perhaps by extension of any interventionist theatre):

> if a play is to be a weapon in the class struggle, then that weapon is not going to be the things you are saying; it is the interaction of what you are saying and what the audience is thinking. The play is in the air. (Hare 1992: 6)

If the aesthetic as a term allows us to place the theatre experience firmly as one that occurs as a meeting between actor and audience, it is also one that offers us a bridge into ideas about education. Just as reception (or response) theory underlines the key role played by the audience in making meanings, so developments in theories of learning have increasingly placed the learner at the heart of the educational process.

Arguably, in this respect, interventionist and other kinds of participatory, educational theatre work have been in the vanguard of both progressive educational and theatre practice, having put audience and learner alike at the centre of the experience. Here is not the place to survey the history of educational theory through the twentieth century, but a number of key themes and developments should be noted if the links with meaning-making and learning in the theatre are to be understood.

Locating the learner

Just as performance theory has increasingly turned much of its attention to the role of audiences in the making of meaning, so, in the education arena, the focus has switched determinedly to the role of the learner in the making of education. Reflecting the recalibrated terminology, we are all learners now rather than people-to-be-educated. As early as 1899, in a lecture given on 'The school and the life of the child', John Dewey was predicting that 'the change which is coming into our education is the shifting of the centre of gravity. It is a change, a revolution, not unlike that introduced by Copernicus when the astronomical centre shifted from the earth to the sun. In this case the child becomes the sun about which the appliances of education revolve; he is the centre about which they are organised' (Dewey 1915: 35).[5] It was a far-sighted prediction and one that still has resonance, but the 'shifting' proved more gradual and more problematic than Dewey might have hoped. None the less it was Dewey, among others (Piaget in particular), whose work inspired what came to be known as child-centred education.

The dominant epistemology in the twentieth century however – one that was largely inherited from the social impact of the Industrial Revolution and the requirements of nineteenth-century capitalism – has undeniably been the positivist view of the world that interprets that world as objectively knowable and knowledge as a set of facts, skills and disciplines, or, in the Platonic view, beliefs about the world that are verifiable by reason or by evidence. In this way, a body of knowledge is rational, it exists outside the individual learner and can be transmitted, received and in turn passed on to others who do not yet possess that knowledge in a recognisably similar form. This then was the business of education. Knowledge can be defined in this epistemology, as Hooper-Greenhill points out (1997: 1), as 'that which can be observed, measured and objectified'. In this positivist, 'transmission' model of education, the student is seen as the empty vessel to be filled with knowledge by the teacher, the transmitter. Of course, the dominant paradigm has been more complex than this summary suggests – and one should be wary of concluding that, for example, the measuring of learning must be rejected simply because it is associated with the transmission model (indeed many radical educationists wish to see some forms of testing built in to child-centred or 'dialogic' education, for diagnostic purposes at least). But the alternative developments in education can be understood only against its pervasive and long-term influence.

The child-centred, 'progressive' educational movements that came to the fore in the 1960s and lasted through most of the 1970s were inspired by the work of many pioneers, not least Dewey and Piaget, and in the UK were prompted especially by the highly influential Plowden Report on primary education, 1967, and the Newsom Report, 1963, on the failures of the secondary modern school system satisfactorily to include and motivate large numbers of secondary school children. These movements attempted to counter the deadening hand of large institutions by stressing, especially at primary school level, the virtues of learning through discovery, allowing for education to take place at different rates according to the ability of the individual child. As Maxine Greene puts it, active learning is about 'beginnings not endings', and tends to be at odds with 'systematisations, prescriptions, with assessments imposed from afar' (Greene 1995: 15). The influence on primary schools was considerable, and had many beneficial results (not least the flowering of creativity and the encouragement of vibrant expressive wall displays and the generation of small group teaching). The trend became much maligned some twenty years later, in the 1980s, as being responsible for the disappointing standards of numeracy and literacy among children moving into secondary schooling. None the less, as the researchers for the *Enquiring Minds* educational research project point out (Morgan et al. 2006), 'the discourse of child-centredness has returned with renewed vigour in recent years, albeit in a new guise'.

Perhaps the most prominent instance of this new guise, and of the way educational practice – formal and informal – has been redefined and reconfigured, is the growing acceptance of the constructivist theory of learning. In the 1990s, constructivist theories of learning, developed from sociology, gained ground, proffering as they did a radically different concept of knowledge acquisition from that of the transmission model – but drawing on theories already in common currency (from Dewey, Piaget, Vygotsky and others). In the constructivist model, knowledge is not merely acquired: it is constructed by the learner as part of the process of engaging with the social world around him or her (Fosnot 1996, Hein 1998, von Glasersfeld 1995). The process of learning begins from the learner and develops as a natural part of interacting with the world: a process of perceiving, digesting, negotiating, adjusting, making meanings for oneself in response to and in interaction with the social and cultural world. Knowledge is in this sense an active process of making sense of the world and one's own place in it. The learner is no longer the passive recipient of information but the active producer of knowledge (Hooper-Greenhill 1997: 1), or, as Usher and Edwards would prefer to phrase it, 'we are all producers of knowledges' (p. 198).

The trends are certainly not new. Dewey was, as already indicated, arguing throughout the early twentieth century for a model of education that valued the learner's own experience as a platform upon which to build. In the 1920s and 1930s, Jean Piaget (1896–1980) was showing how much the process of education, of acquiring knowledge, was to do with personal growth, with internal, biological and psychological processes that were in constant interplay with the external world. Much later, David Kolb (1985) went on to argue that learning was essentially 'an experiential process', an integral part of the way we experience the world and make sense of it by reflecting on it, while at the same time Howard Gardner was proposing that the traditional notions of what constitutes intelligence are outmoded and fail to reflect the observable (and to some extent measurable) variety of intelligences which children possess in varying permutations. (Gardner identifies eight such intelligences and allows for the possibility of a ninth.[6]) Both he and Kolb advocate a re-engineering of the curriculum and teaching methods in schools to allow for that variety of learning styles and ways of expressing and applying different intelligences. Others such as Freire, Illich and Vygotsky have posited social models of learning that stress how vital the social and cultural contexts are to that personal growth – that, in Vygotsky's model for instance, the degree and depth of learning will be stimulated as much by those around you (whether siblings, parents, teachers or indeed artists) as by biological processes. Freire speaks of the individual's 'incompleteness', a state from which he or she will move out 'in constant search – a search which can only be carried out in communion with others' (Freire 1970: 80, quoted by Greene, 1995: 27). Focusing more intently on the political implications of education for older and adult age groups, he powerfully deconstructs the transmission model, which he has described as the 'banking system' of education – a system that involves teachers depositing wodges of knowledge into students' empty accounts for withdrawal later when needed. Against this, he proposes the 'dialectical' system: a learning process that requires genuine two-way dialogue between learner and tutor, in which the tutor has as much to learn from the learner as the other way round. Other radical educationists such as Ivan Illich (1970) and Neil Postman (Postman and Weingartner 1971), have long argued for an approach to education that places the learner centre stage, while John Holt and others have shown how children 'fail' and are failed by the system because schools – and the education policies they are bound to reflect – are by their institutional nature likely to enforce rigid rules, expectations and criteria upon pupils who are seen as a 'mass' that require a degree of regimentation in order for the education to be delivered in an organised way. No matter what gestures are made towards active learning, the very nature of the institution is likely to place impediments in the way of a full implementation of such learning. Ideologically bound into procedures of control, discipline and the meeting of government-set targets and other externally imposed performance indicators, schools operate what has been called a 'hidden curriculum' (Jackson 1968; see also Freire 1972, Holt 1982) which supersedes and drives the official curriculum being followed in the classroom. Hence Neil Postman's argument for a degree of 'subversiveness' in the work of the creative teacher dedicated to the principle of active learning (Postman and Weingartner 1971).

Education beyond school

Education is associated most commonly in popular discourse with schooling. But of course they are not necessarily synonymous – and indeed there are many who would argue that they are mutually exclusive. One of the main premises on which the case for educational theatre is built is the idea that education is not the exclusive preserve of schools. We can all learn from a variety of experiences and in a variety of settings, and theatre may offer certain kinds of educational experiences by virtue of its not being school-based.

One of the main developments since the early 1990s has been the increased recognition – by government as well as by educators – of education as a 'lifelong' process; and a recognition that it can, and must, happen not only in formal, institutional settings (schools and colleges) but, just as importantly, in informal settings too. Informal settings may be taken to include the workplace, museums, theatres and the whole range of cultural organisations available to members of a society. Indeed, today, for all cultural institutions in the UK in receipt of state support of any kind, direct or indirect (through the Arts Councils in particular), it is a requirement of the funding agreement that an education programme should be in place to complement the plays, operas, concerts and exhibitions on offer; alongside which, organisations are expected to show that they are widening access to their work for all sections of the community. Inevitably some schemes are more effective and less 'nominal' than others. But the notion of lifelong learning and the central role that cultural institutions have to play in fostering it has become embedded at a number of levels: in government policy, in funding criteria, and, to greater or lesser extents, in actual arts practice. This is by no means exclusive to the UK. While the detailed policies and practices may vary, an entitlement to lifelong learning is in most western countries an explicit goal, and in many a fact of life.

This is important not only in understanding the place that current educational theatre practice has marked out for itself within the larger cultural, learning and access agendas; it also acts as a reminder of the discrepancy that has often existed, and still exists, between what is allowable and encouraged outside the school system and what so often happens within it. Many have argued, and still do argue, that formal, state-provided education systems tend – implicitly if not explicitly – to coerce students into certain ideological moulds. Pammenter (1993), for example, sees a continuous line from Victorian class-based systems – in which one kind of education was provided for the privileged, to ease them into positions of power, while education for the masses was designed to skill-up the artisans and to ensure that no threat to social hierarchies came from the forms and content of education provision – through the superficial reforms of the Education Act of 1944 (the majority would attend 'secondary modern' schools while those who passed the 11+ exam would go on to grammar schools and fewer still on to university) and into the creation of a national curriculum (1988), serving to pronounce upon every element of knowledge and intellectual skill that teachers were expected to impart. In Foucault's analysis, too, Truth and Knowledge are 'produced' rather than revealed, and both are closely intertwined with power, at the personal, social and economic levels (Foucault 1980). Usher and Edwards (1994), from an assertively postmodern perspective and building on Foucault, argue that 'modern forms of governance and social discipline are secured through education' and that 'in modernity, education replaces pre-modern coercion and subjugation' (p. 84). All very far from the child-centred notions of education embraced by Peter Slade and others in the 1950s and 1960s, and from the emancipatory claims made for education throughout the century. While seeds of truth certainly lie in such interpretations, it is hardly the whole picture, and the National Curriculum is justified by many educationists – in principle if not in every aspect of its practice – as an attempt to equalise the educational opportunities of the many by setting benchmarks that all schools should meet, irrespective of their social catchment area or parental expectations. Recent shifts from an emphasis upon teaching to a concern with the process of learning, with the teacher as an enabler rather than conduit of knowledge, to the approaches inspired by constructivism and multiple intelligence theory, for example, have restored a little of the idealism that lay beneath the child-centred experiments of the 1960s, underpinning it with more sophisticated concepts of how we learn.

In the interests of raising standards of literacy and numeracy in British schools, the introduction by government of the national curriculum, together with the obsession with tests at almost every level of a child's schooling, has constrained and distorted the teaching of the arts in UK schools. Only recently has the volume and rigidity of the standard assessment testing begun to be acknowledged at government level as detrimental to the wider goals of education, and in turn the need to scale it back addressed. The arts sit less comfortably within this test-driven curriculum, and by the same token theatre has often in the course of the last century found itself invited into educational arenas that, at least at the institutional level, were less than welcoming of the idea of informal, extra-curricular education. The intrusion of non-formal education operations (such as touring theatre companies) into formal settings inevitably required negotiation, risked disturbing the rhythms and ideologies of the institutions, and made companies vulnerable to the fluctuating policies and fashions in educational thinking. At other times, companies have found themselves used as convenient sticking-plasters to cover up uncomfortable gaps in the formal school sector, bringing welcome diversions from the daily grind or at best offering entry points into difficult areas of curriculum provision (such as health education and citizenship) that teachers have felt insufficiently prepared, or motivated, to address.

While constructivist, and similar active learning, theories and pedagogies have undoubtedly gained ground in recent years, it is also true to say that there is far from a consensus. As Hein observes (Hein 1998: 21–2), theories of learning and pedagogic practices fluctuate between the two extremes of 'realist' and 'idealist' conceptions of knowledge, between system-centred and child-centred systems, and at any one historic moment it is possible to find educational – and educational theatre – practices at any one of a number of points on that continuum. One reason why many educationists have embraced the opportunities for 'informal' education at cultural institutions outside schools – whether at museums or regional theatres or locally organised youth theatres – is that active-learning practices are more manageable and more acceptable, less constrained by national curriculum demands in those less rigidly organised environments. At the same time, there continues to be lively debate about how far down the road of experiential or 'discovery' learning it is wise to go. In museum education, for example, there is on the one hand an embrace of discovery or visitor-centred learning in which visitors are encouraged actively to engage with the exhibits and to construct their own meanings from them, gaining insights that would be unlikely were they to be following a conventional pre-planned route through the galleries; on the other, a concern that the works of art, intricate tools from another era or culture or products of scientific experiment do need to be explained if visitors are fully to appreciate the significance of what they are seeing: those objects or displays have an existence independent of the visitor. As Hein puts it (1998: 32), 'Any attempt to have the learner figure things out on her own raises the possibility that what will be figured out will not be what is expected'. Likewise, in 'development education' in the Third World, the attempts to move away from top-down to bottom-up educational programmes – from those designed by NGOs or governments and imposed on rural communities irrespective of local needs, to those that reflect those local needs (see for example Hope and Timmel 1999, Frank 1995, Boon and Plastow 2004) – may all too easily allow vital messages, about the transmission of sexual disease and what can be done to prevent or cure, to be submerged in the attempt to get local groups to determine their own agendas or interpret the messages in more palatable ways. Unless handled with immense care and sensitivity, participatory theatre programmes can sometimes end in cementing pre-existing power and gender relations within the community (see for example Frank 1995, Boon and Plastow 2004).

In terms of drama's place in the curriculum more will be said in later chapters, but, for the moment, it will suffice to say that in Britain at least there have been two broadly opposing tendencies. On the one hand there was the move to have drama accepted as a viable, legitimate curriculum subject in its own right with its own sets of learning outcomes and assessment criteria. On the other, there has been the insistence that drama's role is to work from outside – either in opposition to the national curriculum, as argued by many British DIE and TIE practitioners in the 1980s and 1990s as the new national curriculum was being implemented and as the demand for 'rigour' and for measurable learning outcomes became more insistent, or as a complement to it, as practised by many TIE and schools theatre companies, offering programmes to enrich, rather than deliver, the curriculum. Many TIE programmes have for example been designed to bring alternative perspectives into the classroom on aspects of citizenship and personal, social and health education curricula, or on the teaching of Shakespeare. Most drama teachers – wherever they stand on the curriculum issue – see their work as, at least to a large degree, child-centred (or learner-centred) in approach, and the resistance to the 'transmission model' of education has therefore been strong (notwithstanding David Hornbrook's controversial critique of the prevailing orthodoxies in DIE:

Hornbrook 1989, 1991). If, as Maxine Greene suggests, the role of education is 'not to resolve, not to point the way, not to improve', but rather 'to awaken, to disclose the ordinarily unseen, unheard and unexpected' (Greene 1995: 28), then the place for the arts, and especially drama, within education would seem to be irresistible. Resisted it has been none the less.

How does this help contextualise the changing patterns, approaches and assumptions that characterise educational theatre through the twentieth century? Does theatre practice tend to reflect or coincide with, or conversely work at odds with, changes in educational thinking or practice? There is no simple correlation, no simple cause and effect. But the congruencies are telling. Thus, the 1930s theatre was in many respects characterised by its acceptance of the positivist, transmission model of education, evident in the propagandist dramas of political agit-prop, the campaigning dramas exemplified by *Spirochete* and plays for young people such as *Flight* (see Chapter 4). At the same time, just as Dewey was developing ideas of education that put learning through experience at the heart of the educational process, and calling for the student to be placed at the centre of any educational endeavour, so some productions were beginning to experiment with various forms of audience participation, putting the audience literally and metaphorically in the spotlight (see Chapters 3 and 4) – practice that expanded and developed in the 1960s and 1970s, boosted by the trend towards, and the acceptability of, child-centred approaches in schools. The theatre has then found itself (or placed itself) at various times and for various reasons at quite different points on the continuum. It has been used to reach and teach those whom the regular education providers have found difficult to access – for example, the plays used to convey clear messages about drug abuse and HIV/AIDS, or to aid students' understanding of Shakespeare prior to GCSE examinations; and it has been used as a medium of active and critical pedagogy – as, for example, in some of the innovative work about racism in the 1970s and 1980s, and in Boal-inspired forum theatre programmes dealing with aspects of health and citizenship education (see Chapters 7 and 8).

From the vantage point of the early twenty-first century, it is instructive to chart some of the aspirations, ideas, innovative practice and ideological struggles that have characterised the work of those who at various points during the past century sought to use theatre for educational ends. The next group of chapters will begin by looking at some selected examples of campaigning theatre prior to the First World War, seen alongside the emergence of theatre specifically for children, before focusing in more detail on some of the interwar experiments in agitational-propaganda and living newspapers.

Notes

1 'A comparative investigation of educational theatre policy and practice in Finland and the UK: the Helsinki/Manchester Research Project on Educational Theatre', sponsored by the British Council (Helsinki) and the Finnish Centre for International Mobility through its visit grant programme to initiate British–Finnish research collaboration/joint research projects. *Report to the British Council, Helsinki,* August 1998 (unpublished).

2 *Omne tulit punctum qui miscuit utile dulci, / Lectorem delectando pariterque monendo* (Horace, *Ars Poetica* 343f.): 'He gets every vote who combines the useful with the pleasant, and who, at the same time he pleases the reader, also instructs him'. Trans. Leon Golden (Horace 1995).

3 Raymond Williams, surveying the cultural history of the term, notes how 'aesthetic' has tended to emphasise '*subjective* sense activity as the basis of art' as distinct from social or cultural interpretations – an element in the 'divided modern consciousness of art and society' (Williams 1983: 32).

4 *The Max Factor*, by Chris Hawes and the Duke's Theatre in Education Team (Lancaster), later retitled *On His Own Two Feet*.

5 Also quoted in Federal Theatre typescript: 'Article # 1', National Archives, Washington DC; no date, probably 1938/9.

6 Gardner's eight intelligences are: Linguistic intelligence, Logical-mathematical intelligence, Spatial intelligence, Bodily-Kinesthetic intelligence, Musical intelligence, Interpersonal intelligence, Intrapersonal intelligence and Naturalist intelligence. See Gardner (1983, 1993).

Part I

Early warnings: theatre, education and social change, 1900–1947

2

Prelude: 1900–1914 – New Drama, new audiences

There are two main genealogical threads that need to be traced in order to set the scene for the more detailed study of developments post-1918. The first is the emergence of what came to be known as the 'New Drama' at the end of the nineteenth and beginning of the twentieth centuries – exemplified especially in the works of Zola, Ibsen, Strindberg, Hauptmann, Chekhov and Shaw. It is relevant to this study because of the recurring claims made by dramatists, directors and critics that the new theatre for a new century should not only be about the modern world but that it should proceed by means of stripping back the veneer of a society whose values were in the most part dictated by the powerful and the rich. Exposure of injustice, inequality and the hypocrisy of those who proclaimed the moral values and norms of society, and the waking up of the comfortable bourgeoisie to the realities of the world around them – these were the banners flown by playwrights as diverse as Zola, Ibsen and Shaw. Their aims and strategies varied of course. Ibsen famously scorned Zola for descending into the sewer to bathe while his own purpose was to scour it clean (Meyer 1974: 515). Some (such as Shaw) saw their purpose in explicitly educational and campaigning terms while others did not, rather claiming (if a little disingenuously) simply to be dramatising life as they found it. However articulated, the claims made for the revitalising of theatre's social role and for the part it could play in awakening and changing society for the better, and the energies invested in transforming theatre's practice, clearly set a context in which ideas about theatre as an educational medium could be debated, explored and tested. The second, related thread is the development of theatre for children and young people – a dramatic tradition that stretched back to Elizabethan times and even earlier and one that was often put into the service of education. The new

century saw the beginnings of exploratory attempts to harness that
educational potential in a variety of ways and for a wider segment of
society – attempts that came to fruition much faster in Russia following
the Revolution than anywhere else, but which were later to burgeon
across Europe and the United States.

The New Drama

The nineteenth century had witnessed an extraordinary period of rapid
change across almost every field of human endeavour. The discoveries
and advances in science and engineering, and in economic, political and
religious thought, brought about profound changes in the way people
viewed their world. And the Industrial Revolution, as it came to be
called, had created in its wake not only new, faster manufacturing techniques and an expansion in trade but changes in the environment and a
massive growth in the population of the cities.[1] Inevitably the social consequences proved to be far-reaching: not least, the creation of a mass,
urban working class who suffered overcrowding, disease, poverty and
exploitation. The contrasts between rich and poor became inescapable
and gave rise to a wealth of new literature that, in both fictional and documentary modes, mirrored, analysed and castigated: from Shelley to
Dickens to Zola, and from Engels to the reports of the 'social explorers'
(Keating 1976) – the journalists, politicians and clergymen who adven-
tured into the unknown, frightening worlds of the poor in London,
Manchester and other grim cities to expose the dark underside of the
'commercially prosperous centres of Empire' (Keating, p. 6).

   This was the backdrop against which various artistic movements in the
latter part of the century emerged, attempting to record and interrogate
contemporary society 'as it was', through the minutiae of closely
observed details of social behaviour, living conditions and the physical
and mental health of people at all levels of society. The influence of Emile
Zola (1840–1902) in this respect was seminal. His own adaptation of his
novel *Thérèse Raquin* for the stage (done in 1873) and his collection of
essays – written during the 1870s and published in 1880 – provided an
articulate and forceful manifesto and a stimulus to writers of like mind
who believed that theatre desperately needed to get back to real life if it
was to retain any potential as an art form. In his essays (collected under
the title 'Naturalism in the theatre'), he argues that:

> The drama must return to the simplicity of action and unique psychological
> study of character exemplified in early Greek tragedy but combined with a
> location of the drama in a contemporary environment, peopled by human

beings from our own world . . . We are an age of method, of experimental
science; our primary need is for precise analysis. (Zola 1881, reprinted in
Bentley 1968: 361)

Naturalism, then, was not just a stylistic preference, an attempt to make
the scenery, speech and behaviour on stage correspond as closely to real
life as possible; it was, more powerfully, a philosophic statement, an
insistence that the 'real world', when examined under the dramatist's
microscope, would reveal sordidness, corruption, greed and destructive
psychological impulses – behaviours determined in large measure by the
social and economic conditions in which people lived out their lives. Such
revelations were not merely to satisfy middle-class curiosity but to meet
a growing sense among many dramatists of the responsibility they had
to stir the moral consciences and social awareness of their audiences.

The other influential figure was Ibsen (1828–1906). In his 'social-
realist' plays (from *Pillars of Society* to *The Wild Duck*), the preoccupation is with the problems of personal and social morality in the world
immediately around him (Gray 1977). His target is the complacency,
hypocrisy, smallmindedness and lies on which contemporary middle-
class society was built, and the profound, often destructive effects upon
individuals caught up in its web. The 'pillars of society' are shown to be
corrupt, duplicitous, or at best misguided: conditioned by social norms
that have gone unquestioned. The iconic play was of course *A Doll's
House*, in which a conventional marriage based on self-deception is
finally and abruptly ended by a wife who at last begins to see her marriage for what it really is. The slamming of the door at the end of the play,
as Nora finally leaves her husband, children and domestic comfort for a
new life in uncharted waters, reverberated around Europe; its message
was, according to the historian and Ibsen's biographer, Halvdan Koht,
explosive: 'A Doll's House exploded like a bomb into contemporary
life . . . it pronounced a death sentence on contemporary ethics' (Koht
1928, cited by Meyer 1974: 476). And Meyer claims that 'no play had
ever before contributed so momentously to the social debate, or been so
widely and furiously discussed among people who were not normally
interested in theatrical or even artistic matters' (Meyer, p. 476).

The extent to which these social-realist plays can be categorised as
campaigning or educational is however much more problematic. When
asked to address the Norwegian Women's Rights League in 1898 – some
nineteen years after writing *A Doll's House* – Ibsen rather unexpectedly
claimed that 'I have never been deliberately tendentious in anything I
have written. I have been more of a poet and less of a social philosopher
than people generally seem inclined to believe . . . I must decline the

honour of being said to have worked for the Women's Rights movement. I am not even very sure what Women's Rights actually are' (quoted in McFarlane 1970: 169).

In one sense, Ibsen was of course right. He was not merely or even primarily an advocate for liberal reform or votes for women or even for a loosening of outmoded moral codes. He was (as Ronald Gray concedes, in his 'dissenting view') personally involved in these plays and their themes, his whole playwriting output being 'something of an autobiography of his inward self, rather than objective presentations of topics of the moment' (Gray 1977: 20). But, if Ibsen later resisted the interpretation of his plays as didactic works, there is little doubt of the message *A Doll's House* was delivering to the society of its day. Nora's anguished response to the crushing of her deepest hopes and the dawning realisation of her own individuality becomes in the last few moments of the play nothing less than a declaration:-

Helmer   First and foremost, you are a wife and a mother.
Nora   I don't believe that any longer. I believe that I am first and
          foremost a human being . . .

That does not of course reduce the play to the level of a tract: as an exploration of personal self-discovery, it is much more than that. And in the social context of late nineteenth-century Norway (and most of Europe), the fact that the individual here is a woman, whose role in society was vastly more confined than that of a man, intensifies both the process of discovery and the obstacles she has to overcome. Ibsen's rejection of any suggestion of a didactic purpose to his play was in any event made many years later when he had moved into a different playwriting vein, so one must not take his statement as definitive. But it was another contribution to the heated and widespread debates over the real purpose of drama as an art form, and indeed reflected the tensions detectable in the work of many dramatists between their expressed philosophies and the plays themselves.

George Bernard Shaw (1856–1950), perhaps most of all, was unequivocal about the necessity of writing drama that engaged directly and unapologetically with the big social issues of the day. Playful, provocative, wittily subversive and eager to expose the underbelly of English capitalism, his plays owe much to the searching studies of contemporary social life of Ibsen. But they also relish intellectual paradox and celebrate the vitality of the individual spirit when constrained by authority and middle-class conformity to the status quo (Bentley 1967, Meisel 1963, Valency 1983). Were they educational in intent? For Shaw, unlike Ibsen, there was no doubting the moral impact that plays could have. Indeed, in his view, most of the plays to be seen on the popular stage – romantic melodrama, plays populated with 'women with pasts' – were for the most part, if unintentionally, immoral in the views of the world that they imparted, and merely reinforced the hypocrisies and complacencies of middle-class life. Drama had a role to play in changing that world; it had lessons to impart: moral, political, ideological.

Shortly after he arrived in London from Dublin as a young man (in 1876), Shaw had set about educating himself in the political philosophies of Marxism and subsequently the dramatic works of Ibsen; in the latter, he found a playwright who actually seemed capable of dealing with social issues, and especially the injustices and corruption of contemporary society in a radical and powerful way, and above all in an accessible, dramatic form. No play by Ibsen had yet been performed in London: it had taken ten years before *A Doll's House* saw its first performance in the West End (in 1889). But Shaw, in collaboration initially with the critic William Archer, was inspired enough to begin writing a play on Ibsenite lines – which eventually became *Widower's Houses*, the first of what Shaw was to call his 'Plays Unpleasant'. *Widower's Houses* was given its first performance in 1892 at J. T. Grein's privately run Independent Theatre – part of Shaw's response to the intensifying search for a New Drama in Britain to match that of Ibsen, Strindberg and Hauptmann on the continent. During the period between 1890 and 1914 English theatre underwent changes of major proportions. This arose from a combination of factors, social, cultural and economic: the impact of Ibsen on the London stage (an influence that had begun even earlier with the publication of Archer's English translations); the formation of a number of small, avant-garde experimental theatre groups, inspired by André Antoine's Théâtre Libre in Paris, notably the Independent Theatre and later the Stage Society; the emergence of new British playwrights such as Shaw, Harley Granville Barker and John Galsworthy, committed to theatre that was socially engaged and about the contemporary world, working in naturalistic modes and shunning the popular melodramatic and well-made-play forms that had dominated British theatre for over half a century; and the beginnings of a regional repertory theatre movement with the establishment of repertory ventures in Manchester, Glasgow, Liverpool and Birmingham (Rowell and Jackson 1984).

While Ibsen's influence was seminal, and while Shaw towers above all other playwrights in Britain at this time, the transformation of the English stage – and of ideas about what the stage could do and say – was not accomplished singlehandedly. And the plays produced in this period must be seen in the context of the whole dynamic of change that was taking place, culturally, socially and politically. The suffragette movement, for example, had begun to gain serious momentum by the end of the previous century, and campaigning plays about the cause, played to small, dedicated audiences of suffragette supporters, had begun to penetrate the mainstream – *Votes for Women* was played at Granville Barker's pioneering seasons at the Royal Court Theatre in 1907, and plays by male authors reflecting the new mood, featuring 'new women' as protagonists, were soon to be found in the new repertoires of the regional repertory ventures (see Gardner and Rutherford 1992). Manchester's Gaiety Theatre production of *Hindle Wakes* in 1912 was perhaps the most famous and influential example.

Can this outburst of new dramatic energy be said to be 'educational', either in intent or in practice? Shaw's first plays were grouped together as 'Plays Unpleasant' – that is, plays about *social crime*. In each of them, the theme was the need for social and political change – his concern was clearly with society as a whole rather than primarily with the individual characters themselves. Just as he had argued that the great triumph of and justification for *A Doll's House* was its utilitarian value, so in his preface to the 1902 edition of *Mrs Warren's Profession* he went on to argue in detail the need for plays that could, with courage, honesty and uncompromising force, tackle crucial social problems – here that of prostitution and of social attitudes to women.

> *Mrs Warren's Profession* was written . . . to draw attention to the truth that prostitution is caused, not by female depravity and male licentiousness, but simply by underpaying, undervaluing and overworking women so shamefully that the poorest of them are forced to resort to prostitution to keep body and soul together. (Shaw 1946: 181)

He went on to observe that the play had eventually, against many odds, been 'performed and produced mainly through the determination of women . . . [who believed] in the timeliness and the power of the lesson the play teaches' (Shaw 1946: 200). Rather than place final guilt and responsibility upon Mrs Warren, the 'adventuress', for having dared transgress social norms, Shaw places guilt upon the social system in condoning, even encouraging, a world of injustice and exploitation. The purpose of the play is clearly to illuminate a social evil and to persuade others that something needs doing. In part the play was another step in Shaw's campaign to throw shafts of light on the ills of society – middle- and upper-class hypocrisy, the exploitation of women, the poor – in such a way as to awaken his audience, especially the well-to-do audiences that generally attended fashionable London playhouses, from their complacency about the society they were part of and party to. The only conclusion that could be drawn was that the social system was at fault and needed changing. And yet it was not, he was quick to assert, a 'mere thesis play'; rather it was a revelation of the issues at stake, brought about, he claimed, by dramatically depicting the social problem in conflict with the instincts and temperaments of credible flesh and blood characters:

> [O]nly in the problem play is there any real drama, because drama is no mere setting up of the camera to nature: it is the presentation in parable of the conflict between Man's will and his environment: in a word, of problem. (Shaw 1946: 197)

Already, he is acutely conscious of the danger of allowing the 'message' to overwhelm the credibility of the characters – a risk that hovers threateningly above almost all plays driven by educational goals. By using drama to get to the heart of human dilemmas – for Shaw, always essentially social – the playwright could actually create 'real drama' rather than the pseudo-drama that most conventional entertainment offered the Edwardian playgoer.

This play marks out a terrain occupied by many writers since – one in which the playwright is concerned to highlight a number of social issues that need addressing and to forge a drama that will simultaneously expose them, demonstrating the injustice that clearly needs to be righted, and speak to an audience who it is implied will not only recognise such issues but may well be implicated in them. If they can at least be provoked into fuller consciousness of the issues as problems that touch their own lives in the real world, the playwright will have largely succeeded. Whether the audience can be expected to act on this recognition is another matter. But such drama is undoubtedly designed to entertain, engage, inform and, to a degree, 'instruct'. As to *Mrs Warren's Profession*, while the play made ripples in the elite circles who attended private 'club' performances of the play and those who bought the printed text, it was banned from public performance until 1922, and it hardly brought about an end to prostitution or to capitalism. A play that did effect a demonstrable change, if in a smaller key, was *Justice*.

Galsworthy's *Justice*

John Galsworthy's play *Justice*, written in 1909 and staged the following year, is one of the very few plays to which one can ascribe a direct and immediate impact upon the social system.

Galsworthy was already, in 1910, emerging as a considerable 'man of letters', with several significant plays to his credit (*The Silver Box*, *Strife*) and his epic series of novels, *The Forsyte Saga* (1906–21), already under way. Unlike Shaw, he was not a Marxist and politically tended to be on the fence, if with a detectable tilt to the left, but, as his biographer John Ginden has shown, he was enormously sympathetic to the 'New Drama' movement and associated himself with the work of Shaw, Granville Barker and others in promoting ideas for the establishment of well organised and subsidised theatres that would provide a platform for that New Drama, especially for a transformation of theatre into 'a more vital element of contemporary culture' – 'for our drama is renascent, and nothing will stop its growth' (Galsworthy 1912, cited in Ginden 1987: 215).

He did moreover feel passionately about specific social issues and in particular – in the period 1907–10 – that of penal reform. He had visited Dartmoor prison in 1907 and been shocked by the conditions in which prisoners were kept, especially by the solitary confinement that all prisoners, irrespective of the degree of seriousness of their crime, had to undergo at the start of their sentences. Generally, this was for a minimum of three months, more usually six or even nine months. Further visits to prisons in Pentonville impelled him to write a long open letter (published in *The Nation* in 1909) to the current Home Secretary, Sir Herbert Gladstone, complaining about the damaging psychological and physiological effects of solitary confinement. It marked the beginning of Galsworthy's concerted campaign for prison reform. Correspondence with the chairman of His Majesty's Prison Commission followed and he obtained an interview with the Home Secretary of the day, Sir Herbert Gladstone, who granted him permission to visit more prisons and to interview some sixty convicts (Gindin 1987, Dupré 1976). Gladstone intimated that solitary confinement might be reduced to three months for all prisoners, but Galsworthy still felt this to be unsatisfactory. This was the point at which he turned to the drama as a key weapon in his armoury. He determined to write a play that would highlight the injustices and bring them to the attention of a wider public. *Justice* was the result, written at speed (Gindin 1987, Kennedy 1985) and urged on by Granville Barker who wanted to stage the play as part of a series of plays planned for his repertory season at the Duke of York's Theatre early the following year.

The play itself was based closely on the research Galsworthy had been carrying out in the previous three years which explains the almost documentary feel that pervades the scenes set in the courtroom and the prison. At the centre of the drama is William Falder, a young law clerk who forges a cheque in order to raise sufficient money to elope with the woman he loves, the wife of a drunken, abusive husband. He intends to repay the money later but is found out by his employer and prosecuted. We witness his trial, his conviction for embezzlement and scenes from his time in prison. Falder is not an heroic protagonist: distraught and bewildered by the severity of his punishment, he is unable to cope with the brutality of prison life. The most powerful – and, in its time, a quite shocking – scene comes during Falder's initial period of solitary confinement. In a prison cell, we watch a man silently undergoing increasing frustration and despair. There is no dialogue, but we experience Falder's isolation, his anger and by the end of the scene a sense of the larger picture of misery experienced by other prisoners in other similar cells.

ACT III. SCENE III. FALDER'S CELL, a whitewashed space 13 feet broad by 7 deep, and 9 feet high with a rounded ceiling . . .

[At the end of the scene, entirely wordless:] A sound from far away, as of distant, dull beating on thick metal, is suddenly audible. Falder shrinks back, not able to bear this sudden clamour. But the sound grows . . . And gradually it seems to hypnotise him. He begins creeping inch by inch nearer to the door. The banging sound, travelling from cell to cell, draws closer and closer; Falder's hands are seen moving as if his spirit had already joined in this beating, and the sound swells till it seems to have entered the very cell. He suddenly raises his clenched fists. Panting violently, he flings himself at his door and beats on it.

THE CURTAIN FALLS. (Galsworthy 1910: 82–5)

It is a profoundly disturbing moment, and brilliantly staged by Barker if the critics at the first night are to be relied upon. For Galsworthy the scene was not only a depiction of what society regularly consigns its convicted prisoners to day in day out but an image of the wider theme that underpinned his whole play, that is, the inhumanity of which society is capable, indirectly if not directly, arising most of the time not out of deliberate cruelty but rather out of bureaucratic short-sightedness, officiousness or general complacency. Most of us, now as then, are all too happy to let the judicial system 'get on with it' and would prefer not to know too much of the detail – it takes a crisis, a particular case of injustice, usually involving a personal story with which it is easy to empathise, to reach the headlines before most of the public at large become aware of the inequities and brutalities that recur daily and of which the one case is just a symptom. Barker and Galsworthy had both agreed that a major priority was to make the prison scenes 'scrupulously accurate and emotionally compelling' (Galsworthy, quoted in Gindin 1987: 202). According to another of Galsworthy's biographers, Catherine Dupré (1976: 152), the setting directly mirrored his recorded observations of prison cells visited, just as, in the courtroom, the arguments of the prosecution and defence counsels and the judge's summing-up precisely captured the debates about criminology of the time (Nellis 1996: 73).

After his sentence has been served, Falder returns to the outside world but, now a broken man, is incapable of readjusting. He falls foul of the law again, this time for forging references in order to avoid declaring his criminal record when applying for jobs, and is caught. Rather than face yet another spell of prison, in desperation he commits suicide.

Interestingly, while at one on the need for accuracy of detail in the staging, Galsworthy and Barker had disagreed over the ending. Barker felt that Falder should survive his ordeals 'to emerge from his experience in prison morally triumphant over the system'; Galsworthy however wanted 'to make the spectator feel, "Thank God, he's dead" . . . Only by giving him back to nature can you get the full criticism on human conduct' (cited in Gindin 1987: 203). He stuck to his guns, attended most rehearsals and in the end was magnificently served by Barker's direction. The play opened on 21 February 1910 at the Duke of York's – and simul-taneously in Glasgow at the new repertory theatre there. The response was extraordinary. At the first night, when the final curtain came down, there was a long silence, followed by sustained applause and shouts for the author: 'We want Galsworthy – we won't go home until we get him!' (Gindin 1987: 205). People refused to budge, especially in the galleries. Eventually the management turned out the lights, to no avail, and Barker had to come on stage to explain that Galsworthy really was not in the house and would they please go home. The reviews were equally enthu-siastic. Max Beerbohm, in the influential *Saturday Review*, praised both the depiction of the legal and penal problems and the presentation of the horror of incarceration (Kennedy 1985: 107).

Audiences may have been relatively small, but they were influential – they came mainly from the social, political and intellectual elites of the time. Winston Churchill, who had now become the new Home Secretary in the Liberal Government, went to see *Justice* four times. He wrote to Galsworthy: 'I greatly admire the keen and vigorous way in which you are driving forward a good cause. I am in entire sympathy with your general mood' (Kennedy 1985: 106). The correspondence between them continued and they met several times to debate matters further. According to one weekly magazine, Churchill received floods of 'tear-stained letters imploring him to abolish solitary confinement', prompted by the play (*The Bystander*, 9 March 1910, quoted in Kennedy, p. 106). Churchill was already preparing a series of reforms to take to Parliament which now included 'more humane and equitable treatment of prisoners and further reductions in solitary confinement', from three months to one. The bill was passed and Churchill wrote to Galsworthy: 'there can be no question that your admirable play bore a most important part in creating that atmosphere of sympathy and interest which is so noticeable upon this subject' (Gindin 1987: 204, 207).

Although the reform did not go as far as he had wanted, Galsworthy believed his articles and *Justice* together had 'helped to knock off 1000 months of Solitary Confinement per year', a claim which Gilbert Murray, the classical scholar and a close friend, enthusiastically endorsed: 'How much greater it is to have saved a lot of men and women from two months solitary confinement than to have sent any number of over-fed audiences into raptures' (quoted in Dupré 1976: 154). Dupré has suggested that the play derived much of its power from its documentary quality, comparing its impact to that in the 1960s of *Cathy Come Home*, the television docu-drama about homelessness that had an extraordinary effect upon public attitudes at the time and led directly to the setting up of the housing charity Shelter: 'People suddenly realised that Falder existed, that there were men like him enduring hour after hour of solitude, that solitude was driving them mad' (Dupré, p. 153). The concern to get the facts right, to replicate as accurately as possible those very conditions in prison that Galsworthy had so carefully researched, gave the play a particularity and a persuasiveness that was difficult to escape. Galsworthy's own opinion was that the production got the balance between 'realism' and dramatic fiction about right: 'allowing for the necessities of the stage – the vividness and concentration which the stage demands – the play is an *essentially* true presentment of what happens in many cases' (quoted in Marrot 1935: 262 and cited in Nellis 1996: 74). It would be difficult to ascribe the change in the law entirely to the effect of one play of course. It undoubtedly played a significant part – but it was also one element in the author's larger campaign.

In fact, Galsworthy the artist was a little concerned that the play was seen as nothing more than 'a tract on solitary confinement'. For him, this was to miss the point of the 'more fundamental criticism on human life' he was trying to make – the play was a tragedy, and about human tendencies that would remain even if laws were reformed:

> As a whole my play was designed to show the immense . . . disproportion that exists between criminality and punishment in a great number of cases, so that all might be spurred to devise, so far as is humanly possible, machinery of justice that will minimise to the utmost this disproportion. (Galsworthy, quoted in Dupré 1976: 153.)

It is tempting to see the message of the play neatly summed up by Falder's defence counsel at the end of the trial: 'Justice is a machine that, when someone has given it the starting push, rolls on of itself. Is this young man to be ground to pieces under this machine for an act which at worst was one of weakness?' (*Justice*, pp. 49–50). Is this then the real message of the play? Is the appeal to the jury in Frome's summing-up really John Galsworthy speaking? Does Frome in effect stand as the surrogate of the author here? (Author surrogacy is a concept to which I will return at various points in the book.) From a later perspective, the message does appear to be all too explicit, all too neatly wrapped up for us, the ensuing action (the scenes in prison, the subsequent release and suicide) merely confirming Frome's prediction. One commentator finds Galsworthy's technique over-tendentious, with Falder 'as much a pawn of Galsworthy's didacticism as he is a victim of the legal system' (Clarke 1989: 66). If the play was meant to serve as a metaphor for a larger human condition, it was also, undeniably, presenting its audiences with an image of a reality that was 'out there' and verifiable. Mixing veracity with an emotionally powerful, agenda-driven, propagandist call for 'something to be done' produces complex tensions. The metaphorical dimension can sometimes get lost, at least in the immediate aftermath of the production, and, in its time, there is little doubt of the way *Justice* was seen and 'read' – as powerful propaganda.

This raises a series of interconnected questions that will recur in different guises many times through the remaining chapters. What is the relationship between art and campaigning (or any 'interventionist') theatre? Did the social impact of the play distort what the play was really trying to say? When a play is driven by motives of compassion and social reform, does it become overburdened with social imperatives that reduce the meaning in the eyes of its beholders to one of a simple message? If dramatic techniques are deployed that involve emotional manipulation, does this undermine the play's ability to communicate a more profound, and ultimately more persuasive vision of the world?

Emerging as another symptom of early twentieth century beliefs in progress and social change and the role the arts could play in this was the idea that theatre could be a vehicle for the instruction or edification of the young, but only if organised in a more systematic fashion than hitherto.

Theatre for children

Although dramatic performances *by* children have a long and rich history, dating back at least to the late Middle Ages, the provision of theatre *for* children, at least at the professional level, did not begin until the first decade of the twentieth century, and even then only on a relatively modest and sporadic scale at first. The dichotomy separating children's theatre for entertainment from theatre for education was marked throughout the first half of the twentieth century. It was not until the postwar developments in participatory children's theatre and, later, the TIE movement – inspired, in Britain, by Peter Slade, Brian Way and Caryl Jenner, and, in the USA, by pioneers such as Alice M. Herts and Winifred

Ward – that (to adapt Schechner's term) the 'education-entertainment braid' began to be woven in any innovative or sustained way.[2] Of this more will be said in later chapters.

From the late medieval period onward the universities and the public and cathedral schools are all known at various times to have encouraged play readings and performances by their pupils for strictly educational purposes: teaching oral Latin, the classical authors (Plautus and Terence included) and the skills of rhetoric. In Elizabethan times a number of eminent teachers at such schools as Eton, Westminster and Shrewsbury were writing plays in English for their pupils, claiming that drama helped to develop not only self-confidence and oratorical skills but also the moral sense that could be derived from a study of high comedy (see Coggin 1956). With the enforced closure of the theatres from 1642 to 1660 the involvement of children in theatre virtually ceased for some two hundred years, apart from sporadic activity at a handful of public schools. By the second half of the nineteenth century, however, the mood had changed, and the educational value of theatre within schools was being more confidently asserted, even though it was usually confined to after-hours leisure time and to the production of the classics. Bradfield School, for example, built its small open-air replica of a Greek amphitheatre for performances of the ancient classics by boys and teachers together in 1888. For children of the lower and middle classes however theatre remained, at best, an adult experience that they shared with their elders. Thus, by the latter decades of the century, pantomime, hitherto an adult and often satirical form of entertainment, had become a predominantly Christmas holiday entertainment with children forming a large part of the audience. Its comedy became more and more geared to children's tastes, and spectacle replaced the satiric, often anarchistic plot of the old harlequinades. At the same time, a new moralistic tone crept in, clearly aimed at ensuring that children received proper edification along with the fun. Thereafter, Christmas pantomimes, appealing unashamedly to children and to family audiences, became, and have remained, a regular feature of the theatrical scene in Britain.

It was the professional theatre that provided the first play for children of any real quality: J. M. Barrie's *Peter Pan* (1904), a play that achieved its deservedly classic status partly because it avoided the common error of the time, that of patronising its audience, and partly because it was a drama of unusual energy and originality. It was also written by another of the leading lights in the Shaw/Barker 'New Drama' movement (Barrie had had several plays staged in Barker's pioneering season of new plays at the Royal Court Theatre, 1904–7). The famous scene in which Pan appeals directly to the audience for help in saving Tinkerbell's life is often cited as one of the earliest moments of audience participation in children's theatre. Tinkerbell, Pan learns, will only recover 'if children believed in fairies'. Pan then *'rises and throws out his arms he knows not to whom, perhaps to the boys and girls of whom he is not one.* "Do you believe in fairies?" asks Pan. "Say quick that you believe! If you believe, clap your hands!" *Many clap, some don't, a few hiss. But Tinkerbell is saved.* Oh, thank you, thank you, thank you . . .' (Barrie 1928: 71–2). In terms of a large-scale mainstream professional production in a West End theatre, this is probably a correct assertion, although direct address to the audience and even dialogue across the footlights has its own substantial genealogy (from the Elizabethan soliloquy to nineteenth-century melodrama and pantomime). While the participation was felt by some to be closer to coercion than genuine interaction,[3] it became enough of an iconic moment to inspire further forays into audience participation in plays written for children (see Swortzell 1990: xxv, Swortzell 1988: 17, Bennett 2005: 12, England 1990). It would however be misleading to see the play as a revolutionary shot in a campaign to establish a new genre. As Jacqueline Rose has shown (1984), much of its storyline and theatrical style has its roots in the family pantomime tradition of the previous century and, on its highly successful opening night, the audience was predominantly an adult one. Only later did the appeal to children and parents gain momentum and Barrie was constantly revising it in response to its unexpected success (and in part, according to Rose, to erase all traces of the suppressed paedophilia detectable in the earlier short story in which Pan first appeared).

Other plays for children, such as A. A. Milne's *Toad of Toad Hall* (1929), saw successful runs in the West End and the regions, but the main purpose was generally to provide entertainment for children during the Christmas season. The provision of theatre for children with a more explicit educational bias, targeted specifically at young people and run on a more regular basis materialised, not entirely surprisingly, in the form of the production of Shakespeare's plays, particularly for older age groups and toured to schools and colleges. Appreciation of Shakespeare was felt to be an indisputably justifiable and worthwhile activity for which support could be mustered from education authorities and parents. Frank Benson began touring productions of such plays as *The Merchant of Venice* to public schools in 1889, and shortly before the First World War Ben Greet's company presented Shakespeare for London schoolchildren at special low rates at a variety of venues. When Greet became the Old Vic's first theatre director in 1914, he took the opportunity to extend this service and, during the 1914–15 season, instituted a series of 'special matinees for schoolchildren' of Shakespeare's plays relevant to the current examination syllabus; *As You Like It*, for example, was so popular that extra matinées had to be arranged, with four thousand children seeing the play during one week (Coggin 1956, Redington 1983). When Greet left the Old Vic in 1918 he continued to provide Shakespeare matinées for London schools, with the London County Council bearing the cost (despite a temporary withdrawal of subsidy between 1921 and 1924). In 1924 the government's Board of Education agreed that theatre visits by schools to see the works of Shakespeare were educationally justifiable and could legitimately be subsidised by local authorities nationwide – setting a most important precedent. Other companies took advantage of the new opportunity, notably Nancy Hewin's Osiris Players, an all-female acting troupe who toured Shakespeare (and later other classic plays) to schools and community halls in the regions almost continuously from 1927 to 1968.[4] For younger children adaptations of folk and fairy tales formed the mainstay of the work on offer, but it was not until 1937 that grants became available for productions in schools of non-Shakespearean plays – the first being an award to Bertha Waddell's Scottish Children's Theatre Company by the Glasgow Education authority for programmes that included short playlets and dramatised folk songs and nursery rhymes (Coggin 1956: 264, Redington 1983: 31–2). It established another important precedent and recognised the educational worth of drama and theatre in school settings for younger pupils.

In the United States, Alice M. Herts initiated in 1903 a programme of drama productions specifically for immigrant children living in the slums of New York, helping to underpin the emerging distinction between plays for children and plays for grown-ups (Swortzell 1988: 2; McCaslin in Landy, 1982: 193–4). Herts's project, known as the Children's Educational Theatre, set out explicitly to bring an experience of the arts to deprived children in the community, to teach 'the language of the new country', and to provide a welcoming place for all ages in a deprived neighbourhood (pp. 193–4). Mark Twain, visiting the theatre in the early 1900s, was impressed enough to proclaim that 'children's theatre is one of the very, very great innovations of the twentieth century' and went on to praise its 'vast educational value' which, while it was 'now but dimly perceived and but vaguely understood', would he predicted 'some day . . . come to be recognised' (quoted in Swortzell 1990: xiii). The practice of adapting fairy tales and children's classic novels was given new and fresh impetus by the work of Charlotte Chorpenning, a Chicago-based writer who produced a series of lively and eminently stage-able versions of the classics over a period of some ten years, culminating in the immensely popular production of *The Emperor's New Clothes* for the Federal Theatre Children's Unit in 1936 (Swortzell 1986: 10).

While in Britain the developments between the wars remained modest and the education/entertainment dichotomy continued, with the real innovations delayed until after the Second World War, elsewhere in Europe the changes were more marked – and nowhere more than in Russia, in the new Union of Soviet Socialist Republics. Here revolution became the motor for change in all official organisations, on the cultural front as well as the political and economic. The state-subsidised Petrograd Children's Theatre was established in 1918, quickly followed by the Children's Theatre of the Moscow Soviet, both of which initially presented a traditional, apolitical range of fairy tales, songs, marionettes and dance; but by 1923 children's theatre was beginning to be commandeered as a propaganda tool, functioning 'explicitly as an instrument of the totalitarian regime, legitimising and perpetuating the official dogma of Marxism-Leninism' (Water 2006: 9). None the less, as Manon van de Water has comprehensively shown, within the context of a state still hammering out ways of implementing and sustaining the revolution, the subject matter, types of play and styles of production varied considerably, sometimes in response to the passions of particular directors, sometimes in order to meet the latest directives from their political masters as ideological strategies changed. While most productions in the Soviet era kept, or were kept, well away from direct commentary on contemporary issues, some did venture in the direction of veiled political comment. In the work of Yevgeny Schwartz, the stories of Andersen and Grimm were used as vivid, playful, yet sharply satirical vehicles for political comment: *The Naked King* (1933) was one controversial example – a 'comical but doggedly anti-fascist protest . . . that worried the censors enough to prevent its public staging for almost thirty years' (Swortzell 1990: xxvii). Without doubt, the high profile given to theatre for children and young people in Russia set benchmarks for the establishment of children's theatres in many other European cities, in the capitalist west as well as in the soviet satellite countries – purpose built, often prestigious, theatre buildings for children and young people, that were intended to instil public pride as signifiers of a state commitment to making culture available to everyone. There were risks attached however: of ossifying the kind of state-approved culture considered suitable for children, of constraining experiment and innovation, and of creating a hierarchy of cultural practice in which independent companies – if they were allowed to practise at all – received minimal funding. (See Water 2006, Swortzell 1990.)

In Britain, the movements for change – in the repertory theatre movement, in the gathering belief in the power and indeed the necessity of drama as a commentator on social and political life, and in the campaigns to ameliorate the very social inequities that dramatists sought to address – were dealt a crippling blow with the outbreak of the First World War. Churchill's bill to introduce more substantial prison reform was put on hold, as were the campaigns for universal suffrage, for women's rights, for the effective regulation of a rampant capitalism; all suffered delays, compromise or loss of steam, as other priorities loomed. It was the repercussions of that devastating war, however, that, from 1918 onwards, gave new impulse to those movements for change and to the vision of a different, more accessible, more empowering kind of theatre. Of those new post-1918 movements the most energetic, ambitious and innovative were those aligned to political change.

Notes

1 See especially Bruce (1987), Decker (1977), Engels (1892), Furst and Skrine (1971), Stearns (1972), Hauser (1990).
2 Schechner has proposed the notion of an 'efficacy-entertainment braid' in *Performance Theory* (1988: 120–4), or an 'efficacy-entertainment dyad' in *Performance Studies* (2002: 71), as a way of understanding how the two fundamentally distinct goals of performance practice might be both differentiated and 'entwined' on a continuum rather than as binary opposites. Efficacy refers to the types of performance that aim at 'transformations', often involving the participation of the audience, but, in Schechner's terms it is associated more with 'ritual' than 'theatre'; entertainment refers to conventional theatre performances in which the stage action and audience remain separate and 'fun' is one of the main goals. There are, he suggests, many permutations in between these two poles of the continuum. Education, although not referred to explicitly in Schechner's summary of efficacious features, would certainly be a goal much closer to 'efficacy' than to 'entertainment'.
3 Susanne Langer recounts her childhood memory of utter dismay at the sudden disruption of the make-believe by a Peter Pan who turned to the audience and insisted, 'like a teacher coaching us in a play', on the audience demonstrating their belief in make-believe: Langer 1953: 318; see also Chapter 5.
4 See Paul Barker, 'Shakespeare's sisters', *The Guardian*, 26 June 2004.

3

Agitating the audience: theatre, propaganda and education in the 1930s

Radical theatre in the 1930s

In the history of political theatre the 1930s was an extraordinary period. It was moreover a period in which, for a complex array of social, political and economic reasons, the possibilities of theatre as an educational medium distinct from its function as a propaganda tool began to be opened up. The early part of the decade, following the stock market crash of 1929 and the beginning of the Depression years, saw the rapid growth of the workers' theatre movement throughout Europe; it saw the growth of a diverse range of radical theatre groups in the United States, many of them created by immigrant workers bringing with them agit-prop (agitational propaganda) practices direct from Germany and Russia, driven by a widely shared belief that American capitalism was on the brink of collapse and that one last push would result in proletarian revolution; it saw continued interrogation of the broader purpose and function of theatre, which was in turn manifested in a vigorous reaching out to new audiences, the ready embrace of propaganda, education and artistic innovation, and the reshaping of the relationships, physical and philosophical, between stage and audience.

Even when the revolutionary campaigns gave way to the Popular Front against Fascism in the middle of the decade, the innovation and the imaginative re-visioning of what theatre could be continued, and if anything gained new momentum. It was the latter years of the 1930s that produced the achievements of the Federal Theatre Project in America, the launching of Ewan MacColl and Joan Littlewood's Theatre Union in Manchester which was to re-form after the war as Theatre Workshop, and the beginnings of Unity Theatre in London.

None of this came out of the blue, and the seeds of change were sown and nurtured in the 1920s. (See especially Stourac and McCreery 1986, Bradby and McCormick 1978, Davies 1987, and others.) But the crash and the Depression Years gave enormous impetus to radical movements in the arts – and to explorations of theatre's role as a teaching medium.

What follows is not an attempt to survey the history of these movements, and in the space available it would be impossible to do justice to the variety and richness – and indeed the paradoxes – of this area of political and cultural activity. Excellent books on the period provide factual detail and personal insight (Chambers 1989, Davies 1987, Goorney and MacColl 1986, Samuel, MacColl and Cosgrove 1985 and Stourac and McCreery 1986). My aim here is to sketch out a number of features of work in this period that seem to me particularly significant in the evolving ideas about theatre's educational potential, and especially to examine the shift that occurred in the mid-1930s from theatre seen primarily as a tool for propaganda and exhortation to theatre as a tool for communicating ideas and for 'moving' audiences to 'work for the betterment of society' (Allen 1937: 2). By the end of the decade, there was an increasingly widespread recognition that – to quote John Allen again, one of Britain's leading advocates of socialist theatre in the mid-1930s (and later to become, after the war, a significant figure both as theatre director and in the education world as a government inspector of drama and Principal of the Central School of Speech and Drama): 'Few forms of activity can surpass the theatre for combining learning with entertainment and instruction with fun' (Allen 1937: 3).

Perhaps no other form represents the propagandist end of the educational/interventionist spectrum more starkly, and energetically, than agit-prop. My focus will therefore be initially on the agit-prop form, culminating as it did in Clifford Odets's inspirational marriage of agit-prop and social realism in *Waiting for Lefty*; and subsequently on the shift in tactics for reaching out to, engaging and 'teaching' audiences in the changed political landscape in the middle of the decade – the emergence of the Popular Front against Fascism having replaced the revolutionary politics of earlier years, with immediate ramifications for leftist theatre.[1] By the second half of the decade, many politically committed theatre groups – such as London's Unity Theatre – were endeavouring to position themselves, gingerly, on a borderline between revolutionary proletarian theatre and a more inclusive socialist theatre – a theatre of the popular front as it were, building on earlier radical theatre experiments but reaching the convertible rather than preaching to the converted.

Propaganda and education

Propaganda, in its concern with the spreading of ideas and with persuasion, can be seen as a legitimate if extreme point on the broad spectrum of what constitutes educational activity. But, from a twenty-first-century perspective, its primary associations are with the propaganda activities of Fascist regimes in the 1930s and of Soviet regimes before and after the Second World War, with American anti-communist campaigns during the 1950s and with more recent racist campaigns of organisations such as the British National Party or France's Front National. It does not sit comfortably therefore within our current notions of education, no matter how broadly conceived they might be. It can be easy to forget that propaganda has had a more accepted, and indeed central, place in the canon of educational practice. The Catholic Church has, for example, long had its Congregation for the Propagation of the Faith, though 'propagation' is no longer used in its current nomenclature. At root, the word 'propagate' means to *spread* from person to person or place to place; to disseminate (a statement, belief or practice) (*Shorter Oxford English Dictionary* third ed., 1983). And, in today's world, propaganda (even if we call it by a different name) can have a relatively benign and uncontroversial function, as in the television campaigns in the run up to Christmas that aim to drive home the message about drinking and driving. But such campaigns often contain more than a whiff of crisis-management: the intensity of the appeal is in direct proportion to the perceived threat. And the effectiveness of their means has been hotly debated.[2] The feature that constitutes such appeals as propaganda rather than education (at least in the sense we use that term now) is that, as expressed by Pratkanis and Aronson, in their seminal study of the subject, they 'persuade not through the give-and-take of argument and debate, but through the manipulation of symbols and our most basic human emotions' (Pratkanis and Aronson 1991: 5–6). While few would wish to disagree with the primacy that the authors give to argument and debate, this assertion does rather beg the question of whether or not it is legitimate to appeal to the emotions in the educational process, and if so to what degree. If the emotions are to be excluded (other than referentially), then it begs the further question of how far theatre can claim to be a means of learning when the exploration and transmission, perhaps even the manipulation, of human emotion is one of the medium's characteristic ingredients – a point to which we shall need to return. Interestingly, it was in 1937, just as concern was building about the rise of fascism throughout Europe and about Stalinism in the Soviet Union, that the Institute for Propaganda Analysis (IPA) was formed in the USA to promote public awareness of the ever-widening use of political propaganda. In one of its notable publications, *The Fine Art of Propaganda*, it made this significant assertion:

> It is essential in a democratic society that young people and adults learn how to think, learn how to make up their minds. They must learn how to think independently, and they must learn how to think together. They must come to conclusions, but at the same time they must recognise the right of other men to come to opposite conclusions. So far as individuals are concerned, the art of democracy is the art of thinking and discussing independently together. (IPA 1939, *The Fine Art of Propaganda*, quoted in www.propagandacritic.com/articles/intro.why.html, last accessed 15 March 2006)

As Europe lurched towards war, a principled statement about the need to distinguish propaganda from true education, and to stress the importance of individual thought and collective debate, must have seemed particularly timely. It undoubtedly draws on the arguments of America's leading educational philosopher of the first half of the twentieth century, John Dewey, who had for many years been pressing the case for reconceptualising education and for stressing the intricate and indivisible relationship between democracy, education and individual thought processes (Dewey 1918). A decade earlier than the IPA statement, however, propaganda was perceived very differently. In a world still reeling from the ravages of the First World War and from the inequalities and injustices that still plagued and divided western societies, propaganda was a means of spreading the word that the world could be different and that revolutionary ideologies offered hope to those who were at the mercy of capitalist exploitation.

Agit-prop and the influence of Piscator

The origins of agit-prop lay in the activities of the small-scale theatre groups in Soviet Russia formed following the revolution to explain current events and government policy in popular, clear, entertaining ways to a predominantly peasant and largely illiterate population, from west to east. They were known as the Blue Blouse ('Sinyaya Bluza') after the workers' blue overalls which the actors wore for their performances. The style of theatre was in large measure determined by the need to play in a variety of challenging locations: on the backs of lorries, in bars and in ill-equipped community halls, sometimes before audiences of hundreds or of several thousands (Stourac and McCreery 1986: 56–7). It therefore had to be entertaining and highly visual, exploiting such popular forms

as cartoon, circus, carnival and mass spectacles, and drawing on older
traditions too, notably *commedia dell'arte*, as well as on the use of the
rapid montage of images common to contemporary left-wing political
theatre and film. It had to aim at the 'tempo of today, the tempo of
machine technology' in order to achieve the effect of 'an electric current,
so that the viewer gets a shaking up of a psychic and physical character,
and is charged with energy' (*Sinyaya Bluza* 1925, no. 18, pp. 3–5,
quoted in Stourac and McCreery 1986: 57). The 'charging with energy'
was about rousing the masses to 'the struggle for the socialist reconstruction of society', educating them 'in the habits of a class fighter and
builder' and imbuing them with 'confidence in the final victory' (ibid.,
1927, no. 69/70, p. 53; quoted in Stourac and McCreery 1986: 53). It
was seen as imperative to harness the entertaining features of each piece
to the ultimate goal, that of winning over ordinary people to the immediate and urgent task of transforming society and of equipping them with
the knowledge to enable them (it was hoped) to play their part.

Although the Blue Blouse troupes began to lose their popularity by the
late 1920s, the vitality, directness and immediacy of the form quickly
caught on in Scandinavia and, most influentially, in Germany where
support for revolutionary activity had been burgeoning throughout the
fraught decade that followed defeat in the war (Stourac and McCreery
1986: 73–5); and from there spread to Britain, the USA and beyond. Why
did this apparently crude, speedily crafted and culturally specific form
appeal beyond Russian borders? What was it about the agit-prop form
that exerted such a hold on the political and theatrical imaginations of,
for example, so many in British left theatre groups of the time? Ewan
MacColl recalls his first engagement with agit-prop in Salford in the late
1920s from the point of view of an unemployed working-class youth
who had no experience of theatre going or any grounding in theatrical
traditions:

> I saw the theatre simply as a new and exciting form of propaganda, a new
> and exciting way of giving voice to all your . . . political feelings. . . . I
> thought that the theatre should become a weapon, it should be something
> that spoke for all the people like me. (MacColl 1985: 226)

Tom Thomas (writing of his experience with the Hackney People's
Players in the late 1920s and early 1930s) offered a similar rationale:

> Agit-prop . . . has no stage, no curtains, no props. Instead of creating illu-
> sions, it can speak to people's own experiences of life, dramatize their trou-
> bles, present them with ideas. It is mobile – it can be taken to the people
> instead of waiting for them to come to you. And it is a theatre of attack.
> (Thomas 1977: 95)

Plate 1 *Class against Class*: the British Workers' Theatre Movement delegation rehearses an agit-prop piece *en route* to the 1933 Workers' Theatre Olympiad, Leningrad.

Characters were two-dimensional types, points were made swiftly and directly, the action was often choreographed and choral recitation was generally preferred to dialogue, underlining the sense of a collective enterprise in which powerful effects – both on stage and in real life – could be shown to be achievable by ordinary people working together in a common cause. *Class against Class* – a sketch created for performance at the 1933 Workers' Theatre Olympiad in Leningrad by the London-based Workers' Theatre Movement and in response to Hitler's alarming rise to power in Germany that same year – illustrates something of the choric, stylised mode of delivery that characterised early agit-prop. (See Plate 1.) Naturalism, with its more individualistic emphases, could scarcely have been more inappropriate. Plays by Ibsen, Shaw and Strindberg may have offered in their own ways critiques of the social system but their intellectual density and appeal to the middle- and upper-middle-class audiences for whom they were usually written – together with their tendency to offer 'delayed gratification' rather than the spur to action sought by working-class activists – made them mostly inaccessible to those without the cultural and economic capital to appreciate them. Underpinning the dramaturgy, too, was a belief that optimism was an essential part of socialist theatre. Whatever the extent of the oppression, however hard the conditions of exploitation or unemployment, and however great the odds against liberation might appear to be, the message that underlay all such dramatic expression was that in unity there was strength – that the world could be changed and the lot of working people could be bettered. Revolution was the ultimate goal but raising the consciousness of the working class was the first necessary step upon the well-signposted road that the Soviet Communist party had marked out. Hence the move away from the gloomy endings of so much 'realistic' drama. Workers needed to be inspired, not overwhelmed by the 'realistic' (and defeatist) representations of their oppression. For this reason, the Workers' Theatre Movement (London) changed the ending of their production of *The Ragged Trousered Philanthropists* to offer a more up-beat, optimistic view of the future, and to engineer a plot climax that served simultaneously as a direct invitation to the audience to voice their collective assent to a socialist future, a response celebrated in the *Sunday Worker*'s review:

> Finally, Harlow moves a resolution that 'Socialism is the only remedy for unemployment and poverty' and turns to the audience with 'What d'you say, mates?' . . . old Philpott as chairman puts the resolution: 'Those in favour shout "Ay!" (To audience). 'Let it go now! One, two, three, ay!' The success of this device is unquestionable, and the curtain is rung down upon a tremendous shout of 'Ay!' from the audience. (28 February 1928, quoted in Samuel et al., 1985: 55, 58).

Piscator

Agit-prop was by no means a fixed form. It developed, in Germany during the late 1920s and early 1930s, a remarkable variety of techniques in response to the demands of the time and the types of audience being targeted – techniques that took agit-prop beyond mere propaganda and opened up opportunities for different, more challenging relationships between stage and auditorium. More than anyone else, the person to have seen its educational, dialogic, rather than merely didactic, potential and to have done most to translate it into theatrical reality in Germany was Erwin Piscator – in this respect more influential than Bertolt Brecht. As Brecht himself recognised, acknowledging in turn his own debt to Piscator, Piscator's theatre was 'the most radical' of all attempts to give the theatre an educational function: 'every single one [of his experiments] was aimed to increase the theatre's value as education' (Brecht 1964: 130). In the immediate aftermath of the First World War, Piscator, a committed communist, had become a leading figure in the growing workers' theatre movement and in 1920 established the Proletarisches Theater in Berlin (in which the audience were addressed as 'comrades'), from which many productions were toured around the beer-halls and wherever workers congregated. The plays were often hastily devised by the company in the interests of striving to achieve an impact on actual events outside the theatre – for Piscator saw drama as, in his own words, 'a political tool . . . An instrument of propaganda, of education' (Piscator, quoted in Innes 1972: 22). Brecht in 1930 explained the significance of what Piscator was doing (and signalled the influence he had upon his own conception of theatre) thus:

> Piscator . . . might transform the stage into a factory assembly shop or the auditorium into a meeting hall. Piscator saw the theatre as a parliament, the audience as a legislative body. The social problems of the day, so urgently requiring attention and decisions, were enacted before the eyes of this parliament. Instead of a delegate making a speech about certain intolerable conditions, these conditions would be shown on stage. His theatre was designed to enable parliament, his audience, to make political decisions on the basis of what they had seen on stage on the evidence of representation statistics and slogans . . . his first priority was to stimulate discussion. His plays were designed not merely to provide an experience but to force the audience into deciding actively to come to grips with life. He used every means open to him to achieve this end. (Brecht 1940: 31–2)

In 1929/30 one of the plays performed in Berlin and subsequently on tour to packed houses by Piscator's company (the Piscator-Bühne) was *Section 218*, by Carl Crédé. 'Section 218' referred to the current legislation on abortion, which was being applied with great harshness during the economically crisis-ridden years of the Depression and had caused considerable suffering and public discontent (Innes 1972: 138). The play was an expression of protest against this particular law. Very deliberately the dividing line between art and life was challenged by turning the theatre event into a debating-chamber-cum-political-rally. Reports from each day's newspapers were inserted into the play from performance to performance, accentuating the actuality of the play's subject matter. Piscator went to great lengths to involve the audience directly in the stage action, believing that the 'fourth wall' dividing stage from auditorium 'had to be eliminated if revolutionary material was to be communicated as a directly felt experience' (Innes, p. 137; see also Jackson 1980a: 36–7). The performance was to be a political discussion, the outcome of which was to be decided by the audience. Thus, in the words of a contemporary reviewer,

> the public participated through speeches and shouts . . . until finally this (involvement) reached its culmination with a real vote that swept the public into an almost unanimous rejection of Section 218 of the criminal code by a show of hands, through which for the first time the ending of a play corresponded to a public meeting. (quoted in Innes 1972: 137)

One of the methods he experimented with to engage his audiences was to create a sense of immediacy and topicality by placing actors among the audience so that often a dialogue would take place across the foot-lights during the course of the play. Thus, as Rorrison explains, the 'min-ister, the doctor, the district attorney, the factory owner sat and aired their views on the law in the orchestra before climbing onto the stage to act them out' (Rorrison in Piscator 1980: 341). Even, on occasion, rep-resentative members of the local community (actual lawyers, doctors, teachers) would be asked to take part in the debate in the auditorium.

Few productions of the time it seems went as far as this one did in actually incorporating debate and an audience vote within the play itself, but many did provoke heated discussion after the performance – the desired effect. Of course the general thrust of each production was overtly political and the party-line was rarely in doubt. But the methods employed went beyond mere propaganda. While quite openly manipu-lative in the selection of the human stories to dramatise, the play also attempted to persuade by argument. The conclusions may not have been in doubt, but there were points of view that had to be aired, voices from different sectors of public life that had to be listened to, and facts that had to be faced, before any vote could be taken. This was no simplistic appeal to working-class sentiment but a penetrating and full-blooded exposé of the dehumanising effects of an unjust law and its implemen-tation, a probing and exposing of the issues behind the easy rhetoric that characterised much of the political debate. The theatrical methods were innovative and carried out in the belief that didactic theatre could teach and not merely preach. It was, as John Willett puts it, 'a vehicle for Marxist analysis rather than for merely revolutionary exhortation or the . . . exposure of social abuses' (Willett 1971: 11). Audiences were to be engaged as closely as possible, indirectly in the analytic process on stage and directly in the debates in the auditorium that often followed. Piscator's methods have been accused of being little more than theatri-cal trickery and it is difficult to make any final judgements given the inevitable transience of his productions, relying as they did upon topi-cality, tempo and the immediacy of the audience response – a response which, so long after the event, it is impossible adequately to evaluate. Nevertheless his influence was felt not only by Brecht and others in Germany but elsewhere in Europe and particularly in North America – to which Piscator emigrated in 1938.

Meanwhile, Brecht was pursuing a rather different line, one that involved using the stage to present sharp, provocative parables for his time: plays such as the early *Lehrstücke* ('teaching plays') and *The Measures Taken*, which told stories set in other lands, designed to demonstrate dialectically how the world, once understood, was changeable. But, while in *Section 218* Piscator had endeavoured to influence events immediately outside the theatre walls, for Brecht, at this stage in his career, the imperative was to analyse not so much the specific issue but the more invisible power structures that underpinned the operation of all capitalist societies (*The Exception and the Rule*, 1930); or the moral dilemmas faced when opportunities for change beckon (*He Who Says Yes*; *He Who Says No*, 1929–30). This distinction, between the play that seeks to persuade in the here and now with a view to effecting immediate change in the world outside and the one that is designed to provoke uncomfortable questions and insights, in parable form, is one that we shall see in sharper outline – in comparing *The Life of Galileo* and plays dealing more directly with scientific dilemmas – in Chapter 4.

Workers' theatre in America and Britain

Piscator's international influence was perhaps most marked in the United States, and long before his arrival on American shores. Agit-prop theatre techniques were being imported from both Russia and Germany as early as the mid-1920s – especially via the German and Russian immigrant groups, bringing with them new ideas and methods for agitational, revolutionary theatre. Most notable perhaps was the work of the Prolet Bühne, a small but energetic agitational theatre group working initially among the immigrant German communities in New York (Cosgrove 1985: 266). From 1928 the group was led by Hans Bohn, a theatre director who had been well acquainted with Piscator's agitational revues and other forms of worker's theatre in Berlin and who soon began to develop a considerable repertoire of short exhortatory plays, recitations and pageants – all devoted to the propagation of the communist viewpoint – which the group performed at workers' meetings in New York and beyond. The Prolet Bühne soon became one of the leading workers theatre groups in the United States, and alongside the Workers' Laboratory Theatre was a major channel for the dissemination of ideas and information about European agit-prop (Cosgrove, p. 267).

In Britain, the vital force in left-wing theatre during the late 1920s and early 1930s was embodied in the Workers' Theatre Movement (WTM). Born in 1926, of solid left-wing parentage – *The Sunday Worker*, the Central Labour College (London) and The Plebs League – and given new impetus when taken over by Hackney People's Players in 1928, the WTM was in Raphael Samuel's words, 'an exercise in *proletkult*' (Samuel 1985: 37). Looking forward to a Workers' World, it had revelled in the proletarian condition rather than wanting to be emancipated from it, and saw itself as 'first and foremost enacting the class struggle on stage' (Samuel, p. 41). But even the WTM looked west as much as to Russia and Germany for its inspiration. Its first performance was of Upton Sinclair's *Singing Jailbirds*, a realistic play based on an actual American strike (p. 41), but it quickly moved towards agit-prop – theatre that was highly portable, exhortatory in style, provoking the audience to see the truth of their own (or others') oppression and urging them to take action in concert with their socialist comrades.

Interestingly, the Workers' Laboratory Theatre was also at this time (1934) in regular correspondence with Ewan MacColl currently forming, with Littlewood, Theatre Union in Manchester – further pointing to the complex network of relationships and influences that existed in proletarian theatre between Russia, the European mainland, Britain and the USA. While there was considerable direct contact between British and German troupes (the British WTM took up an invitation to tour Germany in 1931 – see Stourac and McCreery 1986: 73–5), the trajectory of influence often did not take the shortest route. Russian- and German-inspired theatrical experiment frequently reached Britain via America, during which process it had of course become further transformed. In 1932, for example, Proltet, the London Yiddish socialist theatre group, performed *Strike!*, a mass recitation piece by Michael Gold – a few years after it had first been done by the New York Workers' Drama League in America (in 1926). Gold describes how many of the performers should be 'scattered in groups or as individuals through the audience'; dressed in 'usual street clothes', there is 'nothing to distinguish them from their fellow workers in the audience'. As the recitation gets under way and voices from the platform are interrupted by voices from the floor, the audience 'is swept more and more into the excitement all round them; they become one with the actors, a real mass; before the recitation is over, everyone in the hall should be shouting: "Strike! Strike!"' (Gold, quoted in Cosgrove: 266). Predating *Section 218*, and influenced by practices in Moscow (to which Gold had earlier gone to learn about Soviet agit-prop), this piece was an undoubted influence on Odets's chosen style for *Waiting for Lefty*. Ray Waterman, writing in 1934, cites one of Proltet's London performances as demonstrating the value of agit-prop in combining propaganda and entertainment: when 'players, mingled in the audience, cry in unison, "We are hungry. Give us bread!"', many members of the audience were taken by surprise, turning to each other to check whether they should join in, but none the less grasped the challenging ideas being presented (Waterman in Samuel et al. 1985: 179). A little earlier, the Hackney People's Players had performed a political revue called *Strike Up* in 1929, 'sprinkling' in the hall a group of its own members who, at the appropriate moment, shouted 'Yes, strike!' so that 'it sounded as if the whole audience in the hall was calling for a strike' (Thomas 1977: 88). Audience participation – whether spontaneous or induced, simplistic or sophisticated – was for many of these groups seen not simply as a device to enliven the drama but as a key goal to be aimed at, and, when participation happened, a vindication of their socialist agenda. Participation in the action and the mood of the piece could be, and was, taken as a sign of engagement with the cause, a token of intent: the stirrings of class-consciousness and the recognition that action in concert with fellow workers was vital to overcoming perceived oppression, and that it could actually feel good. There was tangible power in being part of a chorus of voices, a power unimaginable and unattainable were individuals to act alone. Of course, such commitment had its limits. It was fine so long as you did not feel coerced, and so long as the experience remained fresh and eye-opening. Once the method became formulaic and repetitive, the efforts all too easily became counterproductive. Once the feeling set in that the 'them and us' applied not only to capitalist bosses and workers but, in a different way and just as disempoweringly, to the divide between activists on stage and audiences being cornered into agreeing, or rather ratifying, the messages directed at them, then the local battle was lost before it had begun.

Following the Wall Street crash, workers' theatre in America had grown rapidly. By 1933, over 250 workers' theatre groups were known to exist in the USA; by the end of 1934, there were over four hundred (Cosgrove: 268). As these groups multiplied across industrial North America, the high point – and in many respects the beginning of the end – of this increased activity was undoubtedly reached with that first performance of *Waiting for Lefty* in 1935. Although groups continued for several more years to produce agit-prop pieces (as well as *Lefty* itself), from 1935 on we see a decline in proletarian drama – largely as a result of increased concern over the rise of fascism in Europe. The need to combine the forces of the left and the liberal middle ground to fight fascism, leading to the emergence of the Popular Front, had the effect of undercutting the struggles of the Communist Party and other groups committed to the cause of revolution. As Tom Thomas, of the Hackney People's Theatre, wryly noted, 'in theatre terms, it's much more difficult to present an argument for a constructive line, like building a united front against Fascism, than to write satires and attacks on the class enemy' (Thomas 1977: 94). And, in America, Roosevelt's New Deal programmes for putting people back to work blunted many of the revolutionary arrows.

Waiting for Lefty – from agitation to Unity

Originally written in 1934, this short one-act piece was given its first showing in New York in January 1935 at a private Sunday benefit performance for the New Theatre League and its mouthpiece the *New Theatre Magazine* – a left-wing journal which had selected Odets's script as the best short play on the subject of labour relations. Odets had written the play at the height of the New York taxi drivers' strike and that topical event provided the immediate setting for the action. As soon as the play opens, the audience are addressed directly as an audience of workers at a trade union meeting at which strike action is being debated. Interspersed with the arguments between union leaders and their disillusioned members are dramatic flashbacks to moments from the lives of workers in different walks of life. The play combines with remarkable success the staccato techniques and exhortatory tone of agit-prop with the characteristically American predilection for social realism. A series of five short scenes – among others, a low-paid taxi driver and his wife facing increasing financial hardship, a Jewish doctor sacked as a result of anti-Semitic bigotry – pithily illustrate the different reasons for each having turned to taxi-driving to make ends meet and their consequent politicisation. Between them, the scenes accumulate to provide a powerful dramatic argument for standing up against exploitation, oppression and racial prejudice. As in productions by Piscator, actors placed in the audience added to the sense of reality and excitement generated in performance such that the final moments, culminating in the decision to call for strike action, invariably received spontaneous roars of approval from the audience.

That the audience involvement generated by the play was more than mere excitement of the moment is indicated by Harold Clurman who witnessed that extraordinary first performance and reflected afterwards:

> When the audience at the end of the play responded to the militant question from the stage: 'Well, what's the answer?' with a spontaneous roar of 'Strike! Strike!', it was something more than a tribute to the play's effectiveness, more even than a testimony of the audience's hunger for constructive social action. It was the birth cry of the thirties. Our youth had found its voice. It was a call to join the good fight for a greater measure of life in a world free of economic fear, falsehood, and craven servitude to stupidity and greed. 'Strike!' was Lefty's lyric message, not alone for a few extra pennies of wages or for shorter hours of work: strike for greater dignity, strike for a bolder humanity, strike for the full stature of man. (Clurman 1957: 138–9)

Plate 2 *Waiting for Lefty*, New York, 1935. Production for New Theatre League. The call for strike action at the end of the play: actors placed in the audience are seen in foreground.

Although written ostensibly about one particular strike, the play lost none of its appeal when that strike was long over. Its value – and its danger – was, as Clurman suggests, metaphoric: a vital clue to *Lefty*'s widespread appeal. And one that marked a clear shift in the function and form of agit-prop. It managed to be, at one and the same time, agitational, celebratory of working-class solidarity, and – at another level – educative. It asked its audience to see and to make *connections* between one local, and long-gone, dispute and the bigger picture of exploitation and injustice, between the struggles of individuals and the larger struggle of the working class for control over their own lives and for the betterment of the human lot.

It clearly struck a chord with that first audience, and proved capable of doing the same for hundreds of audiences over the next few years – voicing directly and passionately the mood of many working people of the time who felt themselves to be victims of exploitation. The play was immediately taken up by workers' theatres all over the USA and was the catalyst in starting more such groups; and it soon became a famous theatrical rallying-point for socialist groups in Europe too. In many US cities, its performance caused consternation among the authorities and was often banned under one pretext or another. An article in *Time Magazine* at the time described instance after instance of a 'systematic campaign against a play acknowledged as high art regardless of its political significance' ('*Agit-Prop*' in *Time*, 17 June 1935, p. 38). In England, Merseyside Left Theatre's performance in Chester in 1938 was stopped by the theatre manager who objected to the play's 'extreme profanity' (Chambers 1989: 64).

Lefty's continued pull, long after the heyday of agit-prop was over, can be attributed to a number of factors: to that combination of agit-prop and social realism that made it work so effectively both at political gatherings and in more conventional theatre settings; to the shortage of truly inspirational left-wing drama; and to its rapidly acquired, almost mythic status as an emblem of how working-class theatre could galvanise its audiences. But the scale of its success was unique and it paradoxically heralded not only the death-knell of agit-prop but a move away from performing at picket lines and union meetings and back in to theatre buildings.

One gauge of the play's metaphoric power and its capture of the mood of the moment is the extent of its impact beyond the immediate dispute that triggered its birth, and beyond the particular cultural conditions of East Coast America in the Depression.

Unity Theatre

The shift in attitudes to the function of theatre as a propagandising tool could not be better illustrated, in Britain at least, than in the work of Unity Theatre. It was founded in London in 1935 by members of the left-wing amateur theatre group the Rebel Players and the associated New Theatre League – the members of which were all Communist Party activists and sympathisers. It operated as a democratically run club, determinedly amateur in status, and aimed to be an example of socialism in practice. Unity's stated purpose was, in the words of its rule book:

> to foster and further the art of drama in accordance with the principle that true art, by effectively and truthfully interpreting life as experienced by the majority of the people, can move the people to work for the betterment of society. (Chambers 1989: 19)

The very inclusive wording befitted the mood of the time, but its roots were inescapably in the Communist Party and its aims were dedicatedly socialist. The aims were also broadly educational rather than propagandist.

The WTM in Britain had finally collapsed in 1935. The limited and ultimately formulaic, repetitive style of so much propagandist theatre had already begun to seem increasingly crude and off-putting not only to non-party audiences but to many party members too, even before the Popular Front took hold. Members of the WTM who had taken examples of their work to the Moscow Workers' Theatre Olympiad in 1933 had been chastened by the criticism they received for their 'primitive' style of work (Davies 1987: 108). And in 1935 moves to establish a building-based theatre more in tune with the age gained momentum. It was becoming recognised that there were benefits to be gained from bringing a more professional dimension to the work – a move not to employ professional actors but to find premises for the work that would allow for proper rehearsals and greater control over the style of presentation. Hence the decision of the Rebel Players, hitherto closely identified with the WTM, to create a new workers' theatre club – to be known as Unity – and take over for the purpose a converted church hall in Britannia Street, subsequently (in 1937) transferring to more fitting premises in Goldington Street.[3] The move indoors to permanent theatre premises, no matter how basic, was not without its critics – not least of whom were members of Manchester's Theatre Union (previously Theatre of Action) who passionately argued for the necessity to remain mobile and close to the material living and working conditions of their audiences (Stourac and McCreery 1986: 258).

One of Unity Theatre's early members, and an influential force in the theatre's development, John Allen, wrote an illuminating document at the end of Unity's first highly successful year. It provides some valuable insights into the way the club worked, its roots, its attempts to redefine socialist theatre and its relationship with its audiences. Called *Notes on Forming Left Theatre Groups* and published in mimeograph form in 1937, it was written in response to 'numerous requests' from left-leaning groups all over England and Scotland for 'advice about how to form and conduct amateur theatrical groups' (Allen: 1). It reflects the mood of the period in giving explicit support for conducting the fight against war and fascism 'on the basis of a popular front' and it underlines the widespread conviction that the theatre is an especially effective basis for such activity. It also performs a delicate balancing act between its inclusive, popular front aspirations and its 'proletkult' roots.[4] Allen strongly advances Unity's claims to inclusivity, which he sees as applicable to actors and audience alike, and offers as an example of this Unity Theatre Club's production of *Waiting for Lefty* – its first production and the play that helped to put Unity on the map. The twenty or so actors in the cast, he proudly notes, 'included members of the Liberal, Labour and Communist parties, members of Co-operative Societies, Trades Unionists, and so on'. And the audiences were even more varied: 'they are not solely members of the working class'.

> A theatre such as this is continually presenting left-wing opinions and problems to people who would never dream of attending a political meeting; and if those ideas are presented in a way that is theatrically effective, they will have a considerable influence on those members of the audience. (Allen: 2)

Note the concern to celebrate theatre dedicated to the cause of socialism and at the same time the need to reach more than the converted few. Ordinary people can be persuaded of the virtues of the socialist cause so long as they are not harangued. Simply to participate in a performance, even as just one member of a mass recitation piece, can be empowering:

> In mass recitations, a man can learn the simplest elements of theatrical technique. He can experience . . . the exalting sensation of addressing an audience with words in which he passionately believes, and that of communion with other people on the stage.

Moreover, 'the tremendous amount of co-operation that is needed among the different people concerned in putting on a play, is in itself a splendid lesson in practical socialism' (Allen: 2–3).

The decision to produce *Waiting for Lefty* and to make it the first official production of the new Unity Theatre Club was a significant, if perhaps (with hindsight) predictable, indicator of how Unity was trying to position itself. The play offers an insight into the energy, stylistic experiment and accord with the temper of the age – and simultaneously of the in-built paradoxes – of radical theatre in this period. Ewan MacColl had put on the first performance in Britain (without waiting for a performance licence for it) with his Theatre of Action group in Manchester – not long after its first performance in New York. He recalls that the play was 'an ideal one for us' – it had many of the qualities associated with agit-prop, yet, while 'the slogans were still there', they were 'no longer used as a homiletic epilogue to the main action' (MacColl 1986: xxxv). The Rebel Players also staged an unofficial performance later that same year: it was, according to Chambers, seen as 'essential to the group's survival' if they were to break out of the political and artistic isolation which many workers' theatres were now experiencing as the political climate changed, and prove they were capable of taking on challenging work (Chambers 1989: 42). Unity went on to perform the play – with a licence – over three hundred times between 1936 and the outbreak of war. The play had by 1939 become synonymous with left-wing theatre.

Allen in his *Notes* acknowledges Unity's roots in agit-prop yet simultaneously articulates a philosophy that defines a more politically and artistically inclusive path – and continues his negotiation between past practice and current aspirations. Dealing with the issue of propaganda, for example, he stoutly defends its existence in the plays while expressing wariness about agit-prop itself:

> where is the work of art of value that is not propaganda? To condemn all art that has a message or an axe to grind is to condemn all art that has ever been created. Who is to judge the line between explicit and implicit propaganda?

. . . Is Dickens a lesser writer than Jane Austen because he condemned prisons in virulent and outspoken language? (Allen: 18)

But, on agit-prop he advises:

> these pieces should be used very sparingly. They are useful sometimes . . . to achieve a swift effect, but careful preliminary consideration should be given to the sort of people likely to compose the audience . . . Anything done in the theatre must be done theatrically . . . anything that does not live on stage, however wise, witty or wonderful . . ., will not only leave your audience unmoved: it may even antagonise them seriously. (p. 19)

In other words, the campaigning spirit and belief in changing the world for the better according to socialist principles should still lie at the heart of the drama produced by such groups as Unity; but the *form* is key to the effectiveness of the plays. Agit-prop, he seems to suggest, may now be inappropriate, given the changes in the outside world (in which priority had to be given to defeating fascism, and in which engaging audiences could no longer be taken for granted). At the same time, he acknowledges the value of agit-prop experience, at least for the training in 'outreach' if not for its agitational style:

> Actors who currently form the back-bone of the club spent 5 years rehearsing in attics and cellars, and giving performances at street corners, from the backs of lorries etc; . . . and the quite remarkable strength and vigour of these actors is due entirely to this training. (p. 4)

And he lays special emphasis on one-act plays – 'it is from the performance of one act plays in political meetings that we believe our movement will grow' (p. 10).

There was then an apparent contradiction, between on the one hand valuing the form and style of agit-prop, and indeed its propagandising function, and on the other suspicion of its ability to move audiences, and its theatrical lifelessness, which was itself a reflection of the larger shift in attitude to left-wing causes, to theatre's form and function and above all to the audiences. The need to keep all options open was in part resolved through Unity's decision to establish a mobile touring unit to take precisely such short, politically topical pieces (including *Waiting for Lefty*) to trade union and political gatherings. There was still a demand for such work outside conventional theatre buildings, as evidenced in the up-grading of the unit's means of transport (and no doubt at the same time in the quality of its staging): from two resurrected taxis in 1936 to a lorry the following year to a coach in 1938 (Chambers 1989: 91). Indeed, Allen optimistically claims that in this way, by retaining the mobile units, 'the forces of Socialism are building a theatre of their own, based on their own revolutionary doctrines, and supported by the mass of the people' (Allen: 14). Meanwhile, Unity's work on its main stage developed and for a while flourished, and provided inspiration for the forming of sister Unity groups in towns across Britain – in, for example, Liverpool, Leeds and Bristol. Its repertoire soon included home-grown plays, revues and living newspapers. *Lefty* however remained a mainstay, and production of American dramas continued to enrich and enlarge the repertoire. One of the main sources of continuing inspiration and of actual scripts was The Federal Theatre Project.

The Federal Theatre Project

The Federal Theatre Project (FTP) was launched in 1935 – set up as part of President Roosevelt's New Deal programme for getting the nation back to work in the midst of the Depression. The number of unemployed in the USA had by 1932 – the year of Roosevelt's election – reached 12 million: one in four of the workforce was now jobless; and Roosevelt's response was to inaugurate, through the Works Progress Administration, a nation-wide series of 'job creation' programmes, one of which was to apply to theatre workers. The Project was envisaged on a mammoth, coast-to-coast scale: a government-subsidised theatre network employing thousands of out-of-work actors, directors, designers and stage-hands, with the aim of fostering the talent and vitality of the American theatre and (of more importance to the Roosevelt Administration) of helping to boost the morale of American citizens. It employed some twelve thousand theatre people, and produced some 830 stage plays and six thousand plays for radio. (See Flanagan 1940, O'Connor and Brown 1980.) Commercial considerations were no longer to dictate what plays would be done and where, and performances were to be cheap, and free where possible. In fact, over the four years of the Project some 65 per cent of all seats for performances given by the Federal Theatre were actually free (Flanagan 1940, O'Connor and Brown 1980). The Project aimed to reach and involve all sections of the community, with plays targeted specifically at Blacks, non-English-speaking European immigrant groups, and children, as well as those aimed more broadly at the general public. According to the type of production, these plays were performed in conventional cinemas and theatres, schools and community halls, CCC (Civilian Conservation Corps) camps and in city parks across the country. There were statewide tours, community-based plays and productions in large Broadway theatres; and – an FTP innovation, to break with the traditional notion of New York being at the geographical apex of the American theatre – several of the major new productions opened simultaneously in up to sixteen states. There were new plays, classics, musicals, and – of most direct relevance to this discussion – 'living newspapers'.

Because 90 per cent of the budget had to be used for paying wages, the money available for spending on productions themselves was small, but this generated staging methods that were innovative and imaginative. For its national director Hallie Flanagan, the FTP was not only about getting people off the dole – it was an opportunity to recreate the American theatre and above all to lay the foundations of a genuinely national theatre. Flanagan was a visionary and a realist. As an academic (in the Theatre Department at Vassar College) she had been inspired by much of the theatre work she had seen during two study tours of Russian theatre in the late 1920s and in 1931, but also had proven organisational experience and was known to be a strong supporter of the aims of the New Deal. Thus she saw the offer to direct the Project (made by Harry Hopkins, head of the Works Progress Administration) as a unique opportunity to combine managerial pragmatism with artistic vision. That the Project achieved as much as it did in its four years of existence is testament to her initiative, imagination and enterprise.

From the outset, too, one of the key arguments Flanagan deployed to justify the work of the Federal Theatre was that it was educational. Thus she recalls how, in the early days of planning, Elmer Rice, Philip Barber (the two men who would run the NYC operation) and she were all in agreement about the philosophy of Federal Theatre: that 'theatre was more than a private enterprise, that it was also a public interest which, if properly fostered, might come to be a social and educative force' (Flanagan 1940: 54). It was agreed too that it should, in the words of one of the FTP's early chroniclers, aim to provide 'a certain amount of education in drama appreciation', recognising that 'Audiences . . . can be educated' (Whitman 1937: 143). Later, at the end of the first two years of the project, there appeared the Bair Report. In 1937, Dr Frederic Bair, a consultant to the Advisory Committee on Education in Washington DC, asked for a report on the educational aspect of the FT to be produced for his committee. It appeared in September that year,[5] clearly the fruit of a collective endeavour by the Federal Theatre to show its credentials, at a time when criticisms of the project were beginning to mount (about its cost, its apparent partisanship in respect of Roosevelt's New Deal policies and the left-leaning attitudes which some detected in living newspapers such as *Power* and *Triple A Plowed Under*). But the hard statistics about the sheer range and volume of activities undertaken, about employment, attendance and training, are remarkable. And the supplementary evidence (in Volume E) includes a wealth of testimonials and unsolicited letters of gratitude from members of the public, teachers and youth organisers, together with highly favourable production reviews and evaluations of the project in US and even English newspapers, impressive even allowing for the selectivity that would have been applied. It covered the whole range of work. Thus, in Section V (entitled 'The New Theatre goes out to meet a New Audience'), for example, there are accounts of the use of marionettes in involving and stimulating the imaginations of 'the backward and mentally dormant' children, in teaching English and 'the duties of citizenship' to new immigrants, and in teaching English, history and even 'safety first' in state schools; the use of participatory theatre in psychiatric practice; the work of the Community Drama Units, especially their cross-curricular programmes in schools (drawing on the experimental, active learning advocated by Dewey at the time); the widespread and high-profile activity of the various Children's Theatre Units who brought theatre to community centres and city parks as well as to regular theatres; the adaptations of Shakespeare and other classics for high-school audiences; and the lower profile but vital work of the Play Bureau in cataloguing and making accessible American plays, new and old (*The Bair Report* 1937). There were also sections that dealt with sponsorship, the 'Discovery and training of a New Audience', and 'Training the Theatre for Tomorrow'.

There is no explicit theorising of the term 'education'. In Section I, Hallie Flanagan is quoted approvingly (pp. 8–9) as saying that the Federal Theatre represented the need to 'expand . . . the boundaries of theatre' and acknowledge 'the value of theatre to recreation, education, therapeutics'; and the authors go on clearly to articulate the main premise:

> In the sense that education is that which truly informs and awakens the spirit of a people, the Federal Theatre Project, taken as a whole in its constant activity to make a social and cultural contribution to the nation, can be considered a significant educational effort that may have its effect upon and exert an influence over many communities for years to come. (p. 12)

But in his preliminary report (18 August 1937), J. Howard Miller, Deputy National Director of the FTP, drew attention to the problems of definition and suggested two categories under which Federal Theatre work might be deemed educational. On the one hand, it is seen as a broad category to do with 'the capture of the spirit in the theatre's magic hour of illusion': 'if the spirit of the people were informed and awakened through these presentations', then the project's work could be seen as part of the 'educational activity of the nation' (pp. 1–2). More narrowly, on the other hand, it encompassed 'those special activities of the Federal Theatre in hospitals, schools, community theatre service, the development of children's theatres, the special activities in which units of the

Federal Theatre researched drama and allied fields' (pp. 2–3). Hence the training of professional theatre personnel, the teaching of drama (that is, plays) to children, community drama (including the use of 'animateurs') and drama as therapy. There is a tantalising reference to work undertaken by the New York Project's Community Drama Unit at Belle Vue Hospital, in which audiences were variously observers and active participants; one event involved the staging of a mock trial after an altercation among patients (*Bair Report*, p. 31). Activity in learning and the act of theatregoing (which involves activating the imagination) were seen as necessary ingredients in a much larger process: participation in a democratic enterprise. The influence of Dewey runs through this document, notably in its emphasis upon experience as a key part of learning: theatre provides that experience through its active mode (in the physical participation of children, patients or community groups) and through the more 'passive' participation in theatregoing.

A further example, not discussed in the report, is provided by the CCC Unit, which devised a participatory play for the large numbers of young men encamped out in the national parks, far from home, recruited to perform a range of tasks as part of the New Deal job creation programme such as building and repairing roads. *The CCC Murder Mystery* – 'a unique experiment in audience participation' as one theatre historian has called it (Kreizenbeck 1979: 66) – toured many of these camps during 1936–38 with remarkable success. The camp canteen would be converted into a courtroom and volunteer members of the camps would, with coaching, take on roles of accused and witnesses in a fictitious murder trial, all played in comic vein but with just enough plausibility to intrigue and engage the hard-to-please audience. Deliberately playing with the boundaries between theatre and reality, the piece in many ways anticipated the methods of participatory TIE of the 1970s and 1980s, although on Schechner's efficacy-entertainment continuum there is no doubt that it located itself well to the entertainment end. While the men may have learned little about the intricacies of court procedure (though there was some attempt to follow the main procedures in the interests of credibility), camp commanders remarked again and again in their own reports on the way the piece engaged all camp members, sparked discussion and, most important for the authorities, raised morale.[6] Finally, the report lists the various attempts to reach new audiences – in this respect, the very experience of live theatre is assumed to be of its nature educational – and the production of 'informative plays on current subjects of social significance . . . all of which are directly educational in nature' (p. 13). The most notable and high-profile example of this latter category was undoubtedly the living newspaper.

The living newspaper and *One Third of a Nation*

An American variant of a theatre form developed in the early days of
Soviet Russia by the Blue Blouse, and imported subsequently to
Germany, the Federal Theatre's living newspaper also drew on the
Americanised forms of agit-prop, exemplified by *Newsboy* (1934) and
Waiting for Lefty, and on a range of other techniques as well, European
and American, not least the documentary reportage techniques developed by Piscator, and the *March of Time* newsreels. The American
version developed into a quite unique form, one that dramatised for specific purposes the contemporary world, and at the same time proclaimed
its factual authenticity. Arthur Arent, one of the major writers of living
newspapers for the FTP, in 1938 defined the genre as 'a dramatization of
a *problem* – composed in greater or lesser extent of many news events,
all bearing on the one subject and interlarded with typical but non-
factual representations of the effect of these news events on the people to
whom the problem is of great importance' (Arent 1938: 57). It dealt then
with significant issues and events of the time, making full use of the
theatre's resources in order to show ordinary people how their own lives
were being affected by those events and what they themselves could do
to try to change things for the better. A mix of the campaigning, the
didactic and the interventionist. Subjects treated included the plight of
the American farmer (*Triple A Plowed Under*, 1936), the development
of trade unions (*Injunction Granted*, 1936), the case for state control of
the electricity industry (*Power*, 1937), the problem of syphilis, its history
and how it was being combated (*Spirochete*, 1938) and America's poor
(*One Third of a Nation*, 1938).

By their very nature these living newspapers were topical and designed
to be immediately relevant to the problems faced by ordinary people.
(Arent was rewriting the ending of *Power* every night of the performance
to take in the latest developments in the pronouncements from government and the debates in the Congress.[7]) Few of them would stand the test
of time, but then that is not always the most appropriate test of worth.
Most were fresh, dynamic, theatrically adventurous, frequently (though
not invariably) critical of current policies and constantly stressed the
need for personal involvement and action if social advance were to be
achieved.

As Douglas McDermott has pointed out (1965), the living newspaper
would commonly begin with a recent event that had received headline
attention in the press which demonstrated the problem to be addressed
(the tenement fire in *One Third of a Nation*, for example). Then an 'everyman' protagonist would be introduced – usually a representative of the

ordinary citizen ('Consumer' in *Power*, for example, or Mr Buttonkooper in *One Third*) – who would soon recognise the problem and the need for a solution. After some initial hesitancy, or disbelief, deriving from ignorance or apathy, his curiosity about the cause would be aroused and 'subsequently satisfied by an excursion into recent history' (McDermott 1965: 86). He then becomes part of the investigation until solutions are found or proposed. As a representative of the ordinary citizen, the common man, he was a type – uncomplicated, just enough of a character to make the point effectively and entertainingly and to catch the audience's sympathy and fellow-feeling, and no more. Usually, but not invariably, male, he could be slow on the uptake, grumpy, angry, impetuous, perplexed, but full of questions which he puts with ordinary, common-sense directness. Once forced to grasp the problem, he is unswervable in his commitment to finding answers. He progresses through the drama in effect as an audience-surrogate, and his conversion at the end is clearly meant to stand for the audience's own conversion, as a call on their behalf for action, and as an insistence on the need for citizens to participate. The above pattern, followed by most living newspapers, parallels interestingly, as McDermott has suggested (1965: 12–13), John Dewey's notion of 'the pattern of reflective thinking'.[8] In 1933, Dewey had published his influential second edition of *How We Think* in which he analysed the way in which the human mind tends to solve problems. Genuine thoughtfulness involves, according to Dewey, a state of doubt, hesitation, bewilderment, followed by an act of searching. Rather than jumping at a conclusion because of, say, impatience or laziness, to be genuinely thoughtful we must be 'willing to endure suspense and to undergo the trouble of searching' (Dewey 1933: 16). The pattern through which the protagonist progresses – from bewilderment, curiosity, surprise, to engagement, the hunt for answers, the discovery that the easy answers turn out to be wrong, and the eventual recognition of the need for specific forms of action – matches remarkably closely the process described by Dewey and which he advocates as a central aim of education.

'Voice of the Living Newspaper' and the 'little man'

Perhaps the most striking feature of all was the 'Voice of the Living Newspaper' – usually the protagonist's, and the audience's, guide through the maze of events, facts and opinions (see Arent 1938). It was represented through a large loudspeaker usually placed at the side of the stage – its only physical presence – and was accepted perfectly readily by all the characters on stage. It was both narrator and participant; it could set the scene, provide crucial facts and figures; it could engage in dialogue

Plate 3 *One Third of a Nation.* A living newspaper. Federal Theatre, New York, 1938. 'The Tenement Fire', the spectacular fire sequence at the opening and close of the play.

with onstage characters; it could call new characters and change scenes; it could put on the spot and question public figures who clearly had something to hide and reveal supposedly the 'truth' of the matter; it would often directly address the audience and pose key questions for them to ponder. Its operation in *One Third of a Nation* provides a good example. Following the powerful opening scene ('February 1924') in which a large tenement block, teeming with human life, catches fire with substantial loss of life, scene 2 opens with an announcement from the loudspeaker: 'Thirteen persons lost their lives in that fire . . . What started this fire? Why did it spread? . . .' With the help of the disembodied Voice, the Commissioner's Enquiry begins its investigation. After testimonies have been heard from the Fire Department, Buildings Department, and the Old Buildings Bureau, the Commissioner appears satisfied but the loudspeaker has other ideas:

> Commissioner: That's all gentlemen. Thank you.
> Loudspeaker: Just a moment, Mr Commissioner. Has *everybody* testified?
> Commissioner: Why, yes . . .
> Loudspeaker: How about that empty chair? Don't you think there ought to be somebody in it? Well, you want to get at the bottom of this thing, don't you?
> Commissioner: Certainly . . .

Plate 4 *One Third of a Nation.* 'The City Grows'

Loudspeaker: Then let's call the landlord!

(Rohan 1938: 19–20)

This leads immediately to investigations and dramatic illustrations of how things have come to be this way: the larger picture. The state of New York's housing cannot be blamed on a few individual villains, but has arisen as a result of complex factors, social, political and economic, some of which can be traced back to the city's growth over more than a hundred years. The following scene, 'The City Grows', is a brilliantly conceived theatrical lesson in land economics, which vividly demonstrates – with the aid of a grass mat representing the island of Manhattan – how property on the island became subject to rapidly accelerating, and insatiable, demand, much to the delight of landowners who had bought early and simply waited as demand rapidly outgrew supply.

On its own, however, the Loudspeaker is not a dramatic device that will hold the attention for long; and immediately following the 'City Grows' scene the ordinary man in the street makes his appearance – here it's Mr Angus Buttonkooper. Following a now well-established pattern, from Piscator onwards, a direct bond with the audience is established by having him emerge from the auditorium. During the blackout after the previous scene, he calls out from the audience, 'Hey! Give me some light!', and proceeds up to the stage:

Loudspeaker:	What is it?
Little Man:	I'd like some information.
Loudspeaker:	What about?
Little Man:	Housing.

(p. 39)

Then, apologising for not being an actor, he inserts himself into the play:
'Every time something happens that I don't understand I'm going to stop
the show and ask questions.' We quickly learn that his keen interest in
housing is a personal one, since he has had application after application for a new apartment turned down. Finally he had gone to see
the Tenement House Commissioner and been told that 'the Living
Newspaper was doing a show on housing and I ought to see it . . . So here
I am'. (scene 4: 'Looking Backward', p. 39). The self-confidence of the
living newspaper authors is well illustrated by such self-referential
exchanges: in commenting on itself, the form is also exploring further just
how the barriers between stage and auditorium, between the body of
knowledge to be communicated and the ordinary people for whom that
knowledge is judged most necessary, can be crossed; and how to signal,
unpatronisingly, that the problems and the solutions to them lie in the
hands of the audience. (See Chothia 1984: 30 for further discussion of this
aspect of the staging.) With the help of the Loudspeaker, Buttonkooper's
search for answers begins in earnest, and he is accompanied before long
by his wife who joins him, again from the auditorium. By the end of the
play, the Buttonkoopers have moved from the periphery to centre-stage
and call with passion for action from their representatives in Congress.
The function of the character as 'audience surrogate' could hardly be
better demonstrated, and, as we shall see, is repeated with many variations in educational theatre productions throughout the century.

Those living newspapers which were the most rigorous in their investigative methods as well as theatrically powerful – again *One Third*
stands as the supreme example – managed to raise questions, provoke
debate and challenge politicians to defend their own actions (or absence
of action). The publicity leaflet and programme (see Plate 5) for *One
Third* proclaimed the factual authenticity and accuracy of its subject
matter, claiming to be at least on a par with the best investigative journalism; and its documentation was indeed meticulous – the published
edition was packed with footnotes, every quotation used in the play
being fully documented (Rohan 1938). In this sense its claim to an educational role was well founded. But its political agenda, indeed its bias,
was also undeniable. Morris Watson, one of the editorial staff, argued at
the time that living newspapers aimed at the presentation of objective
fact, at neutrality (1937: 16–17), but we are presented with facts as

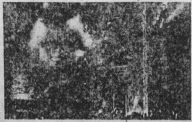

...one third of a nation...

LIVING DRAMA

The Living Newspaper

SPOT NEWS

Vol. V No. 3   ADELPHI THEATRE   Opened Jan. 17, 1938

Slum Housing Dramatized; President Suggested Title

ACCURACY, KEYNOTE OF FACTUAL BASIS FOR HOUSING PLAY

Research Includes Visits To Slum Areas For First-Hand Data

COMPLETE accuracy in documentation, which made the previous Living Newspapers impregnable from attack, has been maintained in the current production "...one third of a nation...."

The research on which the current play is based was even more extensive than that for previous Living Newspapers. Besides the usual study of books, newspapers and documents the research workers, most of them trained news gatherers, were sent into the slums for first-hand observation.

Photos Prove Facts

On some of these slumming trips a member of the Federal Theatre Project photographic staff accompanied the research worker. This made possible a pictorial record of tenement conditions which may be shown to skeptics who might doubt the story presented on the stage.

"Hot Beds" Discovered

Among the numerous startling and interesting facts brought to light by the slum visits was the existence in Harlem of "hot beds." The term refers to beds rented in three eight-hour shifts.

Even the lengthy bibliography printed in other columns of the program does not show the

(Continued on page 4)

Living Newspaper material is compiled by a staff under supervision of Irving Mendell with Richard J. McManus as head of research and Stephen Madigan as head of the library.

STAGE INNOVATION PRESENTED IN SET

A DEFINITE innovation in stagecraft is introduced by the WPA Federal Theatre's Living Newspaper in the construction of the set for "...one-third of a nation...."

Confronted with the problem of portraying slum dwellings, both inside and outside, in a single set, Howard Bay, scenic designer, drew plans for a four-story tenement house with the front walls for the most part torn away symbolizing all slum houses.

Construction presented another technical problem. The house could not be merely a back-drop with suggestion of rooms, hallways and staircases. Action was to take place on all four levels of the set. That necessitated it being a solid and sturdy affair: almost substantial enough to live in.

The "housing" problem was solved by using a patented type of scaffolding such as was used to build the Empire State mooring mast and the Chrysler tower. The framework is of steel pipe with an exclusive coupling device which permits of great ease and rapidity of building at low cost.

(Continued on page 2)

WPA THEATRE SETS TWO-YEAR RECORD

THE WPA Federal Theatre Project is nearing its third year with a record both in attendance and number of productions which even the most optimistic would have doubted at its inception.

Nearly 2,000 plays have been offered the public throughout the country and the attendance figures exceed 20,000,000. Many of the productions have been given free of charge and thereby have introduced to the theatre millions of men, women and children who never before had seen a stage production.

A Caravan Theatre, with its stages mounted on motor trucks, played in public parks all last summer in New York, Chicago, San Francisco and other cities. These open-air performances were attended literally by millions whose enthusiasm was proven by their presence at each new offering in their respective neighborhoods.

Besides the free shows there have been scores of plays presented in regular theatres and it is an old story now that a number of them have been hits. Two of them, "Dr. Faustus,"

NATION-WIDE PLANS FOR NEW DWELLINGS MAKE SUBJECT NEWS

Roosevelt's Program And Wagner Act Enhance Play's Timeliness

AS USUAL the Living Newspaper goes to press with a timely topic — housing. It was a live subject when first considered but since that time President Roosevelt has made his second inaugural speech from which the title of the play is taken. He declared that he found "...one third of a nation ill-housed, ill-clad and ill-nourished."

This was followed by the passage of the Wagner-Steagall Housing Act, extending Federal support of public low-cost housing to replace slums, and more recently by the President's advocating in addition a vast program of private housing construction.

Housing In Headlines

Almost daily the newspapers carry headlines in regard to housing problems and programs. Just as "...one third of a nation..." was ready to open, Mayor LaGuardia presented plans for two huge low-cost slum-elimination projects in New York City to Nathan Straus, Federal Housing Administrator. One of them is for the Red Hook district of

(Continued on page 4)

Past Performances

"...one third of a nation..." is the fifth Living Newspaper presented to the public by the WPA Federal Theatre Project. Earlier ones were:

"Power"
"Injunction Granted!"
"Highlights of 1935"
"Triple-A Plowed Under"

Tenement House Fire

Plate 5 *One Third of a Nation*. The publicity leaflet in the form of a newspaper.

selected and juxtaposed by the living newspaper editors in the interests of making a powerful case for public spending to deal with the hardships and injustices of the poor, ill-housed and under-fed (Flanagan 1940: 207). While the narrative sets out to expose present inequalities and injustices, the method was to structure the drama around a supposedly factual investigation of how current circumstances came to be. Recent history is selectively uncovered and reasons for the present state of affairs are conclusively offered. The Voice of the Living Newspaper appears to stand simply for the things the ordinary sensible common man would say, do and ask for given half the chance. Its conclusions would therefore be the conclusions reached by any sane individual who had access to the information provided in the course of the play.

But the method was hardly that of the neutral presentation of facts. There was an editorial slant (as with any newspaper or broadcast). There was, too, as C. W. E. Bigsby points out, a philosophical premise (if unstated) behind the narrative – that is, that the concern was not with individual psychology but with man governed by environmental and economic forces. This leads Bigsby to conclude that 'the Living Newspaper inevitably offers a naive model of an historical process . . . Private reality is superseded by a compilation of public positions.' Moreover, the editing is revealed in the 'process of selection in the voice of the people for which there is no precise documentary validation' (Bigsby 1982: 220). At its worst, Bigsby concludes, 'the Living Newspaper was a crude device, importing its effects from outside the theatre, substituting the sentimentality and melodrama of fact for that of fiction' (Bigsby, p. 228). But while living newspapers undoubtedly varied in quality (Flanagan was herself highly critical of some because of their leaning towards propaganda), it is also arguable that, in the context of their time, the social analysis offered was not so much naive as calculatedly, even courageously, oppositional. Even in the midst of the Depression years, the dominant ideology of the time was still that of capitalism and the belief that free-market forces represented 'the American way', that individualism was the motor, the driving force that would lead to a better life for all, far superior to the notions of collectivism that infected that dangerous creed from Russia. Hollywood (with some notable exceptions such as *Mr Deeds Goes to Washington*) served to shore up such notions with its common diet of sentimentalised heroes and heroines who 'won through' because of their essential, individual goodness.

The achievement in the best, most theatrically effective living newspapers – and perhaps most impressively and influentially in *One Third of a Nation* – was to create an epic form of drama which gave theatrical shape to the lives of ordinary people and called for public participation in the debates and decision-making of the time by showing how people were willy-nilly participants in the drama of public life. They could choose to be active or passive participants but participants they were: they could not help being caught up in and affected by events of the world around them. In this sense, living newspapers such as *One Third* and *Power* could justifiably claim to be performing an educational function – educational in the sense of promoting debate, of constructing a narrative that blended factual information with a constant stream of questions and with an insistence that audiences made connections with their own lives and considered what actions they could take themselves. As Hallie Flanagan argued, this was the kind of drama which could focus on 'a struggle hitherto infrequently stressed . . . the struggle of a great many different kinds of people to understand the national, social and economic forces around them, and to achieve through these forces a better life for more people' (*Federal Theatre Magazine* (1937), reprinted in Flanagan 1940: 183).

Given that premise – that people should be stirred to action, even within the democratic framework – it is perhaps not too surprising that the activities of the living newspaper were considered subversive by the increasingly hostile right wing of American politics. In 1939 the entire Federal Theatre Project was closed down following hearings by the House Un-American Activities Committee (HUAC) who were convinced that the Project was no more than a vehicle for communist propaganda. It was not only the living newspapers that came under hostile scrutiny. Other suspect elements included the Children's Theatre Unit, not least for its production of *The Revolt of the Beavers*, a play that tells a story of two children who, lost in the forest, find themselves in the Kingdom of the Beavers, and caught up in the struggle of ordinary beavers to overthrow the tyrannical hold of the Chief Beaver – a story that was interpreted by some reviewers (notably Burns Mantle of *The New York Times*) as a dramatisation of the Communist Manifesto for children (see Swortzell 1986: 15). The Project's very embodiment of the New Deal, its energetic attempt not just to boost morale but to engage its audiences as active members of a democracy, to tackle contemporary issues in ways that were critical and insisted on active participation in the world, made it seem, in the eyes of its detractors, a threat out of all proportion to its actual size or influence. In her account of the Project, *Arena*, published the year after the Project was closed, Flanagan argues:

> It was not ended as an economy move, though this was the ostensible reason given: the entire arts program, of which Federal Theatre was one of five projects, used less than three fourths of one per cent of the total WPA

appropriation; and that appropriation was not cut one per cent by the end
of Federal Theatre; the money was simply distributed among other WPA
projects. It was ended because Congress, in spite of protests from many of
its own members, treated the Federal Theatre not as a human issue or a cultural issue, but as a political issue. (Flanagan 1940: 334–5)

As Hallie Flanagan reportedly commented in 1938, while the HUAC
investigations were going on, 'The theatre when it is good is always dangerous' (quoted in Kazacoff 1989: 7).

The impact of the living newspaper format upon British groups was
considerable. In Manchester, Ewan MacColl created *Last Edition*,
dealing with unemployment and injustice, which toured with Theatre
Union in 1940. On a personal note, I recall a chance conversation many
years ago with a friend of my mother-in-law, a quiet charming lady who
confided to me that in her youth she had been an active member of
MacColl and Littlewood's Theatre Union in Manchester, and one of a
small group who had gone over to New York to see *One Third* in order
to report back. Her memory of the event was hazy but she did recall
vividly the tenement fire scene with which the production began and
ended. We sometimes forget how much traffic across the Atlantic there
was during that period and how much solidarity of purpose was generated between socialist groups either side of the ocean; and by the same
token the degree of inspiration that the wholly amateur groups in Britain
drew from the activities of their better organised, and often state-funded,
American comrades. Throughout the decade, and all the more so with
the growing suppression of artistic freedoms under fascism across so
much of the European mainland, American theatre was seen by many as
being in the vanguard of radical theatre, providing a sizeable repertoire
of scripts and models of practice that nourished practitioners in Britain.
Of Unity's productions in its first year of operation, three of the first four
were of American plays, while in 1937/8, although only two were of
American dramas (*Plant in the Sun* and *Bury the Dead*), three of the
home-grown plays were modelled closely on American-style living newspapers: *Busmen*, *ARP* and *Crisis*. *Busmen* (directed by Allen) dealt with
the 1937 bus strike; *ARP* with the looming threat of war and the precautions Britain needed to take in the event of air raids; *Crisis* with the
impending catastrophe in Europe and Britain's reluctance to take a stand
against Hitler. It was perhaps the living newspapers that provided the
most powerful meeting point for the goals of celebration, politicization
and education.

We should not of course over estimate the significance of Unity and its
contemporaneous British left-wing theatre groups. Unlike their American

counterparts, they were small-scale, amateur and rarely impacted on the larger theatre-going population. Indeed, for many years, theatre historians of the decade, at least those writing into the 1960s, such as J. C. Trewin (Trewin 1960), gave them barely a mention. Productions were inevitably mounted 'on a shoestring' by unpaid enthusiasts so standards were variable. And there was considerable tension between the 'inclusive' and 'propagandist' tendencies of the movement (not least between members of Unity and Manchester's Theatre Union). But while their influence at the time may have been minimal, contained, it was in an indirect way longer-lasting than most of the mainstream theatre of the time that drew the large West End crowds. Thus the Red Megaphones of Salford eventually metamorphosed, via Theatre of Action and Theatre Union in Manchester, into Theatre Workshop after the war. And Unity, together with its sister left-wing theatre clubs in the regions, did excite and inspire – and provide experimental opportunities for – a remarkable number of actors who themselves became influential in the development of British theatre after the war (for example, Alfie Bass and later Michael Gambon).[9] If British mainstream drama in the interwar years had been in a relatively static, somewhat lethargic state, certainly in comparison with trends on the continent and the United States; if there had been very few British dramatists of significance capable of doing more than entertain; if even the more serious writing such as Shaw's generally appealed to the comfortable and prosperous upper middle classes and provided few shocks to the system; if theatregoing in the 1930s, especially in the West End and at the major regional touring houses, tended to be not only the preserve of the upper and upper middle classes but almost exclusively *about* those classes, then Unity and the Unity network, Theatre of Action and Theatre Union, stood as beacons of theatrical vitality and social engagement – signposts for the re-energising of the British theatre after the war, manifested in the achievements of Theatre Workshop, the new writing at the Royal Court, the theatre in education movement and other community outreach work, and the political theatre of the 1970s and 1980s.

Before we examine postwar developments, however, I want to look more closely at examples of the way theatre in the late 1930s and early 1940s responded to and attempted to address concerns that, at least on the surface, were not to do with political change – the social impact of scientific advance.

Notes

1　The Popular Front against Fascism was officially launched at the Seventh World Congress of the Communist International in August 1935 – a remarkable change of heart by a party hitherto dedicated to promoting workers' revolution and to opposing all other routes to social change (Stourac and McCreery 1986: 246–7).

2 See the various studies made of the government campaigns to educate the public about AIDS in the 1980s: for example, Singer, Rogers and Glassman (1991); see also BBC Television *Panorama* coverage (2005) 'The 1980s AIDS campaign' at http://news.bbc.co.uk/1/hi/programmes/panorama/4348096.stm# (last accessed 31 July 2006).

3 Chambers provides an excellent, detailed account of these events and of the debates that propelled them.

4 The term 'proletkult' derives from the Russian movement to develop an 'authentic' proletarian culture and a militant class consciousness, given an immense boost by the events of 1917 (Samuel 1994: 37; Stourac and McCreery 1986: 25–6).

5 *The Bair Report: Educational Aspects of the Federal Theatre Project.* National Service Bureau: Federal Theatre Project: WPA, 15 September 1937.

6 See typescripts of letters and summaries of feedback in Federal Theatre Collection, Special Collections & Archives, George Mason University, VA: e.g. WPA press release, 18 December 1936; narrative report, March/April 1937.

7 Producer's memo for revised script: 'Power' t/s: FTP 000 089, 3 January 1938, George Mason University Federal Theatre Collection.

8 I am indebted to McDermott for pointing out the parallel. However, it is worth noting that Dewey's book was published in 1933, not 1938 as McDermott claims; the ideas were therefore in circulation for a period of time sufficient for them to begin to impact upon the public discourses about education at the time when living newspapers were being developed.

9 Chambers notes however how a number of the political playwrights of the postwar period, such as John McGrath, pointedly excluded Unity from their lists of influences (Chambers 1989: 401). Unity became post-1945 far less radical in its repertoire and in its political agenda, and was considered by many to have lost its cutting edge and its ability to inspire a new generation of left-wing writers.

4

Theatre and the challenge of science, 1936–1947: some historical perspectives

The theatre's response to scientific advance

The use of theatre to debate topical issues in science is not new. In this chapter I will look at some of the uses made of theatre during the middle of the twentieth century to explain scientific advance to a popular audience and, in the case of many of the plays, to warn of the dangers of complacency and ignorance. The focus will counter-balance the emphasis in the previous chapter: here the concerns of writers are not primarily oppositional, not primarily with endeavouring to convey clear-cut messages about changing the social order, nor with celebrating working-class solidarity. None the less, in their various ways, the five productions I refer to do have agendas; and each is underpinned by the belief that communicating with an audience is not only beneficial but necessary – whether it be to meet a specific, topical need, or to sound an alarm, or to energise and stimulate the curiosity of a young audience in scientific advances which they need to understand and to which they should feel they belong.

The past hundred years have seen extraordinary, almost unbelievably rapid advances in science, advances that seem to offer simultaneously both promise of the unparalleled betterment of the human lot and serious threat – a threat to our comfortable assumptions about how the world is ordered, to the place of religion, and to the very notion of what human life is and even to the survival of the human species. If theatre's oft-proclaimed educational role is as potent as many claim, then scientific advance poses a challenge to the capacity of theatre to 'hold' and communicate – and indeed explore and throw light upon – conceptions of scientific invention and its social repercussions.

One might be forgiven for thinking that the arts are an inappropriate medium for tackling scientific issues. Even if one resists following

C. P. Snow and F. R. Leavis into debates about the fundamental incompatibility of ways of thinking in the arts and sciences,[1] it is difficult to avoid the contention that artistic forms, in their use of personal stories, creative imagination and emotional response, are simply not the best, or most efficient, way to communicate scientific information. In her recent study of the relationship between science and the arts, Sian Ede argues that it is unlikely that art can 'directly be about science – lectures, books or discussions are more successful at explanations or stimulating debate' (Ede 2005: 3). She goes on to suggest that art can none the less 'engage with [science] and create images which suggest alternative ways of seeing' (p. 3). None the less, science – and the attendant excitement of being at the frontiers of knowledge – has inspired and fascinated playwrights from Marlowe (*Dr Faustus*) to Frayn (*Copenhagen*), and in recent years scientists and scientific organisations committed to promote the cause and public understanding of science, such as The Wellcome Trust,[2] have frequently turned to the arts in order to generate a wider public understanding of scientific advances. They acknowledge areas of common ground – for example, that science requires imagination and creativity in its attempt to conceptualise physical or chemical processes, and to envisage hypotheses (Ede, p. 7). They also value the ability of the artist to capture emotional response and to trigger such response in audiences, and to embed ethical issues in human stories. But others have also seen drama as an ideal medium through which to promote directly a grasp of scientific complexities. Carl Djerassi – novelist, playwright and emeritus professor of chemistry at Stanford University – has argued forcefully for what he calls 'science-in-theatre', a form of pedagogic activity which uses theatre to 'smuggle scientific facts into the consciousness of a scientifically illiterate public . . . intellectually and socially beneficial because the majority of scientifically untrained persons are afraid of science' (Djerassi 2005: 1). In justifying his own mix of didacticism and drama, he quotes Horace who, in *Ars Poetica*, talked of 'delighting the reader at the same time as instructing him' (see note on p. 46). It is a sentiment that has provided a recurring motif for many of those across the centuries who claim an educational role for literature and drama – and was frequently put to the test in the 1930s. Before the arrival of popular television, and especially of the docu-drama genre, live theatre offered one readily available means of trying to make sense of, and communicate, momentous developments in the world beyond the home. And in the 1930s, and in the years immediately following the dropping of the atom bomb on Japanese cities, we can appreciate that the advances in science that were impacting so powerfully upon ordinary lives made it impossible for anyone to ignore them, least of all the playwright.

In considering the selected plays, I will encapsulate my observations under two main headings. First, *Addressing the science*: what are the attitudes to science embodied in the plays? Is science, for example, seen as a body of knowledge to be explained, or as a cause for anxiety? Is it seen as emblematic of the human quest for knowledge, or as a danger, a mechanism for releasing devastating forces upon an unwary public and therefore a threat to be challenged? How is 'the science' represented on stage? Secondly, *Addressing the audience*: what are the attitudes to the audience embodied in the plays? How is the audience inscribed into the ways the plays are written? What assumptions appear to be made about them? Are they, for example, seen as a generalised 'public' who require to be taught factual information (the didactic approach), or as fellow citizens invited to participate in debate (the dialogic), or are they being recruited into a campaign, expected to pass on the message with some degree of urgency (the propagandist approach)?

The five plays I will refer to are: *Flight*, a living newspaper for children produced in New York in 1936, recounting the history of humanity's attempts to conquer the skies; *Spirochete*, a living newspaper produced in Chicago in 1938 and subsequently in Philadelphia and three other cities, which dealt with the widespread problem of syphilis and how to counter it; and three plays that dealt directly or indirectly with the anxieties triggered by the use of the atom bomb to subdue Japan and bring to an end the Second World War: Hallie Flanagan Davis's $E = mc^2$ (1947) a living newspaper written by the erstwhile director of the FTP (when she was known simply as Hallie Flanagan); Ewan McColl's *Uranium 235*, a documentary drama on the same topic written for Theatre Workshop (Manchester) in 1946; and Brecht's *Life of Galileo*, written originally in 1938/9 but heavily revised in 1947 to take account of the bombing of Nagasaki and Hiroshima. (He revised the play once again in 1954, just before his death.)

Of the five, all but one deal with anxieties of the time, anxieties in which science was profoundly implicated. In one play science was seen as the way forward because it offered clear solutions to a severe medical problem, that of the syphilis epidemic (the parallels with artists' responses to the AIDS epidemic in the 1980s/90s are close if not exact); and in three plays from the 1940s, which dramatised the social and moral repercussions of the atomic bomb, science posed a far more ambiguous challenge: the harnessing of atomic power and the dropping of the atomic bomb on Hiroshima and Nagasaki, an advance that was seen potentially as having either calamitous or redemptive repercussions.

The first, however, *Flight*, does not touch on any sense of crisis. In part that is because it is the one play that was designed exclusively for young people at a time when plays for children were expected to be not only enjoyable but also inspirational and carriers of a moral message. *Flight* was a play about aviation, written for the Federal Theatre Project in the form of a living newspaper, a documentary drama with explicit educational goals. It was presented by the WPA Theatre for Youth in New York in December/January 1936/7, and later, in March, by the Seattle Children's Theatre. The publicity for the New York production described the play thus:

> A dramatization of man's conquest of the air.
>   The play opens with a father telling his son the story of how mankind learned to fly. As he reaches exciting events in the history, they are shown on stage. WE SEE
>
> • The CAVEMEN discover fire and the wheel
> • LEONARDO DA VINCI, the painter, experimenting with wings he has made . . .
> • OTTO LILLIENTHAL and his glider
> • The WRIGHT BROTHERS' flying machine, proof that man can fly
> • The FIRST AIR MAIL delivery in America
> • CAPTAIN STREIT blazing the first air trail to Alaska
> • LINDBERGH landing at Le Bourget field after crossing the Atlantic Ocean.
>
>   (FTP Collection, George Mason University)

As this sequence of scenes suggests, there is a straightforward chronological, if highly selective, recounting of scientific progress towards the heroic achievements of the aviator-pioneers of the twentieth century; and by the end of the play (Lindbergh's triumphal homecoming in 1927), the note struck is unambiguously one of celebration, not only of one man's achievements but of human endeavour in general. The dramatic framing and narrative continuity provided by the father telling the story and introducing most of the scenes to his son underlines how much the play relies on the one-way transmission model of learning.

The remaining four plays were designed for adults, and not only do they illustrate particular ways in which theatre has been used as an educative medium to address scientific issues, but the techniques have much to tell us about the strengths and the limits of what theatre can do in the educational arena.

Spirochete was originally written at the height of a campaign that the Surgeon General of the United States had instigated to tackle the disease of syphilis which had reached epidemic proportions – and for which there was now a proven scientific cure. Between 1937 and 1941, a largely successful attempt was made to raise national consciousness about this 'taboo' illness

Plate 6 *Spirochete*. Prologue. Federal Theatre, Chicago, 1938.

and to persuade people to have blood tests and, where necessary, receive treatment at special clinics (O'Connor 1977: 94). This living newspaper follows a common pattern. As is common in many newspaper 'special reports' (and now, in television documentary programmes that draw on investigative journalism), a problem of contemporary social concern is identified through a narrative device which reveals the problem in terms of the particular instance: its impact upon ordinary individuals. The opening scene has a young couple applying for a marriage licence, who are surprised to find that they have to undergo a medical test for venereal disease before the licence can be issued. Their embarrassment and resistance is typical of many and they clearly fail to recognise the seriousness of the disease, especially for their offspring. They need persuading – and the play sets out to do just that, through historical 'flashbacks' which tell the history of the disease traced from Columbus's return from America through to the latest advances in medical science. The figure of the 'eternal patient' repeatedly appears at important historical moments through the play, pleading for a cure: a pathetic, rather sentimentalised version of the 'little man' figure common to most of the Federal Theatre living newspapers.

The culmination of the play is a dramatisation of the recent fights in the Illinois state legislature to get laws passed that would help eliminate the disease, including the requirement of medical tests before marriage. The play ends with the ringing words of the speaker of the legislature:

> The amendment stands adopted! (*There is Applause for this.*) Victory for this amendment is a battle just begun. Votes for a measure mean nothing unless translated into action by the people. This fight must go on until syphilis has been banished from the face of the earth. It can be done and will be done if you and you *and* you wish it so. The time has come to stop whispering about it and begin talking about it . . . and talking out loud!

The satisfactory completion of the narrative is clearly intended to lie with the audience.

Dramatic responses to the dropping of the atom bomb

On 6 August 1946 the United States dropped a uranium atomic bomb on Hiroshima; three days later, a plutonium bomb was dropped on Nagasaki. The numbers of people killed exceeded one hundred thousand and many thousands more were injured. The event undoubtedly hastened the capitulation of Japan and the end of the Second World War.[3] But, as the implications of the unleashing of weapons of such extraordinary force quickly sank in, general anxiety about the future of humankind in this new world rapidly grew. In July 1946, there were mass demonstrations in New York's Times Square against further testing of nuclear weapons. The Soviet Union was known to be developing its own nuclear arsenal; Britain too began independent nuclear bomb tests in 1952 and within a year had its first operational atomic warhead. The wave of opposition led to the formation of the Campaign for Nuclear Disarmament (CND) in 1958 to co-ordinate and advance the protests against nuclear weapons programmes.[4]

Among the responses of theatre makers, the earliest, immediately following the end of the Second World War, were Ewan McColl's *Uranium 235* in 1946 and Hallie Flanagan Davis's $E = mc^2$ (1947). Both plays – as their titles suggest – are concerned to deal with the science head-on. MacColl's play was written for performance by the newly re-formed Theatre Workshop, based in Manchester and led by MacColl and Littlewood, and was one of the first productions to be taken on tour by the company – to community halls in South Wales, to theatre less towns in the north of England, to Glasgow, Edinburgh and even to London (for short runs at the Embassy Theatre in Swiss Cottage and the Comedy Theatre in the West End) (MacColl 1990: 260). It begins in the midst of wartime air-raids and, with two everyman figures, the Scientist and the Man-in-the-Audience, as our guides, traces the history of the human search for knowledge about 'the fundamental nature of things' (MacColl 1949: 11) from the Spartan wars and Democritus' discovery of the atom, through the Dark and Middle Ages to the rapid acceleration of scientific discovery in the nineteenth and early twentieth centuries. Throughout, the struggle for knowledge and truth is constantly checked and diverted by the equally strong human impulse towards power and wealth. Thus, in the early days of the Industrial Revolution, with poverty and disease rife among the exploited factory workers, the Scientist comments: 'They [the poor, the exploited] are the price of the misapplication of the tools which science has provided' (p. 43). By the end, of the play, humanity stands at the literal and metaphoric crossroads. Having witnessed 'the end of the old world' with the atomic bomb explosion, the cast on stage now represent 'the world' who must decide where scientific discovery will take us next. The figure of Energy faces them: 'I will go where you go. If you work for war I will work with you. If you work for peace I will work too. There are two roads . . . It is for you to choose and for me to follow. *The crowd hesitates*. Which is it to be?' The crowd then turn to the audience: 'Which way are you going?' The allegorical style of the play is reinforced by the frequent turn to free verse in the dialogue and mono-logues and the deliberate echoing of the medieval morality play *Everyman* to help give poetic shape to this 'journey through the corri-dors of the mind' (MacColl 1949: 19).

Flanagan Davis's play takes a similar line in its attempts to capture the mix of awe, panic and profound anxiety that the release of atomic forces has provoked. While MacColl's play bears some stylistic resemblances to the living newspaper (not least through its Man in the Audience figure and the use of the disembodied 'microphone voice' to impart news events), Flanagan Davis totally embraces the format she had overseen and advocated less than a decade before. Just as *One Third* had opened with a stunning tenement block fire to capture the audience's attention and highlight the social problem to be addressed, and closed with it to underline the urgency of the matter, so $E = mc^2$ begins with the atomic bomb blast in Hiroshima and ends with the world about to be enveloped in cataclysmic nuclear warfare. The imminent, fictitious catastrophe is interrupted by the Stage Manager – inheriting the mantle of the 'voice of the Living Newspaper': 'sometimes visible and sometimes a voice' (Flanagan Davis 1946: 22) – who warns us that such a war could all too easily happen. He confronts us directly with the question: can we save ourselves? 'It rests not alone with the scientists but . . . with you and me.' As with *Uranium 235*, we are taken through dramatised accounts of 'the past, present and future of the Atom', although the focus is mainly upon twentieth century discoveries and the decisions of politicians. The goal here is more overtly didactic, with choreographic representations of the movement of atomic particles, and 'Atom', dramatised as an unstable, schizophrenic figure who oscillates between docility and hysteria (p. 24). It is Atom who, close to the end of the play, comes down to the audience and pleads with them: 'Somebody's got to take control . . . If *you* don't, then this is what happens.' The nightmare scenario follows. As with *Uranium 235*, there are crossroads, this time marked by three signposts: 'Business as usual', 'To War' and 'To World Peace'.

Finally, *The Life of Galileo* is considered here as an example of a play that shares similar concerns to those of the previous two but departs markedly in its approach and dramatic solutions. Brecht's focus is upon the moral and political relationship of science – and of individual scientists – with society, seen through the lens of Galileo's struggle to sidestep the ideological requirements of his religious paymasters. Brecht revises an already existing playscript to encompass his response but there is no explicit reference to atomic power anywhere in the play; it is firmly set in Galileo's world of the early 1600s. But the changes from the original version – made in collaboration with Charles Laughton, keen to play the eponymous 'hero', which he did in the Los Angeles and New York productions in 1947 – make the topical references clear. In the 1938 version, Galileo recants in order to preserve his freedom to continue his precious work: he may have betrayed science in the short term but he has secretly made a copy of his most recent research, *The Discorsi*, which he passes to his ex-pupil Andrea to smuggle out of the country for the longer term good of society as a whole. As David Edgar succinctly explains, having himself 'translated' the play for the Birmingham Rep Theatre production in 2005:

> Shorter and crisper than the first version, the climactic scene is different in two crucial respects. First, Laughton suggested (and Brecht accepted) that the existence of Galileo's secret book should be revealed before his speech of self-abnegation (so instead of the hidden book outbidding the self-criticism, the self-criticism trumps the hidden book). But the content of Galileo's speech has changed as well. In the first version, he says he has betrayed science by not standing up for rationalism, the principle that fact should always outweigh opinion. In the Laughton version, the principle Galileo fails to defend is the responsibility of the scientist to improve the human condition. The reason for this change was that American scientists had, in the interim, invented the atom bomb . . . In Brecht's hands, a play celebrating scientific rationality changed into a play calling for social responsibility. (Edgar, 'The Italian Job', *The Guardian*, 26 October 2005)

So, then, to first of the two key questions: what are the attitudes to science embodied in the plays?

Addressing the science

In *Spirochete* and *Flight*, 'the science' was not in itself a problem. In one a cure has been found for the disease and therefore the drama brings good news. Scientific research has at last borne fruit and we now have to apply it in the real world. If there is a challenge to be faced, it is not whether science has indeed solved the problem, or whether tests have been adequately carried out, or whether side effects will outweigh the benefits (concerns that dominate popular discourse about science in today's media). It is rather that the application of science requires the persuasion of ordinary people to permit intrusion into their personal lives – to undergo blood tests before marriage for example. In the other, the human conquest of the air becomes an emblem for 'man's quest for knowledge', for a view of history as the story of the advance of humankind – how can one dispute the narrative when planes in the air above us provide a living testament to the gains humanity has made compared with past epochs? Progress is then defined enthusiastically in terms of advances in and applications of scientific knowledge. Written by Oscar Saul and Lou Lantz, *Flight* was described as 'no cut and dried history of aviation . . . "Flight" is as up-to-date, as thrilling, as swift as a modern bomber . . . [it] is all the dreams that man has ever dreamed when he felt the urge to fly.' (FTP Seattle publicity leaflet, George Mason University Collection). The 'onwards and upwards' narrative thrust of the play is inescapable.

As well as the scenes celebrating progress, there is one scene (Saul and Lantz, *Flight*, in Swortzell 1986: 89–92) that hints at the negative impacts of aviation. With some ambivalence, the scene depicts the use of aeroplanes in the First World War, illustrating how war spurred on the technical advances that led at last to superiority over the German machines, but also dramatises the screams of civilians as air-raid sirens sound and bombs drop. We learn how aerial bombardment was more widely and quickly destructive of civilian lives than any previous form of warfare. An implicit anti-war stance may be detected here but it is not science itself that is to blame; the scene is immediately followed by another depicting postwar advance – the use of planes to drop mail rather than bombs. The almost unvaried forward movement of the narrative becomes in the end rather monotonous, lacking any real dramatic suspense. As Lowell Swortzell observes of the play's didactic style, *Flight* remains 'a worthy example of educational theatre at work and also an important reminder of the pitfall awaiting those who use theatre to teach' (Swortzell 1986: 20). Reviewers of the time were generally complimentary if with reservations. Thus, while the reviewer of the *Herald Tribune*

expressed doubts as to the dramatic qualities of the play and to some of
the acting, she found it:

> a skilful and educational entertainment designed to give a comprehensive
> idea of the development of flying . . . Using at times motion pictures to illus-
> trate 'flight', and techniques definitely cinematic in treatment, such as the
> flashbacks into history, it is the experimental quality of the play that is its
> strongest point. (9 January 1937, *New York Herald Tribune*)

She also praised the way the production was 'shaped to a child's imagination without being patronizing'.

Just as all plays for children of the time were implicitly or explicitly
bound to contain a moral message, so *Flight* too embodied a message for
its young audiences: that science should be seen as reflecting the spirit of
enquiry, the urge to know, and the hope for ways of bettering the human
lot. The Father-Narrator locates each of the achievements firmly within
the grand narrative of scientific advance and material and spiritual
progress. When the story moves to Lindbergh's epic non-stop flight
across the Atlantic, it is introduced to us by the Father: 'And now one
man challenges thousands of miles of open sky and sea. One man and his
plane embodying thousands of years of progress.' And finally: ' "He did
it, son . . . He's done a great thing. But he didn't do it alone. And when
he rides up the streets, cheered by a frenzied crowd, behind him, sharing
the ovation will march the ghosts of centuries. . . the pioneers of
progress. . . the men who flew with Lindbergh." *(Music, cheers, silhou-
ettes, sky filled with hum of planes. End.)*' The son (intended no doubt
as a surrogate for all young people in the audience) merely shares in the
glorious affirmation of human achievement. He remains silent here and
indeed throughout the play, the vessel filled by new knowledge – and
informed by a far-from-neutral, ideologically loaded presentation of fact.
The play is not designed to pose questions or provoke debate.

Both *Flight* and *Spirochete* are clearly part of a positivist discourse in
which the progress of history can be confidently expressed and improve-
ments to the human condition can be safely related, explained and, to a
greater or lesser extent, celebrated. Scientific advance is an integral,
unquestioned part of that representation of human progress.

A wholly different tone is evident in *Uranium 235* and $E=mc^2$
which reflect directly and immediately the consternation felt at the time
of the dropping of the atom bomb. Both set out to explain – and to
wonder at – the discovery of atomic structures and the power it has put
in the hands of scientists, but they also sound alarms. Both begin with
attempts to suggest dramatically the bewildering, epoch-changing
power of a nuclear explosion. In $E=mc^2$, on a dark stage, 'A Man' is

seen walking by a wall as a crescendo of sound heralds the first nuclear explosion. He:

> *flings up his hands in a grotesque position so that his shadow is elongated on the wall in this strange and terrifying posture. He falls to the ground. His shadow remains on the wall as the scene blacks out . . .*
> Stage Manager: On August 6 1945, at Hiroshima, Japan, the shadow of a human being was permanently etched on a wall . . . The shadow, symbol of man's terrible power to destroy himself, is still on that wall . . .

Uranium 235 begins with a monologue (in blank verse) from the lone figure of a 'Fire watcher' foreseeing 'destruction's hour' while air-raid sirens moan in the background. Following some brief snatches of contemporary life, full of everyday distractions and obsessions with the gossip columns of the popular press, a crescendo of voices builds to an enormous explosion accompanied by 'a blinding white light' followed by a blackout and silence. When the lights go up again, the figure of The Scientist announces: 'Ladies and gentlemen, you have just witnessed the end of the old world' (MacColl 1949: 18). Interestingly, neither playwright is concerned to set these opening moments overtly in a Japanese setting: the Man in $E = mc^2$ for example 'should register just as Man, not as Japanese' (p.12). The intent in both is to emphasise that the explosion of the atom bomb has repercussions far closer to home than many would like to think. While Flanagan Davis sticks to the well-tried living newspaper formula in $E = mc^2$, simply extending its documentary style through the use of projected film, and some tongue-in-cheek dancing girl routines to illustrate the 'dance' of the atoms, MacColl writes an altogether more sober and sombre documentary play that veers towards verse and highly stylised expressionistic effects as it endeavours to cope with the sheer magnitude of the topic being addressed. The world stands on the brink of either destruction or peace. Never before has humanity had at its disposal so much raw elemental power, or so much capacity to control the forces of nature. Unlike Flanagan Davis's play, the choreography is not designed merely to illustrate the inner workings of atomic particles or the periodic table but to express directly the human forces at work which are affecting society. Hence the 'grotesquely' masked chorus of scientists who disparage Mendelee's discovery in 1875 of the periodic properties of elements (pp. 44–6) and the figures of 'Death' and the 'Puppet Master' (who is seen plotting 'a big show full of laughter and horror', to start in 1914). MacColl deploys a sophisticated mix of living newspaper techniques and allegory, in which the Scientist functions as a kind of everyman figure: knowledgeable but perplexed by the implications of scientific advance. He is not readily reducible as a surrogate figure for either the author or the audience. He sees the implications of the energy scientists have now released; he warns but he also has much to learn. He understands the physics but is as helpless as the rest of us in grasping what it means for the future. The deployment of allegory is an attempt to encompass these enormous themes and a sense of humankind being on the brink of either genuine progress or oblivion.

Early in $E = mc^2$, the Stage Manager brings the focus sharply on to the matter of science and its connection with ordinary people: 'Up until this war, you know, we paid little attention to science . . . After the bomb exploded, however, we had to listen to scientists . . . And it happens some of them are here tonight. *Looks out into audience*' (p. 22). Actors in the audience, playing the roles of key scientists in the development of nuclear fission, then become part of the drama's attempt to explain atomic energy before any debate can be had about how it should and will affect our lives. Science is offered first as a neutral set of facts and processes; once these are grasped, as the Stage Manager says, 'the moral question remains . . . Should we have used atomic energy for the destruction of civilians in the first place?' (p. 38).

For Brecht, his already written but only-once-produced prewar play about Galileo, dealing with the relationship between the scientist and the state, between the search for truth and the contrary interests of the powerful whose interests are in maintaining the status quo, offered a ready vehicle for interrogating what we demand of our scientists. In its second manifestation, it makes an interesting contrast to Davis's and MacColl's responses to the same event. The style and approach are wholly different. In fact, despite being revised after the attacks on Hiroshima and Nagasaki, it remains a dramatisation of events in early seventeenth-century Italy. As with his other great plays of this period (*Mother Courage, Caucasian Chalk Circle, The Good Person of Setzuan*), his aim was to locate the drama in another culture or in another time, and to suggest the parallels with the present only indirectly, as ones which the audience are left to ponder once the play is over. The texture of the story and its historical context are a vital means of examining critical moments in human social history and of provoking questions. An audience may be better able to grasp the issues at stake, the decisions made and the opportunities taken or refused to change things for the better, if granted the metaphoric distance afforded by a play about Galileo or the Thirty Years War, than if encumbered by the plethora of local detail that a contemporary drama about contemporary issues tends to invoke. In this respect, it might of course be argued that Brecht was writing artistically and politically powerful drama rather than didactic theatre. It is true that any pigeonholing of a play as rich and complex in its subject matter and characterisation would be to do it a serious disservice. Whether or not a case can be made for it as educational theatre is a moot point. It certainly stands as a stark contrast to the other two 'atom-bomb plays', and there is little doubt which has best stood the test of time. But if, as Maxine Greene argues (Greene 1995: 28), education is about revealing what may have till this point remained invisible and provoking an audience into making connections between the local (the details of particular events) and the global (the larger picture of the world and the forces that work to drive, or inhibit, change), then a good case can be made for this play being, at least on one of its many levels, educational in both intent and effect.

Brecht chose to embody the whole issue of scientific responsibility in the person of his central protagonist. While there are explanations – for example, of the rotation of the Earth and planets around the Sun rather than vice versa – these are given, not by a narrator, or by a character who clearly voices the play's intended message (an author surrogate), in the interests of informing the audience, but by Galileo as a complex central character whose motivation is wholly to do with his own appetite for knowledge and for communicating that knowledge to those he thinks he can influence. His lecture to Andrea in scene 1, on the motion of the planets round the Sun (with the help of washbasin, chair and an apple) and his energetic, humorous demonstration of the motion of the universe is much more about Galileo's passion for questioning received wisdom and for wanting others to see for themselves instead of blindly following the dictates of their ideological masters than it is about explaining to us, through Andrea, scientific knowledge *per se*. Knowledge is of course communicated in the process – enough for the audience to understand the particulars of the discoveries in which Galileo was engaged. But it is framed dramatically to show us how the mode of discovery was shaped by the material circumstances of the time. Hence the use of everyday objects that locate the exchange between Galileo and Andrea firmly in the world of 1609 and in terms of the teacher–pupil relationship that exists between them, one that matures into a much more balanced encounter by the end of the play. Andrea is here no mere audience surrogate; Galileo no author surrogate. We watch with the hindsight of contemporary understandings, and can appreciate Galileo's courage, inventiveness and insight rather than being ourselves positioned as learners alongside Andrea. The 'knowledge transfer' we witness here is quite unlike that involved in the 'grass mat' scene in *One Third of a Nation* (see Chapter 3) where the economics of land use and rocketing cost of housing is clearly aimed at the audience, or the explanation of the spiral germ in Act I scene 5 of *Spirochete*, or the choreographed illustration of 'free neutrons . . . bombarding the nucleus' in $E = mc^2$ (pp. 30–1). The theme is not the wonders of discovery *per se* but the very act of discovery – the process of looking at the world with eyes wide open and of being prepared to revise one's attitudes when the evidence requires it. The theme recurs and develops with increasing intensity in Galileo's later encounters with the Florentine Court and the professors who refuse to see the evidence of Galileo's findings for themselves through the telescope in front of them. The telescope in this way becomes a metaphor for the very purpose his drama tries to fulfil – a device to help us see with fresh eyes a world we thought we knew till now. Ironically, it is also an instrument that Galileo has plagiarised and turned to his own advantage, both scientific and financial. We are never allowed to read a scene simply for its instructional content: any scientific enterprise is coloured by its intricate entanglement with human desire and fallibility.

Ultimately, this play is not really about explaining science to Brecht's audiences, it is a parable. Scientific discovery is a metaphor for the principle of rational apprehension of the world around us in contrast to the complacency and passivity that most of us settle for most of the time; and a dramatic springboard for the even more urgent questioning of how personal satisfaction and responsibility towards society interconnect, and what happens when they conflict. In Galileo's case, while Brecht celebrates his appetite for knowledge he also abhors the precedent he sets by servilely ceding to politicians and clerics the rights to 'own' scientific discovery and to exploit it for political ends (Esslin 1965: 226, Suvin 1994: 140). In the act of recanting, he sets a precedent: that scientists should bow to pressure from the State. From that precedent, Brecht suggests, came such events as the dropping of the atom bomb and the threat to future generations, inevitable once science becomes the property of those with power. In his 'Postscript to the American version' (summer 1947), Brecht argues that 'Galileo's crime can be regarded as the "original sin" of modern natural sciences . . . The atom bomb is, both as a technical and as a social phenomenon, the classical end-product of his contribution to science and his failure to society' (p. 10). The issue is an ethical and a moral – and a political – one rather than an exercise in explanation. As Esslin puts it (1965: 226), 'the urge for knowledge, the most rational side of human endeavour, science itself, is shown as being merely another of man's basic, instinctive urges'. Galileo is a genius but he also plagiarises and is cowardly; he recants his theories – not (as in the first version) as a cunning act to buy time and complete his treatise before smuggling it out to the free world but as a criminal act of cowardice and self-serving. Still, science is equated with objective truth. To be anti-science is to be corrupt, oppressive and deeply reactionary, unwilling to look at what the evidence shows. To want to exploit science for selfish, ideological or nationalist ends is also to be anti-science.

In all the other plays discussed, much use is made of innovative scenography and choreography to illustrate scientific processes in vivid three-dimensional terms, but with varying degrees of effectiveness. Thus, in $E=mc^2$, 'Atom' is a bouncy, energetic figure, often exhibiting severe schizophrenia (docile/meek, hysterical/comic); and the dancing chorus girls are brought on (with only a hint of self-referential tongue-in-cheek) to illustrate 'free neutrons penetrating or bombarding the nucleus' until the nucleus splits and 'disintegrates with explosive violence', sending the neutrons 'flying violently apart' (pp. 30–1). Atom narrates the sequence in the manner of a Caller in a country dance. The playwright, perhaps with understandable lack of confidence in the scene's dramatic effectiveness, allowed for the possibility that future producers might wish to omit the ballet.

In *Spirochete*, the spread of the syphilis germ across Europe was illustrated by a large illuminated map of Europe at the back of the stage, behind which neon tubes one by one lit up across the map, while simultaneously the silhouette of a scantily clad woman danced across it (the dubious sexist connotations of this were not remarked on at the time). In the final scene of the first half of the play, when Schaudinn and Hoffman discover the spirochete germ, we see what they see in their microscope – a magnified image of the wriggling spirochete projected for us on to a large screen above them (see Plate 7). Although the spiralling motion was done manually, it was one of the scenes almost all reviewers commented on approvingly. In an age when magnification of the miniscule biological organisms was much less commonplace for the ordinary citizen than now, there was clearly a fascination with such close-ups, 'stagy' though they might seem to a twenty-first century audience reared on television documentaries with their cacacity to produce magnified images of minute molecular forms with the sharpest clarity. But, while such a demonstration is pivotal to the very purpose of *Spirochete*, it contrasts markedly with the function of the telescope in *Galileo*. We do not see what Galileo sees because that is not where the real focus of the play lies. The device itself, the means of discovery, matters more in Brecht's play than the actual product of the discovery.

Even allowing for the massive differences between then and now in terms of what stage technology can do, there was then – and is so much more so now – a profound tension between those scientific processes (and the wonder, excitement and astonishment they generated among the scientists who first discovered them) and the capabilities of the theatre to stage such processes. Human stories are easier to dramatise

Plate 7 *Spirochete*. The virus is identified under the microscope. Federal Theatre, Chicago, 1938.

than molecular interactions; the impact of scientific discovery on individual lives and the dilemmas they produce can be contained in conventional dramatic forms. Sundgaard recognised this in moving the dramatic
momentum of the whole of the second half of *Spirochete* to the personal
and social – and political – struggles to get action taken to combat the
epidemic, and to the admittedly sentimental depiction of the blight the
disease had on just one family (a technique frequently exploited by most
tabloid newspaper editors today of course).

The tension between narrative drama and drama as explanatory
vehicle is also acknowledged in the self-consciousness of many of the
staging techniques deployed by the dramatists concerned to explain
science to their audiences. Hence the use of the Stage Manager in $E=mc^2$
who oscillates between being narrator – our authorial, authoritative
guide through the history (an embodied version of the living newspaper's
'Voice') – our representative, as bewildered about the subject as we, and
an actual stage manager whose job is to turn the stage into a theatrical
classroom: 'Look here . . . there's more than one way of releasing atomic
energy – and this is the *theatre* way! (*Calls up into the flies*) Hey, Willy,
haul up Atom's box!' Atom too becomes humanised – when first discovered she is a disembodied voice from within a box on stage, but, in fairness to actor and audience (the Stage Manager informs us), the actor

cannot stay cooped up like that throughout the play, so theatrical licence will be invoked: '*The box is hauled into the flies, revealing Atom, huddled up. . . She springs to her feet, vital and dynamic; turns several cartwheels . . .*' In *Uranium 235*, MacColl is less tempted to explain the key scientific principles by means of popular dance routines, although he does have one choreographed scene when the energy released from the splitting of the atom cannot, it seems, be represented on stage in any other theatrical way.

Addressing the audience

What are the attitudes to the audience embodied in these plays? And how does the playwright (and director) position the audience in relation to the subject matter?

The Managing Producer of *Flight*, Jack Rennick, claimed that this play and the New York WPA Theatre for Youth were endeavouring to close the 'wide gap in theatre offerings presented for children and those for adults' by establishing 'a center for the playgoing young person who wishes to see plays dealing with adventure, history, science, invention, and other subjects which have become part of his world and in which he is vitally interested' (FTP Collection, GMU: Press release: 'Children's lives enriched by Theatre' FTP 000337). The play was presented on Thursday, Friday and Saturday nights at 8.30pm with Saturday matines at 2.30pm, which suggests the age range catered for: Junior High School teenagers and the family audience. In order to capture the excitement of aviation and its sense of modernity, great use was made of light, sound and projections of images of planes on the scrim at the rear of the stage. The play was certainly a bold attempt to produce drama for older children that would engage directly with the contemporary world and capture something of the topicality and innovative form of the adult living newspapers. But its weakness lay in the predictability of its linear narrative and in the sense conveyed of the theatre medium deployed as little more than a set of illustrations for a history lesson. No wonder that all the Son can do is listen and watch.

Spirochete is located too in a very culturally and historically specific context, and exemplifies a type of theatre that has a clear agenda, both didactic and propagandist, in respect of its audience. It operates from a platform of fixed knowledge about the subject matter of the play, that is, the scientific discoveries that produced a cure for syphilis. The object of the play is primarily one of consciousness-raising and of challenging the audience to respond actively to the subject matter and to the call for action, on both the personal and the social levels (by for example changing their attitude to the socially taboo nature of the disease, by 'whispering out loud'; or by actually signing up for the tests). It assumes a positivist notion of cognition and of how we learn: a one-way transmission of knowledge. The play's techniques signal very clearly the kind of journey the audience are to be taken on – it will be a lesson in history and a drama of contemporary life. We witness lives made miserable by misunderstanding, fear and the lack of a medical cure, leading to the unavoidable conclusion that something must and can be done. Meanings are pre-made, and there is little room for the audience to construct their own meanings – other than applying the lessons of the play to the particularities of their own lives. The audience may have different personal takes on the material but they will be in no doubt as to the conclusions they are expected to draw.

The play must be seen firmly within its outer, cultural, frame. Sundgaard did not write *Spirochete* at the request of government officials, this was not initiated as state propaganda (Sundgaard interview, 1976). But, while the play was in rehearsal, the Chicago Health Department did get actively involved, obtaining the Surgeon-General's official approval of the script and providing a great deal of publicity. Not only did the production help them to publicise their own programme of mass blood-testing but they provided a blood-testing cubicle in the foyer of the Blackstone Theatre in order to catch receptive audience members on their way out of the play. Two priests were among the first to take the tests as a show of support for the introduction of mandatory tests. The production was then a semi-fictional, semi-documentary complement to the medical health campaign, a response to the legislation which had just gone through the Illinois legislature and a means of generating further newspaper and radio publicity. The overlap between fiction and reality was even more marked for the author, who found himself being rung up for advice at all hours by members of the public who assumed he was an authority on syphilis (Sundgaard interview 1976). In some cities, however, raw nerves were touched and objections to the play were raised, most frequently expressed in terms of the play's explicit association of the revered name of Columbus with such an abhorrent illness. The naming of a national hero as in any way connected with the disease became the subject of heated controversy in Boston where the antagonism of the Catholic hierarchy was aroused, while in Philadelphia the Knights of St Columbus objected to the use of Columbus's name – he was 'a good Catholic and a very virtuous man and he couldn't have picked up a venereal disease', so he became, in order that the production could go ahead, 'an unidentified explorer who returns to Spain in 1493' (Sundgaard interview).

The play also exemplifies a certain kind of campaigning theatre, not unlike much of the TfD work in AIDS education of recent years, designed to achieve specific outcomes, and supported by a range of campaigning activity, by an infrastructure of advertising, posters, media publicity, newspaper stories – and usually underpinned by a prevailing ideology of 'progress' – the combination of which *can* lead, and *has* led, to change for the better. It is part of a tradition of propagandist, campaigning theatre that dates back at least to the Blue Blouse troupes and one that insists on a direct, precise and targeted relationship with its audience. The difference from agit-prop is that the relationship with the audience in a production such as *Spirochete* tends to be patient and respectful of likely sensitivities. In agit-prop, the 'street theatre' style, the need to make points with speed in non-theatrical settings, and an ideological impatience to get things moving often lead to shortcuts, to stereotyping and sometimes to haranguing – although also sometimes to a powerful sense of urgency. In *Spirochete* there is urgency but there has to be reassurance too. The real task in *Spirochete* – and the driver behind the drama – was how to explain the progress in such a way that it would both be comprehensible to the ordinary public, and, more importantly, persuasive. If syphilis, and all the social and personal havoc it wreaks, were to be eradicated, people would have to change their lifestyles and accept some intrusion into their liberty. The associated risk is of course that, in making assumptions about the audience's pre-existing levels of awareness, it will seem patronising. Contemporary reviews did not make such a charge, though they did criticise the first production for the variable quality of some of the acting.

In the 1938 Chicago production, then, it was the actual staging rather than the acting that drew the reviewers' admiration. It was entirely at the service of the ideological, sociological and educational ends of the play. Thus the scenic devices of the map of Europe illustrating the spread of the epidemic and the projected image of the rotating spiral germ, as seen by the Scientists Schaudinn and Hoffman at the moment of its discovery, were both visually arresting and clearly designed to communicate information. In $E = mc^2$ and *Uranium 235*, as we have seen, explanations of scientific processes are sometimes accomplished through choreography, particularly when words alone are insufficient. This contrasts sharply with Brecht's play, where the staging is part of the overall paradoxical strategy, and where the author is less intent on directly intervening in social behaviour. Dialectical presentation of the conflicting views of how the world works, of what constitutes 'truth' and whose authority should count – the rulers' or the lone scientist's? – shapes the dramatic action and focuses our attention on the momentous choices Galileo is driven to make. Props and furniture are marshalled into performing a key part

in the dialectical unfolding of the play's action, and in the means by which
the audience is stimulated to interrogate both the actions they witness
and the wider social implications of those actions. Thus, Galileo's theories of the Earth's place in the universe – demonstrated for us in the early
scene with Andrea – are shown to challenge not only scientific but religious and political orthodoxy too and the very power structures that hold
contemporary society together. The theories are ridiculed and dismissed
by the visiting dignitaries in scene 4 before they have even been explained
let alone demonstrated. The use of the telescope in the scene becomes
pivotal: it serves to substantiate the theory and is the means by which our
grasp of the political and ideological realities is transformed. We see with
magnified clarity what really drives this society. Galileo's later choice
about conformity or rebellion acquires added weight. Unlike the more
overtly didactic, campaigning dramas, the process by which we learn to
see the world is accumulative and complex rather than illustrative.

The positioning of the audience

The stage audience relationship is in *Spirochete* made even more precise
and unambiguous through the framing devices employed. The common
man – first, in the form of the engaged couple, subsequently, of the 'eternal
patient' – stands as surrogate for the audience. The audience is cast from
the start in the role of 's/he who must be educated'. It is a monologic
process. Despite the resistant voices that are heard in the play (from the
engaged couple to the anxious employer to the reluctant legislators), all
opposition is shown to be flimsy when presented with the hard facts: the
disease creates terrible suffering for the victim and those close to him;
infection does not necessarily reflect a debased life style; and there is a
cure. The real battle is to make people aware of those facts and to encourage them to abandon their residual prejudices. And the cultural capital
upon which an appreciation of its dramatic value is built is not esoteric –
it is about and for the 'little man'. There is no need to induct the audience
into the niceties and customs of traditional theatre because its function
and operation are instrumental and transparent. The audience is clearly
positioned and guided through the narrative, not least by their onstage
surrogates. Clearly part of the strategy to reassure, the engaged couple at
the start are nicely naive. They are even more vulnerable and unaware
than the audience members, who by their very presence are presumably
already alert to the issues being addressed – given the publicity posters
that adorned the outside of the Blackstone Theatre highlighting the
deathly secret of a disease that few wanted to acknowledge (see Plate 8).
These audience surrogates are presented in a stereotypical form that

Plate 8 *Spirochete*. Publicity poster. Federal Theatre, Chicago, 1938.

would be instantly recognised by anyone familiar with stage and film comedy dramas of the early/mid-1930s. From the start the action is located in the contemporaneous 'real world' outside the theatre, even though its first scene is presented in quick-fire dialogue and with 1930s B-movie-type characters and against a minimalist set (see Plate 6). The signifiers of the real world are there: the costume, the 'ordinariness' of the characters, the indicative marriage bureau desk, and, not least, the topicality of the subject matter. The radio show compère clearly acts as a surrogate for the author: a narrator who will lead the couple gently through the history of the disease and the scientific challenges to find a cure.

In all the plays except *Galileo*, there are consistent attempts to make the necessary engagement of the audience explicit. The preface to $E=mc^2$ could hardly be clearer about its goal: it 'tells the past, present and future of the Atom Bomb . . . clearly, dramatically and fearlessly'; the storyline 'is easily followed . . . the message of the play is easily grasped'. On stage characters of various types act as surrogates for the author at key points in the play, imparting important bits of information, guiding us through the narrative, highlighting the issues we need to grasp – for example, the Father-Narrator in *Flight*, the radio show host in *Spirochete*, the Stage Manager in $E=mc^2$ and, intermittently, the Scientist in *Uranium 235*. One might ask whether such an approach could ever produce good drama. Once the message is 'read', what is there left for the audience to do? But these plays do also, with varying degrees of success, try to reach their audiences in ways that invite more open participation, that try to break down the stage/auditorium barrier. The audience is inscribed into these plays in two different ways. Most obviously, certain characters in the play serve as audience surrogates, asking the questions we might have asked, digesting the information and prompting appropriate explanations (hence, the engaged couple and the eternal patient in *Spirochete*; the man from the audience in *Uranium 235*; the son in *Flight*). There is also, often, a direct, physical link established between onstage action and the audience. Thus, echoing earlier agit-prop techniques, actors in the auditorium enter into dialogues with onstage characters, or they get up and cross the footlights and become characters in the play, adding urgency and reality to the debates that lie at the heart of these documentary plays. At the end of *Spirochete*, when the state legislature debate and pass the act to make the blood tests mandatory, the conventional device of having characters on stage as audience surrogates is collapsed in favour of direct address. We have arrived at the here-and-now. Have faith in the science, have faith in those who are applying the science to ameliorate not only the disease but the climate of shame that surrounds discussion of it, have faith in the politicians who wish to put measures into place to make it work. It's now over to you, the audience: now that the subject has been demystified, talk about it, abandon the prejudice and the secrecy that distorts the truth about the disease, and, not least, take the blood test – and the benefits for us all will be tangible. Indeed, a successful campaign may even implicitly offer hope for the eradication for other diseases too. In the Philadelphia production, the director James Light made the involvement of the audience explicit: for the final scene, the Speaker of the House stood before a podium set at the front of the forestage facing the audience, the house lights were brought up, and members of the cast sat in the auditorium in role as members of the legislature, while others of the cast 'became' members of the general public sitting on stage, now the public gallery – a nice stage–auditorium reversal. (*'This scene is played with the audience as the legislature, the speaker on the apron and the actors scattered among the spectators. Entire cast on stage representing "The People"*.' Philadelphia director's report, FTP Collection, George Mason University.) While this is campaigning theatre much in the tradition of agit-prop, the aim now is not to subvert authority but, in this respect at least, actively to support it.

In *Uranium 235*, the Man from the Audience is invited on stage by the Scientist: 'But I am not an actor. Oh, yes you are. We are all actors in this play. There's no audience now. We are all needed to play a part.' Self-referential dialogue pervades the two atom-bomb documentaries – a symptom perhaps of the extraordinary complexity of the subject matter for which naturalism would be wholly inadequate. In $E = mc^2$, the Stage Manager looks out into the audience and asks questions of scientists seated in the auditorium. Following a scene in which the future uses of the atom are contemplated (including with remarkable prescience, 'genetically accelerated crops' and cures for cancer), the Professor proclaims that we have a wonderful future, if we don't destroy ourselves first (p. 50) – which way we go is up to all of us. A voice in the audience calls out: 'You mean – up to *us*?' and is answered, 'Yes . . .'. Moments later, Atom approaches the audience again: 'Somebody's got to take control . . . If you don't then this is what happens. A nightmare scenario is then acted out (anticipating sequences in the much later film *Dr Strangelove*), in which we see an earthquake in San Francisco being misinterpreted by Western Defense Command as an atom-bomb attack on the US, and an unstoppable sequence of mutual mass destruction begins. 'Can we save ourselves? It rests not alone with scientists but . . . with you and me.' *End*. Theatrical self-consciousness can be a way of claiming a degree of freedom to switch styles and methods of approach as the subject matter demands; it can also, if misjudged, become tiresome, a symptom of a loss of imaginative grip on the material. $E = mc^2$'s greatest strength is perhaps in its directness and gathering sense of urgency. But its constant and often clumsy switching from one stage effect to another, its use of rather facile stereotypes and its unsteady balance between frivolity and momentousness severely limits the play's persuasiveness. It is also, at one level, disempowering. The inevitable catastrophe at the end is designed to engender a sense of panic in the face of imminent wholesale destruction. The message that we must all decide, all take control, may help to raise consciousness and may sound an alarm, but it does not actually help the audience do anything about it. The perceived threat to world safety is dramatised in terms of a specific, all too plausible scenario, but the ways in which it might have been prevented are given no dramatic space. The more specific the threat, the greater the need for specific ways out of it. The contrast with *Uranium 235* is telling.

By the end of *Uranium 235*, as the Scientist and the Puppet Master dispute ownership of the allegorical figure of Energy, the onstage crowd call out, to Energy:

> *All.*   Which way are you going?
> *Energy.* I will go where you go. If you work for war I will work with you.
>   If you work for peace I will work too. There are two roads. It is
>   for you to choose and for me to follow. *The crowd hesitates.*
>   Which is it to be? *[The End]*

Once again, the question is thrown open to the audience; but the ending is more abstract than $E=mc^2$, and all the more disturbing for that reason, not only because there *is* no clear-cut answer but because the audience have work to do in, for example, deciding for themselves who the Puppet Master stands for in the world they know outside the theatre, and where they position themselves in relation to him. This is perhaps a more productively unsettling process than Flanagan Davis's, whose rather reductive and, finally, melodramatic, dramaturgy undermines the actual challenge the audience faces. While Flanagan Davis's method is illustrative, coupled with dire warnings of catastrophe (we mustn't let the world be blown up by mistake), but leaves us helplessly wondering: 'what now?', MacColl poses the question more philosophically, abstractly and poetically. His allegorical approach leaves more room for the audience to interpret in their own ways and provides more stimulus for debate. Rather than the sensational ending of $E = mc^2$ – the acted-out nightmare, to which we can only answer: please no! – anything but! – MacColl asks us to examine the power relations that operate in society which influence, but do not have to dictate, the decisions ordinary people face. The audience is urged to act, to exercise their democratic rights, but they can do so only if the social forces above them and around them are understood.

MacColl's account occasionally slips into portentousness but it is less concerned to scaremonger, more complex, more troubled, more solemn. Perhaps it was no wonder that the audience response at one community hall in the mining valleys of South Wales was so muted and reverential: at the end,

> in silence, the audience trooped out into the night. What had offended them? . . . [Minutes later] we found the entire audience gathered outside. One of them stepped forward and thanked us, upon which the rest of them broke into enthusiastic applause. Dazed, we asked why there had been so little applause inside the hall. 'It wouldn't have been right. Your drama, it was like a sermon. And you don't applaud a sermon.' (MacColl 1990: 259–60)

In Brecht's play, there is no easy allocation of surrogacy functions to his characters. Galileo is both teacher and ultimately complicit in the surrender to authority. In his notes to the play, Brecht asks that the characterisation of Galileo

> should not aim at establishing the sympathetic identification and participation of the audience with him; rather, the audience should be helped to achieve a more considering, critical and appraising attitude. He should be presented as a phenomenon, rather like Richard III, whereby the audience's emotional acceptance is gained through the vitality of this alien manifestation. (p. 14)

Andrea is both 'learner' and, later, the one who courageously smuggles out the *Discorsi* so that Galileo's discoveries can benefit the world at large. But Brecht's decision to switch the order in which we (and Andrea) learn of the *Discorsi* marks the clear change in relationship not only between Andrea and his erstwhile tutor but between Galileo and ourselves. The world is now a different place, and the tutor-scholar-'hero' confesses his betrayal to the dismay of Andrea who, both impressed and empowered by the book he has in his hands, is disorientated by the larger betrayal. We are offered a model of the world as constantly in flux and constantly ready for change, but at the same time at the mercy of those institutions and individuals alike who grasp the opportunities for their own (class, hierarchical) interests.

Is Brecht's play an example of educational theatre? Clearly not in any instrumental sense: it does not teach, or set out to teach, a body of knowledge about science; it does not explicitly pose questions in the way that Flanagan Davis and MacColl do at the end of their plays (and in the way that Brecht had done in his earlier *Lehrstücke*). But it does offer a parable from which lessons can be drawn not only about the world of

1947 but also for our own. The dialectic of force and counter-force, emphatically and vividly depicted for us in the penultimate scene of the play culminates in Galileo's long confession and his passing on of the baton to Andrea who must care for it with new understanding of what it entails: 'I have betrayed my profession. A man who does what I have done cannot be tolerated in the ranks of science . . . You yourself are a teacher, now' (p118).

There are, finally, some provisional observations that these plays prompt. Often the urge to dramatise scientific advance comes not out of a general belief that lessons in science are 'a good thing' but rather in response to specific social crises in which science is seen either to offer solutions or itself to be implicated in the crisis – in, for example, the syphilis epidemic in the 1930s which we might parallel with the rush of interest in what medical science could do during the first decades of the AIDS panic of the 1980s and 1990s, and the more recent controversies over genetically modified crops, cloning and BSE. Almost inevitably bound up with the concern to find answers is an associated moral panic, whether this be the anxiety about the future use of atomic energy triggered by the dropping of the atomic bomb in 1945, or by the popular associations of sexually transmitted disease with sexual immorality, depravity or deviance, or by the challenge to settled religious belief systems that our power to shape the genes at the very core of human life poses.

There is a recurring problem of how to explain complicated knowledge and engage the interest and imagination of ordinary people without patronising or 'dumbing down' – of how to make the issues seem 'real' and 'relevant' and comprehensible, and in dramatically viable ways. The solutions may, as we have seen, involve projections of documentary material – cinematic depictions of planes flying, or of an atomic bomb exploding; the magnified microscopic image of a germ; and the setting of a story of the ubiquitous and often sentimentalised 'little man' against the larger picture of scientific discovery and intellectual endeavour. As the science gets more complex and our/society's responses become more problematic, so there is a discernible tendency to resort to non-naturalistic forms, to dramatic poetry, to language and staging techniques that can capture the ambiguities and the complexities more effectively (especially evident in MacColl and Brecht) and can perhaps transcend the messenger–receiver paradigm, cutting across the boundaries that can so easily separate audiences from the images of the world represented on stage.

Through the 1930s and into the immediate postwar years, there is a marked shift detectable, from, on the one hand, science seen as in itself relatively benign (so long as we understand it and embrace the good it can bring) and emblematic of human progress in general, to, on the other, science seen as highly problematic. Science bestows on those who can master its processes enormous power; it challenges our conception of humanity, religious faith and notions of progress; but it can also be seen as implicated in the political, religious, economic and social manoeuvres of the age and thereby tainted. Brecht's dramatisation of Galileo's achievements, intricately bound up with his human weaknesses and his ethical failure, prompts us to ask awkward questions about the relationship between science and society in our own day, not least about the widening gap between scientists and the general public. Brecht blames Galileo not for creating that gap but, through his decision to recant, for appearing to validate it.

The theatre's response to scientific discovery illustrates only too vividly the limits of the models that had seemed to be so appropriate to the inter-war years. The attempts made by educationists and artists alike to close the gap between the external world (rapidly and unnervingly changing as science discovered more of its secrets and how to manipulate them, for good or ill) and the day to day world of ordinary people, were reflected in the theatre's own attempts at more participatory models of audience engagement. Experimented with in a variety of ingenious ways in the living newspapers, those models were to be rethought and re-explored, often radically, in the second half of the century.

Notes

1 See C. P. Snow 1959/1993, *The Two Cultures*; and F. R. Leavis, 1962/1972: *Two Cultures? The Significance of C. P. Snow* (the 1962 Richmond Lecture).
2 The Wellcome Trust, one of the world's largest medical research organisations, not only funds research but also promotes education about scientific advance, and to that end has funded a series of science-oriented performing arts and theatre-in-education programmes. The Trust's most recent initiative, 'Pulse', was a two-year programme of performing arts events created by a range of professional artists working in conjunction with school, youth and community groups across the country, designed to generate interest in and debate about the current advances in medical science (2003–5). The initiative was successful enough to have been repeated in 2005–7. It represented a strategic move away from 'Public Understanding of Science' programmes to a focus upon 'Public *Engagement with* Science', signalling a recognition of the value of participatory programmes. See www.wellcome.ac.uk/pulse for further information and for an evaluation of the initiative.
3 'On a pound-for-pound basis, the Uranium-235 [the nucleus of a heavy atom] in an atomic bomb can release in the order of one million times as much energy

as TNT' (Mark Carson, Los Alamos Scientific Laboratory www.grolier.com/ wwii/wwii_atom.html, accessed 5 May 2006).
4 See Weinberg (1994); Herken (1988), and www.channel4.com/history/ microsites/B/britains_cold_war_super_weapons/nuclear.html (last accessed 3 April 2006).

Part II

Postwar: theatre, learning and participation

5

Audience participation and aesthetic distance

In this chapter, I want to consider one of the characteristic features of much educational theatre, especially following the end of the Second World War, audience participation. When audiences are actively engaged in the event as *participants*, the question of how far such theatre can be considered aesthetic and indeed the viability of aesthetic criteria is thrown into sharp relief. One major field of theatre practice in which audience participation has been pivotal, and which has had education as one of its primary goals, is theatre in education (TIE), and in this chapter the main examples will be from selected TIE and related practice over the past thirty years.[1] However, given the very considerable overlaps now between TIE, theatre in health education, prison theatre and theatre for development, the questions raised and observations made will, it is hoped, be more widely applicable.

The origins of what became known as the TIE movement can be precisely located – in Coventry, at the Belgrade Theatre in 1965. As with any movement, it had its advocates who argued its value, sometimes with almost messianic zeal, and various groupings of companies and individuals who broadly shared the same beliefs. The Standing Conference of Young People's Theatre (SCYPT) was for several decades the driving force behind much of the advance of good practice and the debates about strategy, form, ideological stance (invariably taking a stance well to the left of centre) and resistance to the introduction of the national curriculum. As a movement, it reached its peak during the mid-1980s and early 1990s (O'Toole 1976, Redington 1980, Jackson 1993). TIE still exists in manifold forms, and plays a significant part in both formal and informal education, but the work has diversified, is no longer identifiable as a 'movement' and often goes under other names (interventionist theatre, forum theatre projects, even, in some cases, museum theatre). The specialist TIE companies that do still exist, and those that include TIE as an identifiable part of their port-folio,[2] offer work that covers citizenship, personal and health issues, special needs, children's theatre, and youth theatre (drama workshops and per-formances for and by young people). More will be said later about TIE, its genealogy and its methodologies. But first, the work needs to be set firmly in the context of a number of important social developments and educa-tional trends in the middle part of the twentieth century. Discussion will then move to the concept of audience participation and some of the theo-retical questions it poses for the artistic and aesthetic status of theatre as a medium of education.

Some postwar contexts: cultural renewal and expansion in the UK

The social changes accelerated by, and to some extent triggered by, the ending of the Second World War have been well documented.[3] The opti-mism for a better world that ushered in a Labour government, elected with a landslide majority in 1945, was already latent during the darkest days of the war, as J. B. Priestley had urged in one of his weekly radio broadcasts during July 1940:

> We cannot go forward and build up this new world order, and this is our war aim, unless we begin to think differently. My own personal view . . . is that one must stop thinking in terms of property and power and begin thinking in terms of community and creation . . . We want a world that offers people not the dubious pleasures of power, but the maximum oppor-tunities for creation. And, even already, in the middle of this war, I can see that world shaping itself. (Priestley, 21 July 1940: from his weekly wartime broadcast, 'Postscripts')

And during some of the fiercest bombings, in October that year, he observed:

> Our greatest potential ally is not this power or that, but the growing hope in decent folk everywhere that . . . the seeds of civilisation could be saved to take root and to flower afterwards; that a reasonable liberty along with a reason-able security can be achieved; that democracy is not an experiment that was tried and failed, but a great creative force that must now be released again.
> ('Postscripts')

Priestley had, as playwright, novelist, journalist and radio broadcaster, been an articulate spokesman for the many who sought not just an end to conflict but the beginnings of a new order.[4]

Central among the aspirations towards that new order – shared by many on the centre-right of politics as well as the left – was the creation of better opportunities for the working man and woman, in health, education and social security; and Clement Atlee's Labour administration began a massive expansion of public ownership of key parts of the economy and especially of those areas that affected social cohesion (Royle 1988). A Conservative minister in the wartime coalition government (R. A. Butler) had already steered through the enormously influential Education Act of 1944, setting the pattern of education in Britain for the next twenty years, at least until the phased introduction of comprehensive schooling in the 1960s and 1970s. This act gave an entitlement to full-time schooling for everyone up to the age of fourteen and beyond according to ability; it was however integrally bound up with the new '11+' examination which detrimentally divided the school population into those destined for 'academic' education in grammar schools, and those who were deemed 'technically' or 'vocationally' minded, 'non-academic', and allocated to what was perceived increasingly to be the decidedly inferior 'secondary modern' school. For the Atlee government the major task after the war was the establishment of the Welfare State, particularly in the shape of the National Health Service and the introduction of a universal benefit and pension system, based on 'the positive principles of universality and need' (Royle, p. 206). At a stroke, it seemed, equality of opportunity and the redistribution of wealth in a general levelling-up process had become embedded as fundamental principles in the social hegemony – even if in practice the benefits were far from immediate. The universal welcome for such principles also explains the pervasive sense of disillusion in the mid-1950s, with the Conservatives back in power and Utopia still as far away as ever. None the less, the changes were profound and long-lasting, and their repercussions in the cultural sphere were many.

In this context, there are at least three strands of cultural change that need to be acknowledged: the growth of state-subsidised theatre, focused both in the regional repertory theatre network and in the national companies, specifically the Royal Shakespeare Company and the National Theatre (both of which were established in the 1960s); the increased interest among arts practitioners, and subsequently the funding bodies, in arts in the community and what came to be known as 'outreach'; and the development in schools, especially at primary school level, of child-centred education together with the recognition it afforded of the place of the arts in the curriculum, as a result of which there was a rapid growth in drama as a curriculum subject in schools.[5]

The long haul to reconstruct the country after the Second World War was accompanied by a new expansionist mood in the arts, aided at last by government commitment to financial support for the arts from the public purse. The Council for the Encouragement of Music & the Arts

(CEMA), established during the war, had successfully promoted a wide range of arts activities across the whole country, providing escapism and morale-boosting, celebratory entertainment. The Old Vic Theatre, for example, was relocated temporarily to the North West, and Shakespeare and Euripides were performed for mining communities in South Wales. CEMA's existence was important too because it established the principle of the necessity and social value of the arts, especially at a time of social strain, and laid the ground for government subsidy for the arts in the post-war era. When CEMA was reconstituted as the Arts Council of Great Britain (ACGB) in 1946, its stated objects among others were 'to develop and improve the knowledge, understanding and practice of the arts; and to increase the accessibility of the arts to the public throughout Great Britain' (ACGB 1946). Consequently, one of the first tasks the ACGB saw as needing attention was the subsidy of theatre tickets to ensure that performances were brought more within the range of ordinary people. Theatre gradually became slightly more accessible to the working or lower middle classes and to the young, not only in terms of ticket affordability but in the gradual opening up of the repertoire to newer writing, including plays by writers from the very social groups who had begun to benefit from the welfare state and increased educational opportunities. It was a slow, faltering but noticeable change.

Another of the Council's priorities was the establishment of a buildings fund (Housing the Arts) to help create a new generation of theatres. The first new repertory theatre to be built was the Belgrade Theatre, Coventry (1958), and by 1980 some forty new or rebuilt theatres were in existence, notable examples being those at Nottingham, Birmingham, Manchester, Sheffield and Chichester (Rowell and Jackson 1984). New drama was encouraged, new audiences were sought and many theatres made genuine attempts to become a part of the communities they served. Hence such developments from the mid-1960s onwards as the creation of large, inviting foyer spaces, with café, bar, bookshop and exhibition areas and the formation of TIE and community arts teams and youth theatre groups.

Theatre in education

One of the most important manifestations of the 'outreach' impulse was the TIE movement. Part of a concerted attempt by professional repertory theatres to connect theatre with the lives of ordinary people, the first theatre in education company was formed in 1965 at the recently built Belgrade Theatre, followed within a few years by others at theatres such as Leeds Playhouse, Bolton Octagon and Nottingham Playhouse. Over the subsequent decade similar such units were established at other regional theatres, some became independent companies in their own right and several were formed by local education authorities specifically to serve local schools. The TIE model also generated interest abroad and in adapted form spread to many other countries from the 1980s onwards – notably to Ireland, Norway, Denmark, Nigeria, Kenya, Australia and the United States. It was not, however, a uniquely British phenomenon. The use of theatre as an educational tool, deployed within the very communities and institutions where its impact would be strongest and most effective, was clearly 'in the air'. TIE was therefore interestingly paralleled in many countries by the rise of comparable theatre work that developed wholly independently – most notably (but certainly not exclusively) exemplified by the Brazilian director Augusto Boal's 'Theatre of the Oppressed' (Boal 1979), a form of politically and educationally driven theatre in Brazil that emerged during the 1970s and rapidly caught on in Europe and the United States (Babbage 2004, Heritage 1998, Thompson 2003, Vine 1993). It subsequently became a linchpin of much of the theatre for development work in Africa and the Indian subcontinent (Boon and Plastow 2004, Thompson 2003).

In the UK, TIE companies quickly became among the foremost innovators of participatory theatre. The term TIE refers to the use of theatre for explicit educational purposes, closely allied to the school curriculum and mostly taking place in educational contexts – schools, colleges, youth clubs, sometimes in museums and at historic sites. It tends to be a highly portable form of theatre, using minimal sets and lighting (if any), but practised by specialist professional companies who aim to bring high-quality performance work into the classroom, school hall or other venue.[1] Above all, it will usually involve some element of interaction with the audience: it may be a short play followed by a workshop in which actors and children together will explore some of the issues further, using a range of techniques such as the 'hot-seating' (or interrogation) of characters from the play and 'forum theatre' exercises based on the theatre advocated by Boal; or it may sometimes – for younger children especially – involve the active participation of the children in role throughout the event.[2] Full-scale in-role participation of this latter kind has now become rare, not because of any lack of interest but simply because it operates best with one class of children at a time and is labour-intensive and therefore costly.[3] Occasional revivals and developments of this format have demonstrated its continuing power and effectiveness (for example in recent work by Triangle Theatre in Coventry, and in student productions at various university drama and education departments). The play followed by interactive workshop is today the more common form. Whatever the age or the format, the young people do not, then, watch simply as passive spectators but engage actively with the events they witness – as contemporary investigators, as nineteenth-century cotton workers, as peasant farmers on the estate of a sixteenth century nobleman, or simply as themselves, responding to opportunities to interrogate characters, offer advice or (as in forum theatre) rehearse alternative courses of action in order to try to resolve difficult social dilemmas. The *type* of interaction will usually be governed by the subject matter of the programme and by the targeted age range of the children – and also by the cost and level of subsidy available.

As well as being rooted in, and an extension of, theatre practice, participatory TIE also drew strongly on parallel developments within the school sector in drama in education (DIE). There had been several early pioneers of drama as an educational method, Caldwell Cook (1917) in Cambridge before the First World War being one of the first. Even more influential, however, were Peter Slade (1912–2004), whose seminal study, *Child Drama*, appeared in 1954, and Brian Way (1923–2006; his *Development through Drama* appeared in 1967), both of whom advocated a central place for drama in the curriculum by rejecting the primacy of 'putting on the school play' and emphasising instead the child's own creativity and the development of personal confidence and social skill ('rehearsing for life' as Way (1967) termed it). Slade had begun formulating his ideas and his practice during the 1930s. Although he came to be associated principally with a child-centred approach that eschewed formal theatre production (putting on plays was in his view – especially for younger children – detrimental to the essentially expressive and developmental function that drama, at root, shared with play), he was not as rigidly opposed to performance as some have claimed. For teenagers, working towards production could be a powerful incentive to focus their activities and develop their communication skills. His resistance to the primacy of production-based work was rooted in his opposition to much of the theatre performed for young people in the interwar and immediately postwar years – plays deemed of educational merit (Shakespeare and the classics) but performed in large proscenium auditoria and in a style that Peter Brook (1969) would probably have recognised as 'deadly theatre'. At various points between 1934 and the outbreak of the Second World War, he formed several small-scale theatre companies to tour productions of a more intimate kind to community halls and schools; and in 1943 he founded the Pear Tree Players – according to Coggin (1956: 237–8), the first professional theatre company entirely devoted to education. Inspired by the work of Slade and, later, Way, Dorothy Heathcote and Gavin Bolton, 'drama in education' – also known as 'creative dramatics' in the United States and subsequently and increasingly as 'process drama', a term derived from the work of Heathcote, Bolton, Cecily O'Neill (1995) and others – grew steadily through the 1960s and 1970s. The ideas and innovative practice of Heathcote and Bolton, in particular the approach known as 'mantle of the expert' (Heathcote & Bolton 1995) proved immensely influential in the development of participatory forms of TIE. By the late 1980s the work was further enriched by influences from abroad, not only by Boal's forum theatre methods but also by increased awareness of, and exposure to, exciting work undertaken by practitioners of children's theatre in mainland Europe, which demonstrated the imaginative and multi-layered qualities of which children's theatre was capable, through innovative design, choreography and 'physical theatre'. The growing acceptance of drama as a valid curriculum subject in the UK also helped to validate the practice of TIE as an educational tool, which in turn was able to attract funding from its two principal sources, the regional arts funding bodies and local education authorities (LEAs).

In Britain TIE has always relied heavily on public subsidy for its survival. From the late 1970s on, recession and soaring inflation took their toll; and from the mid-1980s government pushed to make everything – education and the arts included – subject to the 'rigours of the marketplace', so the ability of TIE companies to survive and to continue offering the same level of service for the deliberately small audience-sizes came under enormous strain. This pressure coincided with the devolution of LEA budgets down to individual schools which in turn reduced the scope of LEAs to subsidise TIE work in their respective areas. No longer could TIE be offered free at the point of use, which in turn curtailed much of the (expensive) participatory nature of the work. Many companies had to close, while others had to play to ever-larger audiences, and there is no doubt that there was considerable dilution of TIE practice in the process. But good innovative work still goes on if among fewer companies. Economically, TIE in Britain has had to reconcile itself to the situation faced by similar groups in the United States, Australia and elsewhere, in which public subsidy, if it exists at all, has to be augmented by grants from charitable foundations, commercial sponsorship or box office. (See Chapter 8 for further discussion of the cultural climate within which the work now has to operate.)

In other countries, theatre for educational purposes (whether or not labelled TIE) has developed in differing ways according to cultural need; but perhaps it has been Boal's advocacy of the Theatre of the Oppressed (1979, 1995), and especially his forum theatre techniques, that have had the most remarkable and extensive impact, not only upon TIE but even more so upon the varied practices known as theatre for development (TfD) throughout the 'Third World'. In particular, his concept of the 'spect-actor' has further, provocatively, challenged the notion of a necessary dividing line between audience and stage, and offered the most explicit, direct link yet between what happens within a theatre event and what happens in direct consequence in the world outside. Forum Theatre – the technique through which fictional stories based on real-life problems are enacted and then replayed and reshaped *by the audience* as a means of testing solutions which can be applied in the world outside the theatre walls – has been utilised within prisons as part of rehabilitation programmes, in rural Nigeria to provoke debates about AIDS prevention or drug abuse, and across India to promote literacy. The number of applications has been almost endless, even if the universal efficacy of the method has still to be proved. Debates abound about its effectiveness. To what extent can action for change, rehearsed within the safe confines of a community hall, be readily transferable to the real world? How far is its transferability dependent upon the specific cultural context – will the same techniques work equally well in Brazilian and British prisons, in a South African township and in a remote tribal village in central India? What exactly are the ideological assumptions that underpin its practice – can it, and does it, activate collective action aimed at social transformation, or is it most effective at an individual level?[6]

These and other such questions throw into sharp relief the very purpose of audience participation. Participation has been at the heart of TIE and indeed of much theatre for young people, TfD and other forms that claim to have an educational role. What, then, are the purposes and implications – artistic and educational – of engaging audiences actively in a theatre event?

Audience participation

Arguably, all theatre is participatory at one level or another: the theatre event is always a two-way process, the audience bringing to the event its own experiences and understandings from the outside world, influencing the performance by its very presence, and making its own meanings out of the onstage material. My focus here however is with theatrical activity that sets out to transgress the traditional boundary-lines between stage and auditorium and to generate an engagement from the audience that is overt and direct, and will often be physical, active and sometimes verbal in form. And while audience participation embraces diverse practices across the spectrum of theatre activity throughout the twentieth century, it is the search for an explicit *educational* or *interventionist* role for the theatre that has generated a whole array of new forms, and of ways of directly engaging audiences. It has, as we have seen, been manifested in agit-prop and the workers-theatre' movements of the 1920s and 1930s, in Brecht's *Lehrstücke* of the 1930s and in American living newspapers. It then re-emerged with extraordinary vitality and diversity in postwar theatre for children and young people (Way 1981), in TIE (O'Toole 1976, Redington 1983, Jackson 1993), in community theatre (Erven 2000), in the various forms of 'Theatre of the Oppressed' (Boal 1979, 1992), in the various political and alternative, experimental theatre of the 1960s and 1970s (from the Living Theatre to 'happenings' to 'theatre of mixed means' (Kirby 1965, Schechner 1973, Shank 1982, Tytell 1997, Jackson and Lev-Aladgem 2004).

Audience participation came to be central particularly to theatre created for young people. Brian Way for example records his frustration as a member of the first Young Vic Company, formed after the end of the Second World War to bring theatre to young people across the UK, at the yawning gulf that separated the actors from the serried ranks of schoolchildren in the auditoria, whose enthusiasm to participate became progressively denied as the performance unfolded (Way 1981). Before long, Way had set up (with Margaret Faulkes, in 1953) Theatre Centre in London to experiment with theatre of a more immediate and accessible kind, directly related to young people's interests, performed in the round and incorporating participatory elements. By the early 1970s, at its height, Theatre Centre had seven companies on the road touring the country, playing mainly in schools, but also in arts centres and small theatres. Despite the many obstacles, Way successfully pioneered forms of drama that spoke directly to his audiences and involved limited degrees of audience participation. His collection of *Three Plays for the Open Stage* (1958) and (with Warren Jenkins) *Pinocchio* (1954) demonstrate the style of play for which Theatre Centre became renowned: lively, colourful, simply but intimately staged with minimal barriers between children and performers, although steering clear of any critical view of social reality. No more than two hundred children were permitted at any of the performances which were mostly staged in the round. The key feature of these productions was always the limited but active involvement of the audiences (what O'Toole terms 'peripheral participation', 1976). Classic story-telling techniques, utilising much eye-contact and frequent invitations to contribute sound effects, carefully planned exchanges with the audience at predetermined moments and mime were all characteristic features of the productions.

From there, it was a short step to the creation of participatory TIE programmes in which children were involved more directly in the dilemmas posed by the stories. Types of participation varied. It might consist of schoolchildren taking on the role of participants in the story (for example, as villagers faced by a dilemma over the building of a nearby dam or employees faced with redundancy), and addressed by the characters as such, or slipping into role 'by default' (for example, they are invited to interrogate characters from the play they have just seen – this is not character-playing for they are still themselves but entering into the 'game' of conversing with fictional beings), or visitors to a 'living history' exhibition who encounter and speak to characters from the past, or audiences at a promenade performance who get pulled into the action as 'the crowd' or 'witnesses'. In all these ways, the audience member or visitor or roleplaying participant becomes engaged in an active relationship with the characters. The engagement is actual, more often than not happens away from the conventional auditorium in more neutral or 'open' spaces, and the dialogue at key points in the drama is designed to be genuinely two-way. (The nature and problematics of dialogue in participatory theatre are discussed in more detail in Chapter 7.)

Active audience participation – whether in TIE or in other non-pedagogic contexts, such as the Living Theatre experiments of the 1950s and 1960s – has also, however, been a highly contentious strategy. Some view it as a technique that denies the essential condition of theatre. David Cole has argued – in his influential study *The Theatrical Event* (1975) – that any element of audience participation should be avoided at all costs, asserting that 'Audience participation, in seeming to provide a way of drawing nearer to the theatrical event, in fact abolishes it' (Cole 1975: 79). It is an important argument, which bears closely on the case for and against participatory theatre. For Cole, if a spectator crosses the borderline that separates her from the acting arena, enters into the Stage Image and becomes in effect an actor, then the 'theatrical event' becomes instead an acting class. If by the same token an actor reclaims his body from the Image and 'in his own person' approaches and 'socialises' with the audience, it is not theatre any more, but rather a round-table discussion (Cole, p. 76). Participatory theatre, in toying with the borderlines between fiction and life as a part of its strategy and philosophy, is for this reason, contends Cole, spurious. He argues that theatre 'makes imaginative truth present' (or evokes its presence) by means of a process that is close to that practised by the 'shaman' and the 'hungan' in certain tribal rituals. On the basis of this premise, Cole assumes and indeed insists on a clear boundary between actors and audience so that the 'sacredness' of the acting – the special qualities inherent in the act of theatre – is not compromised by the spectators. There can be no 'area between' spectating and acting: spectators are either spectators or they have become actors – they cannot be both (p. 76).

This is a rather rigid demarcation and fails to allow for the far more fluid notion of theatre as (in Schechner's words) 'an interplay among space, time, performers, action and audience' (1977: 28). In a sense, Cole is arguing for the role of traditional theatre to be understood as an essentially ritualistic event, gaining its power from the ritualistic and physical separation of audience from actor. It is a notion of ritual that differs considerably from what Victor Turner, and subsequently Schechner, has described as the performance of ritual activity for religious or other serious social purposes in the real world (Turner 1982, Schechner 1988). In rituals enacted in the real world, all of those present are likely to be participants at some level, whether priest or congregation, orator or listeners to be won over. 'Aesthetic Drama', on the other hand, is the term Schechner uses to describe the kind of traditional theatre performance to which audiences go, knowing that they are indeed audiences: they are there to watch a theatrical event, engage and respond as appropriate, safe in the knowledge that whatever happens on stage is not real life. They keep their distance, literally and metaphorically. The performed event may look and feel similar to real life, the correspondences may be close, but what is often called 'aesthetic distance' ensures there is no real confusion. As Daphna Ben Chaim summarises it, 'in one there is belief . . .; in the other there is a suspension of dis-belief' (Ben Chaim 1984: 42). Despite the social/ aesthetic distinction that Schechner draws, he does also recognise that 'audiences', like 'performers', do not always have to exist as distinct entities: that the boundary line between them can be crossed, that the theatre practised by artists such as Beck and Malina and indeed by Schechner himself (with the Performance Group) was designed to transgress that conventional divide. Audience and performer could in this sense operate as two basic functions of one communal exercise (Schechner 1966). But on one thing Cole and Schechner agree: that when participation takes place, it changes theatre utterly. In Schechner's words, audience participation 'expands the field of what a performance is' and is 'incompatible with the idea of a self-contained, autonomous, beginning-middle-and-end artwork' (1973/94: 40). For Cole, it ceases to be art; for Schechner (especially as his later, not always consistent, essays suggest), it has become simply different. It may no longer be art in the conventional sense: 'performance', 'social event' and 'social theatre' are some of the terms he has used to describe such practice.

Cole's contention would seem to view audience participation as a process that inevitably denies, or at least severely compromises, the possibility of what is often thought to be an essential ingredient in any true theatre event: *aesthetic distance*. If it is the function of aesthetic distance to maintain a clear distinction between stage and audience, then to blur that distance would also risk blurring the necessary distinction between art and life: as another commentator has put it, 'When distance disappears then art does too' (Bennett 1990: 16). The consequences of blurring that distinction invite risks, not least in respect of the kinds of response one can expect from participating audiences as we shall see in the next two chapters. It is however the argument of this book that audience participation and aesthetic distance do not have to be mutually exclusive: audiences can be actively engaged in ways that retain a degree of aesthetic distance, even if the nature of that 'distance' may appear to be of a markedly different kind from that found in conventional theatre practice.

Aesthetic distance

As the above implies, aesthetic distance between audience and stage is a key factor that appears to operate in any conventional theatre event (or 'aesthetic drama'). As Daphne Ben Chaim puts it, in her excellent study of 'distance in the theatre', our involvement in the stage action 'may be intense but it is different from our involvement in everyday life' (Ben Chaim 1984: ix). It is often referred to as having a protective function – that which saves us from feeling so caught up in the fiction that the dividing line between it and real life gets lost leading to confusion or panic. But while it is often couched in those rather negative terms aesthetic distance is of course much more than a safety-net; as the boundary-line between art and life it would seem to be central to the very business of art. No matter how engrossed in the lives or problems of the characters on stage we may feel, the fact that at the same time we *know* it's also a fiction (we *willingly* suspend our disbelief) enables us to see, reflect, perhaps understand more clearly than we normally might, beyond the noise and flux of everyday life. We may for example, as Ben Chaim suggests, perceive 'ironies, images, and theoretical implications' that the characters in real life probably would not; we have a 'paradoxically involved-yet-removed' relation to the artwork (p. 17).

In any theatre performance then there is likely to be – whether we consciously realise it or not – an element of aesthetic distance which enables the audience both to believe and not to believe at one and the same time. We can imaginatively embrace the fictional world and be caught up in the excitement, fantasy, dangers and dilemmas it may generate, but we are equally conscious of its fictionality. Boal has described this rather extraordinary paradox as *metaxis* (Boal 1995: 42–4). The degree of distance that an author or director strives for, and the purpose to which it is put, has of course varied enormously from author to author, from production to production. The difference between Brecht's highly stylised, poetic depiction of a political dilemma in *The Measures Taken*, played on a raised platform in a lecture-hall setting, and Galsworthy's emotionally charged depiction of prisoners in solitary confinement in *Justice*, presented in a traditional proscenium-arch London theatre, provides just one example. In one, the audience is addressed as comrades, faced with a political choice that has been framed in fictional but 'exemplary' terms. Denied conventional theatre trappings, with no darkening of the auditorium lights and no attempt made to create an illusion of real events happening in a far-off place, the degree of distance is pronounced. In the second, the audience, drawn mainly from the upper-middle classes and Edwardian London's intelligentsia, are won over by the realistic portrayal of the crisis in one man's life, depicted in terms calculated to move them emotionally by means of empathy with the protagonist and shock tactics in the staging. The degree of distance felt by the audience has been minimised by the closest attention to the real conditions signified on stage (for example of the courtroom or the prison cell) – minimised but by no means eliminated, as the gilded proscenium arch of the Edwardian theatre through which the action is inescapably framed would have ensured.

For Brecht, of course, the 'distancing' effect, or *Verfremdungseffekt*, was a central weapon in his armoury for jolting the spectator into a heightened awareness of the theatre in which he or she sat, and of the theatrical devices being employed to represent the world on stage (see Ben Chaim 1984: 25). By this means the spectator would be discouraged from feeling empathy for the characters and encouraged instead to view the events and the dilemmas faced by the characters as 'exemplary', as constructed, the purpose being to demonstrate how human beings have behaved at particular historical moments, and to invite the audience to ask why, to consider whether there might have been alternative courses of action open to them. Thus, the function of art was to re-present reality in a wholly different light from the norm: to distort it in order to understand it better:

> Reality . . . has to be altered by being turned into art, so that it can be seen to be alterable and be treated as such. (Brecht 1974c: 219; also cited in Ben Chaim 1984: 32)

The real world will be represented on stage in such a way that the audience both recognises the world as one that exists or has existed and at the same time is distanced from it, at least enough to enable them to be critical of it, to be curious about why and how things happen: why Galileo makes a stand at one moment and surrenders at another. The intent is clearly that the audience should take up a critical stance towards (be distanced from) the world represented and by extension be empowered to act upon a world that they no longer take for granted. In this sense, it has a highly educational function: the whole purpose of theatre becomes harnessed to transformative goals and the audience itself is invited to learn and to act upon what they have learnt, in particular to be critical of the way their lives are governed by those above, by the powerful.

Distancing was then, for Brecht, about heightening audience consciousness and reflection in an overt, politically orientated and socially purposeful way, in the interests of showing human beings – and the world they inhabit – as changeable, and with the ultimate end of promoting social change. It was a specific rational technique for framing the action, for 'defamiliarising' events in the world that we might in other circumstances have taken for granted, seen as normal, inevitable or 'natural'. At every point, Brecht wishes to place his theatre at the service of an informed, reflective consciousness that will transfer directly into the 'real world' beyond the theatre walls. It is not primarily conceived as an aesthetic concern – in Ben Chaim's words, Brecht's concern 'goes beyond aesthetics' (1984: 32) – but a social, political one. None the less, the implication of Brecht's style of theatre is significant for any appreciation of how aesthetics, education and the practice of drama interconnect. In particular, his utilisation of *astonishment* (rather than empathy) was a key feature of his distancing techniques: the framing of everyday events in such a way that we are taken aback, we are shocked to see things happen the way they do, to see characters make the decisions they do, and are therefore prompted to ask questions: why did this happen, and was it inevitable? – could the characters have made different choices? As Brecht put it: 'What is "natural" must have the force of what is startling' (Brecht 1974a: 71). Astonishment – because it is allied to illumination (Brooker: 191) – is seen as a highly productive experience, and one that can lead to altered perceptions of the world around us, perhaps even to our taking a more active role in addressing similar issues in the everyday world.

In the 1950s, the psychologist Leon Festinger propounded a theory that corresponds remarkably closely to Brecht's notion of the productive effect of astonishment. In seeking to explain some of the circumstances and motives which lead us to change our minds or behaviour or to take action in the everyday social world, Festinger proposed the operation of a process which he termed 'Cognitive dissonance'. In brief, the argument is that a recognition of sharply contradictory cognitions, of two sets of knowledges that are clearly incompatible, will produce a sense of dissonance or psychological discomfort, which in turn will serve as a strong motivating force to try to reconcile those oppositions, to achieve a degree of consonance.[7] The mind may attempt to achieve consonance by seeking new understandings, new knowledge or new beliefs about the situation that gave rise to the dissonance, or by in some way altering existing beliefs to accommodate the new knowledge. Shock, astonishment at seeing things you had taken for granted in a wholly new light, such that existing beliefs can no longer be sustained, is a powerful motivation for learning, and it is one that Brechtian theatre was designed to produce. The key differences from Festinger's theory of course lie in the fictional, overtly constructed framework within which such surprise is induced, and in the political purpose to which it was put.

There is of course no guarantee that the audience will respond in such a way. It is well known that Brecht himself found actors' portrayals and audiences' responses not quite as he hoped and constantly revised his theory and his guidance for actors as a result. Hence his *Mother Courage Modellbuch* in which he laid out guidelines for actors and directors to help them guard against the easy, sentimental or romantic interpretations that audiences might be all too readily inclined to fall for. Hence too his steady retreat from the overtly didactic plays of the 1930s – a move that signalled an acknowledgment that audiences rarely behave in quite the way one would like or expect; and an understanding that art often functions most effectively through a complex distancing process – one that acknowledges the need for closeness, or engagement, and at the same time for a degree of critical and emotional separation. *Recognition* of the issue will not in itself be enough. An audience needs to care about what is happening before them, to see that something is at stake for the character involved – without necessarily falling into what was for Brecht the empathy trap. Distance might need to be coupled with a degree of fellow feeling – if not quite the degree of empathy that serves to 'naturalise' or universalise. Perhaps Brecht's later theatre can be seen as a symptom of a growing acceptance that 'teaching' through art is unlikely to bear fruit if the vehicle is too transparently a didactic one. Change at both the individual and collective levels is – if it is to happen at all – more likely to happen because the audience makes personal connections with the dilemmas depicted, and perhaps the most one can expect is for the audience to be led to contemplate and to question rather than to take action on leaving the theatre. Different styles may of course work more effectively in different cultural moments or different cultural locations. There is no universally applicable method. In the context of a fragmented Germany – still reeling from the defeat of the first world war and subsequently from the impact of the Depression and soaring inflation, and with beliefs in Marxist solutions in full play, inspired by the recent events in Russia – a theatre that worked in a more direct, didactic style undoubtedly caught the mood of the time and was more in tune with perceived needs than the subtleties of *Galileo* or *Mother Courage* would ever have been.

There is one further aspect of distancing that demands some attention before moving on to consider the implications for participatory theatre. That is, the notion of 'under- and over-distancing'. The psychologist Edward Bullough made a pioneering study in 1912 of the phenomenon of what he termed 'psychical distance' in art. His essay has provoked much debate ever since and it served to propel much of the argument in Susanne Langer's seminal study *Feeling and Form*, as well as Ben Chaim's discussion of theatrical distance. Bullough defined distance as the 'aesthetic tension' between two extremes: 'total empathy on the one hand and its complete elimination on the other' (Ben Chaim 1984: 78), and argued that art achieves its fullest impact upon the beholder when there is a satisfactory balance between 'over-' and 'under-distancing'. There is a clear connection here with Aristotle's idea of catharsis, and T. J. Scheff (1979) expands Bullough's argument as a means of further understanding how catharsis might operate. He proposes that catharsis occurs when there is a balance within the audience's mind between distress and security. He refers to this balance as an essential part of the process of 'distancing' and suggests that catharsis will occur 'when an unresolved emotional distress is reawakened in a properly distanced context' (p. 13). When a drama is too vicarious it means that it is 'over-distanced' and therefore does not lead to catharsis. When a drama is 'under-distanced' then the reawakening does not occur in a context which is sufficiently safe, and therefore the distress is experienced as overwhelming (p. 14). Another way of putting it is to suggest, as Ben Chaim does (1984: 76–8), that 'excessive awareness of fictionality can be as dangerous to imaginative participation as too little awareness which endangers "volition" '(volition being the freely-entered-into complicity with the fictional event: the willing suspension of disbelief; the voluntary treatment of the image with seriousness while at the same time aware of its unrealness) (p. 74). Thus one might say that, for example, Brecht introduces and sustains a relatively high level of distance while Galsworthy maintains a low one. But, as Ben Chaim perceptively notes (p. 80), many authors will often achieve their most powerful and effective moments through a reversal of the general level of distance at climactic points (when, for example, Katrin climbs on to the wagon to warn the village at the end of *Mother Courage*, knowing her own life will be lost as a result, one of the most emotionally charged moments in modern drama). One might add that an array of sudden variations in the level of distance is available to the dramatist. Thus, in *Justice*, there is not a reversal but certainly a sudden reduction in distance, from the familiar, orderly, 'safe' setting of the courtroom to the disturbing, wordless scene in the prison cell that quickly follows. When active audience participation is called for, however, this 'satisfactory balance' (if indeed there ever can be such a thing) may be more difficult to achieve.

Is aesthetic distance possible in participatory theatre?

The necessity of distance provokes the most contentious debate when it appears to be threatened or compromised by a call for any audience participation. Thus, Aurand Harris, the eminent American children's theatre playwright, argued that he rarely wrote plays involving audience participation because it prevented him from achieving the 'aesthetic distance' necessary for true art. Without aesthetic distance – by which he implies a clear separation of the stage-world from that of the audience in order that the author's narrative line may unfold unimpeded and uncompromised – Harris believes you lose the essential element of 'make-believe' and end up with little more than an 'informal happening' (Harris 1985: 159). This is an argument that chimes with Cole's, even if 'sacredness' is replaced (as it so often is in writings about children's theatre) by the softer notion of theatrical 'magic'. If, in other words, the audience mixes in with the actors, if they are allowed some degree of influence over what happens and how, the event's claim to being art (so the argument goes) becomes seriously undermined. Perhaps because participatory theatre deploys so many of the devices, techniques and conventions of mainstream theatre – and yet departs so radically in one key respect, that of the stage–audience relationship – it has drawn hostile criticism all the more readily from those who place a high premium upon the rich traditions of children's theatre. Susanne Langer recalls her 'terrible shock' as a young child when taken on her first visit to the theatre to see *Peter Pan*: the illusion was 'absolute and overwhelming' until, at the highest point of the action, the actress playing Pan 'turned to the spectators and asked them to attest their belief in fairies' (to help save the life of Tinkerbell).

> Instantly the illusion was gone; there were hundreds of children . . . clapping and even calling, while [Maude] Adams, dressed up as Peter Pan, spoke to us like a teacher coaching us in a play in which she herself was taking the title role . . . [A]n acute misery obliterated the rest of the scene, and was not entirely dispelled until the curtain rose on a new set. (Langer 1953: 318)

It was, she claims, an extreme example of a 'central fallacy' in many play productions – the belief that the best drama should aim to disregard detachment or distance with the aim of maximising audience belief in the

reality of what they are watching. 'To seek delusion, belief, and "audience participation" in the theatre is to deny that drama is art' (p. 319).
For Langer, following Bullough's lead, art involves 'separating the object
[of our attention] and its appeal from one's own self' – obtained not by
denying its appeal but by 'filtering' that appeal, by clearing the personal
relation we have with the object of 'the practical, concrete nature of its
appeal' (Bullough 1912: 91; cited in Langer 1953: 319). We may be
moved but we are not distracted by having to take any immediate, concrete action to deal with the problem faced by the fictional character –
we do not have to intervene to save Ophelia's life. Art is essentially symbolic not the thing itself, and therein lies its peculiar power and its range
of effects upon our emotions and intellect alike. Langer's recall of that
participatory moment in *Peter Pan* is just one example of the way a theatrical device intended to reduce the distance and engage the audience
even more strongly can have the reverse effect, at least for some members
of the audience; active participation of the audience, far from advancing
our engagement with and understanding of the action of the drama can
all too easily disengage and confuse.

In 1979, John Allen, in his influential *Drama in Schools*, expressed
considerable concern about the 'hybrid' nature of theatre in education in
the UK – particularly for its heavy reliance upon the full-scale participation of its young audiences. It was, he claimed, 'in its very nature, a compromise or . . . fusion between the wholly independent . . . disciplines'
of teaching and acting; and he wondered whether 'the art of the theatre
[was] itself being undersold.' (Allen 1979: 6–7). Allen's concern is one
that has been expressed time and again by both critics and supporters of
theatre in education and especially by those who believe theatrical art
and explicit pedagogic goals are incompatible (see Schonmann 2005).

Do TIE and other forms of participatory educational theatre sacrifice
aesthetic distance in the interests of pedagogy? Do they risk 'under-
distancing' their audiences? Beneath any TIE programme – as with any
good piece of educational theatre – there lies the premise that children and
young people can apprehend, and learn about, the world through
metaphor: through engagement with imaginative material that re-presents
and illuminates aspects of their own lives in the real world. By theatrical
means, a new, fictive space and time scale are generated, separate from the
immediate pressures of their world, within which can be explored matters
that are none the less very much of that world. (It is what Neil Postman
(1994) has called, in respect of creative pedagogy, the creation in the classroom of a 'counter-environment'.) By reshaping, intensifying and fictionalising experience, the possibility is offered of seeing freshly, with new eyes
and new understanding, free from the inhibiting constraints of examina-

tions, institutional authority and externally imposed rules. Permission is given to look again, to reconsider, to find new connections between the actual and the possible, the given and the imagined, the personal and the social; and to investigate alternative pictures of the world, of other, perhaps better, ways of living our lives.

But participatory theatre goes further: it involves its audiences physically, so that the question of aesthetic distance becomes a complicated one. With younger age groups, the participation of the audience can sometimes be one of total immersion, from beginning to end, and an integral part of the event. The children are players in the drama, part of the narrative: without them the event would be pointless, for they are the weavers, or the villagers, the people who are caught up in the clash of economic and political forces and who have to make decisions about where they stand on the issues or on the conflicting views of specific characters who request their support. Many years ago, immediately after a participatory TIE programme about settlers in the American West of the mid nineteenth century (*Land Rush*, Belgrade TIE Company, Coventry), a nine-year old explained to me (with a real sense of wonder) why it was he had enjoyed the experience he had just been through by saying: 'I've never been in a story before!' That was to him an enormously important, and unique, thing to have done. He had valued playing a part inside the story and felt he had had a share in its creation: it could not have proceeded without him. But he was also, I suggest, implicitly recognising the art form in calling it a story. It was not just a rather elaborate form of play which could have gone anywhere, but a narrative with a clear strong structure, a plot, a beginning, middle and end, operating in its own special time and space, transformed out of the otherwise mundane circumstances of school hall and timetable. He could not make the story go his way, but he was a contributor to it, not a passive receiver of an already finished product.

With older groups, the participation may be more detached, allowing the pupils to retain their own identities as teenagers, and on their own familiar territory, but it still requires active engagement with fictional material, having to confront (or 'hot-seat') characters from the play they have just witnessed, to probe beneath the surface actions, to discover why they took the stand they did (or failed to), why their attitudes to others were as they were, and what if anything could be done to rectify or improve their situation. Even in such limited involvement, it is common for the most 'streetwise' youths to be drawn in to the 'hot-seating' convention and enter into a debate with the characters that is as much about their own lives and perceptions of the world as it is about those of the fictional beings they meet. The suspension of disbelief is willing, conscious, because the pupils see (or sense) it to be in their own interest to engage in the 'as if' process. I recall seeing teenage boys, in a forum theatre workshop following M6 Theatre Company's *Trappin'* (a play by Frances McNeil about oppression within a marriage, 1991) readily step into the shoes of the (oppressed) female character to try to help solve the problem she faced. Normal embarrassment, self-consciousness, had been suspended – of their own volition – as they, as well as girls, entered into the fictive world in order to struggle with 'real' interpersonal problems in a safe environment.

Once the pupils consciously (and often cautiously) enter into the contract with the performers, if the programme is effectively and powerfully presented, the engagement will be intense, even with pupils of fifteen or sixteen years of age, and exchanges between them and the characters quite heated. Sometimes it will be a necessary (and carefully gauged) part of the educational strategy of the programme that high levels of empathy are generated and anger aroused in the pupils as a means of taking them from one stage in the process to the next. Such strategies, involving momentary reductions in the spectator's emotional distance from the event (under-distancing), can of course be dangerous if mishandled, but highly productive when handled correctly, when followed by an opportunity to debrief in calm conditions, and can genuinely lead to 'a change in understanding' (Bolton 1993: 40) of the subject being tackled.

If a function of art is to strive for understandings of the world through metaphor (itself a form of artistic distancing), then does TIE muddy its waters by introducing active involvement? – by denying its audience in the process physical distance? The audience in a theatre, watching an action framed by the proscenium arch, scripted and designed to achieve a richly textured vision of the world, views it from a specific vantage point, so that the vision is a shared, controlled experience (just as a painter expects his 'audience', and the novelist hers, to see from one standpoint at a time) . In many of the more adventurous forms of participatory TIE the view is often deliberately partial, with groups of children seeing different segments of the event from different angles, maybe in different rooms; characters will each offer different and seemingly valid perspectives; rarely will there be a neutral, narrator-type figure to confirm or validate one view at the expense of the others. And there will be discussions and information-exchange between characters and children that will inevitably be unscripted and wholly different from one school to the next. Sometimes the programme will deliberately ensure that different groups of children will meet different characters and gain quite different perspectives on the events, leading to an even more heightened pooling of knowledge between them as they attempt to piece the jigsaw pieces together. In the best programmes the jigsaw will be challengingly difficult (if not impossible) to complete. Truth usually proves to be a slippery commodity, resisting neat packaging, and the debate must continue after the drama has finished.

When the children are actively participating, in the midst of the action, in dialogue with the characters, does TIE in effect give up aesthetic distance for a kind of 'team teaching'? Is there a reversion from theatre to pedagogy and back again? In good TIE, my argument is that there is no such reversion, despite what to the observer may seem evidence to the contrary. The theatre is pedagogic and the pedagogy is theatrical. It *is* possible to create strong theatrical moments within a participation framework. But in moving from powerful, staged crisis (when the pupils are a recognisable kind of audience) to small-group discussion, what matters is that the whole experience should be conceived of as an *integrated aesthetic totality* in which the 'audience' can switch to being active participants, engage in out-of-role discussion and move on to (for example) interrogate characters from the play without feeling they are at any point being returned to the classroom.

A brief example from one of the most innovative, and controversial, TIE programmes in the 1970s may help to make the point about how programmes can sustain the imagery, dramatic tension and complexity *through* the participation without subsiding into teaching a lesson or preaching a message. *Pow Wow* was a fully interactive piece about racism for six- and seven-year-olds,[8] designed around stories of the Wild West (a more popular genre with children in the 1970s than now). The children first meet a cowboy, Tex, who in the classroom recounts the story of the pioneering days of pushing back the frontiers and the battles with the 'redskins', prior to their being taken to the school hall to watch Tex's 'Black Elk Show'. They witness a Native American Indian sitting before a small tepee within a padlocked cage, who then – at Tex's commands – demonstrates the ancient customs of his tribe. Later, in the temporary absence of Tex, the Indian is released from his cage with the help of the children and proceeds to show them aspects of the 'real' story of Indian life (the reliance on and respect for the land, for example). Two sharply conflicting pictures of the American West therefore emerge which the children have to deal with when Tex returns angrily to find Black Elk out of the cage. Tex and Black Elk agree to allow the children to help resolve the stand-off, each confident of their support. The children vote on who should keep the artefacts that Black Elk has kept secret from his employer: the pipe of peace, the tomahawk and the ancient map of his village. The vote is open and the teacher is under instruction not to influence the outcome; the script allows for two alternative endings. (See plates 9 and 10).

Plate 9 *Pow Wow.* Belgrade TIE Company, 1973. Black Elk inside the cage.

Plate 10 *Pow Wow.* Tex returns to discover Black Elk outside the cage.

Within the shifting 'promenade' staging of *Pow Wow*, therefore, is contained the strong pictorial image of the Indian imprisoned in his cage which the children view from the single standpoint of a conventional audience, the physical participation involved in learning about the 'Indian''s way of life, and also the highly disturbing imagery which they find themselves part of at the end, caught almost literally in the cross-fire between cowboy and 'Indian'.

These and other like images are powerful and resonant of meaning, immediately accessible to the children's understanding, no matter which of the varied positions they may be seen from – because in each of these cases the positioning of the children is crucially important, planned and carefully staged: being in the midst of the action does not mean being deprived of a controlled perspective upon it. It does not involve the wholesale elimination of distance. Finding oneself surrounded by the action, in the midst of two diametrically opposed viewpoints, may well provide a vivid, almost tangible grasp of the dialectical relationship of those arguments and of one's own, uneasy position between them – not least because that position requires an immediate response. Moreover, the imagery and feelings generated can be recalled and reflected upon long after the event. This is not of course to claim that all immersive theatre experiences of this kind are invariably capable of achieving this particular mix of active involvement and controlled imagery. It is all too easy to mistake frenetic activity for purposeful participation, facile enjoyment for the deeper experience that can be at once enjoyable, challenging and capable of changing understanding. It is a rare programme that achieves such a blend.

For a variety of reasons, philosophic and economic, many companies during the late 1980s and into the 1990s moved themselves closer to the pedagogic practices of classroom drama as advocated by Dorothy Heathcote, Gavin Bolton and others. In part this was a response to the perceived need to ensure a degree of *critical* distance, an opportunity to reflect *within* the programme. Indeed, even by the late 1970s, some TIE work had been showing signs of becoming formula-bound: the participation reliant upon well-tried fail-safe techniques and, especially with the younger age groups, upon the heightened emotional state of the children who could be all too easily led into predictable decision-making. Thus, just as the classroom drama teacher generally saw herself as 'facilitator' of the children's own dramatic explorations and would often, at carefully chosen moments, switch in and out of role to move the drama on, to challenge pupils' thinking and deepen their experience (Bolton 1998, Heathcote 1984, Wagner 1999), so many TIE teams experimented with techniques equivalent to teacher-in-role. At least one member of the team might act as facilitator to 'freeze' the drama at key moments and encourage pupils to discuss and analyse what they had just witnessed. But, while the teacher may comfortably switch back and forth between facilitation and taking on a character, the classroom context will be of course significantly different for an incoming TIE company who cannot hope to do the same job as the teacher who knows the class and its individual needs and abilities (see Bolton 1993).

It is important here to stress that, whatever the format of the participation programme, the TIE team are outsiders. They cannot know the children and their individual needs, and they are on the pupils' territory. It is *as* strangers – as artists – that they can do something crucially different from the teacher. The actor-teachers can provide that 'counter-environment', that controlled, stimulating, theatrically conceived meeting ground – can invite the pupils to contract in, willingly – so that the event can operate at many different levels, narrative, affective and intellectual, and a genuine, shared exploration of issues can take place. The effective TIE team plays to its own distinct strengths; and, unless the difference from classroom teaching is acknowledged and properly signalled, the theatrical stimulus can all too easily get lost amidst inappropriate 'teacherly' techniques. The impulse to want to make explicit statements or to 'sum up' or underline the learning points (a process of cognitive force-feeding) can be difficult to resist, especially when preparing the ground for the children having to make decisions or express views. Over-distancing of the teacherly kind carries the risk of undermining the provocative power and imaginative richness of the metaphor. At those pivotal learning points, as much as at other more obviously theatrical points, it is crucial that TIE sustains its aesthetic momentum. Indeed the educational outcome will be richer and more potent for so doing.

It may be helpful to think of the experience of watching an educational theatre event (whether involving full-scale 'integral' participation or more modest 'extrinsic' participation – see O'Toole 1976) as operating within an *aesthetic framework*, one that embraces the totality of the performance event: the artistry of the performance and the response of the audience. It is this framework, created by the artists involved, that allows actors and audience to meet on metaphoric ground. It becomes even more imperative when the audience has little or no prior experience of live theatre and when the methods of approach involve active participation of some kind – a feature that can for many be unnerving, full of risks, not least of losing face in front of one's peers, and a disincentive to engage. It can be created anywhere (conventional theatre space, school hall or classroom), but its effectiveness will be dependent upon a number of conditions. In particular, there has to be clarity in the ways in which the purpose of the event and the mode in which it operates are signalled to the audience. How the action is 'framed' for us and our points of view established require consistency and sharpness of focus. Secondly, there needs to be, however initiated and however signalled (implicitly or explicitly), an unwritten contract (or agreement) between performers and audience that the event should take place in such a space and in such a way (the original meaning of artistic convention). And thirdly, the physical layout of the space must be appropriate: the arrangement of chairs in relation to the performance space, checking for adequate sight-lines, are as important, if not more so, as the design of the set. The way space is configured and used will directly affect the actor–audience relationship. And aesthetic distance itself can moreover be qualified, sometimes even be determined, by the physical distance between performance and audience spaces. The aesthetic framework, connecting all the key elements of the theatrical event, provides the conditions through which our perceptions and our response can form themselves, enabling us to be fully open to the event and allowing us that degree of pleasure, absorption and heightened awareness, even at the most disturbing moments of the performance. If the conditions are right, we are then in a position to gain a different, more richly distanced perspective on the world we inhabit and take for granted.

Augusto Boal offers a further way of accounting for this framework by setting the notion of distance within what he calls 'aesthetic space'. In *Rainbow of Desire* (1995) he uses this term to refer to the space in which theatre occurs: whether the platform of a conventional theatre or the metaphorical platform which will exist in any kind of performance event, be it ritual, carnival or street theatre. In his later book, *Legislative Theatre* (1998: 72), Boal expands on this idea, speaking of aesthetic space as the area of performance where the action is most 'intense', where 'objects no longer carry only their usual daily signification'. Moreover, 'aesthetic space is the creation of the audience' (p. 71), requiring their 'attentive gaze in a single direction for this space to become 'aesthetic'; he speaks of this space as one of 'enchantment' and 'magic', one that is 'hot', 'powerful' and 'five-dimensional' – that is, it consists of the three physical dimensions plus the subjective ones of imagination and memory (p. 74).

There is then more to this notion of aesthetic space than simply the place of performance, created as much by the gathering of the audience as by the actors. For Boal, the act of theatre involves the creation of 'a separation . . . between the space of the actor and the space of the spectator' (1995: 18). Often there will be an actual platform to delineate that separation but it is by no means necessary. It simply has to be clear that there are one or more people present whose task will be to perform for us and whose role is distinct from that of the spectators. It can happen in informal community venues and inside or out, even on street corners, as well as in conventional auditoria. The psychological and physical worlds of the actor and the spectator will necessarily be distinct in a number of key respects – because, for example, at the beginning of the performance event the actors have come already prepared with scripts learnt and possible scenarios rehearsed, they are already present when the audience arrive; whereas the spectator arrives with, at most, expectations that will be tested by what unfolds. Through the performance, however, those worlds can be brought together in a dialectical relationship, through metaphor, through story, through a shared interest in the outcome of a performed event. It is the 'inter-penetration of these two spaces' which, for Boal, then constitutes the 'aesthetic space' (Boal 1995: 18). Aesthetic space, then, implies a bridge between the two worlds: a communication involving not only the signals emitted by the actor to an audience but the reverse too: a series of responses that will be detected either implicitly (body language, degree of concentration) or explicitly (laughter, perhaps even verbal replies to questions asked by the actors). Moreover, while the actor and the spectator are normally two people, they can also, sometimes, coincide in the same person – hence the notion of the 'spect-actor' and the possibility that actors and spectators can share the same aesthetic space and yet simultaneously be conscious of the distinction between the fictive and the real (*metaxis*). The aesthetic space is, moreover, 'dichotomic' and it 'creates dichotomy': the actor is 'who he is and who he seems to be' (p. 23). He is 'here and now, in front of us, but he is also far away from us, in another place, in another time'. Likewise, for the spectators, 'we are here, seated in this very room, and at the same time we are in the castle at Elsinore' (p. 23). This 'doubleness' lies at the heart of theatre and for Boal is part of its aesthetic and therapeutic power (p. 24). While Boal does not in this essay refer to aesthetic distance *per se*, it is clear none the less that our consciousness of being simultaneously present and elsewhere, made possible by the aesthetic space, constitutes for him what we have been calling aesthetic distance. Aesthetic distance may therefore function as an enabling mechanism, enabling the audience to negotiate its own relationship with the fictional-but-real events as they unfold.

In participatory forms of theatre, the management of this process of negotiation is not as straightforward or as unproblematic as it might at first seem. In forum theatre, much will hinge on the skill of the facilitator (or 'joker') to provide that bridge between fiction and real world, between theatrical performance and active engagement on the part of the 'spectactors', between the signified world and the larger picture. It also presupposes an alert, receptive audience, willing to embark on a journey that is determined by others – by actors or facilitator – who will be far more prepared and (it will seem) knowledgeable than they. The establishment of trust and a process of induction will be vital. Induction may involve (as it often does in Boal's workshops) participation in theatre games, designed to relax and reduce inhibitions and to introduce ways in which imagery, created out of the participants' use of their own bodies, can capture the essence of social tensions and problems (see Boal 1979). Or it may involve informal mixing between performers and audience prior to the performance, or careful signalling during the opening moments of the performance. The work of Geese Theatre offers a useful example of how, in the challenging conditions of prison, actors work to break down barriers, establish a constructive atmosphere and, for specific periods when a performance is required, negotiate into existence a degree of aesthetic distance.

More detailed discussion of Geese's work is provided in Chapter 8, but, in brief, the company's work consists of integrated programmes which combine performance with sustained participatory workshops for prisoners and probationers. When in prisons, their programme will often take the form of three, four or even five day residencies to enable trust to be built and the methods of approach to become familiar and, as far as possible, sustainable beyond the visit itself. As the current Geese director, Andy Watson, explains (interview 2004), the induction process begins before the play itself starts. At the very beginning, as the prisoners come in, the actors are out of role and introduce themselves informally, creating a relaxed atmosphere and establishing the beginnings of a rapport and a building of trust – essential when there is usually very little if any unity among the group (they will all be there for different reasons, often asked to attend while having little real idea of what the event will entail). The informality is largely to communicate to the group, before they 'become' an audience, that no one will be sitting in judgement, or telling them how to run their lives; the company are there 'to pose questions and to listen' (Watson). But this is also designed to be a kind of theatre that is 'really flexible and responsive to whatever comes from them'. As Watson explains, it's partly about 'demystifying theatre': 'we encourage breaking the rules, breaking theatre etiquette'. That does not however mean the elimination of aesthetic distance.

The performance itself will be punchy, humorous and calculatedly provocative. Much use is made of masks (see also Chapter 8) and other non-naturalistic devices in dramatising issues to do with recidivism or the impact upon others of offending behaviour. The skill is in 'making the show and the characters as close to their actual lives and problems as possible *and* in a heightened theatrical way, with a lot of comedy and humour so they don't switch off' (Watson). There is a clear understanding here of the need for an element of aesthetic distance, even if it is not articulated in those terms. The phrase used by both Watson and Simon Ruding, a previous Geese director and now director of the TiPP (Theatre in Prisons and Probation) Centre, Manchester, is 'the one-step-removed approach' (interviews, Watson 2004, Ruding 2004). The central character will be fictional but very close to the situations these prisoners are facing or about to face. The company will not do '*Macbeth* for prisoners' (as some companies do) – Shakespeare's play may be about murder and it may make a valuable contribution to the prisoners' quality of life, but it operates at many steps removed whereas Geese are committed to working intensively with inmates or probationers for whom addressing particular issues is an immediate and direct necessity (Ruding, interview 2004). There is a fine balance that has to be found between the metaphoric function of the story and the direct relevance to the lives of the audience. This does of course place an onus upon the company to 'get the metaphor right'.

The balance is achieved in part through the creation of a world, a set of characters and dilemmas that come straight from the company's own research and experience of working in prisons and in part from the creation of scenarios that have flexibility and responsiveness to particular audiences built in. The characters, in this sense, closely resemble those of *commedia dell'arte*: they are vibrant, alive, and the dialogue is, within the constraints of an agreed scenario, improvised. They are also, on the page, calculatedly stereotypical, or skeletal, in conception; they become fleshed out on the day, in performance, in response to the pre-show informal conversations, and to the mood and the interjections of the audience as the show proceeds. At key points, when the character of the Fool intervenes in the action, to catch the protagonist as he trips up yet again, the dialogue between the two characters is opened up to audience suggestions: what should he do now? Sometimes the advice may be different, even the precise opposite, from that proffered by an audience the previous week: 'You can't do that because . . .' or: the protagonist might lift his mask and say: 'She said this to me and I don't know what to say – what should I say?' In this sense, the audience genuinely become coauthors of the theatre event and of the performance text: 'the characters are created in conjunction with the audience' (Watson). The strategies have the advantage of keeping actors and audience alike on their toes. In the context of improvised and, to some extent, unrehearsable actions, sometimes the actor may be genuinely flummoxed. But the Fool can intervene at any time: 'Stop the show – you can't say that because five minutes ago you said something different . . .' In this way, Geese endeavour to induct their audiences into a theatre event that will be unthreatening and yet provocative: conventions are quickly explained and usually equally quickly understood. But the 'distance' created through the use of masks allows the performance to become at the same time crisp, focused and pulling no punches: not so close to the participants' lives that they feel inhibited or threatened but close enough to be recognisable and productively unsettling.

Aesthetic distance cannot be reduced to a formula which can be applied in a number of permutations to achieve specific effects with specific audiences. It is a problematic notion and requires enormous imagination, understanding of the audience and grasp of artistic forms on the part of the theatre makers, especially in the context of participatory theatre, if it is to be handled well. I want now to turn to the notion of *theatrical frame*, which I hope will extend the ways in which we might understand the functioning of acsthetic distance in this kind of work.

Notes

1 The selection of which TIE programmes to examine has been motivated by the wish to look at a variety of formats, some of which, important and valid as they are, are much less viable financially in today's climate. Discussion of examples from a decade or more ago offers the additional advantages of greater reflective distance and the opportunity to be more critically analytical of practice: the ethical issues involved are significantly reduced by the passage of time. The points raised none the less have continuing relevance to current practice.

2 Among the many notable companies currently offering TIE and related work in the UK, at the time of writing, are: Action Transport (Cheshire), Big Brum (Birmingham), Blah, Blah, Blah (Leeds), Bournemouth TIE, CragRats (Yorkshire), GYPT (Greenwich & Lewisham Young People's Theatre), Language Alive and Catalyst (at the Playhouse, Birmingham), M6 Theatre (Greater Manchester), Nottingham Roundabout, the Schools Company at the West Yorkshire Playhouse (Leeds), Y Touring (London); in Ireland, TEAM (Dublin) and Graffiti (Cork); and in the United States, the Creative Arts Team in New York. Space does not allow a full listing of the many other excellent companies in the UK and elsewhere.

3 See for example Angus Calder (1992), *The People's War: Britain, 1939–45*; E. Royle, *Modern Britain: a social history 1750–1985* (1988).

4 Within a few months, Priestley's broadcasts had built up an unprecedented following and it was estimated that around 40 per cent of the adult population in Britain was listening to the programme (see www.spartacus.schoolnet. co.uk/2WWpostscripts.htm, last accessed 4 August 2006). Extracts from the BBC sound archives can also be heard via the National Media Museum in

Bradford, at: www.bbc.co.uk/bradford/content/articles/2006/07/14/wired_
listen_up_feature.shtml (last accessed 25 August 2006).
5 See especially Bolton 1998, Hornbrook 1989, Somers 1996.
6 See especially O'Sullivan (2001) and Nicholson (2005) for recent critiques of
  Boal's practice. Nicholson has shown how Boal's method hovers uneasily
  between a belief in human beings as social animals, valuing collective action,
  and a focus upon the liberation of the individual.
7 The example sometimes given (see http://tip.psychology.org/festinge.html,
  last accessed 1 July 2006) is of someone who buys an expensive car but dis-
  covers that it is not comfortable on long drives. Dissonance exists between
  their beliefs that they have bought a good car and that a good car should be
  comfortable. Dissonance could be eliminated by deciding that it does not
  matter since the car is mainly used for short trips (reducing the importance of
  the dissonant belief) or focusing on the car's strengths such as safety, appearance, handling (thereby adding more consonant beliefs). The dissonance
  could also be eliminated by getting rid of the car, but this behaviour is a lot
  harder to achieve than changing beliefs.
8 Devised by Belgrade TIE in 1973. In many ways, it was a problematic programme (it allows the children to believe the characters are real rather than
  fictional, until the debriefing with the teacher at the end), but, in its day, it was
  boundary-breaking in its commitment to dealing, imaginatively, with racism
  with children of such a young age, and became highly influential.

6

Positioning the audience: framing the drama

In their placing of the audience within, sometimes centrally within, the theatrical frame, and in their reliance for much of their power and efficacy upon their interactive nature, TIE and other forms of participatory theatre have been notoriously difficult to pin down in conventional terms. They would, for example, seem to fail one of Jurij Lotman's requirements of an 'artistic text', namely that its structure should not be subject to change (Lotman 1977). Likewise, such theatre forms challenge the assumptions of some earlier semiotic theorising about theatre (for example, Elam 1980, Esslin 1987, Aston and Savona 1991) which, for the most part, presuppose a *fixed* theatrical frame, one which, having been set, will predispose its audience to view and 'read' the performance according to a given set of unified 'codes' consistently from start to finish. Much of the success with which theatrical communication takes place will then depend upon the degree of audience competency in being able to decipher those codes. While semiotic theory has provided us with many of the analytic tools with which to analyse conventional theatre, its limitations have become increasingly evident, particularly in relation to areas such as physical theatre, improvised theatre and participatory theatre where 'text' is often, almost by definition, an unstable entity.[1] But the difficulties do not absolve us from at least attempting to propose and test methods of accounting for forms of theatre that lie further away from the accepted norms of what theatre is taken to be.

How then *does* one analyse a TIE performance or a forum theatre event in such a way as to include simultaneously both the interactivity and the aesthetic framework of the event? Can such theatre forms legitimately claim to be considered aesthetic projects? This is not merely an academic quibble, to be dismissed as irrelevant to the work on the ground ('If it works, it works' or 'if it's any good you'll just *know*' or 'what matters is how much the pupils learn', and so on). It actually affects the attitude and approach of those who design, direct and perform these programmes, and likewise influences the way we argue for the validity and efficacy of this work to 'clients' and to funders. If theatre is only the sugar on the pill, maybe it can be done without or with reduced funding and little attention given to the artistry of the project. Other, cheaper kinds of sweeteners can be found.

Consider for example the function of the 'workshop', a frequently used means of moving from conventional play to interaction with the audience. At its worst, it can be little more than an optional extra, bolted on to the end of an otherwise straightforward piece of theatre with little attempt to relate the two: we move in effect from theatre to classroom. At its best, the play will need the workshop to complete the educational process it has begun. Dilemmas and other kinds of unresolved actions, or actions that result in tragedy that might have been avoided, will have been established and cry out for resolution, analysis or consideration of alternatives. The workshop itself will be conducted within a theatrical context, often with actors both in role and as 'facilitators'; critical moments from the play may be rerun for closer investigation and perhaps for reworking as the audience begin to offer alternative routes for the characters to take. But in such workshops, we have to examine very carefully how exactly we use the theatre elements and how we balance the theatre with the 'teaching'. All too often, the theatricality (if any) can become lazily executed, with ill-prepared actors playing to the gallery or skewing their work to the openly didactic; or the facilitator will be an actor who would really rather be acting, or will also be the stage manager, the assumption being that this role has little or no aesthetic function: she or he just needs to chair and control and ensure the message is not lost. In these circumstances, in my experience, the pupils will find they have a diluted experience theatrically and an ineffective, or even counter-productive, experience educationally. TIE will be effective educationally only *if* it's effective aesthetically.

The uniqueness of any theatre experience derives in large measure from the essential part played by an audience in making that experience happen. My argument here is that participatory theatre such as TIE has a full claim to being considered not only the product of artistic intent but a full aesthetic experience, even when, or especially when, the conventional divide between actor and audience is removed. Indeed, the very audience participation that is so central to TIE must be seen as part of that aesthetic; the actor/audience divide may appear to have been eradicated but the 'specialness' of the artistic form remains – not in a blur and not in occasional moments but through a carefully contrived set of frames in which not only the actors but the pupils too can be both immersed in and detached from the action.[1]

Although it may seem to violate Lotman's notion of an artistic text as an entity that *in essence* cannot change from performance to performance, we must also be clear that the changes that do take place – often of a physical, active kind, involving amendments to the script and the stage action at certain key moments as the audience intervene – are none the less planned in. The actual form they may take from performance to performance and from school to school may vary, but the whole *raison d'être* of the programme is that those interventions should happen: they are not accidental, random, uncontrollable, anarchic. In a sense they are the logical extension of what Wolfgang Iser has called 'indeterminacies' or the 'gaps' in the text, necessary if any creative engagement with the work is to be possible. (See Chapter 7 for a fuller discussion of these 'creative gaps'.)

Theatrical frame

In trying to describe and analyse a participatory performance in such a way as to account for the aesthetic dimension of the event, Erving Goffman's notion of 'frame' offers a potent and helpful tool. In his book *Frame Analysis* (1974), Goffman, building on the sociological perspectives of Bateson (*Steps to an Ecology of Mind*, 1973), analyses the way in which all kinds of social encounters are given shape and meaning by the 'frames' that we construct around them, or that are indirectly constructed for us as part of the cultural context in which we live. These frames enable us to decipher the codes of behaviour of other individuals or of the social rituals being enacted (in classrooms, conferences, churches and coronations, to mention but a few). The most obvious theatrical analogy is the traditional practice in western theatre of framing the acting area by a proscenium arch and darkening the auditorium such that during a performance only the action within the frame can be seen, giving heightened significance to whatever signs are generated on stage. But of course frame has connotations beyond the merely technical one of the physical, visible frame. It is often used to describe a key feature of any performed work of art – that which makes it art rather than the flux of everyday life. In this respect, one might argue that it is one of the building blocks in the creation of aesthetic distance (as discussed in the previous chapter). Theatrical frame could then be said to consist of the boundary line, visible or invisible, that theatre artists deliberately draw around the piece of experience that they wish to highlight or to examine. That boundary line enables the artist (writer, director and/or performer)

to craft the action within it in ways that intensify and give particular significance to aspects of human experience. It may be defined by the raised
stage area of the Noh theatre, or the torchlit area reserved for a Kathakali
performance in a Hindu temple, or the cleared space at the front of a
classroom. Within the defined space will be enacted not 'real life' but versions of real life (whether highly stylised or naturalistic), convention-
alised and depending upon the willing contracting-in of the spectators:
the 'willing suspension of disbelief' of the audience.

   All of this is well-trodden ground. But the particular usefulness of the
notion of 'frame' is twofold. Firstly, its applicability to social behaviour
in general and in a variety of manifestations prompts us to test whether
there might also be a variety of different types of frame *within* the theatre
event – in other words, there may be *more than just one frame in play* as
we follow the action from moment to moment. Secondly, it reminds us
that, just as in framing a shot with a camera, we have to account not only
for what is contained within the frame but for the *point of view of the
onlooker* too – the angle of the camera, the depth of field, the distance
from the object and so on. In identifying the frame we must inevitably
consider the position of the audience in relation to it – their point of view,
and the attitude to the events that may be implicit in the frame. Just as
in cinema, we may ask whose eyes the camera represents from moment
to moment, so, in theatre, the director guides, if he or she does not
dictate, our gaze. Where is the protagonist in relation not only to the
other characters on stage but to the audience as well? There is a potentially significant frame-shift in *Hamlet* Act I Scene 2, from our seeing the
prince framed within the public setting of the Court to the suddenly
deserted, apparently private setting for his highly personal 'Oh, that this
too too sullied flesh' soliloquy just moments later, witnessed only by the
audience. In any play, how the set is arranged on stage and the spatial
groupings and relationships of the characters, together with the physical
staging style (proscenium or 'open' for example) will signal to the audience the kind of relationship they have to what is going on. We are positioned in relation to the world presented on stage, and the viewpoint and
perspective offered to us may shift from scene to scene. It is may be possible, then, to analyse TIE and similar styles of theatre, including the
interactive components, by close attention to the frames in operation
from moment to moment – and by extension to the sign-systems at work
within each of those frames, and from frame to frame.

   Though there are many permutations of this form of analysis (see
Bennett 1990, Esslin 1987, Heathcote 1980, Jackson 1997, O'Toole
1992, Schechner 2002), broadly these frames might be summarised thus.
Firstly, the event takes place within an *external, or cultural, frame* that

provides (usually) an institutional context within which the event will be 'read' and understood – thus, the school or theatre studio or prison classroom or museum gallery.[2] Secondly, there is the *theatrical frame* – that which marks out the theatre event itself *as* theatre and signals where and how the audience will position itself and behave (for example, via its formal seating or 'promenade' setting, its proscenium or in-the-round staging, use of lighting, etc.). These frames can, I suggest, be extended further to include a number of *internal frames* within the performance that establish the kinds of dramatic conventions that will operate: they constitute the framing devices used to signal shifts of time, place, character, and relationship with the audience.

Speaking of conventional theatre, Goffman draws a distinction between 'theatregoer' and 'onlooker' (Goffman 1974: 129–30). The theatregoer is the social role we play on our way, or settling ourselves down, to watch the play, full of expectation and knowing at least some of the conventions that will operate. In semiotic terms we are already equipped culturally to decipher the 'external codes' that the performance relies upon to function effectively – such as the darkening of the auditorium, the picture-frame stage, the use of naturalism in the acting and writing, given the predominance of this mode and the popular acceptance that that this is how most plays work. We are prepared but we are not yet onlookers: we become onlookers once the performance proper has begun and we engage with the events on stage. For the purpose of developing a model appropriate to interactive theatre, I will link Goffman's theatregoer role with the notion of what I am calling the 'cultural (or pre-theatre) frame' in TIE: the preparation for the event by teacher or actor out-of-role (or facilitator) in which the learning project is explicitly articulated and conventions that need to be understood in advance are intimated (for example, 'you will meet actors in role, in costume, who will address you as though you were people from the 1890s; but you don't need to act, just be yourselves, answer in your own way: try to remember some of the things we've been learning about the period and just let yourselves get drawn into the actions as they happen'). The pupils become 'onlookers' when the first actor appears: the start of the first frame, the (outer) theatrical frame that will govern the way in which the event as a whole will work. They are expectant but not yet full participants: the action will have to draw them in in ways that stimulate, persuade, challenge but also provide those essential gaps in the action that invite genuine participation. ('Onlooker' is not the ideal term to conjure up the audience's active engagement with the events on stage, but, because it serves to indicate the significant shift in the positioning of the audience compared with being theatregoers, one that suggests a settled

attentiveness upon the action within the frame, I will for now retain
Goffman's terminology.)

In one key respect, however, I do depart from Goffman. Referring to
traditional styles of theatre performance, Goffman describes the relationship between onlooker and performance as one in which the 'central
understanding' is that 'the audience has neither the right nor the obliga-
tion to participate directly in the dramatic action occurring on the stage'
(Goffman 1974: 125). This is of course the norm and it is on this premise
that Langer's argument about symbolic form in the theatre is built (see
Chapter 5). But if one allows for the possibility that a more complex set
of framing devices may exist within the dominant outer theatrical frame,
then direct participation can be seen to have its place. The frames that
are subsequently brought into play will, within the overall, outer framework, help to ensure that the aesthetic dimension is in place and that the
pupils are clear enough about what is expected of them to be able to take
part *on terms they understand*. In participatory theatre we are of course
not merely looking on, no matter how involving an experience that can
be; our *active response* will be crucial for the drama to work. Only if the
actors – through the framing strategies deployed – signal that fact sufficiently to the audience is that response likely to be forthcoming.

I have tried to identify in diagrammatic form the different kinds of
framing that often occur in TIE (see Figures 2 and 3).[3] It is important to
realise that these frames are in a sense windows through which we as
spectators view the action *but* they are not rigid or separate entities: the
boundary-lines are not always visible and the audience may not always
be fully conscious of their existence. The switch from one to another may
sometimes be announced, at other times it may be implicit. One may be
activated as another closes, and two may be in play simultaneously, often
one constituting an outer (or holding) frame, the other the inner or active
frame.

There are two diagrams: one summarising the larger, outer framework
of theatre convention following a strict sequence of frames as the audience encounter them; the second focusing in on the internal frames that
are likely to operate during the course of the performance, but not in any
necessary sequence. Diagram 1 attempts to show the interconnectedness
of all such frames. Both diagrams attempt to characterise each frame in
terms of the two main complementary aspects: (1) the actions and images
that are placed *within the frame*; and (2) the points of view, the *relationship to the frame*, of the audience-participants. In other words, they
indicate the positioning of the audience in relation to the events taking
place within the frame, including those sequences when the audience is
itself within the frame. Different types of programmes will use different

FRAME	ACTION WITHIN FRAME	STUDENTS' POINT OF VIEW / ROLE
A. The Cultural (or Pre-Theatre) Frame	The explicit and implicit preparation for the drama that may be done by the teacher or actor out of role (or stage-manager) and is usually curriculum-oriented. It may happen in or just outside the performance space and in the moments (or even several days) before the event begins.	Students as students, preparing for a clearly-defined learning project, sanctioned by their institution. (Includes their expectations and assumptions derived from the larger cultural context).
B. The Outer Theatrical Frame	The establishment of the theatrical space and conventions that will apply, usually done by first actor to appear (or facilitator) or through use of lights, music, etc. Clear signalling of the start of the performance. An explicit or implicit process of induction. We step into a different world.	The transitional phase, as they move from 'students' to 'spectators' or 'participants'. They begin to enter into the theatrical contract. A state of expectation predominates.
C. The Inner Frames (involves one or more frame, any of which may come first)		
D. The Closing Frame	The formal end of the overall theatre event and clearly signalled as such, e.g. by speech, music, silence, tableau, lights. Usually a return to Frame B but it may alternatively end with a workshop and close in the Investigative Frame. The actors hand over to the tutors or organisers.	Students aware of their 'onlooker' role. Return to 'school' or institutional context.

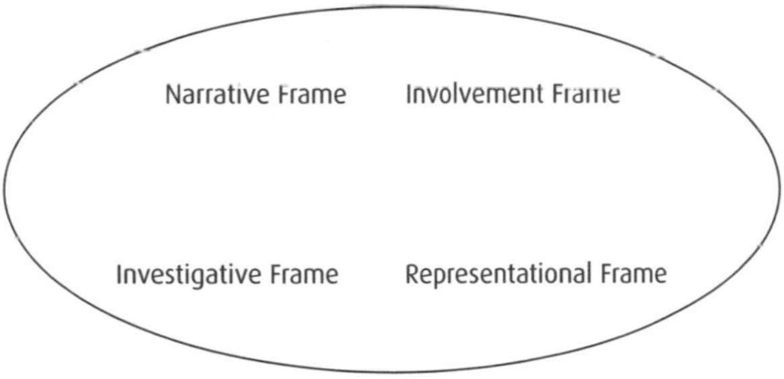

Narrative Frame   Involvement Frame

Investigative Frame   Representational Frame

Figure 2 Framing in educational theatre – the outer framework.

combinations of these frames and in different sequences according to the subject matter and age group involved. Within the diagrams, I have for the sake of brevity referred to the audience-participants as 'students' and, since TIE offers the clearest and widest range of participatory practice,

INNER FRAME (Sequence determined by nature of each programme)	ACTION WITHIN FRAME	STUDENTS' POINT OF VIEW / ROLE
Narrative Frame	Events, background and issues of the drama are introduced and recounted by narrator or facilitator. In story-telling mode, this may form the body of the drama, or it may provide the outer framework of drama and help to establish or reinforce conventions. Also includes direct address by characters within the frame as they advance the plot for us.	As themselves or in role: they are listeners; little interaction at this stage as rapport and trust are built. They do not influence the narrative.
Investigative Frame	Events may either occur in 'real time' with students in midst, or they may be represented as evidence to be analysed and discussed. E.g. a replay of scenes for analysis, interrogation of characters ('hot-seating'), or forum theatre. A facilitator (or 'joker') will usually initiate and link the events.	As themselves or in role (e.g. as 'detectives' or 'journalists') having a task to report on or to investigate events/characters. Often some interaction with characters inside the frame (e.g. 'hot-seating').
Representational (or 'performing-to') Frame	Events representing 'real world' events, enacted by actors in role - characters as in conventional play. Often naturalistic but may be stylised or 'epic'.	Onlookers, as audience, and fully conscious they are watching from a distance, though they may also watch as investigators.
Involvement (or 'performing-with') Frame	Interplay between characters and between characters and students as events unfold. Usually naturalistic and in 'real time'.	As themselves or in role as participants within the frame – interacting and influencing the flow of events, sometimes even the outcome (e.g. via a vote). They may be in the *centre* of the frame, as agents of the action; or within but *at the edge* of the frame, as in a public meeting where they are addressed by characters.

Figure 3 Framing in educational theatre – the inner frames.

drawn on examples from TIE practice to illustrate different aspects of the framing process. Some examples of the framing at work in TIE are given in the subsequent pages.

Theatrical framing in four TIE programmes: *Grounded, Brand of Freedom, Question of Identity, The School on the Green*

Different types of programmes will use different combinations of these frames and in different sequences according to the subject matter and age group involved. A few examples will demonstrate the operation of the frames and their interconnectedness, and the diversity of approach: they are taken from different styles of TIE programme involving different degrees of audience participation – from forum theatre to full-scale 'immersive' participation. The first used a format for the workshop following the play that mixed elements of TIE 'hot-seating' and Boal-inspired replays of short scenes for closer analysis.

A programme mounted for older teenagers, *Grounded* (M6 Theatre, toured in 1994 to classes of fourteen-to fifteen-year-olds), was a fairly straightforward but effective naturalistic piece about teenage sexuality, focussing on the experiences and dilemmas faced by a fourteen-year-old girl as she dates an older boy of whom her parents disapprove and who encourages Joanne to 'go all the way'. There are family rows about staying out late, about her clothes and climactically about her sexual relationship with Adam – intensified by the double dread of pregnancy and AIDS. It culminates, rather predictably but with an uncomfortable logic that was not lost on its audience, in her discovering she is indeed pregnant. What will happen next? A forum-theatre-style workshop then takes place in which key moments from the narrative are rerun and analysed, the students quiz each of the two main characters (girl and boy) and the discussion widens out from the specifics of the narrative to the issues of contraception, abortion, safer sex, relationships with parents and so forth. The performances are 'believable' and the students do not take long before 'contracting-in' to the narrative and subsequently to the workshop. It was a successful programme: teachers *and* health promoters acclaimed it and pleaded for it to be brought back for a second run.

Before the play starts, the 'ethos' of the event has already been established: the creation of an environment and an atmosphere within which everything else will be 'read' and assessed, and of an audience frame-of-mind. The performance will usually be in the school hall, with pupils sitting in no more than four rows of seats which arc round the acting area: they are on their own territory, not that of the actors. There is – deliberately – only a partial concession to the usual requirements of a theatre performance, but just enough to establish that it *is* a performance, it is different, there are clearly (if minimally) delineated acting and audience areas, and it will require a different set of responses from those of the normal classroom. There is a set and recorded music but normal lighting, no stage lights. A short introduction is given, first by one of the teachers and then a member of the company, setting out the purpose of the session and mentioning the workshop that will follow the play. This all constitutes the establishment of the *pre-theatre frame*, although some advance information about the play would have would have been given to pupils and parents several weeks earlier, itself a contribution to pupil expectations and their role as 'theatregoer'. The introduction over, music and the actors taking up position on the set activate the *theatre frame* proper: the performance begins; the students are positioned as the audience. This is clearly a theatre performance and an aesthetic framework has been established. (In Boal's terminology, an 'aesthetic space' exists once the students acknowledge the presence of the actors and the beginnings of a fictional event enacted before them. See Chapter 5.)

More specifically, however, the positioning is quickly given a functional dimension. At the start of the play we see a brief scene between mother and daughter at the clinic, awaiting the results of Joanne's pregnancy test. Unambiguously, we watch through a *representational frame*. Then, before the scene is resolved (before we get to know the test results), the mother gets up and turns to the audience. In effect, through her direct address, as she recalls the events of that day and all that has led up to the current crisis, she reframes the action for us. We are now in a *narrative frame*, and in present time. The clinic scene and most of the subsequent scenes are, we learn, flashbacks – component parts of the evolving story about this particular family and the crises faced, especially by daughter Joanne.

The narration which punctuates the play will contain, direct and – to some extent – interpret the drama for us. The naturalism has already been modified by the direct address convention and the reshuffling of chronological time: clearly this is not to be an uninterrupted, unmediated evolution of events – it helps to reinforce the 'workshop' ethos of having a stage-set within a classroom setting: a frame within a frame. This is important for the culmination of the whole exercise in the workshop. *The workshop*. As soon as the play ends, we are moved straight into a workshop on the themes and issues arising from the play – this offers opportunity for the pupils to be more than just recipients of the drama, to exercise some influence on the characters whom they interview, challenge and advise. Still within the outer *theatre frame* (an important matter; the students are not being returned yet to the classroom), the dominant frame is now the *investigative frame* – established by the facilitator, in this case one of the actors who played a less pivotal role in the play and could thus be more 'neutral'. It is clearly signalled to the students now that they themselves have a distinct role to play – not merely to clarify but to engage with and to test the actions, choices and feelings of the characters (who stay in role throughout). Yet, *even within* the investigative frame, other active frames are brought into play for moments as necessary to advance the investigation – for example, the representational for the rerunning of certain scenes, and, for the pupils who volunteer their physical participation in the forum theatre sequences, the involvement frame. Part way through the workshop there is a rerun of the scene where Joanne and Adam decide after all to 'go all the way'. This time, however, it immediately follows a hot-seating sequence with the pupils and is designed to take on board and try out some of the pupils' suggestions (such as that Joanne should explain to Adam that she doesn't feel comfortable with the situation, or that she's 'not on the pill'). Clearly signalled and sensitively handled, these shifts of frame, which reposition the audience and redefine their role in relation to the drama, serve equally to enhance the learning process and to sustain the aesthetic framework of the event.

In full-scale participation programmes (usually for children up to the age of about eleven, but rather less common now than they were fifteen years ago), the overriding frame is usually the involvement frame. But in order to reach the stage when it can be employed to full effect, it is always necessary to induct the children and take them stage by stage to the point where they are fully 'inside the story', inside the frame, and able to contribute to and learn from the events that take place.

Thus, *Brand of Freedom* (Pit Prop Theatre 1984, toured to the top age groups in primary schools, occasionally to the younger age groups in secondary schools: the ten to twelve year age range) was a classic two-visit programme about the Lancashire Cotton Famine of the 1860s. The story was linked with the contemporaneous slavery issue, based on historically plausible if anecdotal evidence of a female American slave having escaped her bondage by stowing away on a cotton ship sailing to Lancashire and finding work in a textile mill. Different kinds of slavery – and racist attitudes – are encountered on each side of the Atlantic, exacerbated when the cotton deliveries dry up as a result of the American Civil War. The children witnessed first a piece of theatre in the classroom (representational frame) which introduced the themes and characters and stimulated interest in the period. A two- to three-week period followed in which with the class teacher the children carried out research into the period and related it to their own local history, building up at the same time a fictitious but

Plate 11 *Brand of Freedom*. The 'mill workers' pick oakum fibre while assessing the next course of action, Pit Prop Theatre, Wigan, 1984. Pit Prop Theatre Actors: Ray Meredith and Flo Wilson. Director: Cora Williams.

plausible identity for themselves: a role and context which they knew they would be using when the actor-teachers next returned. They were in effect collaborating in setting the elements and broad outlines of the investigative frame that would provide the larger frame that would enclose the dramatic events to come. The culminating session was then wholly participatory. The actor-teachers were in role throughout; the children were wholly inside the story (as 'cotton operatives'). From the moment the first characters arrived in the classroom the involvement frame was dominant. However, as the action progressed and as the children gained confidence in their own roles and views, other frames were momentarily introduced – not to confuse but to clarify and give a sense of direction. Early on, the children in different groups strike up close relationships with specific characters who at quiet moments (often before a dramatic storm) will relate events of the past to explain attitudes in the present, functioning as story-tellers and drawing a narrative frame around the action. At another point a family argument breaks out amidst the community of cotton workers as they struggle with the strains of unemployment; momentarily the children are onlookers, listening intently, watching through a representational frame and gaining insights into the personal nature of the struggle.

By the time the events reach their climax, the children have so fully contracted-in as to be able to intervene and challenge characters who have misled them or persuade others who appear to have less information than do they. Within the involvement frame they achieve a degree of ownership of the events and have a genuine investment in the outcome; they are involved not only cognitively but emotionally too. If the outer, investigative frame seems to have been forgotten by the triumphant end (as fairness wins, at least for the time being), the emotional experience, the detective work and the difficult decisions that they have faced *en route* have been powerful enough to be recalled again and again as the teacher takes over and follows up in the ensuing weeks. There was some criticism at the time that the speed of the narrative and accelerating pressures upon the pupils must have inhibited the kind of detached reflection argued for by Dorothy Heathcote. The team's defence (see Williams interview, 1984) was that the choices and decisions required of the children had to be made under pressure if they were to reflect the reality of the historical situation faced by the cotton operatives (and by implication of any community facing difficult moral and tactical choices at a time of serious social strain). The teacher's role was therefore vital in getting the children to reflect – after the programme had finished and outside the particular dramatic framings deployed.

Also addressing racism, and in a less than obvious way, was a full-scale forum theatre programme, *A Question of Identity*, devised in 1992 by Greenwich Young People's Theatre for teenagers in south London.[4] Boal's rationale and methodology for forum theatre work (discussed in Chapter 5) are well known. Here, however, I will suggest a way in which forum can be seen to operate in terms of the principal frames in operation: the representational and the investigative, and to a lesser extent the involvement frames. The play at the heart of the programme was performed as part of a whole-day event and followed a brief introductory 'real context' (or 'pre-theatre frame') workshop during which pupils in small groups considered a number of questions to do with identity and social labelling. (The three key questions that the whole programme was to address were identified as: 'What gives us our sense of identity? How do we define ourselves? How does one affect the other?') When the students then sat down to watch the play – concerning the experience of racial prejudice faced by three young people from different ethnic backgrounds – there were two frames in operation. The primary one was the representational frame, the students' own role being that simply of onlookers; and a secondary one, the investigative frame deriving from the preliminary workshop and the tacit briefing they had been given: to carry the questions about identity with them *as they watched*. They knew that watching the play was an integral part of their investigation of those issues. Interestingly, racism as such was not the explicit issue: if it had been, the wrong kind of preconceptions and stereotyped notions might have been carried into the watching of the play. Care in setting not only the agenda but also the students' expectations of what the play would deal with was a crucial part of establishing the frame.

The sharp delineation of characters and actions within the representational frame – a strong piece of theatre in its own right – was important for the way it engaged at an intense level the attention of the audience and prepared them to engage with the characters in a different way once the play was over. Of course the play was not 'over' in the usual sense. The events were now reframed: the representational frame gave way to the investigative. With the aid of a facilitator, the students began to explore further the issues arising, to request a replay of key moments, to stop the action for detailed examination, to enter the drama themselves to demonstrate alternative ways of dealing with the pressures faced by the oppressed figure at the centre of the drama. But the representational frame also remained in place: the students themselves could step inside and outside the frame as the occasion (or their own insights, curiosity or passion) demanded. The inside of the frame was now subject to constant readjustment and refocusing as the events and characters' attitudes and behaviour were remoulded or redirected in an attempt to find ways round or to ameliorate the seemingly intractable dilemmas faced. At any one moment there were likely to be at least two frames in operation. For the student who chose to step into the shoes of Tim, the British Asian youth at the centre of the drama, the involvement frame was in place as she confronted the racist behaviour of other characters, underpinned also by the outer, investigative frame. For the rest of the class, the investigative frame also contained within it a renewed representational frame as they watched the confrontation being acted through.

The framing device itself, foregrounded as a device, and therefore by definition changeable, encouraged the students to use the theatre to explore, deepen and clarify their understandings of these aspects of the real world – and perhaps to understand something of the way real life itself is framed for us (often with our tacit collusion) by the social processes of which we are a part. We cannot change social processes overnight, but by understanding that our attitudes, prejudices and behaviour are to a considerable degree 'constructed' by the cultural values and systems around us, that they are not natural, universal or timeless, we may at least see the point of questioning our assumptions and rethinking our own attitudes and actions as a result.

By contrast, *The School on the Green* was a programme aimed at eight- to eleven-year-old children, which examined issues of education and schooling through focus upon the actual events that led up to the

Burston School strike of 1914. The company at the time described it as a 'fusion of presentational and participatory theatre' (GYPT 1987). The pre-frame 'real context' session took place in the classroom during which the four actor-teachers, out of role, met the children to introduce themselves, the material and some of the dramatic conventions that were to be used: notably that of the 'tableau' (or 'freeze-frame': the momentary stopping and unstopping of the action as it unfolded). Some discussion of the children's own ideas about school also took place. The children then transferred to the hall. The drama began – and the first frame was initiated – when they were called together on to the 'Green' (a circle of green carpet) and an actor-teacher 'became' Dossy (the narrator/character who recalls her memories of 1914) 'by putting on the Dossy costume and going into character in front of their eyes' (GYPT 1987: 63). The narrative frame switched quickly to the representational as a series of brief acted-out episodes established the situation in the village and the impact of the two new teachers with their 'new-fangled' ideas. The action was then halted as one of the actor-teachers took on the role of facilitator and initiated a new frame, the investigative. Having at first been addressed as children in their own right, not in role, they now became endowed with the primary role of 'investigators' – they remained themselves (not in character) but with a specific, agreed task: to find out more about a series of strange and perplexing events that happened in an English village in 1914. They knew that the events had actually happened and that they had been significant in the lives of the community for a generation or more; and they were given to understand that the events also posed questions still relevant to their own lives (such as 'what and who is education for?' and 'how best do we learn?'): this was not just a history lesson.

Each of the subsequent six scenes represented not only different stages in the narrative and different aspects of the problem under scrutiny but also different theatrical conventions and different actor–audience relationships: different frames of action. Thus in scene 1 the children are conventional spectators, watching the confrontation between Tom Higdon, the new teacher, and Farmer Sterne who refuses to let his daughter attend school because he needs her labour, from a relatively neutral position (representational frame). The scene finishes and the actors momentarily 'freeze'. With the investigative frame now to the forefront, the children discuss the events witnessed. In scene 4 they are participants in the drama – schoolchildren of the time. The events are part of the same narrative as the previous scene but experienced now from the inside: the 'involvement frame'. In the culminating section (after the historical narrative has been completed) a situation is created in which the children take on the role of parents who must debate the pros and cons of the 'child-centred' teaching methods employed by the 'subversive' teachers and whether or not to support the strike initiated by the pupils: the involvement frame again but with heightened engagement since the children are now not just inside the frame but at its dramatic centre. Underpinning all of these framing devices was the investigative frame. Sometimes it constituted an outer frame within which was contained the inner representational or involvement frames; sometimes it overrode any other frame as scenes were frozen and actions discussed. Again it was through these framing strategies that the artistic process – and its full value in engaging the children and stimulating their desire to know more – came to be at one with the programme's educational aims. Just as the framing devices were introduced, modified, replaced and reinstated according to the varied needs of the investigation, so the degree of aesthetic distance between the drama and the children increased and diminished, without ever being eliminated.

The external world and 'meaning through form'

If framing helps to underline the pedagogic processes in such theatre practices – in particular the kinds of performer–spectator dynamic that intensify and sharpen the learning experience – does it help us in defining the experience as art? It may do if we recognise that the overriding aesthetic in educational, participative theatre is to ensure that whatever the programme is 'about', whatever it is trying to 'teach', must *in some way* be contained within the artistic frame or frames of the drama. While those frames may be interrupted or subverted for specific pedagogic or artistic aims – in for example an attempt to step 'outside' the drama, to derole, and reflect, before returning to the fictitious world of the play – this has to be done with immense care and attention to the artistic whole. If, as sometimes happens, the frames are interrupted in order to *explain* to the children what they have to learn at this point, then the richness of the artistic stimulus is undermined.

This is not to say that the outside 'real' world has to be kept at bay and the fictive world somehow insulated: cosy, secure and neat. Far from it. TIE, forum theatre and prison theatre even more so, will always be at one level or another about the 'real world' and more often than not about the need for change, pressing constantly towards the making of connections between the fictional and the actual. But it can be all too tempting for a company to want to make their meaning explicit before they go lest participants may be under any misapprehension and the point of the programme lost. As Louis Arnaud Reid has pointed out, in his discussion of the philosophical premises on which the arts in education should be based, 'mere referential meaning will not do . . . the full meaningfulness of any work of art is never found simply by referring to something else'. It is to do with finding in the work of art 'something immediate, of intrinsic significance and importance . . . so embodied in what I perceive as a unique and particular and individual thing that I can never say, never translate exactly into (other) terms . . . what the meaning-embodied is' (Reid 1980: 2–3). I take this to imply not a reification of art, in which meanings are pre-set and transmitted intact to its audience, but art as a construct whose meaning will emerge (in theatre contexts) from the coming together of its participants, actors and audience. The meaning has to be made and experienced within the drama. Thus, if the meaning of a TIE piece can be translated just as well into rational terms and the programme is little more than sugaring the moral pill, or illustrating the history or English lesson, then it will have failed aesthetically, that is, failed to have embodied the meaning in the drama. In other words, the piece will not be communicating and transforming in the way that art has the power to do. The message may be clear but it may also be as easily dismissed or forgotten as it was received. Indeed, the medium and the message may even be at odds, producing a self-cancelling effect. The play whose message is 'bullying is wrong' yet inadvertently presents the bully as bad but theatrically exciting is one obvious example.

Reid's argument becomes more problematic for those educational plays designed to be directly about, and to engage with the real contemporary world, where the whole point of the exercise is to use the drama as a stepping stone back into that real world; to use the plays as a means of intervention in that world. Interactive workshops and lively discussion of the play just seen and of its implications, its connections with the here and now of the participants' own lives, characterises much educational work of the last thirty years, in schools, prisons and museums. The boundary lines between the world of the play and the world of the audience are necessarily permeable. Thus, Geese follow their performance of *Gutted* (a play about the troubles and tribulations of a recidivist) with small-group discussions led by the actors who have completely and explicitly deroled. The work moves from theatrical and provocative stimulus to out-of-role group discussion and drama-based workshops in order to enable participants to reflect on the issues raised and to begin to apply the questions and insights to their own lives. Inevitably, some of the points made in the play will be translated into explicit and digestible messages by the participants. But there is also a reason why Geese use overtly theatrical presentations to begin their sessions, including masks, set, music and a distinct acting area. No matter how much the theatre may be seen as a means to an end, as a stimulus for subsequent discussion and roleplay exercises, the company readily acknowledge that the power of theatre resides in something workshops alone cannot provide: its shock value, its representation of patterns of behaviour and dilemmas faced in the real world in a deliberately non-realistic style – energetic, colourful, visually arresting, dangerous in its yoking together of 'realistic' street banter and taunts with performance in the *commedia dell'arte* style. Performance and workshop operate symbiotically; and the theatre performance situated close to the beginning of the session provides an overarching theatre frame which situates the workshops and discussions in a clearly less institutional atmosphere, making them likely to be more open to genuine interaction, challenge and reflection than had the workshops been offered as free-standing events.

The educational ends of any dramatic performance must however be encompassed by the form itself, must not *rely* upon explanations from outside, whether from actors out of role or from tutor once the programme is ended. The drama must certainly allow for, contain, indeed introduce, those elements of the outside world directly relevant to the programme; but they must be contained in such a way that they are accessible and communicable to *all* the participants involved. This is not to call for a narrowing of scope but rather for an aesthetic framework that can be flexible and responsive enough to help make sense of those externals *within the drama*, within the set of frames that the art form has at its disposal. Interestingly, a development in TIE increasingly evident in the work of many companies by the mid-1980s was the move away from polemic, from statement, from single-issue programmes (for example programmes *about* the environment or bullying), to those that embraced a number of issues *within* the art form and offered a multi-layered, complex view of the world in the process. Thus a programme such as *Brand of Freedom*, while it certainly dealt with the issue of racism and the associated themes of slavery, prejudice, class and unemployment, could certainly not have been labelled as merely a programme on racism. It was also an exercise for the children in historical research and, not least, a powerful narrative about justice, about exploitation and about ends and means. Questions raised, implicitly, included for example: whether or not all kinds of actions could be justified in the name of personal material well-being; could it be right to earn money from the mill owner to help him support his case against the Unionists when the mill workers were also trying covertly to support the escaped slave in their midst, whose own destiny lay in the success of the Unionist cause?

TIE highlights a characteristic of much contemporary live theatre in that it problematises the conventional divide between actor and audience. We do not yet have a sufficiently developed, or agreed, terminology, analytic method or theoretical framework which enables us to account for what takes place when that boundary line is crossed. Thus, in the case of TIE, the work is often described in terms of *either* education *or* theatre, rarely both together (except in very generalised terms). TIE, in my view, is not a fundamentally different kind of event, educational rather than theatrical. Rather it is at one end of a wide and richly diverse *spectrum of possibilities* of theatrical art. What I have tried to show in this and the previous chapter is that the removal of the *traditional* notion of aesthetic distance in the theatre, the conventional boundary-line between stage and auditorium, does not throw all into confusion, or devalue the art of the theatre or convert it into 'ordinary' classroom teaching. In effective TIE at least, the aesthetic distance will still be there but in a less easily recognisable shape, and in this respect the notion of 'framing' does I think help. The audience does still have a role that is distinct from that of the actors. The participating onlookers (or 'spect-actors' in Boal's words) will watch with critical faculties sharpened because from a carefully positioned standpoint; sometimes find themselves part of the events, taking their lead from the actors-in-role; at other times (and usually at key moments in the drama) they will themselves be in the pivotal role of influencing what happens next. The notion of frame does *not* explain everything, does not solve all the difficulties of aesthetics surrounding this type of theatre – far from it. But it does I believe help to explain the interior shifts that occur within the theatre event; and it can also act as a memo to writers, actors and directors in TIE to take account of how they are positioning their audience in relation to the action, overall and from moment to moment, and to ensure that those shifts are adequately signalled to that audience.

Finally, the model I am offering may also help to underline the fact that, in the best educational theatre practice, the two components of the experience, the educational and the aesthetic, do not compete – the one enables the other. (Therein lies the unique strength of TIE and similar forms: a twin energy that derives from the best intentions of education – to empower the learner to learn; and from the innate power of theatre art to transform our perceptions of the world, even if only for a few hours at a time.

Closely connected to the process of framing is the matter of dialogue. Within the internal frames discussed above, exchanges take place – between characters, between characters and audience (in or out of role themselves), sometimes between actor-facilitators and audience. The dialogic is a key feature of effective educational theatre, and the next chapter will examine the dialogic potential in both plays and participatory programmes.

Notes

1 See for example Melrose (1994), one of the first extended attempts to explore the implications for semiotic analysis of more complex aspects of 'performance text'.
2 This frame is not intended to encompass the far larger idea of cultural context, which governs most of the everyday assumptions, attitudes, beliefs, habits of thought and customs that an audience will take for granted (Bourdieu's 'habitus' 1977).
3 An earlier version of these diagrams was published in 1997 (see Jackson 1997), but the model has been developed and modified since then, largely to make it more sensitive to the range of practice in TIE and related forms.
4 See also Chris Vine (1993) for a discussion of the rationale for using, and adapting, Boal's format.

7

Creative gaps: the didactic and the dialogic

I want now to focus more closely on the part that an audience plays within the aesthetic framework and in particular on the kinds of exchange that can take place between performer and audience/participant. Drawing again on Iser's reader-response model (Iser 1972), it is arguable that in any work of literature there are what Iser calls 'gaps' designed into the writing, indeterminate elements of the fiction that demand to be imaginatively amplified by the reader (p. 216). The aesthetic process does not consist of a one-way traffic, the reader merely deciphering the codes to unlock the full picture: he or she is drawn into an active and creative relationship with the text. The fiction is in a sense there to be completed by the reader. Louise Rosenblatt offers a not dissimilar theory of the reading process (Rosenblatt 2004), in which every reading act is regarded as 'an event, a transaction . . . The "meaning" does not reside ready-made "in" the text or "in" the reader but happens or comes into being during the transaction between reader and text' (p. 1369).

How applicable is such a model to the audience's experience in the theatre? Well, on one level, it might not seem to fit at all. While the reading of a novel is usually a private, individual experience and the room for various interpretations is wide because of the limited outward form of words on a page, leaving much scope for the imagination of the reader, at a theatre performance many of the interpretative decisions have already been taken – by the director, designer and cast. There is therefore less space for creative gaps in at least some aspects of the presentation (Lear is as old or as mad as the actor makes him). And the reception of the play happens collectively in a way that is fundamentally different from that of the novel, leaving even less scope it might seem for the individual's creative participation. But, of course, that is not the whole story. On another level, the audience plays an essential part in making the theatre experience the unique event it always is. It collectively activates the theatre event, and in various ways participates in the making of meanings at both individual and collective levels. A collective response – such as laughter or deadly silence – will undoubtedly affect the response of the individual spectator but will not dictate it. The power of Katrin's drumming at the end of *Mother Courage* or of Falder's growing panic during the solitary confinement scene in *Justice* will be enhanced by its appearing to have the same outward effect upon everyone else in the auditorium, but the meaning we make of it for ourselves is our own and may not correspond exactly with the meanings made by those around us.

Iser's notion of an essential 'indeterminacy' existing in any work of literature is one that is in my view usefully applicable in the case of participatory theatre: 'creative gaps' are formally built in to the very design of such theatre experiences. Thus, in a TIE programme, such as *Pow Wow* or *Brand of Freedom*, the narrative is constructed so as to lead to moments of choice or decision-making – pivotal stages in the plot at which characters and the children in role are faced with two or more ways forward. Collaboratively and individually, the children must decide on the best course of action. Thus, will they vote for Black Elk to keep his secret possessions (the pipe of peace, the tomahawk and the map) or will these be handed over to his employer, Tex? Will the mill workers in *Brand of Freedom* collude with their employer in supporting the cause of the American South for financial gain (given the hardship faced by their adopted characters and families, and knowing that one of the characters in their midst needs money to care for her baby), or will they refuse and thereby support the anti-slavery cause, or might there be a middle way? Difficult ethical questions are raised as an integral part of the narrative and arguments take place before a decision is reached. The danger comes when those 'gaps' are filled by sub-text – when the actors and facilitators have already decided what ought to fill those gaps, when answers from the participants are sought in order to fulfil the programme's objectives, and when leading questions are then asked that in effect invite students to agree that (for example) in the play just seen the hurtful remark addressed to another pupil in order to impress her peers was the first step to bullying.

The aesthetic and the didactic

A genuine work of art, it is often said, cannot be didactic. The novel, play or poem that sets out to convey information or to preach a message risks surrendering those very qualities we usually value in art – complexity, ambiguity, multi-layered meanings, richness of imagination. Trevor Griffiths – the British political playwright who began his working career as a teacher – once argued that the triggering of a debate in the minds of the audience was more important than any message he might wish to convey:

> One of the hard things you learn from teaching is that you can't expect to see results in front of your eyes. It's very heartbreaking but true that shifts in attitude, let alone shifts in behaviour, are relatively slow. I've come to distrust massive dislocations inside the individual psyche; they are usually Pauline and revelatory, and they last about 20 minutes . . . I'll probably never complete a play in the formal sense. It has to be open at the end; people have to make choices, because if you're not making choices you're not actually living. (Griffiths 1976: 18)

The process of watching a play is ideally one of creative engagement, not of passive reception. If educational theatre becomes didactic, if what it offers is reducible to the one-way conveyance of a message, then arguably it will have failed aesthetically *and* educationally, and for identical reasons. Edward Bond – a writer who has in recent years committed a great deal of time and effort to promoting and enabling theatre for young people in the belief that drama offers them a unique means of discovering the reality of the world and their potential relationship with it – puts it this way:

> The drama does not argue for or against smoking or fashion . . . The drama does not teach right and wrong or create escapist fiction. It confronts the participants' self-module . . . Instead of teaching the lineality of 'do not smoke' the drama creates the dialectic of the self who decides. (Bond 2002)

If the requirements of the aesthetic and the educational sometimes seem irreconcilable, it may be that we need to remind ourselves that, as Griffiths implies, the best education, just as the best theatre, is a two-way traffic business, it is about getting those we teach to become active learners – and to engage in the dialectical process that, for Bond, lies at the heart of real learning. Only by designing those 'creative gaps' into the play, by offering opportunities for the audience genuinely to find their own ways of completing the imaginative and cognitive journey the play has taken them on, will we allow the aesthetic and the educative to coincide, the one feeding the other. Only then do we stand a chance of creating an artwork that can simultaneously challenge assumptions and develop understanding.

Iser proposes one further reason why didactic texts (as opposed to 'literary texts') tend to disappoint us in the act of reading them, especially when they signal their intentions, and their message, from the beginning. '[T]he more a text confirms an expectation it initially aroused, the more aware we become of its didactic purpose, so at best we can only accept or reject the thesis forced upon us' (Iser 1972: 215). Literary texts, on the other hand, are not so rigid or predictable – the act of reading causes the text to reveal its 'potential multiplicity of connections', leading to the creative process of reading. This in turn, one might argue, helps generate a sense of ownership for the reader – having participated in the making of the meaning, he or she can (if so inclined) claim a degree of co-authorship of that fully realised text. The same can be said of watching a play. Peter Brook (1969/1990) has often referred to the process by which plays are 'realised' on stage, in the moment of co-creation of author, performer and audience. Dangers clearly lie in wait for educational theatre once it begins to slip down the road of didacticism. If the TIE programme reveals its didactic purpose too explicitly, if it hammers home a message that the drama is merely designed to illustrate (rather than explore) and provides its audience with little or no creative work to do in 'realising' the text, then arguably, again, it stands accused of betraying its aesthetic status and at the same time its ability to educate. This is where it is important to distinguish carefully between didacticism and education – without at the same time sinking to the rather easy platitude that 'all art is educational' (just as 'all art is political'). It may be but I do not think it gets us very far to say that, and I am trying to stake out a field of theatrical art in which it is possible to have explicit educational objectives without at the same time resorting to the one-dimensionality associated with the word 'didactic'.

Is it then possible to aim at education *and* allow for 'gaps', for creative participation by the students, for genuine dialogue between 'author' and audience? I will argue that it is, and in the following section will test the claim in respect of participatory TIE programmes and theatre for young people, and try to show how the notion of the dialogic is central to both the aesthetic and the educative dimensions of the programme.

Concepts of the dialogic – Bakhtin and Freire

In many respects, educational theatre, especially at the interventionist point on the spectrum, has been in the vanguard of progressive educational and theatre practice. It has put the audience and the learner at the centre of the experience. At the risk of stating the obvious, interventionist theatre – whether or not it has active audience participation formally built into it – always and necessarily operates in close, symbiotic relationship to a specified audience. The audience is inscribed into the play and its performance style from the beginning: its age range, its cultural and ethnic background, its social and economic context, its geographical location, its regional accents, its particular, known needs and concerns (whether they be the confusing and frightening experience of the immigrant in an often hostile community, or drug abuse, teenage pregnancy or AIDS). This careful targeting is certainly one of the defining features of such work. Targeting does have some problematic connotations however. While it implies an awareness of and concern for particular audiences, it does carry associations of 'one-way traffic'. The arrow can only fly one way towards the bull's-eye. Can 'targeting' allow for a genuine dialogue, for listening and responding as well as 'aiming', for offering the audience the opportunity to construct their own inflections upon the subject matter of the drama? When we talk about an 'effective' educational theatre piece, do we mean that it produced the desired or expected outcomes, that its effects were in some degree measurable? Or can 'effectiveness' be gauged from more flexible, responsive criteria? Frequently, the response of the audience or participants will vary from group to group, often the gains will be unexpected or will happen in surprising ways. Students will often pick up and make meanings out of aspects of performance that differ from or go beyond what was originally intended.

Privileging the audience or participants in the making of meanings has as we know been a principle that has informed most of the pioneering work in this field. And as Boal has observed, in reviewing the development of his own practice, theatre of the oppressed has been 'a constant search for dialogical forms, forms of theatre through which it is possible to converse' with his audiences (Boal 1998: 4). That word, 'dialogic', is one I now want to address in a little detail.

It was Mikhail Bakhtin who, in the 1930s, expounded the notion of the 'dialogic' as a feature of social discourse that was also specifically applicable to the arts, and it is a notion that may help us articulate some of the processes that educational theatre practice at its best embodies. It links interestingly too (though it is not identical) with Paulo Freire's concept, some thirty years later, of the dialogic in relation to the learning process. Freire's concern was with the role of dialogic discourse in emancipatory education deployed in the service of the 'oppressed', and it was this concern of course that in turn underpinned Boal's own attempts to shift theatre into a more interventionist, and instrumentalist, mode. For Bakhtin, however, the concept of the dialogic had both a broader, social meaning and, more specifically, a bearing on what makes great literature and, by extension, the arts in general so powerful and so engaging. Integral to his view is the idea that every utterance we make is made within an interpersonal and chronological context: it invariably follows utterances by others and is, directly or indirectly, consciously or unconsciously, in response to them (Bakhtin 1994: 85). Likewise it will, in anticipating a response by others, be shaped by that anticipation. ('Getting one's retaliation in first' is one well-known, if extreme, example of the strategy at work.) Not only the give and take of everyday discourse, but even single, apparently self-contained utterances (public speeches, Hamlet's soliloquies) are responsive links 'in the continuous chain of other utterances which in effect constitute the continuity of human consciousness' (Morris 1994: 5). It is part of what connects us to each other and highlights the dynamic, processual nature of social discourse and meaning making.

By extension, Bakhtin went on to celebrate the active presence of what he termed 'heteroglossia' (or multi-languaged discourse) to be found in many of the great epic novels, in that they contain within an artistic organising framework a diversity of voices, ideas and cultural forces embodied in human actions and feelings (Bakhtin 1994: 113). The voices that Dostoyevsky, for example, releases within his novels are all the more powerful and persuasive because authentic, socially embodied, differentiated and in genuine dialogue with each other and indeed with the author. The usefulness of this notion is that it suggests the dynamic that is at the heart not only of all human interaction but of much (if not all) resonant and aesthetically pleasing theatre – the identifiably distinctive voices given vital human form that provide conflict, tension, debate and intellectual stimulus.[1] It suggests the kind of drama that gives the spectator work to do as well as (aesthetic) pleasure in the doing of it; the releasing of voices upon the stage in ways that make it difficult for us to leave the performance with neat, easily decipherable meanings.

Now, in this respect, it might seem that we hit an obstacle in trying to conscript interventionist theatre into the realm of aesthetics. One of the telltale signs of much agenda-driven theatre can be found in the characterisation, especially in the use of what I have already termed *author surrogate* characters – that is, those that stand for the author, that express the views the writer intends us to sympathise or agree with, or that vocalise the intended meanings of the play. Shaw often will provide us with a Jack Tanner (in *Man and Superman*) who will, to some extent, be the mouthpiece for the author – often entertainingly and stimulatingly so but, for all that, readily identifiable as such; while in living newspapers the function is more explicitly provided by the 'voice of the living newspaper' in the form of a loudspeaker visible to the audience. At the beginning of *Spirochete* the radio show announcer doubles up as the play's narrator and points us towards the history of the disease and the search for a cure. Or several different characters at different moments of a play will temporarily don the mantle of the author and vocalise a message we are to take as at least one of the meanings of the drama – typically, in many theatre-in-health-education dramas, the teenage protagonist who comes to a realisation of the error of his ways: his dabbling in hard drugs or in casual sex with no awareness till now of consequences. There are also conversely the *audience surrogate* characters – those who stand for us, who undergo a journey of enlightenment and can voice our own questions or objections or prejudices. These are the 'Doctor Watsons' of educational theatre – the Angus K. Buttonkoopers or 'eternal patients' of campaigning theatre in the 1930s, or the 'contact characters' in participatory TIE (Kay and Baskerville 1980) or, in performance pieces, the boy- or girlfriend who learns at the same pace as we in the audience and who can voice that learning curve on our behalf. These tendencies often permeate the texture and structure of such plays and can, unless handled with enormous skill in both writing and performance, produce a sense of predetermined outcome, of a message that will out, irrespective of the audience's engagement and attempts to share in the making of meaning. We grasp all too readily who are the bad and the good guys and what the message is that we are expected to take away and apply to our own lives. Far from 'heteroglossic' in their construction of character and plot, such dramas lose their power to grip and challenge, and indeed persuade – and in so doing provide ammunition for those who decry the use of theatre for instrumentalist purposes. But the best aesthetic practice – and the most genuinely pedagogic, in the Freirean sense – lies arguably in a theatre in which heteroglossia is at work throughout, sustaining the complex texture of the drama and the challenge to its audience's preconceptions, requiring active engagement and reflection both during and after the performance. The inclusion of characters and voices that genuinely resist neat categorisation will be necessary if both learning and aesthetic experiences are to take place, if the audience is to be challenged rather than pacified.

How far is it possible to align Bakhtin's notion of the dialogic, and of the artistic power of heteroglossia in particular, with Freire's? Freire places the dialogic at the very centre of his philosophy of emancipatory education. Thus dialogue 'is an existential necessity': the means by which people 'achieve significance as human beings' (Freire 1970/1996: 69). Freire is of course talking about the dialogic as part of 'real-world' encounters between learners and learning enablers (or teachers), rather than aesthetic encounters. But for Freire only certain kinds of encounters are dialogic. In the 'banking' form of education (that is, those traditional methods of education that characterise the teacher as the source of the knowledge to be transmitted to passive pupils who in turn store the cognitive currency they have acquired for future use) the process is 'anti-dialogic' – there is little exchange and little debate. The relationship between teachers and taught is one of domination and, at worst, oppression. Dialogic encounters however are those in which tutor and learner are both engaged equally, in which listening and two-way communication happen in a collaborative spirit, in the interests of 'naming the world' – the process of identifying those aspects of the world that need to be known and understood if teachers and taught alike are productively to act in and, where necessary, on the world – and so gaining a progressive control over social processes. They are encounters in which the educator has as much to learn from the learner as the learner does from the tutor (Freire 1970/1996: 68–70).

The implication for interventionist theatre is clear – as it was for Boal. For Boal the real dialogue in forum theatre is activated *by* the theatre piece, designed specifically with dialogue as the outcome, and takes place when the spect-actors begin to engage directly with the resolution of the problems posed by the actors. The performance leads to the point at which the audience will be motivated to intervene themselves – and where the dialogue will be real and actual. But the Freirean principle of dialogic encounter is actually as important in underpinning the design and performance of the theatre piece as it is in the active participation sequences that follow. Theatre, and educational theatre especially, is not (or should not be) a set of pre-packaged, fixed ingredients. The audience response has to be anticipated, though not predicted (two quite different things) in the very writing, in rehearsal, in the planning of pre- or post-performance workshops too. This is the point at which, in a sense, Bakhtin and Freire/Boal meet. The dialogic does not just refer to the (Bakhtinian) dialogue between characters within the performance text, nor just to the (Freirean) two-way communication that may go on between actors and audience within an interactive performance or related workshop. It also refers to the whole complex process from original conception through to reception and follow-up. It incorporates what is often described as the audience's 'horizon of expectations' (Bennett 1990, Holub 1984, Jauss 1982), that is, the undeniable fact that the audience or community gathering or classroom of schoolchildren never arrive at the event as blank slates: they have their own personal, social and psychological histories and they come invariably with expectations of what is going to happen – determined by teachers, advance publicity, experiences of similar types of shows. Those individual and collective horizons have been preshaped, they already form a stage in the larger, complex dialogue that is beginning to unfold (in what I have called the 'cultural' or 'pre-theatre' frame). And, when the performance begins, the range of dialogues, the levels on which they operate and the content of those dialogues expand and intensify – they do not begin with the turning down of the house lights or the beating of a drum or the entrance of the first player. The performance (that is, the theatrical performance) is the crucible in which existing dialogues are opened up – brought into a particular, heightened and sharpened focus – and new dialogues are added: dialogues between actors and audience; author (the text) and audience; characters and characters; and characters and audience-in-role (as in TIE and forum).

Home and Away

A recent example of interventionist theatre will I hope serve to illustrate the instrumental and the aesthetic at work, the tensions between them and at the same time – in the working through of the dialogic principles that inform both Bakhtin's and Freire's complementary concepts – the potential for unity between them. *Home and Away* was a schools piece created for the fourteen to sixteen age group by the Cardboard Citizens Theatre Company[2] and toured to schools in London and other parts of the UK during 2004. Written and directed by Adrian Jackson, translator of most of Boal's work in English, it utilised Boal's forum theatre techniques and followed a characteristic TIE pattern of delivery: a short play performed in a school hall followed by interactive workshop – in this case forum. It had an agenda. It dealt, clearly and unambiguously, with an issue that has been thrust to the top of the political agenda in Britain in recent years, that of refugees and asylum seekers. Popular tabloid newspapers in particular, together with television newsreel images of asylum seekers being smuggled on to channel tunnel trains at the French terminal, have made it a topic of considerable tension and contention in the UK in recent years, one which politicians of all parties have taken up. Are there too many refugees? Why are they 'flooding' into Britain? Why do they get preferential treatment? Why are they taking our jobs? What can be done about the numbers of illegal immigrants? Unsurprisingly, exaggeration and misconception abound and the 'crisis' trumpeted by the popular press has provided opportunities for extremist right-wing groups to offer their own solutions as though part of the mainstream discourse, legitimising racially biased and socially provocative agendas. *Home and Away* was devised largely in response to this climate of heightened anxiety, crisis and political rhetoric. It was in that sense agenda-driven, and the accompanying teachers' handbook offered a range of exercises, activities, topics for debate and an outline for a teacher-led 'legislative theatre' project as

follow up to the production. Although not explicitly tied into the national
curriculum, there were clear and precise ways in which teachers could link
this into regular drama, personal, social and health education and citizenship curricula. As the teachers' accompanying handbook makes clear,
the main point of the project as a whole was 'to explore and ask questions
about how a refugee child enters a school system in the UK, and how temporary accommodation affects a person's self-esteem' (*Home and Away:
Teachers' Notes*: 4).

But the play itself – the heart of the programme and for the pupils their
first encounter with the specific questions being addressed – carefully
avoided offering explicit messages. It wove together a naturalistically
played story set in a contemporary high school about the arrival of a
refugee boy from Ethiopia with very little grasp of English, and a story
adapted from an Ethiopian folk tale (about the arduous journey undertaken by 'Cruel Man' and 'Kind Man' and their differing encounters with
the tree of the spirits). While there are moments in the play when, clearly,
we are led to sympathise with the boy's predicament, he is not the protagonist. That role is taken by Teri, a teenage schoolgirl who acts as both
narrator and participant in the drama, and who herself undertakes a
journey from ignorance to the beginnings of insight into the boy's plight.
Her insight comes too late, however, to prevent the boy's suicide. She has
the closest link with the audience, communicating to us through direct
address, and in a sense operates as a kind of audience surrogate, standing for us within the drama, whose learning curve perhaps matches ours
as we watch through her eyes. There are too several attempts within the
narrative to correct some of the misconceptions about refugees in the UK
(via the teacher whom we see conducting a class discussion on the theme
of refugees and immigration, acting, perhaps rather obviously, if only
momentarily, as an author surrogate). But the Ethiopian parable claims
as strong as a place in the drama as the naturalistic action – performed
in a stylised, choreographed and orchestrated manner that allowed the
whole company to take part in the story-telling and which served as a set
of brief but compelling narrative episodes that interrupted, yet were
framed by, the classroom narrative. It also provided a richly poetic,
quasi-allegorical counterpoint to the school-based drama, one that
demanded from the audience constant readjustment and refocusing as
they oscillated between the two narratives. The pupils in the story who
mouth the tabloid-type criticisms of refugees and of policies that seem to
favour them over ordinary working English people, are allowed to
vocalise these with energy and plausibility if without drawing our sympathy. The questions are raised but deliberately not resolved. It was in
the telling of the parable and in the voices of these pupils, together with

Plate 12 *Home and Away*. Cardboard Citizens Theatre, 2004. Director: Adrian Jackson. Actors: Aelef Agonafir as Kind Man, Ainsley Stewart and Emma Read as Spirits.

the shy, halting, uncomfortable presence of the Ethiopian boy, that the heteroglossia was especially evident. There was no ready-made moral to take away, no moment of resolution, no character who could offer us closure.

The play was always followed by a forum theatre workshop which attempted to open up the issues to further investigation. (Unlike some TIE programmes, this workshop was not an optional extra.) For forum theatre to work, plausibility of story and a persuasively real dilemma are all important. The questions posed are both simple and complex: could this story have ended differently? What could anyone have done – realistically – to change the outcome? There was no attempt to dismiss the prejudiced taunting and bullying – such things are all too real – but if there were alternatives the pupils in the school hall were the best placed to decide. And, as Adrian Jackson has put it (2004a), 'quality and context are interrelated . . . if the theatre is not good, forum won't work – and if it doesn't then it will merely be an exercise in civic worthiness . . . Good theatre will activate the interventions from the audience.' At the performance I saw (in Trafford, November 2004), the pupils watched with evident attentiveness throughout the duration of the play, despite the far from ideal (though all too typical) circumstances (some sixty pupils seated in four rows of chairs that arced around the performance space with limited viewing from the back rows). For the forum theatre workshop, the acting company split up and became facilitators for each of the four working groups of pupils as they reviewed the story and its possible meanings and discussed alternative endings, before regathering for the forum proper. The pupils' attention was now of a different quality – talkative, active, relaxed, noisy but reasonably focused, and without doubt engaged. The variety and ingenuity of the strategies that they offered and tried out suggested that they were – or at least most of them – fully part of the dialogue.

There were features of the *Home and Away* project in which, momentarily, the dialogic imperative faltered, when author and audience surrogacy became rather transparent. But it was the differentiated voices (not only different viewpoints but different cultural and stylistic voices) that were foregrounded and that provided an experience that was unsettling and resisted simple interpretation. The dialogues within the play – aesthetically resonant and pedagogically challenging – stimulated and enabled the dialogic structure of the event as a whole; they fed the more wide-ranging dialogues that took place in every corner of the room during the group work and subsequently the forum. The ultimate test of the dialogic effectiveness of such a piece must inevitably lie in the actual encounter between performers or facilitators and audience. It is certainly arguable that, despite some minor flaws, the piece convincingly demonstrated the possibility of embracing a number of dialogic forms working at several levels at once – ones that united the pedagogic, agenda-driven concerns of the drama with the aesthetic: the creation of a provocative and compelling (and dialogic) relationship with its audience. My impression of the students' responses is based admittedly on the evidence of just one viewing but is amply corroborated by the teachers' and pupils' feedback from dozens of schools across the country (lodged in the company's files). This account does not in any event aim to offer a formal evaluation of the programme, rather to offer the rudiments of a conceptual framework within which to see how interventionist theatre might and can, at its best, work. *Home and Away* is offered simply as one example of what the dialogic might look like in practice and to stress the artistic, heteroglossic quality of the play itself as a trigger for, and an integral part of, the dialogic experience of the event as a whole.

Another play, dealing indirectly with racism, provides a brief example of another kind of dialogue that a performance can generate. *Two Days as a Tiger* (1996) was the first play in M6 Theatre's multilingual programme of plays and events, under the generic title of *Awaaz/Voice* (1996–99).[3] It was targeted at junior school pupils between the ages of eight and ten, and especially those living in or near the large, inner-city,

Plate 13 *Two Days as a Tiger.* M6 Theatre Company, 1996.

economically poor neighbourhoods of Rochdale, Oldham and Burnley, which contain a high proportion of mixed race or Bangladeshi and Pakistani ethnic groups. The theatre performance drew on stories and performance styles from the Indian subcontinent, weaving them into a contemporary British setting: the acting moved between the naturalistic and the stylised, and the languages spoken by the characters included English, Punjabi and Urdu. The multilingual dimension, accompanied by a visually rich orchestration and choreography of effects, was a key achievement in reaching and engaging schoolchildren in run-down inner-city areas and middle-class suburbs alike. One teacher was greatly impressed at an incidental, unexpected but enormously important moment during one performance in an Oldham Junior School: a white child turned to a very reserved Asian girl sitting next to him and asked: 'Can you understand that language?' The girl nodded shyly, and the boy said: 'Wow!', mightily impressed. For the teacher, the play had done something she spends her working life trying to achieve: raising the status of the Asian children in a mixed-race class and fostering an appreciation of the skill of being bilingual (Wood 2001, interview; 2006 correspondence). Similar statements came from many teachers about each of the productions after they had observed evidence of this shift in power. While this was a performance piece *for* young people, with no overt, active participation, there were clearly several dialogues going on, not only between the ethnically different characters in the play but also with and among the audience, both during and immediately after the performance. That dialogue was also expanded and developed in the follow-up workshops conducted by members of the company and teachers out of which the children created their own responses to the play – in the form of dance, music or bilingual drama. Six schools in each of the three targeted towns were involved culminating in three presentations for multiracial audiences. 'A huge success of these projects was in their power to raise the status of bilingual pupils and the skill of bilingualism. It increased confidence in bilingual children and gave non-Asian children a new appreciation of South Asian languages. Many children learnt some Urdu or Punjabi words by hearing them in the play and then again in follow-up workshops and used them in their response pieces' (Wood, 2006 correspondence).

Creating the right circumstances within which a dialogic space can be opened up is often fraught with obstacles. For in-school shows, we invite our audiences to behave in an appropriate manner, to sit down on these chairs, at this distance from the stage, to be quiet at this moment and listen. We expect them to respond in certain ways: we may structure the work so that it involves them in active role-taking, maybe in their own right, maybe in a role we assign to them (witness or juror or Jerry Springer studio audience); we may place them in the driving seat, as we do in youth theatre productions and workshops, and to a large extent in forum theatre. At the very least we design the work so that it touches (we hope) particular, immediate concerns and offers them fresh ways of examining, perhaps acting upon, those concerns. We expect a lot from them – not least to enter our imagined world, to enjoy it, be moved by it, to be changed by it. Sometimes this happens in the most inhibiting of circumstances, such as being marched in single file down from their classroom to the school hall with severe warnings ringing in their ears about the good behaviour expected of them if they wish to escape summary execution. It can be difficult for students to disentangle the power relations that operate in a large, highly regimented institutional setting from the aesthetic framework the artist-educators try to establish. A range of assumptions is made about young people's needs and the solutions required; and about the appropriateness of theatre as a medium through which to address those needs. And teachers will often announce the message to them in advance. But how often do the host institutions allow for – or create the circumstances which will enable – the 'subversive space' (or that 'counter-environment', as Neil Postman (1994) has termed it) to be created? How often do artists manage to create that rare opportunity to cross a threshold, willingly, into a liminoid world (Turner

1982), opening up liberating possibilities that can be reached through seemingly quite narrow entry points or within tightly constrained frameworks, in which other possible insights and meanings might just become available, the kind that our audiences find for themselves, without regimentation and that become all the more resonant because they are *theirs*? Those meanings do not have to be boxed or put into categories, nor even expressed verbally before the session ends. Art, on at least some of its levels of meaning, needs longer to work. It is of course not only institutional settings that can militate against that aesthetic experience, that opportunity for genuine dialogue. The anti-dialogic impulse can sometimes be found within the work itself, and often the slippage is at its most counterproductive in the supposedly participatory workshop.

Between performance and participatory workshop: some problems

I want to look now at the function of the interactive workshop, the section of the theatre event in which the audience is invited to participate actively in an investigation of the chosen themes. These interactive sessions normally constitute the most explicit mechanism for opening up the issues raised by the play, developing its learning potential and generating actual dialogue between performance and audience. The relationship of 'performance' to 'workshop' can however be an uneasy one, illustrated by the practice of some theatre in health education companies who offer a 'bolted-on' workshop after the play proper has ended (often driven by economic considerations, allowing schools to opt for the cheaper, performance-only package). If the two are not conceived of as an integrated whole, it is quite possible for the one to undermine the other, with confused pupils oscillating between two quite different sets of conventions and expectations, between 'theatre' and 'classroom'. At its best, the theatre provides the imaginative stimulus, empathy and motivation that in turn gives impetus to the workshops: the play will need the workshop to complete the educational process it has begun. Usually, the workshop will follow (though it can sometimes precede and even interrupt) the performance of the play. It may involve 'hot-seating' (questioning) the characters, or – as with Boal's forum theatre – key scenes may be rerun in an attempt to pinpoint moments of choice and to rehearse other ways of resolving the crisis and (in its original conception) liberating the oppressed protagonist. But, whatever form these interactive workshops may take, we have to examine in what ways they feed and are fed by the performance element and how far they operate as part of the aesthetic framework.

There was a moment in a recent TiHE programme – toured to high schools, targeted at fourteen- to fifteen-year-olds and dealing with sexual health and AIDS awareness[4] – that illustrates precisely the kind of difficulty that can occur. It was in many respects an excellent production in which the performance was carefully structured to allow examination of issues to do with sexual health, drug abuse and personal relationships *within* the event. By means of a series of interventions during the play, a neutral facilitator would 'freeze' the action and initiate various forms of interaction between pupils and the characters. At three points in the play, therefore, the action was deliberately (and mostly very successfully) interrupted and the 'facilitator' led a brief discussion on the events just witnessed, particularly about the turning point or crisis that had just occurred, sometimes inviting pupils to fire questions at one or more of the characters involved (a series of switches between the representational and investigative frames). The purpose was to provide an opportunity for them to check their reactions, clarify the nature of the problem being tackled and reflect on the options faced by the character before the consequences are known.

One problematic moment stood out however at three of the performances I witnessed. During the early part of the run, the actors became concerned about the hostility many of the audience were showing towards the one gay character in the play. It was decided, rather hastily, to insert a new intervention immediately after a heated exchange in the play in which the gay character finds himself on the receiving end of a torrent of abuse from the play's central protagonist. The aim was to address more head-on the subsidiary issue of homophobia within the narrative. The facilitator stopped the play and asked the audience how they thought the character had felt, inviting 'Gary' back to respond to their initial observations (for example, that he must have felt 'gutted'). The actor playing Gary then in effect took over the intervention and proceeded to conduct the debate himself, and 'in role' confronted the audience with their own prejudices. However, the distinction between the character and the facilitator role rapidly became blurred. While the actor held on to his role (as Gary), he also became his own facilitator, in role and out of role at the same time: character and facilitator. But it had not been adequately thought through. It became clear that he (the actor) felt strongly about homophobia, so was also *himself* as well as the character and the facilitator, yet another persona for the students to cope with. At each of the performances I observed, the pupils dried up during this particular workshop while the actor struggled to get them to be more responsive. It seemed to me that the pupils were genuinely confused: they were unsure exactly who they were talking to – Gary from the play or the actor himself who may or not have been gay? The actor was in fact gay and his evidently strong feelings about the issue gave this intervention an interestingly urgent flavour, but it also left no doubt in the audience's minds what the 'right' point of view was supposed to be. A 'creative gap' had been filled by the actor instead of the audience.

Young audiences usually understand there is safety in talking to and arguing with a *character*, but, as soon as they think the views expressed are what the actor himself or herself really thinks, an aesthetic dividing-line has been crossed: drama gives way to polemic. Distance becomes minimised, the boundaries between fiction and reality blurred and the possibility of dialogue rapidly evaporates. The pupils are no longer sure of the terms on which this event is taking place, they may wonder how they can disagree with the actor's views if he really is homosexual himself. Indeed, such a workshop can be counterproductive. Pupils are not going to learn if they feel, 'This is what he wants us to think': the possibilities of disagreement, reflection or choice will have been closed down. Unsurprisingly, audience response to this highly interactive sequence was muted; the actor became increasingly frustrated by the lack of response which in turn was reflected in a body language that was dominating, often confrontational, his questions becoming more and more rhetorical and declamatory, accompanied by much use of fingers pointed at the audience. The 'game of theatre' had become too close to reality for comfort, the audience were unsure where the boundary-lines (if any) were. The 'rules of the game' appeared to have changed, but no one had told the audience. The intervention therefore became a kind of power game in which the actor had all the cards – except that, finally, it was the unresponsiveness of the audience that was most telling. The opportunity for the audience to participate genuinely in their own voices had been unintentionally hijacked by the actor. Consequently genuine dialogue – which did take place at the other interventions in the play – was thwarted, and the risk was that homophobia may have been reinforced rather than challenged. School pupils, many of whom will have never seen live theatre before, whose 'horizons of expectations' are determined largely by their familiarity with television soap opera and cinema, will be uncomfortable with an actor who breaks the frame and suddenly operates in a world where the 'rules' of the game seem known only to him. Any heteroglossic qualities the play may have had (such as the expression of two very distinct views of the world embodied in the protagonist and antagonist) became jettisoned at this moment. Here too was an example of how, in the workshop, the author surrogate became – unintentionally and inappropriately – suddenly overt and transgressed what the art form could contain. Most of the pupils I spoke to (some weeks later) volunteered that they believed the character's point of view was also the actor's and several thought this a problem: 'if they think he's gay then people aren't goin' to pass their views over to him . . . they don't want to hurt his feelings' (Jackson 1995a). Good intentions had been undermined by a confused grasp of the nature of the art form.

And this is only a more extreme example of a weakness observable all too often in otherwise well-executed TIE performances. When it comes to audience participation, the all-important, finely honed theatricality of the event will often become blurred. Otherwise fine actors become thrown by a lively, vocal audience and begin to play for laughs or, probably worse, to preach. Sometimes the facilitator of the workshop will be the stage manager, or an ill-prepared member of the cast, the assumption being that this role has little or no aesthetic function: she or he merely has to chair the debate, control the hubbub, keep to schedule and make sure the message gets across. In such circumstances, there is little doubt that the pupils lose out – the quality of the theatre is compromised and its educational potential seriously stunted. It is my contention that, if we want theatre to function as a genuinely effective educational instrument, then we must make sure we have got the aesthetics right – in workshops as much as in the performances.

I have argued that the dialogic process must be at the core of interventionist theatre practice, whether that be the giving of finely honed theatre performances or the running of interactive workshops which include within them moments of performance (forum theatre, hotseating), or which are themselves included within the framework of a larger performance event. It is in those multi-faceted, spoken and unspoken dialogues – within the play and between play and audience – that the aesthetic and pedagogic impact of the performance event will lie. Evidence of the actual responses of audiences suggests there is more, much more, to a successful interventionist performance than 'messages' or measurable outcomes – that there is a quality of experience that is to do with the 'liveness' of the event, the emotional resonances it can offer, the dialogues that can be generated and the complexity of texture that defies easy closure. It is that quality of theatre experience that we have to describe, articulate, research and communicate to those who provide the funding and set the agendas. The relationship between given, externally set agendas and the theatre experience itself is the subject of the next chapter.

Notes

1 Bakhtin's stress was upon the unique ability of the epic novel (rather than poetry or drama) to express fully the dialogic quality of social and cultural intercourse since it could be sustained and elaborated over substantial passages of time and across a range of geographical, political and social settings.

None the less, the application of his concept to drama, if on a smaller more concentrated scale, offers some productive lines of enquiry, which can only be touched on here. See also Carlson (1992).

2 Cardboard Citizens Theatre Company consists of professional actors, dedicated to working for the homeless and against homelessness, many of whose personnel are recruited from the homeless people they serve.

3 *Awaaz* or *Voice* was the overall title for the project as a whole which also included other plays such as *Grandpa's Jinn* (1997), together with the linked workshops and presentations. The plays were also toured to schools in other areas of Greater Manchester.

4 The programme, *Love Trouble*, was evaluated by the author in 1995 as part of a research exercise to test out suitable methods of approach for evaluating TIE. See Jackson (1995a).

8

Targets, outcomes – and playfulness

In many parts of the world (in 'First' and 'Third' World countries alike), the funding of the arts in education has increasingly been driven by notions of value for money and cost-effectiveness, and content is often determined by agencies who prioritise 'crisis management' (tackling drug abuse or teenage crime, for example) or narrowly conceived notions of 'development', and who set rigid briefs for the theatre companies they employ. Evaluation of such work is likewise often conducted according to restrictive and readily measurable criteria. And funding is usually tied to the fulfilment of those criteria. Against such a background, consideration of the creative and aesthetic nature of the work done frequently gets sidelined – and this consequently devalues the very medium through which the 'messages' are communicated. Any advocacy of the role theatre might play in educating young audiences also needs to ensure that the full potential of the art form is recognised. Finding effective ways of describing and articulating and accounting for the aesthetic dimension has become in my view more necessary than ever.

At this point in the book, I want to pose against each other two contrasting notions: that of the 'targets and outcomes culture' against that of the 'playful culture'. And I will argue that it is often the ludic qualities – the 'playfulness' – of the drama (an integral part of the aesthetic experience) that impact upon audiences and participants far more than the overtly serious, message-driven elements. This is a vital dimension of the work which we have to find more persuasive ways of demonstrating. The two cultures are not necessarily incompatible but they often seem to be, and the tensions between these two extreme points on the spectrum, between two mind-sets, can often create difficulties in implementing effective, transformative interventionist theatre practice. Those tensions are not ones that we should necessarily try to eliminate. In fact, as Kershaw persuasively argues (1999), they may often prove fruitful. It is sometimes the case that performance in non-theatre spaces (or at least non-traditional theatre spaces, such as classrooms or school halls or open-air sites) can find ways of negotiating ways around such tensions to good advantage, of being not so much oppositional in the binary sense of the term but able to 'transcend' or sidestep the normative values of a society driven by the pressures to commodify and control. Such performance can perhaps, in the process, create what Kershaw has described as 'a space and time beyond the dominant' (p. 219) in which alternative voices and alternative ways of seeing can be explored and celebrated.

Agenda-driven theatre: the targets and outcomes culture

First, then, the 'targets and outcomes culture'. Education policy in the UK has been dominated for some twenty years by an obsession with results and league tables – ever since the introduction of the national curriculum in 1988 and subsequently the progressive implementation of performance indicators for teachers and pupils alike. Subject benchmarks, detailed assessment criteria for every learning outcome and a barrage of tests to be undertaken at almost level of the child's progression through school have led to a mountain of forms to be completed and boxes to be ticked. The resulting bureaucracy, together with the omission of drama as a formally recognised curriculum subject (except under the umbrella of English), has contributed to the marginalisation of the performing arts in many schools. When a defence of the arts has been required, many advocates of the arts have, wittingly or unwittingly, turned to arguments that are complicit with the prevailing orthodoxy, justifying the arts in terms of their development of 'transferable skills' or their use as tools for the teaching of other subjects such as languages (see Furedi 2003, Best 1999). As a result, the actual value of the arts within education (their ability to develop empathy, creativity, empathic engagement with the experience of others, an appreciation of artistic expressive form) all too often gets overlooked. State directives favour curriculum subjects that will improve numeracy, literacy and skills for the workplace. As one commentator has put it, 'an argument rages about the significance of the different goals of the government's education policy: standards and league tables on the one hand, and a genuine commitment to social justice and inclusion on the other' (Fanshawe 2006). The concern with setting targets and measurable outcomes has had an impact upon the arts at all levels. It is not all doom and gloom. There have been significant strides made to counter the tendency: a select number of high schools across the UK have successfully applied for 'performing arts status', giving the arts a higher profile and obtaining resources to match. While the rationale for the allocation of such status is often framed in terms of vocational and transferable skills, in practice, on the ground, it has contributed to experiment and a widening opportunity for pupils of all abilities to develop their skills in and experience of the performing arts. The Creative Partnerships scheme, led by the Arts Council (England), has also brought professional artists to work in a much greater range of schools within and alongside the official curriculum, prioritising schools in the more deprived areas of the country.[1]

Ironically, despite the decimation of TIE companies between the mid-1980s and mid-1990s, there is now probably just as much money going into TIE and related work as there ever was, but the *structure* of that funding has changed radically. Much education-oriented theatre in Britain (like many educational theatre projects around the globe) now relies increasingly for its funding upon contracts with health education authorities and other such agencies, replacing the previous system of LEA annual grants for a broad range of work. Dependence upon commission for so much of the work, or upon funding that has to be bid for competitively from charitable foundations of one kind or another, has led to the work itself becoming more and more driven by national policy and crisis-management agendas. It survives, largely by learning to live with and within this commissioning and competitive bidding environment – this outcomes-driven culture. Companies have learnt to adapt and diversify according to the latest national and local strategies and priorities, generate new income from sponsorship and respond to commissions from various charitable and government-funded agencies set up to promote health education, AIDS awareness, discouragement of drug abuse and teenage pregnancy and, more broadly, 'social inclusion' and citizenship. (See Whybrow 1994 and Sexton 2003.) The demands for accountability, value for money and proof of effectiveness, are unremitting. Inevitably, and not unreasonably, commissioned work has to meet very specific briefs and criteria. TIE, as with all such 'interventionist' work, has therefore had to redefine itself far more broadly and reposition itself, flexibly if sometimes reluctantly, within a more competitive, market-driven economy.

Two brief examples taken from recent practice – and from the more enlightened sectors of arts commissioning – will serve to illustrate the way agendas and the corresponding claims are articulated. Firstly, a press release from the Wellcome Trust,[2] announcing a sponsored TIE production by the Y Touring Company (London):

17 February 1999. Science Minister launches new theatre-in-education initiative with attitude-changing play . . . to tackle serious health issues,

including misconceptions about mental illness . . . *Cracked* [is] one of four plays which form the initiative. The three-year programme is being funded jointly by the Office of Science and Technology and the Wellcome Trust, the world's largest medical research charity . . .

Cracked, a play focusing on mental illness, has been written to specifically engage young adults and aims both to challenge these fears and to raise awareness of mental health issues, especially those affecting young people. Research shows that particular points in the play, and the subsequent discussion which forms an integral part of the educational experience, can generate a major shift in attitudes.

After watching *Cracked*, pupils' attitudes towards, and understanding of, mental illness underwent a radical change. Before watching the play only 12 per cent of 2,035 students questioned disagreed with the statement: 'schizophrenia is dangerous'. After the play that figure rose almost four times to a remarkable 45 per cent. At the launch Peter Finegold, Wellcome Trust co-ordinator of the initiative, said: 'We need to tackle untruths about mental illness head-on, especially as the stigma and shame attached to mental health problems can prevent people asking for help. Our aim is to ensure that important health issues get aired, discussed and on the agenda.'

. . . Each performance of *Cracked* is followed by a lively, pro-active discussion of the issues raised and a special teachers pack has been produced which builds on the play's messages.

Table 1 shows the list of 'Learning outcomes' for the Nationwide Foundation funding agreement with M6 Theatre for its sponsored production of *Forever*, a theatre in education programme for fourteen- to sixteen-year-olds which dealt with teenage pregnancy and parenting issues. It originally toured schools within Greater Manchester during 2000 and early 2001, but was then revived and retoured to meet demand and funded by the Foundation, a charitable trust linked to the Nationwide Building Society, as part of a larger three-year programme of work (the 'New Generation Initiative') dealing with these issues and this age group. The first column lists the learning outcomes specified by the NGI; the second is M6's indication of how they will be achieved in respect of the TIE programme (Table 1).[3]

The objectives of such programmes are admirable and I do not wish for one moment to sound dismissive of them – quite the contrary. However, it is worth noting that the criteria for assessing and valuing these quite typical examples of TIE are primarily sociological or related to national policy objectives to do with personal and social health, rather than artistic. The artistic is implied only in words such as 'engage', 'challenge'. And of course such criteria prevail in much of this type of work across the world – promoted under the auspices of charitable foundations, non-governmental organisations (NGOs) and government agencies in

Table 1 Example of learning outcomes expected from a TIE
programme – M6 Theatre: *Forever*

Learning outcomes	M6 production: 'Forever'
Increase knowledge of parenthood	Young people learn: that parenthood involves complex relationships that bring both difficulties and joys
Develop appropriate attitudes about parenthood	Young people learn: that parents' needs may have to be considered alongside the needs of other family members
Develop appropriate skills for parenthood	Young people learn: that they need to develop a range of responses to family difficulties
Feel more prepared for parenthood	Young people recognise: the full-time responsibilities and demands of parenthood

developing countries; and reflected in the contracts that American arts-in-
education companies such as New York's Creative Arts Team negotiate
with grant-awarding bodies, driven by not dissimilar agendas. This is not,
I stress again, to dismiss those agendas, rather to note the understandably
limited and limiting framework of priorities within which companies
have to operate and by which they have to explain and justify their work.
Experienced companies such as Y Touring and M6 generally produce
work that has its own artistic integrity while at the same time meeting the
goals set out by their funders; but artistic worth tends to be ignored in the
formal, public justifications of the work or, at best, tacitly recognised and
taken for granted. As M6's general manager has put it, 'the imposed structures can be very rigid/one dimensional and not reflective of the more
multi-layered and creative world M6 inhabits' (Palmer, 2006 correspondence). The discussion of *Forever* later in the chapter will illustrate some
of the ways that, in the actual setting of a school performance, the qualities of the drama transcend the bald list of objectives to be met.

What kinds of impact have these pressures had over time? In the UK,
a combination of soaring inflation in the mid-1970s and the arrival in
1979 of the Thatcher administration, ushering into all walks of public
life an energetically applied 'market forces' philosophy, marked the
beginning of an erosion of arts funding from central government. Small-
scale community, TIE and political theatre companies struggled to
survive. TIE was especially vulnerable. The inventive and often challenging nature of the programmes devised, involving active participation
of the audience, was aided by the fact that performances could be given
for one or at most two classes of children at a time (thirty to sixty pupils).
This was a costly form of theatre (in terms of the ratio of pupils to theatre

personnel), and, perhaps predictably, the progressive whittling away of money for the arts and especially for the arts in education in the 1980s and through most of the 1990s, exacerbated by the devolution of education budgets from LEAs to schools, led to a steep decline in the number of specialist companies and range of work produced.[4]

Paradoxically, the volume of activity in the broader field of educational theatre and children's theatre has not significantly diminished. Indeed, there has even been an expansion in the field of theatre in health education, a branch of TIE which emerged during the 1990s in direct response to the growing need for innovative approaches to educating young people in matters of sexual health, AIDS awareness and drug abuse. One indicator of this trend was the setting up of the Theatre in Health Education Trust early in the 1990s to act as a 'broker' between sponsors and theatre companies prepared to tour into schools, youth centres and community groups (mothers-to-be centres, refuges for battered women and so forth). After a decade of valuable support for an increasingly specialised field of work, it was closed in 2004, as a result partly of its rather limiting regional location in the Midlands, but more so of the constantly oscillating policies and structural reorganisations within the National Health Service – a further symptom of the rapidity with which the cultural and economic landscape has been changing. Another indicator of current trends is the recent publication of a 'good practice guide' on using theatre in education to deliver sex and relationship education (SRE), issued in 2003 by the UK government's Health Development Agency and the Teenage Pregnancy Unit. Its purpose was to help a range of health and social care commissioners, teachers, youth workers and teenage pregnancy co-ordinators, as well as theatre companies, make the best use of TIE, which was seen as 'a dynamic, sensitive and interactive way of delivering and supporting SRE for young people' (2003: 5).[5] The guide hearteningly recognises the artistic and performative strengths of the medium, as well as the need for clear parameters regarding 'style, tone and expected outcomes' (p. 6), and draws attention particularly to the medium's ability to 'challenge rather than reinforce stereotypes . . . related to image, sexual behaviour and sexuality', and its effectiveness in engaging boys and young men (p. 9).

Schemes abound to promote, monitor, account for and of course control arts programmes that are designed to be socially beneficial, most of which require competitive bidding. In consequence, substantial time and personnel have to be committed by theatre companies to fund-raising, applying for sponsorship and marketing, and a wider, regional rather than local, focus tends now to be factored in to all TIE business plans. Small tranches of National Lottery money have been made available via the Arts Council for arts-in-the-community projects; thus, under what until recently was called the 'Arts For Everyone' scheme, for example, companies have been able to bid for extra support for community and school-based work. Similar schemes still exist to promote social inclusion through the arts. M6's multi lingual theatre programme, *Awaaz/Voice* (1996–99) (see Chapter 7), targeted at the multi-ethnic communities in Rochdale, Oldham and Burnley, was so funded. These plays, incorporating dialogue and song in Punjabi, Urdu, Bengali and English, aimed to 'celebrate cultural and linguistic diversity', 'raise the profile of South Asian languages' and promote 'positive role models', and were 'accessible to both multi and monolingual audiences' (M6 Annual Report 1999/2000, p. 5). Financial support for the productions came not only from the 'Arts For Everyone' grant scheme but from a number of other agencies that promote multi-racial education and support for community regeneration, but the energy and resonance in the performance lay in the stories, not in any *overt* attempt to spread the news about how racially different communities should learn to live together. The considerable degree of artistic freedom allowed by the funders in this case is a reminder of the all-important lever that a company has at its disposal if it has a track record of working effectively with outside agencies and has built a solid basis of trust over time with teachers, education officers, community liaison workers and health promotion personnel.

None the less, as one research team found, when attempting to conduct a detailed evaluation of a TIE programme in 1999, there had been a 'further turn of the wheel in the move to an ideology of accountability' and 'the two related factors of the contemporary culture, of assessing whether value for money has been achieved in employing a TIE company and the shortage of public service resources' had led to increased pressures both on the companies themselves and on those who are asked to demonstrate 'proof' of its value (Allen, Allen and Dalrymple 1999: 34–5).

While the longer-established companies have, with greater and lesser degrees of success, had to find ways of adjusting to the changed circumstances while retaining their core values, other companies have emerged out of, and thrived on, the competitive-bidding and target-based culture. One such company is CragRats, now probably the UK's largest company offering a range of TIE products and related training programmes for a clientele that ranges from schoolteachers to large multinational corporations. Formed in 1989 initially to use theatre to 'inform and motivate pupils about their career choices', the company subsequently created 'CragRats ReAct' to meet the growing demand from schools for 'issue-based theatre-in-education' dealing with such issues as substance misuse, homophobic bullying and raising achievement (www.cragratsreact.com/

pagesreact-history.asp, last accessed 1 August 2006), and at the same time the growing interest among potential funders in supporting such work: charitable organisations such as The Children's Fund and Police Authorities and corporations such as the drinks combine Diageo Great Britain. According to the company's own publicity, CragRats is 'uniquely placed' to help large business organisations meet their 'corporate responsibility' goals: 'We work with young people, the wider community, your employees, the media and your shareholders to communicate your key messages' (www.cragratsreact.com/pages/csr.asp, last accessed 1 August 2006). In 2004, the company was commissioned by Diageo to deliver a 'Responsible Drinking Education Programme' for the eleven to fourteen age group in secondary schools in Scotland, Nottinghamshire and London. The result was a programme that included a free performance of a play, *Wasted*, together with a forum-style workshop and associated teaching materials, designed 'to convey key messages including personal responsibility, personal safety and making informed choices' (www. cragratsreact.com/pages/csr-diageo.asp, accessed 1 August 2006). The programme was considered highly successful, not only by Diageo but, according to the independently conducted evaluation, by many of the pupils and teachers (Research Works 2005). Consequently, it was toured to other parts of the country and in 2006/7 there were three teams of actor-teachers on the road all performing the identical show to audiences of up to 120 at any one time. The scale of the opearation brought its own drawbacks. Only if schools booked the linked workshop, for which pupils would be subdivided into more manageable groups, would there be any serious opportunity for genuine interaction; for the many that booked the play alone (usually for logistical reasons), the final question-and-answer session, conducted with the aid of a roving microphone, offered little more than a token gesture towards participation. The practice underlines again the significant changed nature of the cultural climate in which the work now operates, and the risks attendant on embarking upon educational programmes the goals of which are set by the varied organisations now providing core funding, not all of whom will necessarily share the values and understandings of the artist-educators they commission. It should however be noted that, for this particular programme, all communication with the schools was conducted by the theatre company and was free of Diageo branding, in order to avoid any perception that the project was driven by marketing imperatives.

The difficulties of arguing the case for the creative, playful, aesthetic aspects of the work to be given full recognition – rather than readily measurable learning outcomes – are as prevalent now as they have ever been, and the dilemmas and challenges for companies in the current climate have undoubtedly become much more complex. How best does a theatre company survive and develop, artistically and in ways that are genuinely responsive to changing social needs, while working to strict briefs set by commissioning bodies? (The challenges may also, it has to be said, have pushed many into being more responsive to the changing world around them than they might otherwise have been.) Commissioning agencies often, understandably, insist upon playing an influential role in the creation of the programmes and many – with honourable exceptions – signally fail to recognise the nature of the art form they are making use of: separating all too easily the vehicle from the message.

To give just one example: some years ago, a TIE programme about HIV/AIDS and sexual health (*Love Trouble*) had been commissioned from a theatre company by the regional Health Promotion Service.[6] However, the actual script and the 'health messages' which it, and the workshops, incorporated failed to meet expectations at the first read-through with health advisers. The disagreements were apparently heated. The agendas and priorities of the company and of the health promotion team differed widely and misunderstandings were rife. One side came expecting a series of messages to be coming through loud and clear (this is how you can contract HIV; these are the precautions you should take; if you're worried this is what to do or whom to see) – what else happened in the play was entirely subordinate to that. The writer and director had however attempted to embed the messages within a drama about believable characters and their oscillating relationships. As such the messages had become implicit – in the eyes of the health promotion team, lost. Considerable rethinking was done; the workshop sequences designed to accompany the performance were reworked to ensure basic information could be given as needed; and the processes of rehearsal and translation of the script into three-dimensional, human and emotionally charged story-lines, culminated, fortunately, in a production judged to be a great success by all concerned, and further collaborations followed (Jackson 1995a). Not all such partnerships turn out so well.

Flawed though that early draft may have been, the company's instincts were right. The theatre is too often seen as the icing on the cake rather than as an integral part of the educative process. There is a great deal of work to be done in reclaiming for TIE the status of theatrical art rather than merely a walking-talking visual aid. And work to be done too in educating the educators into understanding that theatre without the art will not have the power to engage, to move, to give pleasure, to stimulate the senses, to provoke and to change, that it does. It is this power which explains precisely why young people will often listen in drama in ways that that they do not in other forms of education. All too often the plays written for young people that seek merely to transmit a message will be taken for what they are – messages in the guise of drama, not true drama.

One very clear, obvious, but all-too-often-overlooked fact emerged from my own series of interviews with the fourteen- to sixteen-year-olds who had seen *Love Trouble*.[7] When young people experience a piece of educational theatre, they will generally experience it holistically and process it as an immediate, unfolding entity – not content followed by form, but a dramatic narrative peopled by 'real' characters who will be more or less convincing as they progress through that narrative. Believability, empathy, clarity of story-line, relevance to their own lives and concerns, enjoyment of the vitality of the performance and indeed of the moments of recognition – these are the factors that weigh in their minds, rather than 'learning outcome' or behaviour modification. Any evaluation of this kind of programme has to take account of the way young people actually experience theatre.

What was particularly striking was the pupils' ability to talk openly, argumentatively and freshly about the experience they had had – about their aesthetic response to the play which was *not* the same thing as their identification of the message. They were interested in the story, found the characters and events believable ('because you know it can happen like that'; it was about 'a world we know'; the play was 'more like real life than learning about it in class or from books'), enjoyed the music and the 'streetwise' language and were engaged in the debates that were generated. Several commented approvingly that the actors seemed very close to the ages of the characters they were playing. Interestingly, many of the older pupils claimed they really did not learn anything new – 'it was like a different way of putting it across'; it 'reinforces what we'd already heard about'. They were however much more taken with the matter of personal relationships, with how one tackles sensitive issues with a new boy- or girlfriend – with concerns and choices they were having to confront on a daily basis and for which no textbook answers were available; with watching people very like them struggling with their lives and making the kinds of mistakes they could so easily imagine making themselves.

There was, clearly, a close connection established between the fiction and the 'real world' as the pupils knew it and the process of their 'contracting in' to the event (engaging with it voluntarily) had been effectively realised. A genuine sense of ownership seems to have been engendered – an essential prerequisite for that special kind of knowing that, as Dewey, Best, Boal and others have argued, can be achieved through engagement in the arts (see Chapter 1). The effectiveness of the piece was, then, far more to do with reinforcing what was generally known, initiating debate

and provoking more focused thought about the issues dramatised, than
with communicating facts. This type of response was further substanti-
ated in the extensive evaluation of a TIE programme undertaken in
Plymouth in 1998/9 (Allen, Allen and Dalrymple 1999). It is important
to stress how much time and space we need to give to audience response,
to the voices of the young people who receive the work, especially in any
attempt to assess the value of the whole experience, of which the aesthetic is a key part. Exactly *how* we evaluate the aesthetic dimension is
of course another matter and beyond the scope of this book, but learn to
evaluate it we must.

In such a culture, where there *is* money for the arts but subject now to
external pressures demanding proof of its social benefits, and where mea-
surement of value for money holds the upper sway, profound problems
are posed for the artist – and especially those theatre artists who believe
passionately in the important role the arts have to play in meeting today's
social challenges, who do not want to isolate their art from the needs of
the marginalised, the oppressed, the young. How do you avoid producing safe, formula-bound work that merely promotes facile messages for
a health education agency that provides substantial funding and expects
to evaluate the outcome against the criteria it has laid down?

I now want to narrow the focus again – from the outer, cultural frames
within which any theatre performance has to operate, to the inner frames
(see Chapter 6) – to what goes on within the performance and particularly the oscillating and slippery interaction that takes place between the
act of performance and its reception by an audience. It is often within
these frames that any negative, counterproductive or diversionary impact
from the 'outcomes culture' can be neutralised or even turned to good
purpose. And it is within these frames that we can see at work a quite
different process – that of the playfulness that lies at the heart of theatre.

The playful dimension

The concept of theatre as part of a 'playing culture' is opposed to, though
not necessarily incompatible with, that of the 'outcomes culture'. The
notion of playfulness at the heart of performance is one that is familiar
to theatre and drama practitioners, but one that we need to keep re-
stating, and to find fresh ways of articulating, in today's cultural climate.

In his book *The Theatrical Event* (2000), and in subsequent writings,
Willmar Sauter suggests an approach to theatricality that springs in part
from the general rethinking of theatre studies that has been taking place
over the past decade (Carlson 1996, Schechner 1992, 2002), one which
has in some quarters led to theatre being 'demoted' to the category of a

sub-species of 'performance' (see Introduction). Sauter however argues for a way not of redefining theatre but rather of highlighting fundamental qualities that have too often been subsumed under the traditional focus upon authors, directors, theatre buildings and literary analysis. In particular, he sees 'a very sharp dividing line between theatre as written culture and theatre as playing culture', and goes on to claim that 'an adequate understanding of what constitutes the Theatrical Event' must include 'a concept of theatre as part of a Playing Culture' (Sauter 2004: 4). He takes his cue from Hans-Georg Gadamer, who claimed (in *Truth and Method*, 1960) that all art has its basis in 'playing'; that playing, involving as it often does a 'presentation of self' and carrying the 'potential of a presentation for someone' (Sauter 2000: 81), becomes art 'when a communicative act between player (in the widest sense) and observer (onlooker, listener) takes place' (2004: 5). But, of course, the observer does more than observe. As Sauter insists, the 'player and the observer participate in the playing' and 'the processes of creating and experiencing theatre are united through the act of playing, through the mutual contact between performer and spectator' (2000: 5). Moreover, 'theatre becomes theatre by being an event, in which two partners engage in a playful relationship' (2004: 11) – the performer and the spectator are united as 'two indispensable partners of the theatrical event' (p. 4). The concept of playing can therefore be seen as the basis of the theatrical event, with spectators in this respect participants as much as they are spectators – partners in the creation of that event. Likewise, the audience at a play does more than decipher pre-packaged meanings. To follow Gadamer again, 'there is not first a sender and then a receiver; it is the simultaneous encounter between performer and spectator in the situation of playing which constitutes theatre as an art . . . as a theatrical event' (2000: 82).

This concept recognises theatre as essentially an *interactive* activity, characterised by such elements as immediacy, impulsiveness, playfulness, entertainment, make-believe, physicality, and by a consequent resistance to being appropriated as a message delivery vehicle. It also underlines the part that spectators play in the making of meaning and indeed in the making of the theatre event itself – whatever agenda may lie behind the commissioning of the script, an analysis of the impact made by the play must take account of the processes that lie at the heart of any theatrical experience.

The 'performative' and the 'referential'

There is a further duality that usefully complements that of the 'playing' versus the 'written culture', and that is the productive distinction which

Erika Fischer-Lichte draws between two fundamental qualities of theatrical art, a distinction prompted by the rapid expansion and range of experimental performance in the latter half of the twentieth century and by the rethinking of the very meaning of 'texts' (inspired in part by Barthes's famous claim that 'the author is dead'). It is the distinction between the 'performative' and the 'referential' (Fischer-Lichte 1997). The performative refers to any kind of theatre which derives its power and impact primarily from its *performance* qualities and the specialness of the *relationship with the audience* rather than from the text – the theatre of ritual or carnival for example. The referential indicates the type of theatre which is primarily *about something else*, for example, about historical figures or events, or which dramatises a pre-existing story, or which sets out to communicate a message about an identifiable issue (prison reform, scientific discovery, sexual health, drug abuse and so forth). Its effectiveness will usually depend upon the audience having some prior knowledge of the thing the play refers to and responding accordingly. It can involve the audience in a more cognitive process (a concern with social problems for example) or, at the simplest level, merely in a recognition of an already familiar (or supposedly familiar) world – such as the drawing rooms of the well-to-do classes which formed both the backdrop *and* content of so much British theatre from the Edwardians to the 1950s. The recent renewal of interest in documentary or 'verbatim' theatre (exemplified in such plays as *Guantanamo*, *Talking to Terrorists* and Hare's *The Permanent Way* and *Stuff Happens*) suggests that vitality and directness of impact can still be found at the referential end of the spectrum.

Instead of giving primacy in our analysis of plays and their reception to the intentions of the author (or director), the distinction proposed by Fischer-Lichte draws in the *performativity of the text* and the two-way traffic of the *stage/audience relationship* as well as the intentions of the playwright. Performative and referential should however be seen not as alternatives to each other but rather as opposite ends of a spectrum which also allows for overlap. Plays rarely fall neatly into one category or the other. And, although most of the experimental theatre of the past forty years has tended to emphasise the performative at the expense of the referential, *all* theatre will by definition possess performative qualities, even in its most referential mode – Hare's *The Permanent Way* being one excellent example. Even a play so referentially about the world outside as *Justice* does gain much of its power from one particular scene that, while it represents in documentary detail an actual prison cell, is highly performative in its sheer physicality, its wordlessness and its use of orchestrated sound, rhythm and crescendo (see Chapter 2).

In respect of educational theatre, this distinction helps to highlight a key difference between two types of drama that on the surface might appear rather similar but in practice, and in terms of their impact upon their audience, differ significantly. There is the play that serves as a vehicle for a message, one that will be explicit within the play, or at least that pupils will readily identify: referential in the sense that the play refers outwards to an aspect of social reality that they can immediately recognise and signals explicitly that this is what has to be learned and applied. It tends to produce in students a response along the lines of: 'Ah, now I know what they're getting at; now I know what it means – it's what I get told by teachers or what I hear about on radio or TV, and I can put this meaning away in this bit of my filing system: it's sorted!' On the other hand, those plays that stress the performative aspect (and the 'playing culture') may embody certain similar messages but will not be dependent upon them for their effectiveness in connecting with their audiences. Something else happens: the performance, the acting, the set, the chemistry of an event taking place and communicating on many levels at once (some of which may be quite contradictory, encompassing for example the celebratory, the emotionally unsettling and sheer enjoyable fun), elements that take the eye, stimulate the senses, engage the emotions, absorb the mind and deny the easy extraction of a pre-packaged meaning.

It also links closely to much twentieth-century fascination with and analysis of the forces at work in popular culture. In Bakhtin's notion of the 'carnivalesque', for example, laughter, parody and excess often, throughout history, function as subversive forces, as a celebration of alternative worlds that retain 'an identity and vigour even in the midst of ideological tyranny' (Morris 1994: 194). (Bakhtin's treatment by Stalin no doubt gave his analysis a certain edge.) When present in literature, that element of the carnivalesque tends to produce multiple languages within the one work ('heteroglossia' again) and it can generate liberating laughter. In this way, it is able to function as 'a complex system of meaning existing alongside and in opposition to the dominant, authoritarian orthodoxy' (p. 194), playfulness and the generation of meaning going hand in hand. Huizinga, from a different perspective, allows that the play-instinct can be 'instrumental towards the acquisition of knowledge', but reminds us too that, at root, 'true play knows no propaganda; its aim is in itself' (1945: 238).

This concept is especially relevant to a discussion of how we articulate our relationships with audiences for TIE and other forms of interventionist and community development theatre, since it firmly shifts the focus from persuasive, coercive, objectives-driven work to the understanding of theatre as a pleasurable interactive experience, one that, grounded in elements such as *playing, entertainment, pretence, physical activity* and *potential subversiveness*, unites performers and spectators in a playful engagement (Jackson and Lev-Aladgem 2004: 207). It leads to a focus on the 'eventness' of the theatre as an actual, 'here and now' real happening involving living people – and as a vital, alternative means by which meaning can be generated (p. 207).

In the next section I want to offer two examples of educational (or interventionist) theatre that illustrate how, if in a small key, the playful dimension can be an integral part of an agenda-driven piece of theatre, and how the constraints of working to a brief negotiated with an outside, non-arts agency can still allow for creativity, surprise, playfulness and learning.

Geese Theatre

Geese Theatre[8] is employed almost exclusively by the prison and proba-tionary service to deliver educational drama programmes for offenders, probationers and 'youth at risk'. It could hardly be more 'outcomes-driven'. But the company's work illustrates well the opportunity to deploy the art form with imagination and verve without compromising the given agendas they serve. At the heart of its practice is a belief in the sheer power of theatre in its elemental form to provoke imaginations and trigger different ways of seeing the world, and by extension to influence attitudes and, where possible, behaviour. Its styles of performance are assertively non-naturalistic. What the company is perhaps best known for is its use of that highly theatrical device, the mask. Geese's approach is summed up well by Alun Mountford, one of the company's longest-serving actor-educators, who explains that, influenced by Meyerhold, and drawing on older traditions that have roots in Roman mimes and *commedia dell'arte*, the company created a series of half-masks which represented the 'front' that an offender might use to keep harsh reality at bay:

> With the mask down, the character can lie, cheat, manipulate or do what-ever he needs to do to maintain his self-image. When characters on stage wish, or are requested by the audience, to say what they really think and feel . . . they lift their masks . . . Theatrically, the mask allowed the actor to represent dynamically the 'inner voice' (the thought process), emphasis-ing thoughts, beliefs, rules and values and their effect on behaviour'. (Mountford and Farrell 1998: 112)

The British company, building on the work of Geese Theatre USA, devel-oped a repertoire of some eight masks that reflected the 'behaviours and manipulations' identified by sociologists as characteristic of criminal behaviour. These 'Fragment Masks' included among others: 'The Fist' (an aggressive-looking mask with a three-dimensional clenched fist thrusting from the forehead, signifying intimidation and a denial of vulnerability: 'Don't mess with me!' is its message); 'The Brick Wall' (the bored, indifferent, uncommunicative and blank mask, signified in the image of a brick wall across the forehead); and 'The Victim' or 'Target' (a mask that pleads for pity and shirks responsibility, superimposed this time with an image of a target – 'Poor Me!', 'I didn't have a choice', and 'the system's against me' are its messages). (See Baim et al. 2002: 184–5.)

Exploring further the sheer complexity of masks we all wear in everyday life, the company went on to look for a mask that lay behind the more obvious masks: one that would represent the impulse that lies beyond cognition (Mountford and Farrell 1998: 113), the urge to attack or steal or abuse, one that offenders often describe as impossible to control: 'the beast within'. From this was born the character of the Death Bird – a large mask resembling 'a skeletal vulture skull' and donned at moments of crisis to help offenders identify that supposedly uncontrollable impulse and at the same time create a space in which it could be challenged, in both performances and workshops.

The process Geese take their participants through is well documented in terms both of the theory (specifically cognitive behavioural theory and social learning theory, drawing on Bandura 1977, McGuire 1995, Vennard et al. 1997, Utting and Vennard 2000) and of the practice (see Baim et al. 2002). The work is always interactive and often extends over a three-day (or more) period of residence in a prison; the extended period of time allows offenders to progress through the workshops that follow the performance in the search for ways of identifying, understanding and modifying behavioural tendencies that have brought them back into prison time and again. The sessions are designed to activate the participants into recognising and exploring issues that relate directly to their own immediate situation. As Andy Watson, current director of Geese UK, explains, the recurring questions tend to be: what happens to me when I get out? will I re-offend and risk returning to prison? how do I deal with the impulses within me that got me here in the first place? how do I deal with my immediate family and friends whose attitudes and lifestyles may well have changed in the intervening period, having got used to my absence? (Watson, interview 2004).

Theatre is usually the stimulus from which the workshops emanate and on which much of the discussion and practical explorations will hang. But less discussed has been the sheer theatrical power that emanates from a performance such as *Gutted*. This piece consists of a

45-minute performance which precedes an intensive workshop, usually lasting three days. It deals with recidivism and follows the fortunes of Craig, the play's protagonist, who stands for the 'eternal recidivist' who will not face up to his own responsibility for his continual offending and who dons and raises his defensive masks accordingly. While he functions undoubtedly, on one level, as an audience surrogate, there is an absence of any figure that might be seen as a corresponding author surrogate, or of any moments that could be identified as offering the message of the play. The character who appears to be the 'stage manager' and controls the action, present throughout the play, is a type-figure referred to by Geese as the 'Con-smith'. He is one of a number of permutations of the 'Fool' character, who jest, provoke and needle the protagonists into ignoring pleas from wives, victims or police, appealing in some of the plays to the 'Death Bird' impulse within them. Quite unlike Boal's 'Joker' (though often confused with it), the Fool's task is to provoke by taking a deliberately confrontational line, both with the protagonist and with the audience themselves; he will sometimes be the audience's best friend, sometimes quite antagonistic. He has to be a 'good facilitator and have a knowledge of offending behaviour – and of how to ask the right ques- tions' (Watson, interview). Ruding (interview, 2004) avers that experi- ence in stand-up comedy can be an excellent preparation for the challenges of such work, and of the Fool's part in particular. The 'Con- smith' is a less aggressive figure, content to watch for much of the time from the sidelines, intervening simply to gather the protagonist up as he hits yet another 'brick wall', providing an inner voice – that of the offend- ing side of the character – to urge him on to further offending behaviour: 'get your own back, make sure you're always number one'. The protag- onist does as the Con-smith says – and it doesn't work. The consequent unhappiness and frustration is likely to correspond closely to the unhap- piness felt by the men themselves. But it is up to the audience to construct their own individual (and sometimes collective) meanings from the expe- rience, with the aid of the workshops and roleplay exercises that follow the play.

Is there none the less an overriding message that the prisoners are expected or encouraged to take from the experience? The work is undoubtedly agenda-driven. Watson agrees that, while they do every- thing in their power to avoid moralising, the process is loaded. The company works consistently to achieve the overall goals that underpin not only its official charitable status but everything it does in practice. Those goals are: to reduce recidivism; to reduce criminality; and to reduce the number of victims (Watson 2004, interview). There is an agenda but it has 'got to be about self-learning'. And if there is a message

Plate 14 Geese Theatre, 2001. Craig is urged on to take a violent stance by his peers, *in Gutted*.

Plate 15 Geese Theatre, 2001. In *Lifting the Weight*, the Fool goads the offender into raising his mask.

that runs through the sessions, it is probably no more, no less, than, in Watson's words: 'Take responsibility for your own actions', based on the tacit belief that 'most people have the desire to change, even if only a little bit'. The company therefore tries to tap into that ambivalence that people have towards their own behaviour: wanting things to be different while at the same time believing there are all kinds of reasons to explain, perhaps justify, what they have done. The positive, constructive aspect of the message is that, while we all have masks, it is possible to 'lift the mask and admit there are other things going on, you can be honest about yourself' (Watson). It is a simple metaphor, but its implications and the personal meanings likely to be constructed from it are complex. Lifting the mask is not *the* solution. What about the mask beneath the mask? What happens if 'being honest' doesn't work? Do you put the mask back on? Or is there another route?

A quite different Geese play, in which the theatricality is by comparison quite understated, but potent, is *Stay*. The play, dealing with domestic abuse, forms a pivotal part of a package of work that Geese offers to the probation services, and is constantly subject to adaptation as it plays to different audiences with different needs and in response to the requirements of different probation services. At one performance I witnessed (at a probation centre in the Midlands in 2003), the stunned silence with which a group of adult male probationers watched the steady downhill progress of a marriage into violence and abuse was, for me, a testament to the galvanising power of theatre in making concrete the usually unspoken and, till too late, the invisible processes that lead to violence in a relationship and to a trap from which none of the parties can readily escape. The play was brilliantly yet simply played on a minimal set – a transverse acting area with, at either end, a screen representing entrance to a domestic interior and an internal door to other parts of the flat, a space that also became, as needed, pub and school playground. The two protagonists (husband and wife) do not wear masks. The mask-wearer is a doll: their son who has to deal with the warring factions as each seeks control over him at the expense of the partner, who learns to wear different masks simply to survive, and who in turn learns the behaviours from his parents that seem inevitably destined to land him in the same traps in which his parents are already enmeshed. The actors position the audience with immense care. There is no explicit hot-seating of the characters during or immediately after the play, but there are specific, carefully designed points at which the male character turns to the audience to justify his behaviour (his 'denials'), done in a disturbingly seductive manner, for example, at a scene in a pub, where the character turns to the audience as though his regular drinking mates, bantering over whose turn it is to buy a round. As he tells his story (about the difficulties he's going through with his wife), he invites comments, interjections, questions – and the audience may or may not enter into the dialogue. 'Those denial moments are vital for the audience to have the opportunity to challenge not just the character but themselves', Watson explains. There is a 'horrible inevitability' about what the man says, but 'it's what you hear in pubs – these are the excuses people use to justify their behaviour all the time'. For the audience it is a 'no win' situation – 'no matter what they say, nothing will get through to this guy, until the very end'.

Here was a dramatic structure that was driven by an unrelenting logic, a logic that becomes unavoidable through the course of the drama and one that was not in the slightest reliant on an authorial message. The strategy of the performance and the workshop that followed was based on the principle that the best person to challenge the distortion (that is, the abusive male's belief that he has every justification for doing what he does) is the person that holds such distorted beliefs (Watson, interview). The aim is therefore to engage those men in the audience who want to change. The man is not portrayed as a monster– there has to be a possibility that the outcome could have been different. An opportunity to see the 'softer' aspects of his character is given in a flashback to a moment from the man's childhood, when we see him reliving the experience of being bullied and humiliated in the playground. He has been a victim himself; but he is also in desperate need of someone else in his life: 'If I can control this person, they won't leave me' is the belief that needs challenging. The piece offers a further example of how a powerful dramatic experience can engender what Festinger has termed 'cognitive dissonance' (see Chapter 5) – the sudden realisation that the beliefs you have (or the beliefs you share with the play's protagonist) are completely at odds with the world as seen from another's perspective (here that of the wife and the son). This experience provides rich material for the participants then to follow up in the ensuing discussion and workshop.

In ways such as this, theatre as an aesthetic experience is capable of reaching people who probably have little if any prior experience of live theatre, and can be used as an aid to interrogating personal experience. But within that agenda-driven context, it gives space to those qualities that lie at the root of all effective, live theatre: playfulness, surprise, danger, unpredictability, spontaneity, emotional engagement, performative skill, 'eventness'. These qualities have often been a key factor in successful TIE. For theatre in prisons, one might think such qualities – especially those that carry with them associations of dissent or loss of control – would have been difficult to utilise, if not anathema to those in institutional charge. In fact, while there are inevitably occasional difficulties and always new people to persuade, the company's unique style is one of the very reasons why Geese's work has managed to sustain itself for so long. Highly skilled and carefully pitched playing, extended into the lives of offenders (or ex-offenders), and used as a springboard for workshops in which the participants can (at one remove) investigate and reflect on their own behaviour and belief systems, together with the company's proven track record of effective working in prisons across the country, enable Geese to negotiate those apparently contradictory requirements of prison institution and of live theatre.

Forever

This section draws on recent audience research undertaken by the author into the theatre-in-education programme already referred to (p. 201), *Forever*, dealing with parenting and teenage pregnancy. The research focused upon the nature of the 'theatrical event', audience recall and 'ownership', and the interplay between art form and social purpose. It attempted to offer a different perspective from the one commonly offered by official evaluations which stress the behavioural or attitudinal impact of such programmes. Above all, the multi-layered impact of a piece that deliberately combined seriousness of topic and playfulness of treatment proved to be the most enduring quality identified by the young audiences interviewed.

There have been many evaluations of theatre-in-education and especially theatre-in-*health*-education programmes, most of which, commissioned by funding bodies, tend to stress the behavioural or attitudinal impact of the programmes on their target audiences. (This tendency is further discussed by among others Allen et al. 1999, Jackson 1996, Robinson 1993 and Winston 2005.) But, in the UK at least, surprisingly little independent research has been conducted into the value and validity of educational theatre as *theatre* as opposed to its function as an instrument of social or educational change. The concern is almost always (with some notable exceptions) with what happens after the event rather than with the event itself. The interplay between art form and 'social purpose' is one that requires a great deal more attention than it has hitherto received. (Classroom or 'process' drama, less constrained by the requirement to fulfil briefs set by outside agencies, has fared better – there is now a sizeable body of research into drama in education in its various manifestations, as the work of Bolton 1998, Taylor 1996, Somers 1996, Wagner 1998 and many others amply testifies.)

The primary aim of this particular research project was therefore to try assess the impact upon young audiences of one professional theatre programme that set out explicitly to educate. It focused upon the nature of the 'theatrical event', audience recall and 'ownership', and the extent to which the 'aesthetic dimension' was perceived to be an integral part of the process by recipients (pupils and teachers), creative team and funders alike. One of the key questions driving this research then was: what constitutes a 'theatrical event' in circumstances when traditional boundary-lines that separate audience from actors are deliberately blurred or reconfigured, when the company are clearly performing on 'school territory', and when a 'teaching' agenda provides the play's initial *raison d'être*?

Sauter's notion of the 'playing culture' at the heart of any theatrical event was one particular factor that shaped the research questions I was asking. Hence my wish to give some prominence in the research to the part that spectators play in the making of meaning and indeed in the making of the theatre event itself – a recognition that, whatever the agenda that lay behind the commissioning of the script, an analysis of the impact made by the play must take account of the processes that lie at the heart of any theatrical experience.

The case study

The specific production selected for analysis was *Forever*, written by Mary Cooper, a theatre-in-education programme for fourteen- to sixteen-year-olds, commissioned and toured by the M6 Theatre Company, Rochdale, to schools in Greater Manchester and elsewhere in the North West during the spring and autumn of 2000; then again in spring 2001 and 2002; and for one final tour in autumn 2003.

The play – a performance followed by an interactive workshop, which allowed pupils to interrogate characters from the play they had just seen – was commissioned in response to increasing concern nationally, and not least in government, about the extent of underage sex and teenage pregnancy in Britain, which now has one of the highest rates of teenage pregnancy in western Europe. Carefully targeted schools in Rochdale and certain other boroughs of Greater Manchester, all of which were considered to be priority areas (that is, within the top 10 per cent of boroughs in which the incidence of teenage pregnancy is particularly high), were invited to participate as part of a government-subsidised educational programme. Teachers simply had to agree to take the play and the accompanying workshop and participate in a number of follow-up activities: ensuring that each pupil who saw the performance completed a questionnaire (mainly on the provision of support services relating to sexual health and pregnancy), organising time for an outside evaluator to conduct class interviews following the performance, and submitting an evaluative report. My own research lay outside the official evaluation and was geared more to assessing the *theatrical* impact of the programme upon its audiences, though there were obviously overlaps in the findings that emerged.[9]

Using a qualitative method of enquiry based primarily upon observation and semi-structured small-group interview, I focused on just four schools, talked briefly to pupils (in groups of roughly 12–15) before they saw the play to ascertain some of the expectations they had before the event took place; talked to them again (this time in groups of between three and five) shortly after the performance – sometimes on the same day, sometimes two to three days later; and yet again some two to three months after the event, this time to gauge the extent of their recall and how far their views now coincided with what they had expressed immediately after the event.

The interviews were based on a set of semi-closed questions amplified and adjusted from group to group according to what each group wished to talk about, and moving from question to conversation as and when appropriate to allow, as far as possible, for pupils' own unforced responses (it was important to try to get beyond what the pupils thought I wanted them to think). For triangulation purposes, at one school, in addition to the interviews, pupils were asked to express their views individually in a 'video box' format (that is, in front of a camera with just a few prompts from the interviewer), the point being to see if a different technique produced any variation in the views expressed. (In fact mostly it did not.) At another school, the performance was videoed, first from behind the audience, and then at a subsequent performance by means of a camera placed at the side of the acting area, focused upon the audience in order to track general audience response in visual terms. From some of the schools, it was also possible to read a sample of reviews that students taking drama had been asked to write – again offering another means of checking students' views when expressed in a different medium. Finally, the class teachers, members of the company – director, actors, stage manager and facilitator – and the LEA teenage pregnancy education co-ordinator were interviewed as a check, firstly, on how their intentions and objectives corresponded with what the pupils said they actually got out of it; and, secondly, on how their own views of the event coincided with those of the pupils. Subsequent analysis of the interview transcripts enabled me to identify key categories into which to place pupils' responses (for example, 'recall'; 'identification of the message'; 'sense of ownership'; 'eventness', 'playfulness') – categories that on the one hand related to the original research questions and the semi-closed interview questions and on the other reflected directly, if and where appropriate, the pupils' own differing perceptions.[10]

The event

The play had already had a highly successful run during spring 2000 when it was toured to Year 11 (fifteen- to sixteen-year-old) pupils; this particular production was targeted at Year 10 (fourteen- to fifteen-year-olds) and was staged by the same director (Greg Banks). Two professional evaluations had been undertaken after the first tour which confirmed that the production had effectively fulfilled the brief set by the educationists and that demand for it had been far greater than could be met by the one tour (McCarthy 2000, Sharland 2000).

In the play, a nineteen-year-old boy (Adam) tells, and re-enacts, a story about meeting up with his long-lost father (Liam) and hearing his account of what happened when, as teenagers, he and his mother (Gemma) first met, of their reaction on realising they were going to have a baby, and how that affected their relationship. Much of the drama was enacted through flashbacks to the first date, the arrival of the baby and the deteriorating relationship as the baby made demands upon their patience and their budgets, leading to Liam's desertion of his family. The versions told by mother and father were shown to be sometimes significantly different. Perhaps the most effective device used (certainly if students' response was anything to go by) was that the large actor playing the nineteen-year-old also played himself as the baby (which the audiences found very funny). The play ends with Adam discovering that a 'one-night-stand' has led to his occasional girlfriend (whom he clearly has no desire to continue with) becoming pregnant, and so the cycle begins again. His newly acquired grasp of what his parents went through has been gained too late. What will he do now? In the following workshop, led by a neutral facilitator (Gill Baskeyfield), the pupils had a chance to investigate further: they were asked what they thought the play was about and were then shown a number of key moments from the play, replayed by the actors, and invited to discuss the themes and subsequently ask questions of each of the characters in turn about why they did what they did, and offer advice to them.

The whole event usually lasted about 1 hour 40 minutes: one hour for the play and between 30 and 40 minutes for the workshop depending on the school timetable. (In today's more constrained funding climate, this format – a play followed by a workshop – tends to be the most common one for school audiences. At its best, the performance is

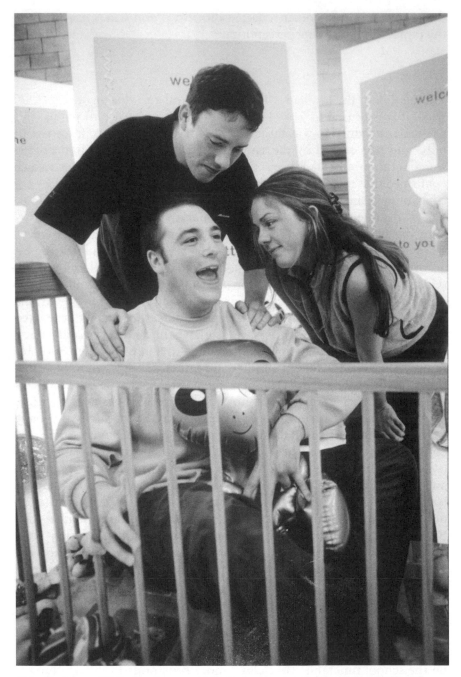

Plate 16 *Forever.* M6 Theatre Company, 2000. Performers: Guy Christiansen (as 'the baby'), Mark Wadsworth and Nicola Maxfield.

designed with the workshop in mind: the two elements are in productive symbiosis, with the audience participation in the workshop generated as much by the direct style of the performance as by the role of the facilitator.)

Interpreting the pupils' responses

The research amply confirmed what the company – and indeed the teachers – knew already: that the great majority of the pupils had enjoyed the play immensely; that they had readily understood the more obvious 'messages' of the play (e.g. that underage sex and teenage pregnancy are full of risks and should be avoided, not least in the teenagers' own interests, that 'thinking things through' is vital). There were however some rather more interesting points to emerge from the interviews, 'video box' sessions and written assignments, which bear particularly on the question of 'ownership' and the interplay of art form and social purpose, and which suggested the strong dialogic and playful levels on which the experience had worked for them.[11]

Making meanings: message versus ownership. What was the message in the pupils' view and how far did they absorb it, translate it into their own terms? To what extent did the event go beyond being the one-way transmission of that message? Did they, in other words, learn anything that mattered to them? It appeared that they did. 'You could relate to it', 'You saw it from all points of view', 'You have to think twice', 'I don't want a kid!' were some of the comments students proffered. The play showed 'there are responsibilities with having a child and you don't know what they are until you actually have a child' (interview 2000) and it 'shows an audience what situations they would have if they were in that position: it is a learning play' (written review 2001). Interestingly, a running theme through many students' responses was the value of seeing the issues and the dilemmas played out in front of them: 'I have heard it [the message] a lot of times . . . don't get pregnant when you are young, but I think it were more descriptive . . . It didn't like give you a message, it showed it to you in a different way . . . you had to watch it to realise what it were like.' Several gave anecdotal examples of 'friends' who had changed their minds about having babies and using condoms.[12] The complex resonances of the play are well suggested by one girl's comments that 'It made people think about the consequences: everything, not just about being pregnant, it made you think about being young and what you want to do with your life' (interview 2001).

There were other indicators too of the extent to which the pupils felt they had some ownership of the event (and wanted to talk about the issues in their own terms). After two to three months the play was still vividly in their minds – the names of the characters may have escaped them, but the impact on them of the characters' short-term thinking appeared to be resonating still. And in the consultations conducted as part of the sexual health education programme, students frequently referred back to the play (without prompting) for examples of what can go wrong in casual relationships (Baskeyfield 2001). While several teachers, and several company members (including one of the cast who had performed for Year 11 in the first tour as well as for Year 10), averred that the Year 10 pupils may have been in some ways (emotionally) a little too young for the play, all the pupils interviewed without exception were insistent that it was pitched just right for them (some indeed angrily rejected the idea that they were too young for this material); and that they could see how easy it would be to find themselves in similar situations to the ones presented. They readily translated the 'message' into their own terms: 'When the performance finished, I felt confused for Adam. It made me think what I would do in . . . his situation. Would I go and see my dad if he'd left . . .? What would I do if I was going to become a parent with someone I didn't even like?' (written review). Although girls tended to be more critical of the fathers than were the boys, there were many exceptions. One boy was angered by Liam's behaviour: 'You can't just turn away from that problem. It is his baby, he can't go "right, I have finished with you now" . . .' (interview 2000). The use of strong language and strong feelings was commented on favourably because 'it got across to us better', 'They didn't treat us like kids' (interview 2000).

Theatricality (the representational frame). What was special about it being a piece of live theatre in their own school (as opposed to a conventional lesson or a video)? The performance of the play in their own hall with the actors and the action literally only a few feet away from them had added to their engagement and sense of 'ownership' of the event. Its very closeness gave them a sense of immediacy and directness which they felt was powerful. They thoroughly enjoyed the 'liveness' and 'fun' of having the performance take place in front of them. And no, they would definitely *not* rather have seen it on video: 'It has more power if it is acted in front of you instead of the television' (written review 2001). 'It is better watching it in a play than . . . on TV, you pay more attention' (interview 2000). They spoke of how 'believable' the story and the characters were: 'I liked the fact we were so close to the stage. It made the performance much more personal . . . I felt more like a friend of the actors and could understand the characters' feelings and emotions' (written review 2001); and 'When Adam narrates he makes direct eye contact with the audience which adds to the sense of involvement for them' (written review 2001). Above all, it made the issues (and the warnings) seem 'real' to them: 'It shows the consequences . . . to help us avoid doing it' and 'You can remember it more as well, put a face to what happened' (interview). Interestingly, a running theme through many of their responses was the value of *seeing* the issues and the dilemmas played out in front of them: 'I have heard it [the message] a lot of times . . . don't get pregnant when you are young, but I think it were more descriptive . . . It didn't like give you a message, it showed it to you in a different way . . . you had to watch it to realise what it were like.' 'Usually when teachers say stuff it just goes in like but, because you are watching, it was allright, it made you watch it. I like watching, it were good' (interview 2000) and 'You understand it more if you see it' (interview 2001) were characteristic of comments made in all four schools. The value gained from *watching* the dilemmas unfold, expressed by a considerable number of respondents, underlines the quality of engagement and empathy that seems to have derived directly from the play being in their midst – qualified only by the frustration of some sitting at the back who suffered from a poor view of the acting area and by the distaste felt by several on the front row when on the receiving end of some of the baby's all-too-realistic choking and spluttering!

Interaction (the involvement frame). Feelings were more mixed about the interactive workshop. Some viewed it as essential because it added information, increased their understanding of the characters' dilemmas and gave them a chance to test their responses out on the characters themselves and sometimes challenge the attitudes they expressed. In the workshop, 'people could ask them things perhaps actually they want to know themselves'; and it dealt with 'real-life issues, talking to you properly, it gave you proper answers' (interview 2000). Others however found that it added little, that all the points had been made by the play; that it was less fun; that it made the event too long (and many were sitting on floor mats or wooden benches some two to three rows back, often with limited sightlines). The implication may be that participation for its own sake is not axiomatically 'a good thing'. It will work if and only if it is conceived as part of the whole, not a 'bolted-on' appendix, and handled in a way that acknowledges the practical limits of how long pupils can sit through a play and workshop combined. Several teachers felt that the participatory session would have worked better had the group of sixty or so pupils been divided into, say, three smaller groups allowing a change of atmosphere and closer contact with each of the three characters. Other factors were beyond the company's control and varied from school to school and even according to the time of day. At some schools, where the 'outer (or pretheatre) frame' of the school environment, the prior expectations aroused by teachers, and indeed the actual management of the event by teachers on the day (trying to achieve that difficult balance between control and the encouragement to enjoy) were more appropriate, the participatory session worked extremely well, marked as much by the energy, absorption and involvement of the pupils when given the opportunity to ask questions of the characters as by the comments given in interview. 'During the workshop . . . you could tell the audience felt as though they were talking to real people instead of fictional characters . . . everyone felt strongly towards them'. . . (written review 2001). Often it was the opportunity to put questions to Liam, the father, that generated the most remarkable upsurge of raised hands. 'I did feel angry towards Liam, but understood why he left' (written review 2001). Invariably, pupils displayed no awkwardness or confusion during these interactive sessions: the opportunity to talk to the characters seemed simply to be a logical outcome of what the play had set in motion. In this respect the two sections of the programme were fully integrated, the play being as much a part of the participatory whole as the workshop itself.

   Playfulness. The play ended on a disturbing note, the cycle was beginning again. Adam was trapped in an all-too-similar way to that experienced by his own parents 19 years earlier. The students found that totally believable. But was it depressing? Did they feel trapped? Their response in interview suggests that emphatically they did not. It was 'not depressing, it were sad. You can't feel the depression inside because they put humour in it as well' (interview 2000). Depressing? 'Not really. It was too bubbly . . . the way they did it , like 'oh, my baby!', then next minute they were saying they were sick of the baby!' (interview 2000). The implication of what they said *seemed* to be that their responsiveness, their engagement with the story and the characters, was bound up with the sense that it was a play and simultaneously serious and playful: watching it was fun and they were fully aware that the drama was both 'real' and 'pretend' at the same time.[13] 'I thought it was brilliant and I thought it were silly' (interview 2000); 'It was funny but it was serious' (interview 2000). The portrayal of the baby by a big, six-feet-tall Liverpudlian actor – physically as inappropriate a piece of casting as it was possible to imagine – who captured brilliantly the movements, facial grimaces and noises of a three-month-old baby, was the highlight of the play for many. 'Having an adult playing a baby was practical, comical, [it] physically exaggerated the impact a baby has on people's lives, and helped us to appreciate the child's point of view' (written review 2001). The director explained that, in restaging the play after its first run, he had wanted from the opening moments of the play to communicate immediately to his audience that this was going to be an enjoyable experience[14] – that they could relax and take it as it came – that if there was to be a message (as many had already been told) then it was not going to be a laborious illustration of what they got told by adults day in, day out. He was all too aware that young audiences, once they have deciphered what a play's message is, then quickly 'turn off': 'Always at the beginning of a piece of theatre you need to shake up people's expectations so they don't get what they thought they were going to get' (Banks interview). In part, this constituted a further element in the induction process, this time an internal device, strategically placed at the very start when audiences were especially receptive but equally very ready to make snap decisions about whether or not they would 'buy in' to this event. As one girl expressed it, 'I thought [at] the very beginning . . . it was going to be fun and totally different than anything I had ever seen before' (interview 2001). What was crucial in reaching this sceptical audience, then, was the element of *playfulness* with which the stories were enacted: that is, the invitation offered to the audience to 'play' with the cast as the story unfolded, to enter into a game in which the actors would tell a story – serious, funny, disturbing, sad as it was from moment to moment – but which, at the same time as alarm-bells were being rung, was also saying: this is not real, it's a story, it's believable and very close to your own lives, but it's not actually you. The very (serious) playfulness with which the actors switched roles and humorously, ironically, highlighted the gullibility and shortsightedness of the characters, enabled the students to see that things were not fixed – that the privileged perspective offered them by the fiction was potentially liberating. The participatory workshop, even if added little to their knowledge of the characters, certainly confirmed the idea that things were changeable, that there were always choices to be made. The participatory 'playing culture' that the performance initiated and the workshop developed, was clearly at work here.

Interestingly, the play was subsequently adapted for television by the Channel 4 network (4Learning) for its education service to schools. Some brief comparisons between the two productions may help to highlight the distinctive qualities of a piece designed to work as a 'theatrical event'. The television producer after much debate decided to replace most of the theatrical conventions with a television-documentary style of realism ('we wanted to play on "reality" and give the film the texture of a documentary – camera hand-held, moving round finding the shot, shooting against windows, very little lighting etc.', Parker 2001).

The gain in pace and authenticity of setting was, however, paid for by the loss of credibility in the casting. Realistic drama on television conventionally requires near-perfect casting: we are far less tolerant of age inaccuracies than we are in the theatre, not least because of the need for close-ups. As it was, the actors offered convincing portrayals of the mother–son sequences in the present but for the teenage love affair the merciless gaze of the television camera exposed the casting of (older) actors as wholly inappropriate. Indeed, it undermined the whole 'teenage pregnancy' theme of the play. Even more problematic was the casting of the baby. The Adam-as-narrator device was retained (Adam often turns to speak direct to camera as though telling the story to his best mate) but the baby was shown as a real baby with grown-up Adam's voice over to indicate the flash-back connection (again television's inexorable pressure to 'cast for real'). In the theatre piece, the playing of the baby by a superb adult actor had been integral to its style and content, as was the actor's ability to generate a strong rapport with an audience only feet away from him. Inevitably, the television version, while strong on pace (rapidly cutting between scenes), could not begin to match the playful, transformative, in-front-of-your-eyes process of the live event. And it had several repercussions. It partly displaced Adam from the centre of the narrative: because we could not see him 'being' the baby as the discovery of what happened between his parents unfolded, we lost the direct connection between baby and teenage selves and the self-discovery Adam undergoes. And the baby itself never became the dominant force in the drama and the relationship that it did in the stage version. It remained an object that people did things to or with. And finally, perhaps inevitably, in the transfer from stage to screen, we lost the brilliant playfulness with which the original Adam switched from being nineteen years old to one year old (so hugely enjoyed by the young audiences) and thereby engaged those audiences at several levels. Lost was the invitation to a live audience to actively engage in the making of meaning, to become virtual players in the 'game' of theatre and in the process to 'own' their share in the creation of the event. Lost too of course was the opportunity to extend that engagement into an even more active, verbal interrogation of the characters.

Mary Cooper, author of *Forever* and of many TIE plays (for M6 and other companies), takes a positive approach to working to a given agenda, even when set by a non-arts-based commissioning body. The condition simply has to be that the brief is set with an understanding of what makes good theatre. Theatre is not, she says, 'about passing on information', and cannot be a 'living leaflet'. It is an emotional medium. If she is to shift her teenage audience from the position of 'This is remote and alien' to 'This is about me', she can only do that 'if you touch them emotionally, make them feel something . . . bring them in this way closer to the issues'. Her aim is to 'enable young people to become subject rather than object' – something that counters what many children experience at school (Cooper interview, April 2004). The challenge in *Forever* was to make teenage boys understand that parenting is as much about fathers as about mothers. It was commissioned as a play about parenting, but it clearly could not be a play about how to change a nappy! It had to be about the emotional lives of the characters, and it had to make a connection with young men. From her own experience and research, Cooper recognised that there were two shocks involved in having a baby:

> First, you have a baby – they're totally dependent on you and there's this other thing in the room with you; secondly, it will be with you forever, and that is a profound emotional shock. Women experience both; men often don't experience the second. All too often, they do not see themselves being around forever, and find it scary, difficult to deal with. And they are often pushed away by that relationship with the baby, by the emotional intensity of the mother . . . I wanted to get across that rawness of experience, emotional nakedness, and the difficulty men have in dealing with it, especially if you're eighteen.

Can theatre change behaviour? Cooper argues that

> If [the teenage audience] do feel, 'this is me', that the issue is not just 'out there', if you can get them to make an investment in the issue themselves, if the play gets them to 're-view', to look again at a situation they thought they knew . . . then they may change, may reach different conclusions . . . But change may take years and theatre won't change people on its own . . . But it can be a part [of the process]. You also have to 'hook' people at the right time. A play about teenage sexual identity and relationships when they're trying to work it out for themselves anyway may be a very helpful thing for them; they can talk about things more freely and maybe as a result behave rather differently. (Cooper 2004)

Did *Forever* have any measurable impact on teenage conceptions in Rochdale? No one can say definitively. But the official figures are as follows. As of 2005, and using as a baseline data from 1998, the national figure for conceptions of under-eighteens had been reduced by 9 per cent. In the North West the reduction was approximately 4 per cent. In Rochdale, the reduction was 15 per cent, almost three times better than the regional average. This change cannot be attributed directly to M6's work, but – according to Rochdale's Teenage Pregnancy Strategy Officer, Mark Limmer – 'research has shown that the places with the greatest positive change have been in those areas where there has been a variety of creative initiatives' (Limmer and Wood correspondence 2005). Throughout this period, M6 toured and retoured productions to all Rochdale high schools both of *Forever* and of various dramatic monologues (with accompanying workshops) relating to teenage parenting.

The evaluations produced by the commissioning body (the Teenage Pregnancy Unit of the local education authority) and the evaluators of the first tour stressed first and foremost the effectiveness of the play in raising awareness, provoking questions and (apparently) leading to some attitudinal change, at least in the short term (McCarthy 2000, Sharland 2000). The strength of the programme as a piece of theatre was recognised and praised, not least for the enjoyment it generated and its lack of 'sermonising', but – quite understandably – it was the impact on pupils' attitudes to unprotected sex and under age pregnancy that constituted the primary agenda. My own research attempted to offer a rather different though complementary perspective, looking at the theatre not just as the means to an end but as 'the thing itself'. The pupils' readiness, in their later reflections, to elide form and content, theatrical medium and message; their recall of the play as much for its performative qualities as for the (referential) issues it explicitly addressed; their absorption in and engagement with the dilemmas each of the characters faced; and, not least, the tough task they set the researcher looking to categorise their responses, are all, I suggest, heartening measures of the effectiveness of the programme as educational theatre. There was a playfulness at the centre of the piece which allowed real engagement at emotional and intellectual levels, quite different from deciphering 'the message'. For that reason, if the play's effect on the pupils' attitudes and behaviour were indeed to prove to be durable, then it is likely to derive as much from its complex, multi-layered and interactive (or dialogic) impact on those audiences, from its 'eventness', as from the explicit messages being communicated.[15]

The school student who found the play was 'silly' and 'brilliant' was in part acknowledging the 'in between' nature of resonant theatre performances in which 'message' becomes side-stepped by the multi-levelled and multi-vocal processes of drama, all the more powerful because they offer a subversive space in which audiences are freed to make up their *own* minds on where they stand. If the messages on offer are worth hearing, they will be picked up by the audience in their own way and at their own choosing. Forcing the message down their throats is, as we all know only too well, not only counterproductive; it denies the liberating power of drama to move us in surprising ways. Maybe that student knew something about drama.

The interconnection between the playful and yet another form of institution, often perceived to be rigid and unbending in its goals and *modus operandi*, and antipathetic to live performance – the museum and, equally emblematic of 'heritage' and resonant of a fixed past, the historic house – is the subject of the final chapter.

Notes

1 See www.creative-partnerships.com/aboutcp/, last accessed 31 May 2006.
2 From the website www.wellcome.ac.uk/en/1/awtprerel0299n113.html, last accessed 10 October 2001. See also Chapter 4, note 2, for note on the Wellcome Trust.
3 Reproduced by permission from the M6 Theatre submission to the Nationwide Foundation, October 2001.
4 See National Campaign for the Arts Report, 'Theatre in Education: 10 Years of Change', 1997; also Whybrow 1994.
5 The Teenage Pregnancy Unit is a cross-government unit located within the Department for Education and Skills which was set up to implement the Social Exclusion Unit's report on Teenage Pregnancy: www.dfes.gov.uk/teenagepregnancy/dsp_Content.cfm?PageID=85 (last accessed 21 August 2006).
6 *Love Trouble* was promoted to schools as 'a two-hour Theatre in Health Education programme on HIV/AIDS and relationships'. The programme was toured by Action Transport Theatre Co. throughout Cheshire in Autumn of 1995 and seen by about six thousand young people in schools and youth clubs; it was re toured, owing to demand from schools, in autumn 1997. The broad aims may be summarised as:

- to provide a quality theatre experience that emotionally engages and challenges its audiences
- to empower young people and offer strategies in order that they can take responsibility for their own health and well-being
- to provide an active forum in which young people can check out facts and information in a safe and non-judgemental environment
- to actively engage the audience with the characters in the play in order that the individuals can explore their own understanding of the behaviour, emotions and experiences of the characters involved
- to give clear information on the facts around HIV/AIDS and challenge misinformation surrounding HIV/AIDS
- to explore some of the wider issues around HIV/AIDS such as prejudice, fear, confidentiality, responsibility, gender, homophobia, and 'risk-taking'
- to provide a comprehensive resource pack for teachers/youth workers complementing the play and integral workshops in order that the learning experiences offered by *Love Trouble* can be reinforced and developed further.

7 My own evaluation of the programme was conducted alongside but separately from the company's own evaluation; space does not permit any detailed analysis of the data, but the report as submitted to the North West Arts Board (now Arts Council North West) is available from the author. The quotations from school pupils that follow are extracted from transcripts of the series of small-group interviews conducted three to four weeks after each performance. See Jackson (1995a).

 8 Geese Theatre was founded in the United States in 1980 by Clark Baim, who
    formed Geese Theatre UK in 1987.
 9 The research was aided by a grant from the UK's Arts & Humanities
    Research Council.
10 The methodology was not foolproof. Apart from the usual problems of
    school timetabling, classes disrupted by sudden intrusions of other groups
    'on their way through', pupils away sick or called out of class, or of tape-
    recorder malfunction, it was not always possible for pupils to be drawn from
    the cross-section of ability and social background I had looked for. And,
    while the small-group interviews often worked well in providing mutual
    support and stimulus (on occasion debates broke out within the group as
    they argued the rights and wrongs of the father's part in the story), at other
    times the group dynamic slipped too readily into the 'leaders and led' syn-
    drome, generating I suspect more uniformity of views than may actually have
    been the case. See Cohen and Manion (1994) for discussion of some of the
    research methodologies which guided this project.
11 These and the subsequent quotations are taken from a series of small-group
    interviews conducted by the author with pupils from four high schools in
    Rochdale between November 2000 and March 2001, and from related
    written work (reviews) produced by pupils from one of those schools. Details
    are given in Jackson 2002.
12 One of the teachers responsible for the personal, social and health education
    syllabus asserted that every year a number of girls with very low self-esteem
    do try to get pregnant for status-raising purposes.
13 One must however be wary of attributing such positive response too readily
    to *all* the pupils who saw the play. Some may well have 'switched off' or reacted
    with cynicism to the very act of having to sit through a school-organised event,
    so of course they were not engaged enough by the narrative to be depressed
    by it.
14 Toys were randomly thrown from backstage over the set on to the acting
    area, sound effects of a baby's rattle and gurgling noises were quickly fol-
    lowed by the appearance of the 'live' baby crawling into the set.
15 The most recent evaluation of the CragRats programme *Wasted* (see
    pp. 204–5), has also, interestingly, found that the play 'stimulated pupils
    through the use of laughter and "silliness" as well as shock and concern –
    all were used effectively to show both the enjoyable and more problematic
    aspects of drinking alcohol at a young age' (Research Works Ltd 2005).

9

Inter-acting with the past: the use of participatory theatre at museums and heritage sites

One area of contemporary educational theatre that has received relatively little attention compared with more high-profile work such as theatre in prisons is the use of theatre in museums and historic sites. In many ways, however, it is at the sharp edge of the debates about how theatre relates to learning. The target audience is often very difficult to predict. While organised groups of visiting schoolchildren can be prepared for in advance, the 'independent' or 'casual' visitor and family groups invariably just turn up on the day. How many, where they are from, their age range, their reasons for coming, the extent of their prior knowledge – all are unknown factors. The subject matter (of the exhibition or site) will generally seem, at least at first glance, to be fixed, predetermined and confined by the particular exhibition or guided tour designed to elucidate it. A historic house communicates an extraordinary sense of 'the past' as strange, awesome, perhaps rather forbidding and the bearer of secrets that are hard to unlock without the help of experts. The museum – in its impressive, often rather old-fashioned and intimidating premises – will seem to many to be the authoritative source of all knowledge about the content of its collections which in turn may well seem remote, evoking a far-off or long-ago world, fascinating in its very disconnectedness from the day-to-day world from which the visitor has momentarily turned.

Traditionally, the mission of the museum has been seen in primarily conservationist terms: as 'an institution that collects, documents, preserves, exhibits and interprets material evidence and associated information for the public benefit' (Museums Association definition – 1984). This role would seem to place the museum firmly in the modernist tradition in which 'grand narratives' are told about the evolution of humankind and the wonders of scientific discovery, and to ally its educational function with positivist, one-way transmission models of learning. But museums have been redefining that role over the past two decades: the Museums Association 2002 definition now also includes recognition of a far more visitor-centred approach, claiming that 'Museums enable people to explore collections for inspiration, learning and enjoyment' (http:// ictop.f2.fhtw-berlin.de/content/view/42/56/, accessed 26 July 2006). The museum world in Britain especially has made remarkable strides to engage visitors and to prioritise less the authoritative imparting of fixed knowledge but rather the stimulation of curiosity, questioning and active learning. Changes in government policy since 1997 – prompted in part by the findings of a major government report into the nation's cultural heritage, specifically within the museum sector, and the ways it might be developed (Anderson 1997, 1999) – have prioritised *accessibility, inclusiveness* and *lifelong learning* for all arts and educational organisations in receipt of public funds. The report noted:

> Museums have entered a time of change. They are being asked to justify their funding and to define the terms of their contract with society . . . Education provides museums with a renewed purpose and enables them to contribute to cultural development in society. (Anderson 1999: 1)

and went on to claim that 'Museums can no longer justify their existence, as many have done in the past, principally in terms of the care and display of their collections' (p. 10). As one commentator put it, 'these days . . . museums take accessibility and inclusiveness far more seriously . . . [partly] because their funding agreements with the Department of Culture, Media and Sport depend on them doing so . . . [partly] because of a cultural shift on the part of both the curators and schools' (Crace 2001).

That shift was accelerated in December 2001 when extra state funds were provided to enable museums to abolish entrance charges, leading to a significant increase in attendance figures. National Lottery funding has had an influence too – it has fostered the extraordinary expansion and modernisation of museums of recent years, and has also brought further pressure to *demonstrate* that museums are for everyone. George Hein, from an American perspective, describes an almost identical and 'increasing pressure on museums to justify their existence' (Hein 1998: 3). In the process, education has been pushed to the top of the agenda for many such organisations. One of the first tasks of the new Director-General of the National Trust, Fiona Reynolds, when appointed in 2001, was to give precedence to education in almost every sphere of the Trust's operation, a policy she progressively implemented during the ensuing years, reiterating in 2003 that one of the Trust's key goals was 'to make sure that education and lifelong learning are at the heart of everything we do' (Reynolds 2003: 5). A recent initiative from the government-funded Museums, Libraries and Archives Council, entitled 'Inspiring learning for all', introduced in 2004 (MLA 2004), further underlined the priority given to education. It sought to promote and expand the range and quality of education activity in museums in response to theories of learning, such as Gardner's 'multiple intelligences' (1983, 1993) and Hein's notion of the 'constructivist museum' (1998). As Helen Rees Leahy points out:

> No longer the 'poor relation' to the core function of curating, the educational role of the museum is now regarded as essential in justifying public investment in the sector, and as a key tool in developing culturally and demographically diverse audiences. Today, education in UK museums is used both to fulfil institutional objectives of audience development and to realise external public policy objectives of ameliorating social exclusion, promoting lifelong learning and increasing access to culture. (Rees Leahy, in Jackson et al. 2002: 11)

This has not been exclusive to the UK but reflects wider international trends. In the United States for example, as Hein and others have noted, 'the last three decades have witnessed a shift in both the definition of education and its relative importance within museums' (Hein 1998: 6), evidenced in a series of reports from the American Association of Museums (1969, 1984, 1992) which have 'consistently elevated and fine tuned museums' educational function' (Hughes et al. 2006: 3).

With these developments has come a renewed interest in ways of using theatre, especially interactive performance, to help meet these new objectives. Theatre can be a means not only of interpreting the collections or the site but of connecting with visitors, engaging their interest and provoking them to reassess their own relationship with the past, or with the subject matter of the exhibition. But it is at the same time a contested practice. While other educational activities (such as workshops, trails and object-handling sessions) are relatively inexpensive to implement and are to be found in most museums, the use of theatre as an interpretative tool in museums in Britain is constrained by a variety of factors, both practical and philosophical. Good-quality museum theatre can be relatively expensive to produce and stage; and many museum professionals resist the use of what they regard as 'an inherently fictionalising medium of interpretation' (Jackson and Rees Leahy 2005: 305), which runs the risk of trivialising or simply distracting attention from the very exhibits it is designed to interpret. There was a salutary warning offered in 1991 by a leading practitioner in museum interpretation at a conference to discuss the future of live interpretation and theatre in museums: 'Museums are not theatres. Visitors are not audiences. History is not Drama. Character interpretation in museums is not Acting.'[1]

No matter how strongly one might believe in the educative power of drama, there are risks in assuming that drama – whether the use of inter-active roleplay, character monologues or full-scale theatre performances – will transfer readily to institutions with their own very distinct goals. The warning was offered, not to deter but to insist that such practice should be seen as a specialist form of interpretation rather than as a branch of the acting profession. The skills required of the costumed interpreter may overlap with, but are not identical to, those of the actor.

None the less, theatre (with or without interaction) is being used increasingly and in a variety of ways at heritage sites and museums, in many countries in Europe, the United States and beyond, in order to enliven the experience of the visitor and to illuminate the past or the gallery exhibitions on display.

'Museum theatre' and 'live interpretation'

The field of work tends to be discussed under one of two main and often interchangeable umbrella titles: museum theatre and live interpretation[2]. The field may broadly be defined as the use of theatre and theatrical tech-niques as a means of mediating knowledge and understanding in the context of museum or heritage education (Jackson et al. 2002). It may take place in museums (in galleries or auditoria) or at historic sites and is gen-erally presented by professional actors and/or interpreters, occasionally by volunteers. It may involve the performance of short plays or monologues based on historical events or materials exhibited on-site; it may be an inter-active event using performance and roleplay, tailored to the curriculum needs of visiting schoolchildren; or it may be designed for family groups and/or the independent visitor (Jackson and Rees Leahy 2005). It may take place in and around original historic buildings or in *reconstructions* of his-toric locations, either on open sites (such as the Blists Hill Victorian Village at Ironbridge, UK) or within large dedicated museum buildings (such as the Victorian streets reconstructed at the Milestones Living History Museum in Hampshire, or the Victorian schoolroom built within the Wigan Pier Heritage Centre, itself a converted canal warehouse close to the original 'pier'). Dramatic approaches are employed for many purposes: education, publicity, marketing, entertainment. Although far from ubiq-uitous, and indeed shunned by some museums, these various forms of dra-matic enactment or 'living history' are now a common, and a popular, feature of visits by public and school pupils alike. The deployment of museum theatre varies across the world and its practice is almost as diverse as the sites in which it takes place.[3] Probably the most common style in museums however – for cost-effective reasons as much as artistic or educational – is that of the single-character monologue, used to tell the stories associated with the collections (Jackson et al. 2002).

In the UK, the use of performance as a means of engaging with visitors has its roots in two main traditions: the theatre-based practice of theatre in education and related 'process drama' techniques (including storytelling), and that of museum-based 'first-' and 'third-person' interpretation. In respect of the first, actors, directors, writers and education officers have frequently turned to participatory theatre methods to provide both interactivity and dramatic structure – through techniques such as roleplay, 'hot-seating' and even on occasion forum theatre – which can then be adapted to the particular collection, site, audience and budget available. Some museum educationalists, on the other hand, have preferred more traditional, non-interactive styles of performance in the belief that a strongly delivered, theatrically-conceived monologue played to a gathered audience gives much sharper focus to the subject matter. Interaction is therefore confined to audience questions-and-answers with the actor out-of-role after the performance (see Jackson et al. 2002).

First- and third-person interpretation is less overtly performance-based and its genealogy is more aligned to the interpretative strategies developed after the Second World War at historic sites in the United States, inspired particularly by Tilden Freeman's seminal 1957 text *Interpreting Our Heritage*. It generally involves interpreters (with or without actor-training) in appropriate period costume interacting with visitors to interpret a heritage site or museum collection. The 'first-person' interpreter assumes a specific role or character (for example, a seventeenth-century pilgrim or nineteenth-century mill worker) and talks to visitors as though they too are from the same period; the 'third-person' interpreter may be in period costume but remains herself, in the present, while talking about the past (Hughes et al. 2006). Some of the more adventurous 'first-person' work has been pioneered at major heritage sites in the USA such as Colonial Williamsburg and Plimoth Plantation, Massachusetts, and more recently in the UK at historic houses such as Clarke Hall (Wakefield), Kentwell Manor (Suffolk) and Llancaiach Fawr Manor (South Wales). This particular form of live interpretation (or 'living history') can incorporate elements of traditional theatre (character impersonation, costume, improvisation around a given scenario, even a stage set, as in the replica seventeenth-century Pilgrim village at Plimoth), while simultaneously prioritising conversational interaction, in role, with visitors.[4]

Museum theatre and its various permutations constitute, then, an eclectic medium, drawing from the whole range of performative and role-based styles of interpretation. But the practice also raises many questions: ideological, historiographic and aesthetic. What view of history do these dramatic encounters propagate? What and whose agendas are being followed, and to what end? How far is the art form of theatre identifiable in such events? Do theatrical techniques always get deployed to best advantage? Do they serve genuinely to enlighten people about the past, enabling them to 'read', to rethink their 'heritage'?

The remainder of this chapter will investigate the kinds of theatricality that can be found within the museum or heritage site context, explicating some of these questions and considering ways in which theatrical practices of various kinds – including both overt and 'borderline' (or invisible) forms of theatre – may enhance the learning experience of the visitor. The field of study is a diverse and expanding one and can here be examined only very selectively. For present purposes, therefore, I have chosen to focus less on the use of drama in the conventional museum building than on *site-based* work and at the particular theatrical dynamic that arises from the relationship between actors or interpreters in role, the specific historic location they operate within and the audience of visitors. To narrow it down further, I will look at just two contrasting examples of such work: the replica Puritan-settler village, Plimoth Plantation, in Massachusetts, USA, and a project undertaken, in Britain, by the Young National Trust Theatre (YNTT), the National Trust's professional theatre-in-education company;[5] and, rather than analyse each in detail, ask of them three interrelated questions: in what ways is the history *theatrically represented*, what kinds of *visitor interaction* are generated, and how do these techniques serve (if at all) the *educational aims* of the programme?

Why select these two programmes? Each makes full-scale, tried and tested use of active 'visitor participation'. Each is committed to clear, well-articulated educational goals. Each bases its work in historic settings of one kind or another (though one is more site-specific than the other). Each is committed to throwing fresh light upon historical events through the medium of live, costumed portrayals of characters from the past. But there are significant and illuminating differences too – notably in respect of the target audiences (one primarily geared towards tourists, one designed for school pupils of a specific age range) and of the degree of explicitness of the theatrical means employed. In focusing upon these two programmes my purpose is not to propose a hierarchy of practices but rather to raise further questions about, and suggest ways of acknowledging and trying to understand, this fascinating meeting-point of theatre, education and museum practice. Any conclusions drawn must inevitably be highly provisional: while the study of the Plimoth programme is based on the author's own experiences and observations as a visitor/participant (in 1994 and 1998), supplemented by interviews with staff and reading of secondary sources, the study of the YNTT programme is based on a formal evaluation exercise undertaken by the author as an outside, non-participating observer, supplemented by interviews with teachers, pupils and practitioners. While this obviously limits the scope for direct and detailed comparison, the common ground between them offers some useful pointers to the complex relationship between educational purpose and theatrical method; and the focus on two contrasting uses of site-specific performance for explicit educational ends adds a further strand to the general themes explored in this book. Not least, it acknowledges the ways in which our ideas of what constitutes educational theatre have, perhaps inevitably over the course of a century, undergone substantial revision.

But, firstly, I wish to establish briefly the nature of the debates about 'heritage', as a cultural phenomenon of the latter part of one century and the beginning of a new, which provided much of the impetus for this particular enquiry.

The 'heritage industry' debates

In 1987, Robert Hewison published his now well-known diatribe against what he termed disparagingly the 'heritage industry' – seen as both a 'distortion of the past' and a 'stifling of the culture of the present' (1987: 10). This, together with a coincidence of other articles and books on similar themes around the same time,[6] provoked lively debates, conferences, even television programmes; it was followed a few years later by Raphael Samuel's important counter-reading of the meaning of heritage and the array of 'living history' activities that it has engendered (Samuel 1994). More recently still, Barbara Kirshenblatt-Gimblett's *Destination Culture* (1998) has provided a wide-ranging American perspective on the inter-relationship of tourism, museums and culture. All of these have made important contributions to assessing the culture we inhabit. And they raise interesting questions too about the ways drama is used in cultural expression and redefinition. At the time of writing, too, in Britain, ideas and debate about 'heritage' have come to the fore with new vigour as the country endeavours to respond to the challenges of a post-'9/11' world: to the implications of 'multiculturalism', immigration, national identity and citizenship.

Hewison's argument was that heritage, in the UK at least, has been exploited to such an extent by the tourist industry, the National Trust

Plate 17 Wigan Pier Heritage Centre: the Victorian Schoolroom.

and government agencies such as English Heritage that it has actually become a measure of Britain's decline – indicative of a cultural vacuity, of escapism and of a resignation to permanent malaise. Moreover, by privileging the past and wishing to preserve our country houses, castles and estates in aspic, we fail to recognise that the past is by definition something that evolves and cannot be recaptured without deception. For that reason, he argues, heritage is, for all its claims, implicitly anti-educational: it offers tourists and school children alike a facile, ready-made and wholly unreal view of the past as a substitute for the complex twists and turns of historical processes. Putting interpreters, guides and, perhaps worse, actors in period costume to explain the past is sympto-matic of a shallow popularising tendency; and it encourages a highly suspect empathy with past lives – inviting today's pupils to identify with, for example, artisans of the 1830s in order to gain an understanding of the social history of the period – and the 'fantasy that it is possible to step back into the Past' (1987: 83). Hewison's critique is certainly given weight by the occasional instances of well-intentioned theatre companies who stage 'history-based' programmes that are little more than fancy-dress romps into worlds owing more to pseudo-Dickensian stereotype than to genuine research. More typically, in the early years of the Wigan Pier Heritage Centre – in the late 1980s – it was often possible, at the extraordinarily popular 'Victorian School Room' exhibit, to find the actor in role as the schoolteacher playing knowingly, tongue-in-cheek, to the voluble, 'naughty' adult males at the back of the 'class', exhibiting the tension implicit in much of what is now often in popular discourse referred to as 'edu-tainment'.

Samuel's alternative view of heritage essentially sought to value the myriad forms that the re-presentation of history can take, and saw 'living history' as one vital part of the 'ensemble of activities and practices in which . . . a dialectic of past-present relations is rehearsed' (Samuel 1994: 6). He suggests that the critics oversimplify and underestimate the extent to which the ordinary public can bring a healthily sceptical intelligence to the packaged history they visit – we do not consume heritage in the same way we consume a bar of chocolate (p. 271).[7] And, pedagogically, 'heritage has been a brilliant success, making 'history on the doorstep' into a normal teaching resource, and opening up whole new terrains for those activity-based . . . forms of learning which have been . . . the unifying thread of the progressive tradition in English education' (p. 278). (Kirshenblatt-Gimblett offers a similarly catholic reading of the variety of 'tourist productions' across the world and the range of contributions they make, positive and negative, to the cultures they seek to illuminate.) So, *do* these 'living history' programmes, especially those that have costumed role-playing at their core, contribute to an understanding of the past? How far do they genuinely seek to counter the facile, nostalgic tendencies that Hewison identifies in much heritage activity? In part, this study was motivated by a desire to test how far Hewison's criticisms or Samuel's defence were borne out in practice. If truly educational approaches to history are to do with generating a spirit of curiosity, enquiry and engagement, a recognition of the differences and similarities between present and past, and with showing that history is as much about lived experience as it is about dates, buildings and artefacts, then what function might theatrical techniques have in achieving such educational ends?

Since a detailed account of the ways in which history is theatrically constructed in each of the projects in question is beyond the scope of this book, my focus here is not on performance analysis, or primarily upon the issue of whether or not such reconstructions might be said to constitute theatre. (Interestingly, Plimoth has been the subject of a number of essays in performance and cultural theory, the most significant being Richard Schechner's now-seminal essay on 'restored behavior' (Schechner 1985) and Snow's monograph on Plimoth (Snow 1993; but see also Roth 1997, Kirshenblatt-Gimblett 1998 and Kershaw 1999.) Instead, I want to argue that, when claims are made for the *educational* function of participatory 'living history' programmes, then certain questions about how they work are thrown into sharper focus. Bland claims of educational intent are not enough. Above all, whether designed for the casual tourist, organised groups or more specifically targeted at and 'customised' for school parties, these programmes will necessitate the most

careful attention to how the experience is *structured*. The structuring of
the visit – the taking of the visitor on a journey (back in time, to
encounter characters of the period and learn about some of the issues and
struggles they faced) and the use of theatrical means to stimulate interest, engage the visitor interactively and thereby enhance understanding
of the period – involves a fine balance between, on the one hand, pleasing the casual tourist or sceptical thirteen-year-old ('heritage industry
entertainment' as Hewison might call it) and genuine pedagogy on the
other. It is in the interactive sequences where the test is most acute –
where the opportunities for discoveries about the period and for genuinely 'dialogic' encounters are at their fullest; and at the same time
where the risks of getting it wrong, of triggering a counterproductive,
anti-educational experience, are at their greatest.

In what follows, then, I will try to identify the processes by which each
project attempts to ensure that education through theatrical (or para-
theatrical) means takes place and the problems and further questions that
those processes generate. I will look, first, at Plimoth, and particularly at
the site as 'stage set' – the way in which the venue contributes to, and
provides a theatrical frame for, the events, sights and sounds to be witnessed; at the use of characterisation and narrative content; and at the
opportunities thereby created for visitor interaction with the world of
1627. I will then turn to the YNTT programme and focus on the different, more transparently theatrical uses made of the historic setting and
of dramatic narrative (including the balance struck between 'fiction' and
'authenticity'); and finally suggest, comparatively, some of the implications that arise for an assessment of their educational impact.

Plimoth Plantation

The 1627 village as stage set

The *Mayflower*, as most will know, brought Puritan settlers from
Plymouth, England, in 1620 to the coast of Massachusetts, where they
founded a settlement which they named Plimoth. It was an epic journey
that before long became enshrined in the American cultural consciousness
as one of the defining moments in the emergence of a nation. In 1957, that
first village, as it might have looked seven years after the first landing, was
reconstructed on a 'green field' site in Plymouth, Massachusetts, near but
not on the original site. It has been rebuilt several times in response to
developing historical research and since the late 1970s has established a
reputation for its imaginative use of 'first-person' interpretation (See
Snow 1993: 24–40).

Plate 18 Plimoth Plantation: entrance to the village: 'Welcome to the 17th century'.

One of the striking moments in a visit to Plimoth is the walk from the Visitors Center (with its usual array of food outlets, souvenir shop and exhibition spaces) through the trees towards the 1627 village. As you near the surrounding wooden palisade, a sign greets you with the words, 'Welcome to the 17th Century'. (See Plate 18.) The (theatrical) framing of the experience is complete when, seconds later, you walk through one of the simple but imposing gateways into the village. At one level, you are indeed in 1627, or at least a late twentieth-century approximation of how that settlement might have looked based on years of painstaking research, peopled by 'ordinary' villagers going about their business (cooking, rethatching a roof, conversing with a neighbour), dressed in authentic period costume and speaking in a dialect that, while comprehensible, is clearly not contemporary American or British English. The village is contained within its well-defined boundary fence; outside is 'our world', inside is 'theirs', a world we are invited to amble through at our own pace. We are encouraged to be curious, to sneak inside a low-roofed cottage to watch as the woman of the house prepares a broth or bakes bread, to let ourselves be drawn into conversations about life in the village.

Is this theatre? It is not advertised as such. The villagers are styled 'interpreters', not actors. But, as soon as the village gates are opened at the start of the day, the staff are in role and remain so for as long as they are in the village (on stage) and so long as visitors (the audience) are about. (On a recent visit, my out-of-role conversation with an interpreter ten minutes before the official opening of the gates ('curtain-up') was interrupted by the sudden arrival of early visitors; the interpreter

Plate 19 Plimoth Plantation: the village.

Plate 20 Plimoth Plantation: encounter with a village resident.

switched immediately and seamlessly into role and I continued my conversation with a seventeenth-century villager.) Conversations are spontaneous but there is undoubtedly a scenario, if not a script. The
make-believe is sustained throughout and in turn sustains the sense of the
village as an inhabited, working, 'real' community. The theatricality may
not be overt but it is none the less pervasive, and inescapable as soon as
one begins to look for it – it is both progressive (the journey into, through
and out of the village) and environmental. The Associate Director of
Interpretation speaks of the village as a kind of historical 'envelope'
within which a quite different time-frame and set of social relations

operate;[8] and Schechner describes encounters in the village as 'environmental theatre' (Schechner 1985: 89); a point reiterated by Snow (1993:
8). The theatricality of the space is designed to complement, rather than
replace, the demonstration mode of conventional museum practice. It
also provides a structure for the visitors' experience that defines and
signals the 'rules of the game' they are being asked to play, even if it does
not control what they actually do. There is here no sense of accidentally
wandering into just another museum exhibit. You are prepared, your
appetite is whetted. In Goffman's terms, you arrive as 'theatregoer' and
are inducted into becoming an 'onlooker' (Goffman 1974: 129–30; see
also Chapter 6) – and by extension into an onlooker-participant since
you enter on to the set, not into an auditorium where you can settle back
into comfortable anonymity. The theatricality does then have a significant part to play in enabling the visitor to get the most out of the experience. A process of contracting-in to the game is undertaken in the very
act of progressing from Visitors Center through the palisade gates.[9] The
rationale is not however a primarily theatrical one: it is rooted in one of
the most interesting, and controversial, postwar developments in heritage education, that of first-person interpretation.

'First-person' interpretation at Plimoth

Those who advocate 'first-person' interpretation claim that it 'creates a
sense of immediacy that makes the past seem real' to the visitors (Osterud
1992: 18). Plimoth Plantation outlines its rationale in its *Visitors Guide*
(1998) as follows:

> Living History is a . . . communications technique [which] seeks to repre-
> sent and interpret a historical context in its entirety, placing people, live-
> stock and material culture within the actual . . . environment [or a
> reproduction] which supported them originally. To accomplish this, an
> entire culture needs to be investigated and understood – what the inhabi-
> tants thought of their world, their hopes and fears, and how they interacted
> with their environment. Staff members who present this information to vis-
> itors are called interpreters, as they explain or interpret the historical
> context. . . . 'First Person' interpretation . . . makes the staff living artefacts
> within the recreated environment. They take on the characters of persons
> from the time and place being represented.

The counter view is that this claim is at best misleading ('because it
creates a false sense that it is possible to "know the truth" about past realities') and at worst deceptive ('because it substitutes contemporary fan-
tasies about the past for artefacts and evidence') (Osterud 1992: 18).
Many curators and museum educators have severe qualms about 'creating

fictional characters from the past and having them speak dialogue which, in order to be comprehensible to people today, could not be a true representation of the times' (Giles 1997: 2). Even at Plimoth, this is a concern that is acknowledged, and in part lies behind the policy there to use only 'third-person' interpretation (demonstrators in period dress but out of role, speaking to us as themselves) at Hobbamock's Native American home site situated just outside the palisade. Here, this method is considered more appropriate in that it allows opportunity for explanation in modern English of a culture that would otherwise be quite inaccessible to the average visitor, given the native language, and the attitudes to the white intruders; and it avoids the risk of engendering stereotyped images of 'alien' and 'savage' Native Americans.

There is much debate, too, about how far first-person interpretation actually achieves what it sets out to do. Thus, for the casual visitor, a live encounter with characters from the past can be enlightening and enjoyable, or it can be deeply embarrassing (Bicknell and Mazda 1993, Giles 1997). The costumed interpreter who demonstrates the spinning jenny and responds to visitors' questions as and if they arise presents no threat: 'the visitor feels in control, free to watch or move on, to ask questions or listen passively' (Giles, p. 2). But the use of actor-interpreters in role can create anxieties for visitor and curator alike. Research some years ago into visitor response at the Science Museum in London showed that some visitors – adults in particular – found first-person interpretation inhibiting and were uncomfortable about being drawn into the spontaneous interchanges with scientific pioneers from the past while surrounded by more conventional museum exhibits (Bicknell and Mazda 1993: 40–2). Children on the other hand, particularly younger age groups, were invariably willing to get involved.

The effectiveness of character-based story-telling and interaction with 'believable' characters in gallery spaces was also confirmed by recent research conducted at the Imperial War Museum (London) and the People's History Museum (Manchester).[10] Despite statistically small samples[11], some clear patterns emerged. Both short- and longer-term recall and understanding were enhanced; the dramatic narrative served as an organising force; and the children were able to relate personally to and empathise with characters in the performances (Hughes et al. 2007: 687). Children, in particular, enjoyed and developed a sense of personal engagement with the subject matter – they felt a degree of 'ownership' in other words – when they were addressed not as 'pupils' in a classroom but as 'investigators' or 'friends and neighbours' whose advice is sought by the character. In *No Bed of Roses*, for example (People's History Museum since 2000), the character of Gabrielle – a Caribbean woman who re tells, and re-enacts, the story of her emigration to Britain in the 1950s – sought advice from the children on the pros and cons of leaving St Kitts for England; and, in a piece created (by Spectrum Theatre Company) for an exhibition about wartime London, the character of Muriel, a wartime housewife, addressed her young audience in the back-yard of a reconstructed 1940s house, as though friends of her own children. In both settings, the children generally responded strongly to, and had vivid recall of, events, struggles and dilemmas presented to them in *narrative form* by the fictional character whom they encountered in their journey through the galleries. Drawing on the embodied narrative as their most immediate source, most (if not all) of these children evidenced a more coherent grasp of the information imparted and sense of the period than did those who followed more conventional pathways (such as guided tour and activity trail).

With adults in mind, some museums and heritage centres (such as Wigan Pier and the Royal Armouries in Leeds) now deploy theatre only at advertised times and in designated spaces, 'providing the familiar concept of theatre and yet managing to be both immediate and intimate' (Giles 1997: 2). The rules of the game are in this way made clear, the experience is clearly framed and signalled *as* theatre, and the aesthetic distance generated allows for stress-free engagement in the subject matter of the event. The opportunities for interaction are however, in this solution, diminished in direct proportion to the overtness of the theatricality.

At Plimoth, within the village palisades, the approach is quite different. There is a real concern to draw visitors into the experience sufficiently to be able to communicate without intimidating and the theatricality is therefore never made overt, never signalled as 'theatre'.[12] The experience is therefore difficult to describe in aesthetic terms. Artistic structure, in the terms used by Jurij Lotman (see Chapter 5), is here by no means fixed or stable. If one views what happens within the palisade as at some level a theatrical event, one would have to acknowledge that, more than almost any other form of artistic event, the experience offered is likely to vary considerably from visitor to visitor, even in the course of one day. To try to push and pull its characteristics into a form that would lend itself to definition as art – at least in the terms outlined by Langer or Cole for example (art as symbolic form, shaped by its own internal laws in which audience participation would be intrusive, inappropriate or even destructive) – is an exercise that would be considered irrelevant to the goals set by the organisation.

Aesthetic distance in this context might at first sight seem to be non-existent. I say 'seem' because the framing strategies that precede, govern and to a large extent sustain our attitude to the site, together with the

people we meet, ensure we cannot confuse these seventeenth-century settlers with real life today – no matter how 'real' our actual encounters may
be. The carefully constructed, precise and consistent framing strategy
gives the experience the kind of resonance that is congruent with the aesthetic framework discussed in Chapter 5, and with Boal's notion of the
'doubleness' at the heart of any theatre experience. None the less, it is in
the very forging of an active and stimulating relationship with the visitors that many of the ingredients and devices common to other, more
obvious forms of theatre performance are pressed into service.

Characterisation, narrative and visitor interaction

Drawing in the visitors and preparing them for the encounters with figures
from the past is done by various means – most overtly by the information
provided at the Visitors Center; more subtly, by the careful framing devices
already referred to as the visitor progresses into the village itself, and
by the 'characterisation'. The Plimoth interpreters (only a few of whom
will have had professional acting experience) are organised and trained
with immense rigour and concern for authenticity. They are employed,
according to their experience and expertise, as Apprentice-Interpreters,
Journeymen-Interpreters or Master-Interpreters. Thus, you may early on
encounter a villager tending sheep or scything grass, possibly one of the
apprentice-interpreters still learning the trade but perfectly capable of
telling you about her work and inducting you further into the early sev-
enteenth century. At various points in the village, more encounters follow
and greetings lead to conversations. You are welcomed as an outsider visiting the village and deserving both explanation, perhaps a little homespun
philosophy, and yarns about the journey from the old world and the challenges of the new. The performance of these narratives is contrived to seem
spontaneous, conversational, arising naturally from your casual questions,
but at the same time offered as an integral part of the texture of the
experience to which you have now become connected. Especially effective
are the more wide-reaching and complex narratives told by the 'master-
interpreters' which provide insight into the lives, values and motivations
of these people. During one visit, I found myself in conversation with a
woman who, in response to a question about her accent, explained that
she was a member of a group of Separatists (a reformist sect) originally
from East Anglia who had fled persecution to Holland where they lived (in
Leiden) for 12 years until they resolved to emigrate to North America to
establish a new colony where their beliefs could be freely practised. (See
Plimoth Plantation manual: 6.) Her accent was indeed, when I listened
carefully, a mix of Suffolk and Dutch influences. She listened to my

queries, registered my puzzlement and adapted her story in response. In the process, gradually and unselfconsciously, I found myself drawn into her carefully researched (and yet imagined) world without having to pretend I was part of it. This fusion of fact, make-believe and improvised dialogue exemplifies well Schechner's notion of how, in certain kinds of performance, the indicative (the historically verifiable 'as is') world can be permeated and interpenetrated by the subjunctive (the imaginary 'as if') world (Schechner 1985: 92–3). In pedagogical terms, it also exploits most effectively what sociologist Robert Witkin[13] has described as the learner's ability to be in two worlds at the same time, to be a participant *and* an observer – arguably, in its promotion of reflexivity, the most productive kind of learning experience.

As one historian observed during her visit, the interpreters managed to belong

> both to the 17th century and to the present . . . [and] made a real effort to communicate with contemporary visitors. Instead of feigning ignorance of 20th century concepts, they helped visitors translate them into terms appropriate to the 17th century . . . [Their] ability to articulate their thoughts and express their feelings, to project a particular character's perspective within a coherent world view, made 17th century culture seem a lived experience rather than a collection of objects.

This of course runs counter to most museum interpretation, which tends to focus on objects and activities and 'rarely explores the subjectivity and consciousness of people in the past' (Osterud 1992: 19).

The educational process: unsettling the visitor?

Part of the educational rationale of the Plimoth programme is a concern not only to reconstruct and to inform, but also to demystify and to challenge visitors to rethink their preconceptions about the Pilgrims (see Snow 1993: 33). Thus, the great Pilgrim Myth that is so deeply embedded in American consciousness is carefully deconstructed. The commemoration of Thanksgiving is shown in its early seventeenth-century form: when tourists stream over to Plimoth Plantation in November they are often surprised to find that the Pilgrims celebrated a traditional English form of Harvest Festival, bearing little resemblance to the modern Thanksgiving celebration instituted by Abraham Lincoln two centuries later. As Osterud notes, too, 'freedom' was not the great rallying call of New Plimoth – there was as much bias, intolerance and strict enforcement of rules as anywhere in England, although the rules were at least set by the community and not by the monarch. The narratives we engage with during our random encounters with the 1627 'inhabitants' are designed precisely to confront us with unromantic realities, highly selective though they may be. My own conversation with a shipwrecked Bristol sailor was a case in point. Angry about the long-drawn-out wait for a ship from England and his continued isolation in a village whose practices he was at best tolerant of, his frustration was expressed in many ways, not least in his irritation with all things Irish (blaming his shipwreck on the pre-dominantly Irish crew). Clearly, the racism was factually authentic and there was no attempt to hide it – it had the effect of shocking his listeners momentarily and then of reminding them of the variety of voices and points of view that made up the community. 'Unsettling the visitor', as Osterud reminds us, '. . . is one of the first requisites of interpretation' (Osterud 1992: 18). And, in a way that Bakhtin probably did not envis-age, it might be argued that such experiences are heteroglossic: one might of course stumble across these differences in world view in a random manner – if at all – but when they happen they unsettle precisely because they cannot be neatly packaged into a uniform, completely consistent reading of life in a seventeenth-century colonial outpost.

There is, however, little control over how visitors will make their way through the village, nor how they will 'read' what they encounter. If they peruse their leaflets and watch the 15-minute 'orientation' video at the Visitors Center before going 'back in time' to the 1627 village, then they will have some idea of what to expect and how to make the most of the experience, how to relate to the characters they will meet. But no one will force them to do so (rightly). They will progress through the village at their own pace, in their own way – there is no guarantee that tourists in a hurry or school parties equipped with workbooks to complete will pick up more than a fraction of the information and insights potentially avail-able to them. At the end of their tour, there is no debriefing (except perhaps for the school parties via their teacher in class next day). Questions may remain unanswered because there are some that you just cannot ask a 1627 character ('what happened to the village fifty years later?'), and some preconceptions or confusions may remain. There are plans to post out-of-role guides near the exit points to deal with such queries. But the randomness of it all is, arguably, a strength too. The unexpected conversation with the 'woman of the house' about religious persecution while vegetables are being prepared in her dark, rather smoky kitchen can provide genuine insight into a small corner of a complex world, a resonant counter-image to the prettified story-book idea of Puritan life still current in many quarters. As Kirshenblatt-Gimblett (1998: 194–5) remarks of Plimoth, 'learning here is all process and discovery. It is partial, negotiable, polyvocal.'

Such randomness contrasts sharply with the tightly controlled and narrative-driven experience offered by YNTT.

Theatre in education on-site – the Young National Trust Theatre (YNTT)[14]

The work of this TIE company, designed specifically for presentation at historic sites, shares many of the features that characterise Plimoth Plantation.[15] While the company's work was not wholly site-specific, in that each programme was toured to a variety of historic houses across the UK and was only partially adapted for each location, every effort was made to maximise the sense of place and make it integral to the story being told. The programme discussed here involved the visitors (school-children) entering a past world, meeting and conversing with historic characters as though they were real, and the setting of the stately home exerted a powerful influence over the children's responses, their level of belief, the sense of authenticity of place and action, and of what life then might have been like. But there are significant differences too. The YNTT programme is clearly more overtly theatre-based. While the Plimoth experience encourages the visitor to engage with a community that *seems* to exist quite autonomously, irrespective of the visitor's presence (if you visit on 15 April, it's 15 April 1627 in the village), YNTT planned for a captive audience of a specified size and age range who are present for a precise period of time (usually 90 minutes), and schools book their classes in months ahead. Each visiting group becomes involved in a narrative that, while based on fact, is fictitious, and meets a variety of costumed characters, both invented and historically 'real'. The events are largely scripted, with sections left open for pupils actively to engage in the debates, and are structured towards a major crisis at which, with the pupils' help, judgements and decisions will have to be made. There is a beginning, middle and end, and the children know in advance they are to be involved in a story; and, even more, that they will themselves be in role. The children are very often encouraged to come to the event with token elements of period costume.

YNTT's programme *For any Field?* illustrates the approach well. Set in 1895 and marking the centenary year of the National Trust,[16] it was toured to 17 National Trust venues throughout the UK during 1995. The programme was designed to enhance delivery of aspects of the history national curriculum for Key Stages 2 and 3 (mostly within the nine to thirteen age band) and, more specifically, to offer pupils the chance to 'explore the motives and behaviours of people in the past' and, 'through direct and sustained participation in a piece of interactive and carefully

researched theatre, . . . gain an insight into the period [and] develop their
own skills in communication and enquiry'. Rather than propaganda on
behalf of the Trust, it was to be 'an exploration of the issues and concerns in late Victorian England that brought the charity into being'; and
it 'investigates rural life in the aftermath of the agricultural depressions
of the 1880s, and allows [the] children to decide for themselves about the
dilemmas which faced those who cared about the countryside and the
people who lived in it' (Teachers Resource Booklet 1995).

The narrative turns on the attempt of the local County Council to buy
up land from Lady Exwood's estate in order to build new houses for
urban slum-dwellers from the nearby city. Lady Exwood is in need of
money because of the debts left her by her recently deceased husband.
The children come already prepared for the role-playing they will do,
pre-divided into three groups. One group of pupils becomes the
Councillors; another consists of the Ramblers and Cyclists: outdoor
enthusiasts from the city (the aspiring working and middle classes) who
have come to protest at Lady Exwood's decision to fence off public rights
of way across her land; the third is the Villagers: local people, poor, living
in low-quality housing in the village owned by Lady Exwood, whose
own fortunes have declined with the estate.

Following an introduction to the event out of role by the company's
director, the pupils, already in costume (usually emblematic rather than
whole costumes: enough to distinguish one group from the others and to
indicate their social class), set off in their groups towards the house and
are in turn intercepted *en route* by the three 'contact' characters who will
each draw their group into the dilemmas, debates and opposing perspectives that are the subject matter of the drama. By the end the children are faced with some challenges. What is the best use for this land:
rehousing slum-dwellers, or maintaining open countryside? They cannot
of course determine who should buy the estate – that would be impossible to reconcile with historical reality: it could only be Lady Exwood's
decision. But, although a vote is not taken, the actor playing Lady
Exwood gauges the children's views, checks whether or not a consensus
exists, identifies shifts of opinion that might have taken place, and makes
her own decision accordingly – to sell to the Council or to Miss Octavia
Hill on behalf of the new National Trust. Whichever way the decision
goes (and the decision varied from performance to performance), recon-
ciliation takes place and a celebration ensues to mark the end. The pupils
in this respect are not 'visitors', nor are they 'audience'; they are participants – prepared weeks in advance, they come ready to go at the pace the
company set; they have already created their own personal narratives
and rehearsed the telling of them. The event itself is carefully built

Plate 21 *For any Field?* The final debate in the Great Hall (at Rufford Old Hall, Ormskirk). Young National Trust Theatre, 1995.

around a clear narrative, a series of pivotal and theatrically conceived moments (such as the arrival of unexpected characters, or the final debate in The Great Hall) and a resolution. There is briefing and debriefing. The theatrical pretence is on one level never in doubt. But the level of engagement, the heatedness of the debates that develop between pupils and characters and between different groups of pupils, will often be intense.

One moment from one performance stands out as an illustration of the complex mix of dramatic, historical narrative and intense engagement in the present. It was the culminating sequence when the pupils in groups converged on the grand reception hall (chandeliers and all) to debate the pros and cons of the proposal to sell part of the country estate to the county council for building new homes for slum-dwellers from nearby Liverpool (see Plate 21). Each group had gained a different perspective according to the roles they were playing and the characters they had met. The debate was heated, the issues (environmental, economic, social, political) difficult and the various points of view each perfectly defensible. How far if at all did theatrical art have any part to play in what was going on? For these pupils at this moment, the theatre *seemed* irrelevant, the arguments were 'real', the characters were human beings, with specific standpoints, who needed to be won over or supported. The awesome surroundings *seemed* for the time being to be forgotten. It could have been a classroom debate or a public meeting. The earlier, more overtly theatrical parts of the narrative (which the pupils had watched and listened to and played a seemingly minor role in), although barely an hour before, had been overtaken by events as a sense of crisis

and a moment of decision loomed and the level of the pupils' involvement intensified. Precisely at the climactic point of the event, the theatre
seemed least in evidence.

And yet, the closer I looked and listened from the sidelines, these young
people were *not* merely engaging in classroom activities. Despite the
reality of their debate, they were still arguing within a quite specific historical framework, consciously framing those arguments in terms that corresponded, more or less, to the conditions of the day: trains of the time
were not electric but steam-driven, noisy and dirty; working on a farm was
not automated as now nor as idyllic as city-dwellers imagine; you could
not advise someone living in appalling housing to appeal to a Department
of Social Security which had not yet been invented, and so on. Perhaps,
after all, the historic setting and the costumes of the characters, as well as
the way that the characters were framing their opinions, were still exerting a constant pull. Realism and the real were intertwined. (There was
perhaps that willing, conscious suspension of disbelief that Coleridge
referred to when trying to explain the puzzling hold a theatre performance
can have for an audience.) How, though, once again, does one describe and
account for such an event? Is it not still closer to the classroom than
drama? How important to the success of the event *were* the costumes and
the clearly fictitious characterisations? How far was the country-house
setting functioning as a real nineteenth-century location, how far as a the-
atricalised nineteenth-century backdrop for a realistic play? When you can
no longer easily see the usual dividing lines between actor and audience,
between set and 'real world', when the audience seem to have become the
actors, what kind of theatre is this, if indeed it is still theatre?

More particularly, what exactly was the value of the location? Even if
the plot and characters have to serve seventeen different venues, from
the *pupils'* point of view the house they enter is inevitably perceived as the
natural setting for the events they witness – integrally related to the stories,
people and arguments they encounter within it. The complex texture of
the social fabric, the class, status and jobs of the various characters, the
question of whose territory they are on and where power resides – all of
these inform and influence the course of the debate and the pupils' grasp
of the period. (While the Councillors were allowed instant access to the
Hall, the Villagers spent much of the action in outbuildings until invited
in by special favour.) No longer is historical fact kept separate from the
humanity of people's ordinary lives and concerns. If the National Trust is
sometimes accused of freezing a moment of time, and with it a particular
set of social relations, in the way it preserves its houses – and of thereby
misleading visitors about the nature of history – then YNTT was arguably
helping to redress the balance.

History and experiential learning

How far did this project go not just in enlivening a period of history but in enabling pupils to gain a real understanding of issues as seen by people in 1895? The evaluation undertaken[17] certainly confirmed that teachers and pupils alike were universally agreed on the value of taking part in the project. And it clearly had a strong motivational effect – at this event their engagement was wholly different from classroom learning: 'When you're acting, it was exciting, you get involved.' The Year 8 pupils (twelve- to thirteen-year-olds) claimed they knew more about the period now than they would have done from conventional teaching. Some also volunteered that they felt they had more of a say in this event than they did in the 'real' world because they were listened to and their views actually had an influence. 'Nowadays young people who have to live in this world for the next fifty years or more don't have a vote or a say.' But that of course was less to do with learning about the past than an observation about their own place in the present and, perhaps, a sign of the quality of their involvement. While all the teachers interviewed booked the event as a resource for teaching history, and were convinced it helped generate interest in the past as lived experience, even more insistently they valued the programme's contribution to the pupils' social education – particularly the incentive it gave for genuinely co-operative working, for decision-making and for developing articulacy and self-confidence.

Had the experience affected the pupils' thinking about nineteenth-century life and the differences from today? All pupils interviewed claimed they had learnt about how people lived and cited the more obvious differences between then and now (the lack of cars, the old-fashioned houses, the different clothes, the lack of toilets in ordinary people's houses; people's greater proneness to disease; the ownership of land by the 'higher people' – such as Lady Exwood). For some (ten- and twelve-year-olds alike) the impact was as much affective as cognitive: 'You feel what sort of problems they had'; while others agreed: 'We did feel like we were going back into the past.' Some of the younger pupils, though, admitted they were not thinking about History at all, just about what was happening from moment to moment in the story. That is not in itself a bad thing (immersion in a story is a powerful means of generating engagement and curiosity), given that it was the task of the teacher to tease out the historical implications of the story after the event, back in the classroom. Several however may have come away with a distorted view of how accessible the powerful were to the mass of ordinary people: 'Then, you could actually go up to the high person and argue whereas these days you couldn't go up to the queen and argue

with her. It was better in those days – you could argue with the council
and [people like] that.' On the other hand, on the issue of whether or
not the Council should be allowed to build new homes on the estate,
one twelve-year-old pupil reckoned that, whatever we might think now,
'At the time, you'd stick with the councillors because it's all cramped
there [in the cities] – if there's a nice new village getting built, you'd be
all right, there'd be less cramped people there.' But another immediately
counteracted, 'It's like that now though, isn't it? They're always building new houses in the countryside, polluting rivers and so on.' They
were still, over two weeks after the event, arguing heatedly for and
against building in the countryside. Here was no neatly packaged,
unified view of historical events. The story had raised issues that were
not only alive to the students but offered a valid way in to thinking
about the past.

     There were, though, undoubtedly areas of the pupils' historical under-
standing that the programme did little to advance. For example, they had
difficulty with casting themselves into the frame of mind of those
Victorian idealists who argued for protecting the natural environment
for moral and spiritual reasons. Many of the younger pupils especially
equated saving the environment with saving the animals who lived there,
rather than seeing the moral point that people required fresh air, relaxation, good exercise and a 'free' environment in which to 'be themselves'.
But, then again, many were at least aware of how the different conditions
of the time would have informed their attitudes to change and to authority: the anxieties the 'villagers' had about how their own livelihoods were
going to be affected by the selling of the land were probably very close
to the historical reality.

Historical authenticity and 'narrative closure'

The two programmes under discussion differ markedly in their
approach to 'authenticity'. While *For any Field?* had a clear narrative
structure and freely (though responsibly) mixed fiction and fact within
a historically authentic setting, Plimoth shuns narrative except at the
level of the characters' own story-telling: a high premium is placed upon
the *everydayness* of the village life and the necessary randomness of the
encounters between character and visitor. Of course, authenticity is a
problematic notion, as much at Plimoth as in the YNTT programme,
and Plimoth goes to considerable lengths in its exhibition and printed
material at the Visitor Center to stress the *relative* authenticity of the
reconstruction, in accord with current knowledge and with the need to
ensure accessibility for modern tourists. (As Schechner puts it, history is

'not what happened but what is encoded and transmitted', 1985: 51.)
But if 'randomness' is an inevitable feature of the Plimoth experience,
by contrast one of the most problematic aspects of the TIE programme
lay in its opposite: in its narrative 'closure', that is, in the means by
which the narrative was brought to a conclusion, the action wound up
and the visitors returned to the 'real world'. The resolution of who was
to buy the land was always followed by the celebratory singing of one
of the songs that had been prepared in advance and a simple country
dance (usually outside). This celebration was felt by the company to be
an important way of drawing the threads together, of providing a satisfying ending for all pupils, irrespective of which argument had won the
day. As a piece of theatre and as a conclusion to a rewarding day out
(for teachers and pupils alike) this section usually worked well, though
more for the younger pupils than for secondary pupils. But it also highlights the problem of how to conclude a narrative in which several
strong, competing and wholly legitimate (and authentic) demands have
been in play. The final, rather contrived expression of unity was hardly
an accurate representation of the tensions and divides that existed at the
time. And at the level of the children's own roleplay, it risked glossing
over the gaps in perception and ideological standpoint that existed
within and especially between the groups. The challenge in designing
such narrative-based programmes must be to find a way of reconciling
such tensions without at the same time slipping into a 'happy ending'
mode that undercuts the real achievements of the event in 'bringing
history to life' and without underestimating the pupils' ability to take on
board the contradictions of the world they have been witness to, contradictions that cannot quickly be overcome by a song and a dance. The
company readily acknowledged the dilemma and, interestingly, its later
work (notably, *God and My Right*, 1998, about the impact of Henry
VIII's dissolution of the monasteries) concluded without the celebratory
ending that had characterised most of the company's programmes for
over a decade: the separate groups were left discussing the crisis they
had been through with their associated 'contact' characters. Divided
loyalties and contrasting perspectives on the event were then left for
the teachers to pursue in the classroom as part of the follow-up (an
advantage not available of course to the 'random' visitors at Plimoth
Plantation). There is in any 'living history' programme a delicate and
difficult balance to be struck between the telling of a good story and
opening up the period to complex and often contradictory voices
and opinions, between the understandable wish for 'closure' and an
explicit drawing-out of the lessons to be learnt, and (on the other hand)
leaving your audience full of unresolved questions and confusions.

Is the education enhanced or hindered by the use of theatrical techniques?

There are many who see the use of theatre in museums as a threat to the real business of educating the visitor about the past. Theatre *can* dilute, distort, even sabotage the educational intent of the curator. Dramatisation *tends* to impose narrative structure on history – tidying it up, reducing it to cause and effect. And there is the further danger of trivialising in the process of popularising, and making fun out of fashions, behaviours and beliefs far removed from our own.

'First-person' interpretation, however, unlike other more theatre-based techniques, occupies an in-between territory in which visitors are often quite unconscious of being acted to, let alone being in role themselves. There is no denying that 'first-person' is a form of acting, even though partly disguised by the spontaneous nature of the exchanges between character and visitor. It might indeed be argued that the very 'interactiveness' of 'first-person' makes it more vital still that it be undertaken by specialist interpreters who are equally adept in interpretation and in *performance*. If the visitor is to be persuasively taken on a journey to another time and place, there does need to be a complex combination of highly skilled character portrayal, naturalistic plausibility, an ability to tell a good tale, a Brechtian capacity to 'demonstrate' the character, and the TIE performer's ability to be both teacher and actor at the same time.[18] The school pupils I observed at Plimoth who stayed buried in their worksheets instead of interacting with the characters they met would have benefited from a more skilful dramatic stimulus; more attention by several of the interpreters to the performative, *improvisational* quality of their impersonations might have helped focus the pupils on the experience of listening, looking and responding instead of merely seeking factual answers.

While there would be no point in forcing all types of staged historical reconstructions into a single mould, there is undoubtedly a need to understand the array of current practices better, and to explore ways of using theatrical techniques more effectively. Thus, the research into visitor response at the Science Museum referred to earlier (suggesting the value of clear signalling and framing of the theatre events, at least for adults), the shifts in emphasis and strategy that have taken place at such museums as Wigan Pier, Plimoth Plantation's current experiment with performed pieces toured into local schools (following a more TIE-based model) – all are healthy symptoms of a constant process of reviewing, rethinking and redefining the nature of that practice, above all of clarifying and testing how theatre can best illuminate, and how it can in other ways impede.

If Hewison and other critics are right to call attention to the dangers implicit in bringing history 'back to life', the variety of living history projects and methodologies demands at least an open-minded as well as a critical account of what they actually do. Those projects that have education – of the general public or of schoolchildren – genuinely at the heart of their endeavour are perhaps able to generate more engagement with and insight into the past than the safer and more traditional methods which privilege the word, the document, the encased artefact and the well-packaged textbook. The use of participatory theatre *can* open up the past precisely to those multiple perspectives and to the complexities and minutiae of the social context that most historians now stress. Of course, educational objectives do not in themselves guarantee the quality of the practice, and one must be wary of projects that paste educational labels on to ill-conceived or shoddily researched work in which both performances and participation pander to stereotyped notions of the past or to conceptions of history as something to be illustrated rather than interrogated.

Above all, Samuel is right, I think, to stress the *dialectical* relationship we can have with the past as embodied in the imaginative, carefully researched reconstructions of places, events and social interactions. The YNTT event may have been problematic in its narrative 'tidying-up', but also provides an example of how a dynamic interplay between present and past can be promoted by a genuinely complex and provocative experience, enhanced through a building-in of contrasting perspectives not only to the dramatic narrative but to the very design of the audience participation itself. The pupils learnt much about past events, living conditions and the lives of those who, like us, had to negotiate their particular ways through particular contexts and constraints; they also learnt something about the ways decisions are made, compromises reached and communities divide, in the past and in the present, and were able to articulate their own, often varied, meanings from it all. As Kershaw argues, the close interaction between actor and spectator can, even in rigorously researched historical reconstructions, 'make the past available for . . . a range of different interpretations . . . about its relevance to the present' (1999: 171).

In a different way, Plimoth Plantation stands as an accomplished example of a site-specific project in which attention to detail is used not merely to reproduce the past but, sometimes, provocatively to make us look again at the past we take for granted – a past that in substantial, often mythic, ways can exert an enormous influence upon the present. In its planning for the passing visitor, Plimoth has structured the framing and the unfolding of the experience in carefully stage-managed and educationally productive ways – even if the lack of dramatic closure, or of any debriefing process, runs the risk of leaving some visitors with mis-apprehensions or, at worst (though probably rarely), with prejudices confirmed.

Each of the projects in different ways manages to sustain both a respect for the reality of the past (in so far as we can ever know it from documents, artefacts and place) *and* a concern to unsettle their audiences' prior assumptions. A commitment that is especially important when the pressures to package heritage into easily consumable products and 'a good day out' are so strong. It marks them out from those examples of heritage drama (such as the Wigan Pier School Room in earlier manifestations) that may divert but do nothing to enlighten.

To what extent are such programmes enriched by their theatrical dimension? It may be instructive to remind ourselves of what the anthropologist Victor Turner has argued lies at the root of all theatre, that is, its ritualistic and life-enhancing potential. Drawing parallels with tribal ritual, Turner argues that theatre contains at the heart of its processes the 'liminoid' qualities that enable both performer and audience to cross a 'threshold' into a 'ludic world' – a threshold that releases them momentarily from the normal constraints of the social world outside and generates forms of 'cultural creativity' that can subvert or at least offer alternative pictures of human behaviour and interaction.[19] Its playful liberties with social reality allow us, the audience (and in certain instances the museum visitor), both the enjoyment and stimulus we associate with any good theatre and the opportunities for genuine learning and rethinking which can be taken back over the threshold and inform our everyday lives. We can be both observers and participants in the game, reflexive and engaged.

Playfulness and historical accuracy may seem poles apart. But, as most historians themselves are quick to argue, the notion of historical accuracy is itself fraught with problems. And if, in the interests of accessibility and the stirring of curiosity, factual accuracy does sometimes get compromised, this should not in itself be a cause for condemnation. I am inclined to agree with John Fines, one-time President of the Historical Association and himself an advocate of drama as a teaching tool, who argued (Fines 1996: 11): 'Drama is in many ways very close to what historians do – they say, "What if?" and "How come?" and "Maybe we got it wrong – let's put it another way and see how it looks." ' Moreover, 'historical knowledge *per se* is not of the slightest use. It is when we apply it that it becomes valuable'; and if it can be applied 'to learn to respect diversity – the fact that in different times and different circumstances and different places people may respond in ways that at first strike us as strange', then that is indeed 'real education' – a point on which Hewison and Samuel might well have agreed. Rather than historical accuracy as the measure by which to judge the success or otherwise of these varied and challenging programmes, it is surely more helpful to develop criteria that at least acknowledge the value that theatre and theatre techniques can have in forging an empathic awareness of, and – even more important – provoking reflexivity and puzzlement about, the lives, beliefs and struggles of people of an age fundamentally different from our own.

Notes

1 Jane Malcolm-Davies, speaking at the Theatre & Museums Conference ('What's the catch?'), Liverpool, 1991.
2 IMTAL-Europe (the International Museum Theatre Alliance) offers the following definitions of some of the key terms of work in this field on its website (www.imtal-europe.org/, last accessed 25 August 2006):

First person interpretation: where an interpreter assumes a particular role, often (but not always) in appropriate costume, either from the premise that he/she has moved forward through time to the present, or that his/her audience has moved backwards through time to his/her past.

Interpretation: a communication process designed to reveal to a specific audience the significance of a historic/cultural/natural site or museum (and the audience's relationship to it) through a first-hand experience involving interaction with another person, a place, an object or an artefact. Live interpretation and museum theatre are just one, highly effective form of interpretive technique.

Living history: a very broad term used to describe historically authentic activities in an appropriate context, often an open air museum. Interpreters engaged in living history may be in role (see First Person below) or simply in costume (see Third Person below).

Live interpretation: a broad term used to cover many aspects of living history-type activities, ranging from non-costumed demonstrations of historical craft to storytelling and costumed first- and third-person interpretation.

Museum theatre: a specific kind of interpretation that employs fictional activity to communicate ideas, facts and concepts. A museum-theatre performer assumes the role of a character (as a solo gallery character, an interpreter or as part of a play or scenario) in order to entertain and educate visitors. They take on the role of a particular character in a particular circumstance in order to help visitors appreciate and understand the story in hand and, through that, some aspect of the host museum or site.

Re-enactment: a detailed recreation (often by a large number of people) of a single short-term historical event (such as a battle, designed to attract a large number of spectators), where action, costume and combat often take precedence over the spoken word.

Role-play: where the audience as well as the interpreter takes on a role or roles within a particular scenario or performance which supports the plot, which may or may not involve advance preparation and the wearing of appropriate costume.

   Story-telling: where the interpreter focuses on relating a particular story rather than on wearing an authentic costume or playing a particular character.

   Third person interpretation: where an interpreter dresses in appropriate costume and has a full knowledge of the life of a particular character or a specific era, but does not assume that role (i.e. can speak authoritatively of the character's life and times, but remains a 21st century person discussing the past).

3 The American practices are well summarised by Roth (1997), Bridal (2004) and Hughes (1998).

4 See especially Roth (1998) and Snow (1993).

5 The company no longer exists in its original form. See note 14.

6 See especially Ascherson (1987a, 1987b, 1992); Lowenthal (1985); and Wright (1985).

7 This point is reinforced by Gaynor Bagnall's study of visitor response to performances encountered at Wigan Pier. The boundaries between consuming and producing frequently became blurred, especially in the performances that relied upon audience interaction: 'visitors were not passive consumers but skilful and reflexive performers' (Bagnall 2003: 95).

8 I am indebted to John Kemp, Associate Director of Interpretation, who has been an invaluable guide to the theory and practice at Plimoth.

9 Snow identifies the implicit protocols of behaviour involved in such a contract: 'there are . . . expected modes of behavior for both performers and spectators if the game of living history is to be successfully played' (Snow 1993: 171).

10 The research, funded by the AHRC and led by the author, involved collaboration between the University of Manchester's Centre for Applied Theatre Research (CATR) and the Centre for Museology and was conducted in 2001–2 in London and Manchester; it set out to investigate the effectiveness of theatre and theatre techniques as a medium of learning in museums. The report can be accessed at www.plh.manchester.ac.uk/research/index.htm, and the outcomes are further discussed in Jackson and Rees Leahy 2005 and Hughes et al. 2007.

11 The research tracked the experience and responses of eight classes of junior school children in their visits to two museums and in their encounters with a variety of stimuli, including, for 50 per cent of the groups, interaction with a character in the galleries.

12 There are occasionally staged events, such as official processions and marriages, which are more overtly theatrical in their separation of performance from spectator.

13 A point made in Witkin's keynote speech given at the 'Researching Drama & Theatre in Education' Conference, University of Exeter, 1999. See also Witkin (1974).

14 The Young National Trust Theatre, from 1977 the TIE arm of the National Trust, regularly toured educational theatre programmes into National Trust properties. In 2000, the national touring company was replaced by a more site-specific strategy, using both professional and non-professional (students, volunteers and participants from the local communities).

15 Although the company no longer operates, the TIE style of work characterises much of the approach of a variety of professional and non-professional groups aided by the Trust, and indeed of companies that produce work at other heritage locations. For a list of specialist companies see the IMTAL-Europe website www.imtal-europe.org/, and, for American companies, www.imtal.org/.

16 The National Trust was founded as a campaigning body to preserve and care for areas of the countryside and historic buildings of special importance.

17 The evaluation was undertaken by the author as a small-scale project using a qualitative research methodology: observations were made of three performances at Rufford Old Hall, Lancashire, and of classroom preparations and follow-up; interviews were conducted with teachers, actors, the director and company administrator, and with the pupils themselves in small groups at a selection of schools (two junior schools and one secondary) some two to four weeks after the event. The quotations are taken from the evaluation report (Jackson 1995b).

18 As Schechner puts it, 'Inside the village, all is naturalism, but taken as a whole the Plantation is like the theatre of Brecht or Foreman' (Schechner 1985: 90); Snow argues that the performance within the village has to be 'naturalistic' (Snow 1993: 43–4) but that there must also be a corresponding Brechtian element in the acting for pedagogic purposes (180–1). See also Williams (1993) on the skills required of the TIE actor.

19 See Turner (1982: 33, 55). Snow (1993: 204–11) takes Turner's theory further and argues that the experiences offered by programmes such as Plimoth Plantation constitute a new 'blurred genre': 'cultural performance' – a term developed further by Schechner, Carlson, Kershaw and Kirshenblatt-Gimblett.

Afterword

'This book is a plea for the recognition of the theatre as an educational force.' So wrote Harley Granville Barker, in the opening paragraph of a book called *The Exemplary Theatre*, published in 1922. Some 85 years later, the plea still has resonance and certainly forms one of the running themes of the current study. But Barker's advocacy, written in different times, also highlights the profound paradigm shifts – in theatre and in education – that have taken place since the 1920s. Barker was, in the early decades of the twentieth century, undoubtedly Britain's leading theatre director and a prime mover in the fostering of the 'New Drama', the development of the regional repertory theatre and plans for a National Theatre. He was a not insignificant playwright himself and later, in retirement, produced a highly influential series of books on Shakespeare that attempted to set the dramatist firmly in his theatrical context, as a writer of plays for performance (*Prefaces to Shakespeare*). Barker's idea of an 'exemplary' theatre, an extension of his campaign to get a national theatre established, was based on a conviction that the theatre was a necessary part of a healthy, liberal society and needed to be recognised, and financially supported, by the state. Hence much of the early discussion is presented in the form of a debate between the 'Man of the Theatre' and the 'Minister of Education'. While the minister doubts that theatrical activity, a medium of entertainment, should be the concern of government, Barker (through his author surrogate) makes a sustained and sometimes impassioned (if occasionally imperious) case for the theatre as a form of cultural expression that has a philosophical basis and offers significant moral, social and of course educational benefits.

Drama is above all, he claims, 'a social art in a sense that the novel can never be' (1970: 70), and he places great store upon the collaborative skills that drama is uniquely placed to foster: collaboration between author, director and actors of the kind that produces great theatre, but equally of the less immediately obvious kind that connects audiences with the actors and the author, a collaboration that happens both during and, more indirectly, after the performance. There is, he argues, a need to train the audiences of the future as a means of developing their discernment and their collaborative abilities in the interests of the betterment of the art form. A state-funded 'exemplary theatre' would therefore not only function as a producing house with the highest aspirations but would combine under one roof several performance spaces with varied stage–auditorium configurations, an actor training school and classrooms for the general public interested in learning more about theatre history and criticism and debating the future of theatre – in the community as much as in the regular theatre buildings. It would be a living testimony to the art of theatre as an expression of social democracy – 'It is upon the possibilities of this collaboration . . . that the theatre may best base its claim to consideration as an educative art' (p. 76).

Of course the cultural context in which that plea was made has changed almost beyond recognition. The theatre in the era after the First World War was still dominated by the commercial combines in the West End and in the majority of the towns and cities throughout the country; repertory theatres dedicated to providing a genuinely varied fare of classics and new work were still finding their feet; and the very idea of subsidy from the public purse was still a pipe dream. A theatre that was to take its rightful place at the centre of a nation's culture, against the odds stacked against it, required, it seemed to Barker, institutional status. And its educative function likewise required to be located and manifested in a prestigious building that would be recognised by politicians and public alike as officially blessed and to be taken seriously. In a very different world, while we may in Britain be able to boast not one but two national theatre organisations and a moderately well subsidised regional theatre network, our aspirations for theatre as an educative art are likely to be framed somewhat differently and probably argued out in less 'gentlemanly' contexts. In 1986, for example, there was a chorus of noisy dissent from the 'alternative theatre' practitioners – those working in community arts, political theatre and TIE – in response to the Arts Council's new strategy document, *Theatre Is for All*. It had advocated substantially increased funding for 'centres of excellence' but severe cuts in grant aid to 'minor' or 'declining' companies. While it certainly argued strongly for support of the 'wider theatre of tomorrow', it was precisely this that drew the protests. The wider theatre of tomorrow was already here – and the Arts Council strategists had failed to recognise it! It was here in the form of the community outreach and TIE companies and in

the whole array of groups and individuals, some attached to larger theatres, many operating independently, who toured locally and nationally,
usually playing in non-theatre spaces, in schools, small community arts
centres and the like. The work was not high-profile, often invisible to the
general public and the London theatre critics, but was, in the view of the
many who benefited (audiences, participants, the artists themselves), just
as important in its own way as that of the National or the major regional
theatres. It took another fifteen years before a strategy emerged that won
widespread if qualified support and which fully acknowledged the vital
role that regional and more local community-based enterprises had to
play in a fast-changing cultural landscape. One of the key elements in the
Arts Council's *National Policy for Theatre in England* (published in
2000 following the seminal ACE-commissioned Boyden Report earlier
that year) was the recognition of education as an activity central to
theatre's relationship to its various communities, not as an added-on
bonus but as something that should pervade the very fibre of its being:
'We expect most forms of funded theatre to place education at the heart
of their work. Involving young people in theatre is key' (ACE 2000: 5).
Hand in hand with this priority were requirements that the 'interaction
between art and audiences and practitioners' had to be 'central', and that
the theatre community should 'continue to build on its work to engage
with people who have felt excluded from theatre' and 'engage with audiences and artists from a broader, more diverse range of backgrounds'
(pp. 4–5). The practice on the ground rarely matches fully the aspirations, and some theatres have paid little more than lip-service to the
requirements for wider access and integrated learning policies, but in
most cases the new funding agreements did lead to education officers,
sometimes full teams, being drafted in to contribute significantly to the
overall programme of the theatre and not merely to offer occasional
peripheral backup to main stage productions.
    The tensions between the function of a theatre whose identity and
purpose are integrally bound up with its bricks and mortar, seeing itself
as a flagship of artistic enterprise, and the function of 'theatre outreach',
operating in non-theatre spaces (rehearsal rooms, studios, school halls,
prisons and the like) are probably inevitable and in need of constant rene-
gotiation and reassessment. Institutional theatre, just as institutional
education, is always likely to play a key role in the cultural life of
the community. Its attention to well-organised, carefully planned programmes of plays and events, its ability to cater for large audiences,
its local visibility, its relative permanence and ability to look at least to
the medium if not the longer term, all mean that it can at its best be a
powerhouse for well-crafted, high-definition theatre and can command

a loyal, local following. At its worst it can constrain, play safe, commodify, centralise, exclude and constitute a drain on cultural resources that might better be deployed elsewhere. Theatre that places education at the pivot of everything it does (whether units within an established building or the specialised touring companies) none the less needs to work simultaneously and insistently both within and outside the large cultural and educational institutions. It needs on the one hand the freedom to experiment, to play, to generate fresh ideas and approaches, to engage in dialogues with its likely audiences and continually to interrogate its own practice and that of the cultural institutions that dominate the landscape. But, on the other, it cannot work only at the margins. If its work is to be able to connect with and enhance the lives of the audiences it serves, it also needs to work inside, with and for, all those institutions that impinge on those lives: the schools, prisons, museums and regular theatres; to locate itself as part of the cultural mainstream and to respond (even if it does not wholly subscribe) to the policy agendas and curriculum targets that drive so much institutional practice. The educational goals, in this respect, bind theatre companies such as Geese and the specialist TIE companies into the network of cultural institutions that provide the funding and the opportunities to work, while simultaneously requiring extraordinary balancing acts as the practitioners endeavour to retain a degree of independence, critical distance and non-institutional playfulness – the very qualities that are at the heart of many effective educational programmes.

So, what we expect from our theatre makers, particularly in terms of the physical, sociological and ideological relationships between 'stage' and 'auditorium', between actor and participant, has changed since Barker's formulation of an 'exemplary theatre', as has the world in which they are situated. We have seen those changes evidenced in the shifts from, for example, the large-scale theatrics of *Spirochete* and *One Third* to the more fluid and more genuinely interactive forms exhibited in *Pow Wow* and *Gutted*; while first-person interpretation – as a form of 'cultural performance' – offers visitors opportunities for engagement with, and learning from, actors in role without even realising theatre is involved at all. The changes were to some extent anticipated in the experiments with audience participation seen in agit-prop and *The CCC Murder Mystery* and the man-from-the-audience in the living newspapers – and indeed in Barker's celebration of theatre's essentially collaborative function. 'Collaboration' as Barker saw it within his exemplary theatre presupposed, however, some very fixed parameters within which it could take place, not least of which would have been the theatre's geographical fixity – audiences and potential students (of whatever age) would have to come to the centre rather than expect the centre to come to them. And, for all Barker's talk of this benefiting 'the common man', it likewise assumed a degree of 'cultural capital' already acquired by those likely to take up the opportunity.

The didactic models from the 1930s and 1940s, and the modernist narratives of progress on which most were predicated, are no longer appropriate just as the complexities and implications of scientific knowledge are now much more problematic than they seemed to be seventy years ago, and just as a mediatised world invites us to plug in to its playful, postmodern and often highly manipulative representations of reality (whether television reality shows, radio phone-in talk shows, live webcam broadcasts or promotional campaigns), accompanied by contentious claims of the 'real', 'active' and 'live' participation of the public. Scientific discovery of the genetic codes that make up our very being has opened up an extraordinary set of challenges to our moral, religious and political assumptions; matters of religious, ethnic and cultural diversity have taken on a new, more urgent edge, posing uncomfortable questions about national identity, territorial borders and citizenship; climate change and globalisation challenge us to look beyond the immediate short-term future and consider the kind of world we will be leaving for our grandchildren.

Drama as an explicitly educational medium has of course undergone at least as much change as all other forms of cultural expression. The one-way traffic models of education have long ceased to have intellectual currency even if they still get applied in all too many classrooms, and even if they still get wheeled out by politicians and the popular press as ways of dealing with crises about drug abuse, obesity and bullying. Participatory models of education, constructivist theories of learning and aesthetic theories that emphasise the readers' and audiences' roles in making meaning have all helped to create a very different climate – even if they are in turn becoming subject to interrogation and qualification. Interestingly, the leading organisations dedicated to the public understanding of science have now shifted the nature of the discourse, subtly but significantly, to a concern to promote public *engagement with* science, underlining the increased perception that engagement places the public in the centre of the process rather than merely on the receiving end of scientists' attempts to explain their work to us.[1]

Is participation the correct term for the kind of 'social theatre' that seems more appropriate to today's needs? – or is 'transaction', as favoured by Kolb (1985) in educational contexts and Rosenblatt (2004) in literary contexts, a more useful one, suggesting as it does genuine exchange between those involved (teachers and taught, artists and audiences), rather than a predetermined programme in which others are invited (allowed) to participate? It certainly suggests the dynamic quality at the heart of real engagement – the possibility that things may change as a result of the encounter: for the performer or artist or facilitator as much as for the participant. Just as Freire argues for programmes of learning in which tutor and pupil can learn from each other rather than reinforcing the hierarchies of traditional styles of knowledge transfer. If the move towards transaction in various forms of 'applied' or 'social' theatre programmes really does involve a degree of co-authorship, however, what are the implications for the art form and for education?

The very notion of participation has been subjected to scrutiny and scepticism in recent years. Cooke and Kothari (2001), for example, question whether, in social development programmes, participation has become 'the new tyranny'. Etherton and Prentki (2006) similarly note how in applied theatre generally and TfD especially 'the emphasis upon participation' (p. 147) has become paramount, but has brought with it increased awareness of the contradictions often inherent in the practice – the tensions between, for example, personal transformation and social impact. Facilitating the 'self-development' of the participants can sometimes conflict with the 'intervention' thought necessary to effect social and personal change, and it becomes problematic when that change 'may not coincide with the desires of the community in which [the facilitator's] process is located' (p. 141). Activity that notionally appears to be about 'empowerment' can so easily, in reality, and whether intended or not (and more usually not), end in cementing pre-existing power relations and actually disempower the very people least able, or least inclined, to stand up for their right to be heard. These tensions are mirrored in the debates in educational circles about child-centred learning as opposed to the benchmark-driven requirements of the official curricula.

Against such a background, of rapid change and contradiction, it is not unreasonable to ask whether there is still a role for an art form that many consider outmoded and elitist. Indeed, it might be thought to be an irrelevant or diversionary exercise to insist on putting the aesthetic at the heart of a discussion of theatre as an educational medium. I hope that this book has gone some way to suggesting the contrary, that recognition, and understanding, of the aesthetic dimension in this field of work are vital. Within artistic encounters, and within theatrical encounters especially, the aesthetic is pivotal in developing an understanding of the world around us on a number of levels, visceral, emotional and cognitive, in seeing it from multiple viewpoints, and in being challenged to think afresh those values, assumptions and attitudes we thought were fixed. If many have consigned the art form of theatre to the margins in favour of broader, supposedly more responsive and more participatory work, in which the arts and 'artistry' are seen as secondary or decorative (the use of song, dance, design incorporated to provide colour or a touch of the 'exotic', or to exemplify a message already declared), then, at such a point, it is I believe timely to reinsert a discussion of the aesthetic back into work that sets itself educational or transformational goals.

It may be that the aesthetic dimension offers an essential space (Postman's 'counter-environment' again) for negotiating the tensions between real life and its imagined alternatives. Participation within a performance context, whether immersive TIE roleplay or forum theatre workshop, may not make the same far-reaching claims as those made for participatory approaches to development (increasing the involvement of marginalised people in decision-making over their own lives, for example, leading to 'sustainability, relevance and empowerment', Cooke & Kothari 2001: 5); it will be limited because 'bracketed' off from the real world through its artfulness and its overt or implicit aesthetic appeal. If honestly presented, it will not (or should not) raise inappropriate or unreal expectations about *direct* transference from the experience of the drama into the literal everyday, 'real' world. If it does, it is likely to have slipped from its anchorings within an aesthetic framework and veered towards didacticism, propaganda or wishful thinking. Through its ability to work at the level of conscious story-telling, of metaphor, the aesthetic framework of an educational theatre performance event can involve its audience or participants because they know (or sense) that the event is both real and not real simultaneously. The *connections* with the everyday are real and significant but indirect, framed, demanding individual and collective processing rather than offering ready-made solutions. The making of meaning cannot be equated with the delivery of messages. As this book (and others before it) has tried to demonstrate, meaning making in the arts is an immensely complex, fluid process: we find ourselves stimulated by an artwork (of whatever kind), we respond intuitively, emotionally and sensorally, and begin to piece together, consciously or subconsciously or both, an understanding of the world presented to us together with the issues that may be raised; our response is shaped by the experiences and mental predispositions we bring with us from the 'real world', predispositions themselves constructed and conditioned by the culture that surrounds us, and is further modified when shared with others. Learning – and making meaning – through drama (whether that be classroom drama or conventional theatre) is, as John O'Toole (1992) astutely reminds us, essentially processual and accumulative. At any one moment of perception and response, the meanings we construct will be unfixed, provisional and negotiable in form. If the impact upon us resonates, if it has any longer-term effect upon our attitudes, behaviour or utterances or our perceptions in the real world, or upon the bank of knowledge on which we can draw in the future, it will not be the message, explicit or implicit, that resonates, but what we ourselves have taken from the experience, how we have reconstructed it, made sense of it to ourselves and applied it in our own ways to our own lives. In this sense, meaning making and learning are synonymous – they both involve (as Falk and Dierking point out in their study of learning in museums, 2001: 61) making sense of the world around us, endeavouring to exercise 'control over the events in [our] lives' and 'making the unknown known' (p. 61). This accumulative and never-ending process is consonant with what the playwright Trevor Griffiths (1976) refers to as the calculatedly 'unfinished' endings of his plays, what Thompson (following on from Boal) describes as the presentation in applied theatre work of 'doubt and not certainty' (2003: 126) and what Taylor (2003) refers to as the 'incompleteness' of applied theatre. This 'incompleteness' is likely to be at once a dramaturgical strategy, a philosophical belief and a recognition of the way 'reception' and 'engagement' work in practice. It relates back to Iser's notion of the 'indeterminacy' at the heart of compelling literature: the 'creative gaps' (see Chapter 7 above) that draw the reader or audience in to an active, collaborative relationship with the text. And, as Helen Nicholson puts it, citing Merleau-Ponty's argument that, in the arts, we must look for meanings in 'the blanks the painter leaves between the brush-strokes, or the silences between the words', those gaps are 'expressive', they invite 'multiple interpretations' and offer 'an aesthetic space in which meanings are made' (Nicholson 2005: 167). At the heart of all effective educational theatre practice, and more critical even than the active participation of the audience, is the existence, in whatever form, of that 'aesthetic space', those 'creative gaps', within which audiences and participants can forge, negotiate, and own, meaning.

One of the main tasks I set myself in writing this book was to consider the challenges involved in trying to describe, explain, analyse and justify what goes on in certain kinds of theatre productions and in performance events that claim to educate their audiences. The discussion throughout has not been an attempt to define art, nor has it been concerned to *prove* that theatre can play a valuable role in educating young people about AIDS, sexual health, citizenship and the like. It is rather the means by which we try to understand and develop the practice that has concerned me, not only in terms of its educational efficacy but, just as importantly, of its aesthetic qualities too. I believe this to be not a 'merely academic' question but one that has a direct bearing on the business of writing, directing and performing these programmes; and likewise on the way we argue for the validity and efficacy of this work to 'clients' and to funders and on the way in which the work is evaluated – both formally (officially) and informally. For that reason, setting the practice within a larger historical context, and tracing and opening up some of the many genealogical links and discontinuous congruities that connect work as disparate as *Justice* and *Spirochete*, *One Third of a Nation* and *Home and Away*, has been an important part of the exercise. Neither *Justice* nor *Galileo* could be seen as obvious examples of interventionist or applied theatre; but they both in different ways illuminate significant points on the theatrical spectrum and pose pertinent questions about the ways in which theatre can engage, and has engaged, with issues of the day and sought to win audiences over to a cause or to promote critical thinking about the ways the world works and about how it might be other than it is, and finally how we, individually or collectively, stand in relation to it. Just as importantly, the ludic qualities of theatre evident in the work of, for example, Geese Theatre, and in a play such as *Forever*, and in much of the live interpretation at sites such as Plimoth, point to the ways theatre can still retain its ancient power to surprise, entertain and provoke, qualities essential to any medium of art that seeks to promote genuine learning rather than merely setting out to inform.

If we are to fully understand and advance the practice of theatre as an educational medium, we do I think need to see it in the context of past achievements, experiments and failures, not because the history lesson will reveal magic solutions to us but rather because the earlier struggles to balance and mesh the 'social' and the 'aesthetic' are revealing and may throw more light on what those fraught but recurring terms mean, and may in the process help us to interrogate current practice with greater alertness to the aesthetic power of the medium. I have argued that the supposed dichotomy between 'aesthetic' and 'instrumental' theatre, often implied if not stated, is a false one. But the very fact that it is perceived to be a dichotomy, that the two are so often posed as alternatives, is every reason why we have to attend more than we do at present to the art at the heart of educational theatre. It certainly happens in the best practice. But only if we articulate and embrace the artistic core of what we do with sufficient energy and conviction, will the best practice *really* be understood by the agencies who fund the work and, more importantly, only then will it be possible to share and celebrate that practice for the powerful theatre, and the 'educative force', we know it can – sometimes – be.

Note

1 See for example Tim Boon's account of the changing nature of the relation-ship between scientists and the lay public ('communication is now much more two-way') in the Wellcome Trust's recent publication *Engaging Science*, ed. J. Turney, 2006, pp. 8–3.

References

Abbs, Peter (1987), *Living Powers: The Arts in Education*. London: The Falmer Press.

Allen, G., Allen, I. and Dalrymple, L. (1999), 'Ideology, practice and evaluation: developing the effectiveness of Theatre in Education', *Research in Drama Education*, 4.1, 21–36.

Allen, John (1937), *Notes on Forming Left Theatre Groups*. Mimeograph published by the Left Book Club Theatre Guild, copy in National Museum of Labour History, Manchester.

—— (1979), *Drama in Schools*. London: Heinemann.

Anderson, David (1997, 1999), *A Common Wealth: Museums in the Learning Age – A Report to the Department for Culture, Media & Sport*. London: Department for Culture, Media & Sport.

Arent, Arthur (1938/1971), 'The techniques of the Living Newspaper', *Theatre Arts*, November; reprinted in *Theatre Quarterly* 4 (1971), 57–9.

Arts Council England (ACE) (2000), *National Policy for Theatre in England*. London: ACE (available at www.artscouncil.org.uk/documents/publications/300.pdf; last accessed 30 August 2006).

Arts Council of Great Britain (1956), *The First Ten Years*. London: ACGB.

—— (1986), *Theatre Is for All*. London: ACGB.

Ascherson, Neal (1987a), 'Why "heritage" is right-wing', *The Observer*, 8 November 1987.

—— (1987b), ' "Heritage" as vulgar English nationalism', *The Observer*, 29 November 1987.

—— (1992), 'Reminders from the past to suspend our disbelief', *The Independent on Sunday*, 26 April 1992.

Aston, E. and Savona, G. (1991), *Theatre as Sign-system: A Semiotics of Text and Performance*. London: Routledge.

Babbage, F. (2004), *Augusto Boal*. London: Routledge.

Bagnall, Gaynor (2003), 'Performance and performativity at heritage sites', *Museums and Society*, 1.2, 87–103.

Baim, C., Brookes, S. and Mountford, A. (2002), *The Geese Handbook*. Winchester: The Waterside Press.

The Bair Report: Educational Aspects of the Federal Theatre Project (1937), National Service Bureau: Federal Theatre Project: Works Progress Administration, Washington DC, 15 September.

Bakhtin, M. (1981), 'Discourse in the novel', reprinted in *The Dialogic Imagination: Four Essays*, ed. Michael Holquist (trans. Caryl Emerson and Michael Holquist). Austin: University of Texas Press.

—— (1986), *Speech Genres and Other Late Essays* (trans. Y. McGee). Austin: University of Texas Press.

—— (1994), *The Bakhtin Reader*, ed. Pam Morris. London: Edward Arnold.

Balfour, Michael, ed. (2004), *Theatre in Prison: Theory and Practice*. Bristol: Intellect Books.

Bandura, A. (1977), *Social Learning Theory*. Englewood Cliffs, NJ: Prentice Hall.

Banks, Greg (2001), personal interview, 6 November.

Barker, Harley Granville (1922/1970), *The Exemplary Theatre*. Freeport, New York: Books for Libraries Press.

—— (1930/1963), *Prefaces to Shakespeare* (repr. in 4 vols), London: B. T. Batsford.

Barker, Paul (2004), 'Shakespeare's sisters', *The Guardian*, 26 June.

Barrie, J. M. (1928), *Peter Pan and Other Plays* (first edn). London: Hodder & Stoughton.

Baskeyfield, G. (2001), *Consultation with Young People in Rochdale* (unpublished report for the Teenage Pregnancy Task Group).

Belgrade TIE Company (1973/1980), *Pow Wow*, in P. Schweitzer, ed. (1980), *Theatre in Education*. vol. 1, London: Methuen.

Ben Chaim, Daphna (1984), *Distance in the Theatre*. Ann Arbor, MI: UMI Research Press.

Bennett, Stuart, ed. (2005), *Theatre for Children and Young People*. London: Aurora Metro Press.

Bennett, Susan (1990), *Theatre Audiences*. London: Routledge.

Bentley, Eric (1965), *The Life of the Drama*. London: Methuen.

—— (1967), *Bernard Shaw*. London: Methuen & Co.

—— ed. (1968), *The Theory of the Modern Stage*. Harmondsworth: Penguin Books.

Best, David (1991), *The Rationality of Feeling: Understanding the Arts in Education*. London: The Falmer Press.

Bicknell, S. and Mazda, X. (1993), *Enlightening or Embarrassing? An Evaluation of Drama in the Science Museum*. London: National Museum of Science & Industry.

Bigsby, C. W. E. (1982), *Introduction to 20th Century American Drama*, vol. I: 1900–1940. Cambridge: Cambridge University Press.

Boal, Augusto (1979), *The Theatre of the Oppressed*. London: Pluto Press.

—— (1992), *Games for Actors & Non-Actors*. London: Routledge.

—— (1995), *The Rainbow of Desire*. London: Routledge.

Boal, Augusto (1998), *Legislative Theatre*. London: Routledge.
—— (2006), *The Aesthetics of the Oppressed*. London: Routledge.
Bolton, Gavin (1998), *Acting in Classroom Drama: A Critical Analysis*. London: Trentham Books.
—— (1993), 'Drama in education and TIE', in Jackson, ed., *Learning through Theatre*, pp. 39–47.
Bond, Edward (2002), *The Cap: Working Notes on Drama, the Self and Society*. Typescript of unpublished address given to the 2002 Conference of the National Association of Teachers of Drama.
—— (2005), 'Something of myself', in D. Davies, ed., *Edward Bond and the Dramatic Child*, pp. 1–8.
Boon, R. and Plastow, J., eds (2004), *Theatre and Empowerment: Community Drama on the World Stage*. Cambridge: Cambridge University Press.
Boon, Tim (2006), 'A historical perspective on science engagement', in J. Turney, ed., *Engaging Science: Thoughts, Deeds, Analysis and Action*. London: The Wellcome Trust, pp. 8–13.
Bottoms, Stephen (2003), 'The efficacy/effeminacy braid: unpicking the performance studies/theatre studies dichotomy', *Theatre Topics*, 13.2 (September), 173–87.
Bourdieu, Pierre (1977), *Outline of a Theory of Practice*. Cambridge: Cambridge University Press.
—— (1979), *Distinction: A Social Critique of the Judgment of Taste*, Cambridge, MA: Harvard University Press.
Bradby, D. and McCormick, J. (1978), *People's Theatre*. London: Croom Helm.
Brecht, Bertolt (1940), 'On experimental theatre' (trans. M. Vallance), in Hoffmann, L., ed. (1971), *Erwin Piscator: political theatre 1920–66*, pp. 31–2.
—— (1974a), 'Theatre for pleasure or theatre for instruction' (trans. John Willett) (c. 1936), in Willett, ed., *Brecht on Theatre*, pp. 69–76.
—— (1974b), 'The modern theatre is the epic theatre' (trans. John Willett) (c. 1930), in Willett, ed., *Brecht on Theatre*, pp. 33–42.
—— (1974c), 'From the Mother Courage model' (1958), in Willett, ed., *Brecht on Theatre*, pp. 215–20.
—— (1947/1963), 'Postscript to the American version', *The Life of Galileo* (trans. D. I. Vesey). London: Methuen, pp. 9–15.
Breitinger, E., ed. (1994), *Theatre and Performance in Africa. Intercultural Perspectives*. Bayreuth: Bayreuth African Studies.
Bridal, Tessa (2004), *Exploring Museum Theatre*. Walnut Creek, CA: AltaMira Press.
Brook, Peter (1969/1990), *The Empty Space*. Harmondsworth: Penguin.
Brooker, P. (1994), 'Key words in Brecht's theory and practice of theatre', in P. Thomson, ed., *The Cambridge Companion to Brecht*. Cambridge: Cambridge University Press, pp. 185–200.
Bruce, M. (1987), *The Shaping of the Modern World*. London: Edward Arnold.
Bullough, Edward (1912), 'Psychical distance as a factor in art and an aesthetic principle', *British Journal of Psychology* 5 (June), 87–118.

Bundy, Penny (2003), 'Aesthetic engagement in the drama process', *Research in Drama Education*, 8.2, 171–81.

Calder, A. (1969), *The People's War: Britain 1939–45*. London: Cape.

Cardboard Citizens Theatre Company (2004), *Home and Away: Teachers' Notes*.

Carey, John (2005), *What Good Are the Arts?* London: Faber & Faber.

Carlson, Marvin (1990), *Theatre Semiotics: Signs of Life*. Bloomington, IN: Indiana University Press.

—— (1992), 'Theatre and dialogism', in J. Reinelt and J. Roach, eds, *Critical Theory and Performance*. Ann Arbor, MI: University of Michigan Press, pp. 313–23.

—— (1996), *Performance*. London: Routledge.

Chambers, Colin (1989), *The Story of Unity Theatre*. London: Lawrence & Wishart.

Chothia, J. (1984), 'One third of a nation: introduction', in *'Busmen' and 'One Third of a Nation'*. Nottingham: Nottingham Drama Texts, pp. 29–32.

Clarke, Ian (1989), *Edwardian Drama*. London: Faber & Faber.

Clurman, Harold (1957), *The Fervent Years*. New York: Hill & Wang.

Coggin, P. A. (1956), *Drama and Education: An Historical Survey*. London: Thames & Hudson.

Cohen, L. and Manion, L. (1994), *Research Methods in Education*. London: Routledge.

Cole, David (1975), *The Theatrical Event*. Middetown, CT: Wesleyan University Press.

Collinson, D. (1992), 'Aesthetic experience', in O. Hanfling, ed., *Philosophical Aesthetics: An introduction*. Oxford: Blackwell/The Open University, pp. 111–78.

Cook, H. Caldwell (1917), *The Play Way*. London: Heinemann.

Cooke, B. and Kothari, U., eds (2001), *Participation: The New Tyranny?* London: Zed Books.

Cooper, Mary (2004), personal interview, 26 April.

Cosgrove, S. (1985), 'From shock troupe to group theatre', in Samuel, MacColl and Cosgrove, eds, *Theatres of the Left 1880–1935*, pp. 259–79.

Counsell, Colin (1996), *Signs of Performance: An Introduction to Twentieth-Century Theatre*. London: Routledge.

Crace, J. (2001), 'Playing to the gallery', *The Guardian: Guardian Education*, 13 November 2001.

Cremona, V., Eversmann, P., van Maanen, H., Sauter, W. and Tulloch, J., eds, (2004), *Theatrical Events: Borders, Dynamics, Frames*. Amsterdam: Rodopi.

Davies, Andrew (1987), *Other Theatres*. London: Macmillan.

Davies, D., ed. (2005), *Edward Bond and the Dramatic Child: Edward Bond's Plays for Young People*. Stoke on Trent: Trentham Books.

Decker, C. (1977), *The Victorian Conscience*. Westport, CT: Greenwood Press.

Dewey, J. (1915), *The School and Society*. Chicago: University of Chicago Press.

—— (1918), *Democracy and Education*. London: Macmillan.

—— (1933), *How We Think: A Restatement of the Relation of Reflective Thinking to the Educative Process* (revised edn). Boston: D. C. Heath.

Dewey, J. (1980/originally published 1934), *Art as Experience*. New York: Perigree Books.

Djerassi, Carl (2005), 'Contemporary "science-in-theatre": a rare genre', The Dennis Rosen Memorial Lecture. www.djerassi.com/sciencetheatre.html, last accessed 1 May 2006.

Dupré, C. (1976), *John Galsworthy*. London: Collins.

Eagleton, Terry (1983), *Literary Theory: An Introduction*. Oxford: Basil Blackwell.

Ede, Sian (2005), *Art and Science*. London: I.B. Tauris & Co.

Elam, K. (1980), *The Semiotics of Theatre and Drama*. London: Methuen.

Engels, Friedrich (1892/1999), *The Condition of the Working-Class in England in 1844*. Oxford: Oxford University Press.

England, Alan (1990), *Theatre for the Young*. London: Methuen.

Erven, E. van (2000), *Community Theatre: Global Perspectives*. London: Routledge.

Esslin, M. (1965), *Brecht: A Choice of Evils*. London: Heinemann.

—— (1987), *The Field of Drama*, London: Methuen.

Etherton, M. and Prentki, T. (2006), 'Drama for change? Prove it! Impact assessment in applied theatre' (editorial article), *Research in Drama Education*, 11.2 (June), 139–55.

Falk, J. and Dierking, L. (2001), *Learning from Museums: Visitor Experiences and the Making of Meaning*. London: AltaMira Press.

Fanshawe, S. (2006), 'What you see is what you get', *The Guardian*, 11 April 2006.

Fines, J. and Verrier, R. (1974), *The Drama of History*. London: New University Education.

Fines, J. (1996), 'To catch the conscience', in Tinniswood and Woodhead, eds, *No Longer Dead to Me: Working with Schoolchildren in the Performing & Creative Arts*.

Fischer-Lichte, Erika (1992), *The Semiotics of Theater* (trans. J. Gaines and D. Jones). Bloomington: Indiana University Press.

—— (1997), 'Performance art and ritual: bodies in performance', *Theatre Research International* 22.1, 22–37.

Flanagan, Hallie (1940), *Arena: The Story of the Federal Theatre*. New York: Duell, Sloane & Pearce.

Flanagan Davis, Hallie (1946), $E=mc^2$. New York: Samuel French.

Fortier, M. (1997), *Theatre/Theory: An Introduction*. London: Routledge.

Fosnot, C. T., ed. (1996), *Constructivism: Theory, Perspectives and Practice*. New York: Teachers College Press.

Foucault, M. (1971), 'Nietzsche, genealogy, history', reprinted in P. Rabinow, ed. (1984), *The Foucault Reader*. London: Penguin, pp. 76–100.

—— (1980), *Power, Knowledge and other Writings*. Brighton: Harvester Press.

Frank, Marion (1995), *Aids Education through Theatre*. Bayreuth: Bayreuth African Studies.

Freire, Paulo (1996), *Pedagogy of the Oppressed*. Harmondsworth: Penguin Books (originally published 1970, New York).

Furst, L. and Skrine, P. (1971), *Naturalism*. London: Methuen (The Critical Idiom series).

Gadamer, Hans-Georg (1975), *Truth and Method*. London: Sheed & Ward.

Gallagher, K. and Booth, D., eds (2003), *How Theatre Educates*. Toronto: University of Toronto Press.

Galsworthy, John (1910), *Justice: A Tragedy in Four Acts*. London: Duckworth.

Gardner, Howard (1983), *Frames of Mind: The Theory of Multiple Intelligences*. New York: Basic Books.

—— (1993), *Multiple Intelligences: The Theory in Practice*. New York: Basic Books.

Gardner, V. and Rutherford, S. (1992), *The New Woman and Her Sisters: Feminism and the Theatre, 1850–1914*. Ann Arbor: University of Michigan Press.

Geertz, Clifford (1997), 'Art as a cultural system', *Modern Language Notes* 91 (1974); reprinted in S. Feagin and P. Maynard, eds, *Aesthetics*. Oxford: Oxford University Press, pp. 109–18.

Giles, Honor (1997), Report on the 'Peopling the Past' Seminar, *Newsletter of the International Museum Theatre Alliance* (IMTAL), 8, 1.

Ginden, J. (1987), *John Galsworthy's Life and Art*. Basingstoke: Macmillan.

Glasersfeld, Ernst von (1995), *Radical Constructivism: A Way of Knowing and Learning*. London: Routledge.

Goffman, Erving (1974), *Frame Analysis*. New York: Harper & Row.

Goorney, H. and MacColl, E., eds. (1986), *From Agit Prop to Theatre Workshop*. Manchester: Manchester University Press.

Gray, R. (1977), *Ibsen: A Dissenting View*. Cambridge: Cambridge University Press.

Greene, M. (1995), *Releasing the Imagination: Essays on Education, the Arts, and Social Change*. San Francisco, CA: Jossey-Bass.

Greenwich and Lewisham Young People's Theatre (GYPT) (1987), *School on the Green*, in *Six Plays*, ed. C. Redington. London: Methuen.

Griffiths, Trevor (1976), Interview, *The Times Educational Supplement*, 25 June 1976, pp. 18–19.

Hare, David (1992), 'On political theatre' (based on lecture given at King's College, Cambridge, 5 March 1978) reprinted as 'Introduction' to *The Early Plays*. London: Faber & Faber.

Harris, Aurand, (1985), 'Plees make more', reprinted in N. McCaslin, ed., *Children and Drama*, third edn. Lanham, MD: Rowman & Littlefield, pp. 117–27.

Hauser, A. (1990), *The Social History of Art, Volume 4: Naturalism, Impressionism, The Film Age*. London: Routledge.

Hawes, Chris, and the Duke's Theatre in Education Team (Lancaster) (1980), *The Max Factor*, later re-titled, *On His Own Two Feet*. Unpublished playscript.

The Health Development Agency (2003), *It Opened my Eyes: Using Theatre in*

Education to Deliver Sex and Relationship Education. London: Department for Education and Skills.

Heaney, Seamus (1993), 'For Liberation: Brian Friel and the use of memory', in A. Peacock, ed., *The Achievement of Brian Friel*. Gerrards Cross: Colin Smythe, pp. 229–40.

Heathcote, Dorothy (1980), 'Signs and portents', reprinted in L. Johnson and C. O'Neill, eds (1984), *Collected Writings on Education and Drama*. Cheltenham: Stanley Thornes.

Heathcote, D. and Bolton, G. (1995), *Drama for learning: Dorothy Heathcote's Mantle of the Expert Approach to Education*. Portsmouth, NH: Heinemann.

Hein, George (1998), *Learning in the Museum*. London: Routledge.

Heritage, P. (1998), 'Theatre, prisons and citizenship: a South American Way', in J. Thompson, ed., *Prison Theatre*. London: Jessica Kingsley, pp. 31–42.

Herken, G. (1988), *The Winning Weapon: The Atomic Bomb in the Cold War, 1945–1950*. Princeton: Princeton University Press.

Hewison, Robert (1987), *The Heritage Industry*. London: Methuen.

Hoffman, L., ed. (1971), *Erwin Piscator: Political Theatre 1920–66*. London: Arts Council.

Holledge, J. (1981), *Innocent Flowers: Women in the Edwardian Theatre*. London: Virago.

Holt, John (1982), *How Children Fail*. Harmondsworth: Penguin.

Holub, Robert (1984), *Reception Theory: A Critical Introduction*. London: Methuen.

Hooper-Greenhill, Eilean (1997), 'Museum learners as active post-modernists', *Journal for Education in Museums* 18.

Hope, A. and Timmel, S., eds (1999), *Training for Transformation: A Handbook for Community Theatre Workers*. St Albans: TALC.

Horace (Quintus Horatius Flaccus) (1995), *Ars Poetica*, trans. Leon Golden in *Horace for Students of Literature: The 'Ars Poetica' and Its Tradition*. Online at www.english.emory.edu/DRAMA/ArsPoetica.html, last accessed 21 August 2006.

Hornbrook, D. (1989), *Education and Dramatic Art*. Oxford: Blackwell.

—— (1991), *Education in Drama*. London: The Falmer Press.

Hughes, C. (1998), *Museum Theatre: Communicating with Visitors through Drama*. Portsmouth, NH: Heinemann.

Hughes, C., Jackson, A. and Kidd, J. (2007), 'The role of theater in museums and historic sites: visitors, audiences and learners', in L. Bresler, ed., *International Handbook of Research in Arts Education*. Dordrecht: Springer, pp. 677–93.

Huizinga, J. (1949), *Homo Ludens: A Study of the Play Element in Culture*. London: Routledge & Kegan Paul.

Ibsen, Henrik (1879/1974), *A Doll's House* (trans. M. Meyer). London: Eyre Methuen.

Illich, Ivan (1970), *Deschooling Society*. New York: Penguin.

Innes, C. D. (1972), *Erwin Piscator's Political Theatre*. Cambridge: Cambridge University Press.

Institute for Propaganda Analysis (1939), *The Fine Art of Propaganda*. New York: Harcourt, Brace and Company, quoted in: www.propagandacritic.com/articles/intro.why.html, last accessed 22 July 2006.

Iser, Wolfgang (1972), 'The reading process: a phenomenological approach', reprinted in D. Lodge, ed. (1988), *Modern Criticism and Theory: A Reader*. London: Longman.

Jackson, Adrian (2004a), Keynote address given at the Interventionist Theatre conference, University of Leeds: Bretton Hall, July.

—— (2004b), *Home and Away*. Unpublished typescript. Cardboard Citizens Theatre Company.

Jackson, Anthony (1980a), 'Can theatre teach?' *Critical Quarterly*, 22.4 (winter), 29–41.

—— ed. (1980b), *Learning through Theatre: Essays and Casebooks on Theatre in Education*. Manchester: Manchester University Press.

—— ed. (1993), *Learning through Theatre: New Perspectives on Theatre in Education*. London: Routledge.

—— (1995a), '*Love Trouble:* an evaluation'. Unpublished report for North West Arts Board.

—— (1995b), '*For any Field?*: an evaluation'. Unpublished report for North West Arts Board and National Trust.

—— (1996), 'Anecdotes are no longer enough: academic research and the evaluation of theatre in education', in Somers, ed., *Drama & Theatre in Education: Contemporary Research*.

—— (1997), 'Positioning the audience: inter-active strategies and the aesthetic in educational theatre', *Theatre Research International* 22.1 (spring), 48–60.

—— (2000), 'Interacting with the past: the use of participatory theatre at heritage sites', *Research in Drama Education*, 5.2 (September), pp. 199–216.

—— (2002), ' "You had to watch it to realise what it were like": researching audiences for educational theatre', in Bjørn Rasmussen and Anna-Lena Østern, eds, *Playing Betwixt and Between: The IDEA Dialogues 2001*. Bergen: IDEA Publications, pp. 168–77.

—— (2004), 'Del Agit-prop al Unity: el teatro radical de los anos treinta y los origins del Unity Theatre de Londres' ('From Agit-prop to Unity: radical theatre in the 1930s and the beginnings of Unity Theatre, London'), *Cultura Moderna*, 0 (launch edition) (spring), 71–90.

—— (2005), 'The dialogic and the aesthetic: some reflections on theatre as a learning medium', *Journal of Aesthetic Education* 39.5 (fall), 104–18.

Jackson, A. and Lev-Aladgem, S. (2004), 'Rethinking audience participation: audiences in alternative and educational theatre', in V. Cremona, P. Eversmann, H. van Maanen, W. Sauter and J. Tulloch, eds, *Theatrical Events: Borders, Dynamics, Frames* (International Federation of Theatre Research). Amsterdam: Rodopi, pp. 207–36.

Jackson, A., Grant, I., Korhonen, P. and Rainio, E. (1998), *A Comparative*

Investigation of Educational Theatre Policy and Practice in Finland and the UK: Report to the British Council, Helsinki. Unpublished.

Jackson, A., Johnson, P., Rees Leahy, H. and Walker, V. (2002), *Seeing It for Real: The Effectiveness of Theatre & Theatre Techniques in Museums.* Report for the Arts & Humanities Research Board. Manchester: CATR. Available at: www.plh.manchester.ac.uk/research/resources/Seeing_It_For_Real.pdf.

Jackson, A. and Rees Leahy, Helen (2005), ' "Seeing it for Real . . .?": authenticity, theatre and learning in museums'. *Research in Drama Education* 10.3 (winter), 303–25.

Jackson, Philip (1968), *Life in Classrooms.* New York: Holt, Rinehart & Winston.

Jauss, Hans R. (1982), *Aesthetic Experience and Literary Hermeneutics.* Minneapolis: University of Minnesota Press.

Kay, M. and Baskerville, R. (1980), 'The actor-teacher', in Jackson, ed., *Learning through Theatre*, pp. 51–68.

Kazacoff, G. (1989), *Dangerous Theatre.* New York: Peter Lang.

Keating, P., ed. (1976), *Into Unknown England, 1866–1913: Selections from the Social Explorers.* London: Fontana.

Kennedy, D. (1985), *Granville Barker and the Dream of Theatre.* Cambridge: Cambridge University Press.

Kershaw, Baz (1999), *The Radical in Performance.* London: Routledge.

Kirby, M. (1965), *Happenings: An Illustrated Anthology.* New York: Oxford University Press.

—— (1974), *New Theatre: Performance Documentation.* New York: New York University Press.

Kirshenblatt-Gimblett, Barbara (1993), 'Foreword' to Snow, *Performing the Pilgrims*, pp. xi–xvii.

—— (1998), *Destination Culture: Tourism, Museums & Heritage.* Berkeley: University of California Press.

Kolb, David (1985), *Experiential Learning: Experience as the Source of Learning and Development.* Englewood Cliffs, NJ: Prentice-Hall.

Kreizenbeck, A. (1979), 'The CCC Murder Mystery', *The Drama Review* 23.4 (December), 59–66.

Landy, R., ed. (1982), *Handbook of Educational Drama and Theatre.* Westport, CT: Greenwood Press.

Langer, Susanne (1953), *Feeling and Form: A Theory of Art.* London: Routledge & Kegan Paul.

Leavis, F. R. (1962), *Two Cultures? The Significance of C. P. Snow* (The 1962 Richmond Lecture), collected in Leavis (1972), *Nor Shall My Sword.* London: Chatto & Windus.

Levy, Jonathan (1987), *A Theatre of the Imagination.* Charlottesville, VA: New Plays Inc.

Limmer, Mark (2005), correspondence with author and Dorothy Wood, 13 December.

—— (2006), correspondence with author, 9 August.

Lotman, J. (1977), *The Structure of Aesthetic Texts* (trans. G. Lenhoff and R. Vroon). Ann Arbor: University of Michigan Press.

Lowenthal, David (1985), *The Past Is a Foreign Country*. Cambridge: Cambridge University Press.

Lyotard, J. F. (1984), *The Postmodern Condition: A Report on Knowledge*. Manchester: Manchester University Press.

M6 Theatre Company (2000), *'Forever': Teachers' Notes*.

McCarthy, Julie (2000), *Evaluation of 'Forever'*. Unpublished report for the Teenage Pregnancy Task Group.

McCaslin, N., ed. (1999), *Children and Drama* (third ed.). Studio City, CA: Players Press.

MacColl, Ewan (1949), *Uranium 235: A Documentary Play in 11 Episodes*. Glasgow: MacLellan.

—— (1985), 'Some origins of Theatre Workshop', in Samuel, MacColl and Cosgrove, eds, *Theatres of the Left 1880–1935*, pp. 205–58.

—— (1986), 'Introduction' to Goorney and MacColl, eds, *Agit-Prop to Theatre Workshop*, pp. ix–lvii.

—— (1990), *Journeyman: An Autobiography*. London: Sidgwick and Jackson.

McDermott, D. (1965), 'The living newspaper as a dramatic form', *Modern Drama* 8.1, 82–94.

McFarlane, J., ed. (1970), *Henrik Ibsen: A Critical Anthology*. Harmondsworth: Penguin.

McGrath, John (1979), 'The theory and practice of political theatre', *Theatre Quarterly*, 35.

—— (1988), 'The process and product of theatre', reprinted in Holdsworth, N. (ed.) (2002), *Naked Thoughts that Roam About: reflections on theatre*, London: Nick Hern Books, pp. 175–8.

McGuire, J. (1995), *What Works: Reducing Reoffending*. Chichester: Wiley.

McNeil, Frances (1991), *Trappin'* (play with workshop notes), in R. Robinson, ed., *Ask Me Out*. London: Hodder & Stoughton.

Mamet, David (1994), *A Whore's Profession: Notes & Essays*. London and New York: Penguin Books.

Marrot, H. V. (1935), *The Life and Letters of John Galsworthy*. London: Heinemann.

Matarasso, Francois (1997), *Use or Ornament? The Social Impact of Participation in the Arts*. London: Comedia.

Meisel, M. (1963), *Shaw and the Nineteenth Century Theatre*. Princeton: Princeton University Press.

Melrose, Susan (1994), *The Semiotics of the Dramatic Text*. London: Macmillan.

Meyer, Michael (1974), *Ibsen: A Biography*. Harmondsworth: Penguin.

Miller, J. Howard (1937), *Preliminary Report of the Educational Activities of the Works Progress Administration Federal Theatre Project*. Memorandum to Dr F. H. Bair, Advisory Committee on Education, from Deputy Director,

FTP. Washington DC: typescript dated 18 August 1937 (National Archives, Washington DC, FTP 000 039).

Morgan, J. et al. (2006), *Enquiring Minds Guidebook*. Accessed at www.enquiringminds.org.uk/programme/context/references.html, last accessed 21 July 2006.

Morris, Pam, ed. (1994), *The Bakhtin Reader*. London: Edward Arnold.

Mountford, Alun and Farrell, M. (1998), 'The house of four rooms: theatre, violence and the cycle of change', in J. Thompson, ed., *Prison Theatre*. London: Jessica Kingsley, pp. 109–26.

Museums, Libraries and Archives Council (2004), 'Inspiring learning for all', www.inspiringlearningforall.gov.uk/default.aspx?flash=true, last accessed 28 August 2006.

National Campaign for the Arts (1997), 'Theatre in education: 10 years of change'. Report by the National Campaign for the Arts. London: NCA.

Nellis, M. (1996), 'John Galsworthy's *Justice*', *British Journal of Criminology* 36.1 (winter), 61–84.

Nicholson, Helen (2005), *Applied Drama: The Gift of Theatre*. London: Palgrave Macmillan.

O'Connor, J. (1977), ' "Spirochete" and the war on syphilis', *The Drama Review* 21.1 (March), 91–8.

O'Connor, J. and Brown, L., eds (1980), *Free Adult and Uncensored: The Living History of the Federal Theatre Project*. London: Eyre Methuen.

O'Neill, Cecily (1995), *Drama Worlds: A Framework for Process Drama*. Portsmouth, NH: Heinemann Drama.

O'Sullivan, C. (2001), 'Searching for the Marxist in Boal', *Research in Drama Education* 6.1, 85–97.

Osterud, Nancy G. (1992), 'Living living history: first-person interpretation at Plimoth Plantation', *Journal of Museum Education*. 17.1 (winter), 18–19.

O'Toole, John (1976), *Theatre in Education: New Objectives for Theatre – New Techniques in Education*. London: Hodder & Stoughton.

—— (1992), *The Process of Drama: Negotiating Art and Meaning*. London: Routledge.

Palmer, D. (M6 Theatre Company) (2006), correspondence, 14 August.

Pammenter, D. (1993), 'Devising for TIE', in Jackson, ed., *Learning through Theatre*, pp. 53–70.

Parker, Tony (Real Life Media) (2001), correspondence, October.

Peoplescape Theatre (2000), *No Bed of Roses*. Unpublished playscript; created for People's History Museum, Manchester.

Peter Boyden Associates and Arts Council England (2000), *Roles and Functions of the English Regional Producing Theatres: Final Report* (The Boyden Report). London: Arts Council England.

Piscator, Erwin (1929/1980), *The Political Theatre* (trans. H. Rorrison). London: Eyre Methuen.

Plimoth Plantation (1994, 1998), *Visitors Guides*. Plymouth, MA.

—— (c. 1998), In-house manual for interpreters (undated typscript). Plymouth, MA.

Postman, Neil (1994), Lecture given at Steinhardt School of Education, New York University (July).

Postman, N. and Weingartner, C. (1971), *Teaching as a Subversive Activity*. London: Penguin.

Pratkanis, A. R. and Aronson, E. (1991), *Age of Propaganda: The Everyday Use and Abuse of Persuasion*. New York: W. H. Freeman.

Priestley, J. B. (1940), *Postscripts*. London: Heinemann. Also BBC sound archives at: www.bbc.co.uk/bradford/content/articles/2006/07/14/wired_listen_up_feature.shtml.

Redington, Christine (1983), *Can Theatre Teach? An Historical and Evaluative Analysis of Theatre in Education*. Oxford: Pergamon Press.

Reid, L. A. (1969), *Meaning in the Arts*. London: Allen & Unwin.

—— (1980), 'Meaning in the arts', in M. Ross, ed., *The Arts and Personal Growth*, pp. 1–15.

Research Works Ltd (2005), *Diageo Great Britain: Evaluation of CragRats Theatre in Education Project – Qualitative Research Report*. London: Research Works Ltd (May).

Reynolds, Fiona (2003), 'Continuing to inspire and delight: the Director-General's Statement', *The National Trust Magazine: Summer*. London: The National Trust, pp. 5–6.

Robinson, K. (1993), 'Evaluating TIE', in Jackson, ed., *Learning through Theatre*.

Rohan, Pierre de, ed. (1938), *Federal Theatre Plays*. New York: Random House.

Rose, Jacqueline (1984), *The Case of Peter Pan, or the Impossibility of Children's Fiction*. London: Macmillan.

Rosenblatt, Louise (2004), 'The transactional theory of reading and writing', in Robert B. Ruddell, Norman J. Unrau, eds, *Theoretical Models and Processes of Reading* (fifth ed.). New York: International Reading Association, pp. 1363–98.

Ross, Malcolm, ed. (1980), *The Arts and Personal Growth*. Oxford: Pergamon.

—— (1984), *The Aesthetic Impulse*. Oxford: Pergamon.

Roth, Stacey (1998), *Past into Present: Effective Techniques for First-Person Historical Interpretation*. Chapel Hill: University of North Carolina Press.

Rowell, G. and Jackson, A. (1984), *The Repertory Movement: A History of Regional Theatre in Britain*. Cambridge: Cambridge University Press.

Royle, E. (1987), *Modern Britain: A Social History, 1750–1997*. London: E. Arnold.

Ruding, Simon (The TiPP Centre, Manchester) (2004), personal interview, 23rd March.

Samuel, R. (1985), 'Theatre and socialism in Britain', in Samuel, MacColl and Cosgrove, eds, *Theatres of the Left 1880–1935*, pp. 3–76.

Samuel, Raphael (1994), *Theatres of Memory: 1: Past & Present in Contemporary Culture*. London: Verso.

Samuel, R., MacColl, E. and Cosgrove, S., eds. (1985), *Theatres of the Left 1880–1935*, London: Routledge & Kegan Paul.

Saul, Oscar and Lantz, Louis (1936), *Flight*, in Swortzell, ed. (1986), *Six Plays for Young People from the Federal Theatre Project (1936–1939)*.

Sauter, Willmar (1997), 'Theatre or performance or untitled event(s)? – some comments on the conceptualization of the object of our studies', *Gestos* 12.24 (November), 27–40.

—— (2000), *The Theatrical Event: Dynamics of Performance and Perception*. Iowa City: University of Iowa Press.

—— (2004), 'Introducing the theatrical event', in Cremona et al., eds. *Theatrical Events*, pp. 3–14.

Schechner, Richard (1966), 'Approaches to theory/criticism', *TDR* 11.32, 20–53.

—— (1973/1994), *Environmental Theater*. New York: Applause Books.

—— (1977), *Essays on Performance Theory*. New York: Drama Books Specialists.

—— (1985), *Between Theatre and Anthropology*. Philadelphia: University of Pennsylvania Press.

—— (1988), *Performance Theory*. London: Routledge.

—— (1992), 'A new paradigm for "performance" in the Academy', *The Drama Review* 36.4.

—— (2002), *Performance Studies*. London: Routledge.

Schechner, R. and Thompson, J. (2004), 'Why "Social Theatre"?', *The Drama Review* 48.3 (fall) (T183), 11–16.

Scheff, T. J. (1979), *Catharsis in Healing, Ritual, and Drama*. Berkeley: University of California Press.

Schinina, G. (2004), 'Here we are: social theatre and some open questions about its developments', *The Drama Review* 48.3 (fall) (T183), 17–31.

Schoenmakers, H., ed. (1992), *Performance Theory, Reception and Audience Research: 3*. Amsterdam: ICRAR.

Schonmann, S. (2005), '"Master" versus "Servant": contradictions in drama and theatre education', *Journal of Aesthetic Education*, 39.4, pp. 31–9.

Sextou, P. (2003), 'TIE in Britain: current practice & future potential', *New Theatre Quarterly* 74, vol. xix (May), pp. 177–88.

Shank, T. (1982), *American Alternative Theatre*. New York: Grove Press.

Sharland, Penny (2000), *M6 Theatre Company: Evaluation of 'Forever'*. Unpublished report for M6 Theatre Co.

Shaw, G. B. (1895), 'The problem play – a symposium', in *The Humanitarian* VI. (May) (reprinted in E. J. West, ed. (1959), *Shaw on Theatre*. New York: Hill & Wang, pp. 58–66.

—— (1946), *Plays Unpleasant*. Harmondsworth: Penguin.

Sheppard, A. (1987), *Aesthetics: An Introduction to the Philosophy of Art*. Oxford: Oxford University Press.

Singer, E., Rogers, T. and Glassman, M. (1991), ' Public opinion about Aids before and after the 1988 U.S. government public information campaign', *Public Opinion Quarterly* 55.2, (summer), 161–79.

Snow, C. P. (1959/1993), *The Two Cultures*. Cambridge: Cambridge University Press.

Snow, S. E. (1993*), Performing the Pilgrims: A Study of Ethno-historical Role-playing at Plimoth Plantation*. Jackson: University of Mississippi Press.

Somers, J. (1994), *Drama in the Curriculum*. London: Cassell.

—— ed. (1996), *Drama & Theatre in Education: Contemporary Research*. York, Ontario: Captus Press.

Stearns, P. N. (1972), *The Impact of the Industrial Revolution: Protest and Alienation*. Englewood Cliffs, NJ: Prentice-Hall.

Stourac, R. and McCreery, K. (1986), *Theatre as a Weapon: Workers' Theatre in the Soviet Union, Germany and Britain 1917–34*. London: Routledge & Kegan Paul.

Sundgaard, Arnold (1938), *Spirochete*, in Rohan, ed., *Federal Theatre Plays*.

—— (1976), interview with John O'Connor, 5 September. Transcript in FTP Collection, George Mason University, VA.

Suvin, D. (1994), 'Heavenly food denied: *Life of Galileo*', in P. Thomson and G. Sacks, eds, *The Cambridge Companion to Brecht*. Cambridge: Cambridge University Press, pp. 139–52.

Swortzell, Lowell, ed. (1986), *Six Plays for Young People from the Federal Theatre Project (1936–1939)*. Westport, CT: Greenwood Press.

—— (1988), 'Theatre for young people: fifty year prologue to what?', in J. Klein, ed., *Theatre for Young Audiences: Principles and Strategies for the Future*. Lawrence, KS. University of Kansas University Theatre, pp. 1–20.

—— (1993), 'Trying to like TIE', in Jackson, ed., *Learning through Theatre*, pp. 239–50.

—— ed. (1990), *International Guide to Children's Theatre and Educational Theatre: A Historical and Geographical Sourcebook*. Westport, CT: Greenwood Press.

Taylor, P., ed. (1996), *Researching Drama & Arts Education: Paradigms & Possibilities*. London: Falmer Press.

—— (2003), *Applied Theatre: Creating Transformative Encounters in the Community*. Portsmouth, NH: Heinemann.

Thomas, Tom (1977), 'A propertyless theatre for the propertyless class', reprinted in Samuel, MacColl and Cosgrove, eds (1985), *Theatres of the Left 1880–1935*, pp. 77–96.

Thompson, J. (2003), *Applied Theatre: Bewilderment and Beyond*. Oxford and Bern: Peter Lang.

Tilden, Freeman (1957/1984), *Interpreting Our Heritage*. Chapel Hill: University of North Carolina Press.

Time Magazine (1935), 'Agit-prop', 17 June, 38.

Tinniswood, A. and Woodhead, S., eds (1996), *No Longer Dead to Me: Working with Schoolchildren in the Performing & Creative Arts*. London: The National Trust.

Trewin, J. C. (1960), *The Turbulent Thirties*. London: Macdonald.

288 References

Turner, Victor (1982), *From Ritual to Theatre*. New York: Performing Arts Journal Publications.
Tytell, J. (1997), *The Living Theatre: Art, Exile and Outrage*. London: Methuen.
Unity Theatre Trust (2002), 'The Story of Unity Theatre', Video-cassette. London: Unity Theatre Trust.
Usher, R. and Edwards, R. (1994), *Postmodernism and Education*. London: Routledge.
Utting, D. and Vennard, J. (2000), *What Works with Young Offenders in the Community? (What Works?)*. London: Barnardo's.
Valency, M. (1983), *The Cart and the Trumpet: The Plays of George Bernard Shaw*. New York: Schocken Books.
Vennard, J., Sugg, D. and Hedderman, C. (1997), *The Use of Cognitive-behavioural Approaches with Offenders: Messages from Research. Part 1*. HORS 171. London: The Home Office.
Vine, Chris (1993), 'TIE and the Theatre of the Oppressed', in Jackson (ed.), *Learning through Theatre*, pp. 109–27.
Wagner, Betty J., ed. (1998), *Educational Drama & Language Arts: What Research Shows*. Portsmouth, NH: Heinemann.
—— (1999), *Dorothy Heathcote: Drama as a Learning Medium*. Portsmouth, NH: Heinemann.
Water, Manon Van de (2006), *Moscow Theatres for Young People: A Cultural History of Ideological Coercion and Artistic Innovation, 1917–2000*. New York: Palgrave Macmillan.
Watson, Andy (Geese Theatre) (2004), personal interview, 30 March.
Watson, M. (1937), 'Editing the living newspaper', *Federal Theatre Magazine* 15, 16–17. In FTP Collection, George Mason University.
Way, Brian (1967), *Development through Drama*. London: Longmans.
—— (1981), *Audience Participation: Theatre for Young People*. Boston: W. H. Baker.
Weinberg, G. L. (1994), *A World at Arms: A Global History of World War II*. Cambridge: Cambridge University Press.
Wells, G. (c.1998), 'Dialogic enquiry in education: building on the legacy of Vygotsky'. Ontario: University of Ontario Institute for Studies in Education. http://tortoise.oise.utoronto.ca/~gwells/NCTE.html, accessed 31 January 2005.
Whitman, W. (1937), *Bread and Circuses: A Study of Federal Theatre*. Oxford: Oxford University Press.
Whybrow, N. (1994), 'Young people's theatre and the new ideology of state education', *New Theatre Quarterly* 39, 267–80.
Willett, John, ed. (1964), *Brecht on Theatre*. London: Eyre Methuen.
—— (1971), untitled essay in Hoffman, ed., *Erwin Piscator: Political Theatre 1920–66*.
Williams, Cora (1993), 'The theatre in education actor', in Jackson, ed., *Learning through Theatre*, pp. 91–107.
Williams, Cora (Pit Prop Theatre) (1984), Interview included in *Brand of Freedom*: a three-part video-recording. Manchester: Manchester University Media Centre.

Williams, Raymond (1977), *Marxism and Literature*. Oxford: Oxford University Press.

—— (1983), *Keywords: A Vocabulary of Culture and Society*. London: Fontana.

Winston, J. (1996), 'Emotion, reason and moral engagement in drama', *RIDE* 1.2, 189–200.

—— (2005), 'Between the aesthetic and the ethical: analysing the tension at the heart of theatre in education', *Journal of Moral Education* 34.3 (June), 309–23.

Witkin, Robert (1974), *The Intelligence of Feeling*. London: Heinemann.

—— (1999), conference keynote address, at 'Researching Drama and Theatre in Education' conference, University of Exeter (April).

Wood, Dorothy (M6 Theatre) (2001), personal interview, 21 June.

—— (2003), personal interview, 2 October.

—— (2006), correspondence, 23 August.

Wright, Patrick (1985), *On Living in an Old Country*. London: Verso.

Young National Trust Theatre (1995), 'Teachers resource booklet for *For Any Field?*'. London: The National Trust.

Index